Fundamentals in Christian Education

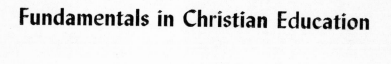

Fundamentals in Christian Education

Theory and Practice

by

CORNELIUS JAARSMA

Professor of Education

Calvin College, Grand Rapids, Mich.

WM. B. EERDMANS PUBLISHING CO.

Grand Rapids   1953   Michigan

DEDICATED

to the memory of my father.

*To him I owe, by the grace of God,
my love for the Reformed Faith.
It was his example of faith and life
that was used of the Lord
to recapture my life for Christ
when going seemed difficult
because of intellectual problems.*

Preface

The extensive growth of Christian schools, elementary and secondary, especially during the past decade is a source of great joy to all who recognize the need of Christian education today. When schools about us are increasingly becoming secular or transpose the Christian faith into human action, our democratic society as well as the Christian home and the Christian church stands to benefit from God-centered education in the Christian school. The Christian school is the need of the hour for home, church, and state.

The rapid growth of and great need for Christian schools in our time catches us as Christians ill prepared to meet the need.

First of all, there is a great shortage of competent teachers. By competence we mean academic and professional competence to be sure. But we must include much more than this. We need teachers who in their wholehearted commitment to the Lord and His service plan to make teaching their life task and mature in this great mission by continued study and personal development.

Furthermore, we have not worked out a reasonably well-defined concept of education for the Christian school. What constitutes a Christian school? We have not been without answers, and good answers, to this question. Neither have we failed to make serious application of our thinking to practice. But when we stop to examine critically what we have done, we are embarrassed to find how vague our notion of Christian teaching and learning still is.

The tremendous importance of the work of the Christian school for the kingdom of our Saviour and Lord demands the strictest honesty with ourselves. We have not arrived. As a matter of fact, we have seriously erred at times; not purposely, but really erred just the same. We must take stock.

One of the major purposes of this book of readings is to help us take stock. The readings have been selected with this end in view. Some may not agree with the choice of selections made by the author. We will all admit, I am sure, that the men of Reformed faith here speaking about

Christian education give us food for thought. Summaries of key thoughts of each selection and accompanying comment aim to help us focus our attention on crucial issues in Christian education. In adapting the readings to this end, portions have been omitted from the originals.

Another purpose of this collection of readings is to make available to teachers, to prospective teachers, and to the Christian community at large, some fundamental discussions on Christian education. While Christian schools are increasing rapidly, we must do all we can to think soundly on Christian education. We must build internally even more than externally. The modern school has come to occupy a most strategic position in the education of our youth. We must do all we can to assure the covenant youth of a Christian education founded upon Christ and the recorded Word, and promoted by the fellowship of love characteristic only of a community where the Spirit of God dwells. Such a community too, the Christian school must be.

In the preparation of this volume the writer and compiler owes a special debt of gratitude to Dr. J. A. Van Bruggen and the National Union of Christian School office for their co-operation. Likewise he desires to acknowledge the following publishers in the Netherlands for permission to quote from their publications: J. H. Kok, Kampen; P. Noordhoff, Ltd., Groningen; J. B. Wolters, Groningen.

May the Lord bless this humble effort to challenge our thinking about Christian education today.

CORNELIUS JAARSMA

Grand Rapids, Michigan

Table of Contents

SECTION THREE
Organization and Implementation of the
Program of Christian Education

SECTION FOUR

Conclusion

The Contributors

LOUIS BERKHOF. Emeritus President of Calvin Seminary.

A. S. DE JONG. Late principal of Christian schools, Chicago.

EDWARD HEEREMA. Pastor of Plymouth Heights Christian Reformed Church, Grand Rapids; formerly Public Relations Secretary of National Union of Christian Schools.

G. W. HYLKEMA. Late pastor of Christian Reformed churches.

CORNELIUS JAARSMA. Professor of Education, Calvin College.

A. JANSE. Principal of Christian schools, The Netherlands.

W. HARRY JELLEMA. Professor of Philosophy, Calvin College.

P. LANKAMP. Supervisor of elementary schools, The Netherlands.

HENRY J. RYSKAMP. Dean of the Faculty, Calvin College.

HENRY SCHULTZ. Professor of New Testament, Calvin Seminary.

J. K. VAN BAALEN. Pastor of First Christian Reformed Church, Edmonton, Canada.

L. VANDER ZWEEP. Supervisor of elementary schools, The Netherlands.

J. W. VAN HULST. Supervisor of elementary schools, The Netherlands.

CORNELIUS VAN TIL. Professor of Ethics and Apologetics, Westminster Theological Seminary.

HENRY VAN ZYL. Emeritus Professor of Education, Calvin College.

D. H. WALTERS. President of the Reformed Bible Institute.

G. WIELENGA. Supervisor of elementary schools, The Netherlands.

SECTION ONE

THE BASIS FOR CHRISTIAN EDUCATION

1

Authority of the Scriptures

In addition to fundamental differences in theology between Roman Catholicism and Calvinism, one can point to philosophical differences too, though both form common front against modern philosophical thinking. The core issue is found in what has been called the formal principle of the Reformation: the highest and final authority of the Holy Scriptures. In the Word of God only do we find the norm for our philosophical thinking. Both philosophy and theology are subject to it, while for the rest they differ in object and purpose, and are critically independent in mutual adoption of each other's propositions.

P. LANKAMP AND L. VANDER ZWEEP
General Introduction to a Course of Study for the Christian Schools, p. 35.

Comment:

The above statement is basic as we turn our thinking to Christian educational theory and practice. Only in the Word of God do we find our infallible norm. This does not mean that the normative value of theology, philosophy, ethics, logic, and esthetics, guided by the light of the Word are excluded. In the light of the Scriptures they too contribute to the principles of education.

2

Religion and Education

The following is an appraisal of the "new education" as expressed in the principles of the French International League for the New Education and of the English New Education Fellowship. These principles are similar to those of the American Education Fellowship (formerly The Progressive Education Association).

We should make it emphatic at the very outset that these principles are not acceptable for our Christian education. We cannot ally ourselves with this movement educationally, psychologically, or sociologically.

Earlier we pointed to the long struggle of the Christian school with Herbart and his followers.

When we read the articles in this statement of principles, we recognize at once that for educational purposes all positive religion is excluded, and hence, we have not gotten one step further. Herbartianism is severely criticized on the ground of research resulting from the study of the child, the school system that developed on Herbartian grounds is rejected, but the criticism is not directed against the secularism in education. The leaders of this new movement ignore religion. Herbart left religion to the church and the parents. But the new movement has no place for religion anywhere. It gives an educational "declaration of rights of the man and citizen."

We are listening to a modernization and modification of Rousseau, psychologically extended and sociologically enriched. As in Rousseau, man is given the central place, or rather, the child as holding the promise for the future. It is the continuation of a revolution in education, adapted to our time.

If we were to formulate an educational credo on the basis of these principles, it would read something like this:

> "I believe in the omnipotence of education;
> I believe in the disappearance of all egoism;
> I believe in the future for an improved humanity;
> I believe in man!"

Over against this faith in evolution with its naturalistic and humanistic outlook upon life, we declare our credo: "I believe in God, the Father of our Lord Jesus Christ"; for Christendom of all ages recorded in the apostolic creed.

It is necessary to give this all the emphasis because to ignore God and the worship of God is to deprive education of its one true foundation, for psychology and anthropology cannot be separated from religion, and a sociology that denies the law of God can never indicate the direction of true social life.

Hence, educational theory and practice, though it embodies scientifically established fact in psychology, will go wrong without the one true foundation.

P. LANKAMP AND L. VANDER ZWEEP
General Introduction to a Course of Study for the Christian Schools, pp. 87-88.

Comment:

What is suggested here by the authors is that the new education of today represents no improvement over the Herbartianism or intellectualism of the nineteenth century school. The better insights in learning are offset by the secularism of the new education. The challenge of Christian education is to give a true setting to a better understanding of the learning process.

3

Principle and Fact

It is important that when we reflect on educational practice principle be placed in the foreground and that we have the courage to accept the responsibility of implementing the principle in practice. We proceed according to principle when we study the findings concerning child life in its psycho-physical development, though they are the fruit of research by modern psychologists. We shall have to dissociate these findings from the life and world view in which they are expounded. They are for us no more than so much technical apparatus that we can use in the construction of our educational practice.

Also in the momentous times in which we live, God in his "common grace" maintains the temporal order and continuous to reveal in His creation what belongs to the structure of this creation, and to the structure of child life. He wills that we accept these gifts of grace too and make them serviceable for the education of our baptized children, that they may as adults be the more able to cultivate more fully their strength to His honor.

In a sense, we can understand why many a Christian teacher assumes a defensive attitude when we speak of educational reform and at the same time quote unbelieving educators in defense of new ways. But this fear need not arise if we see the right relation between principle and fact. In theology Dr. F. W. Grosheide has thrown much light on this relationship, and much of what he has said is applicable to education. "Not facts," says he, "but principle gives certainty. This knowledge will prevent our overrating fact. But likewise we must guard against overrating principles. Understand me well, I do not say overrating our principle. We can never be fundamental enough. I am speaking of principles in general, and we should remember that they are principles, that is, something must follow. It is well that we hold to our principles, but these principles acquire meaning only when they find ever wider application, when facts are related to them. Principles as such give me nothing, the word itself indicates this. Now, it is clear that there is no man who has principles only; he relates them to something; life requires this. But I am speaking of scientific knowledge (wetenschap).

18

No more than we can speak of scientific knowledge when facts only are involved, can principles alone be called scientific knowledge. One who would confine himself to principles only can only blame himself when he is not taken into account, despite his diligent effort. He remains without influence. . . . Principle values fact. Or we might say, what I do with facts, to what end I shall use them, depends upon my principles"

P. LANKAMP AND L. VANDER ZWEEP
General Introduction to a Course of Study
for the Christian Schools, pp. 94-95.

Comment:

As new insights are gained in the ways of child life and the development of child life into maturity, the distinctions drawn in this passage become increasingly pertinent. Studies in psychology and education have frequently proved so confusing and often contradictory because we fail to orient them in what Scripture clearly teaches about man. Armed with the Word as God's directive of and corrective for life we can give our principles wider application by relating them to fact.

4

The Covenant of Grace and Its Significance for Christian Education

Advocates of Christian education have always maintained that the Chrisitan school is an outgrowth of the covenant idea, and is absolutely necessary in order to enable the child to appreciate its covenant privileges and to understand the solemn significance of its baptism in the name of the triune God. They are convinced that the Christian school, as well as infant baptism, finds its main support in the doctrine of the covenant, and are therefore unalterably opposed to the tendency of some to slight this doctrine and to relegate it to the background.

In the American ecclesiastical world the doctrine of the covenant is almost entirely unknown. You can take up one work on systematic theology after another without finding a single chapter devoted to it. Such works as those of the Hodges, Thornwell, and Dabney form exceptions to the rule. Moreover, it is quite evident that in most of the churches of our land, even in those who theoretically subscribe to the doctrine of the covenant, this doctrine has no grasp on the life and the conscience of the people in general, and fails utterly to have a determining influence on the education of their children.

In the present controversy between the Modernists and the Fundamentalists the hearts of all serious-minded Christians naturally go out to the latter, because they take their stand on the infallible Word of God; but unfortunately they are nearly all Premillennialists, who drive a wedge in between the Old and the New Testament, claim that the covenant made with Abraham and sealed by circumcision includes only the natural descendants of the patriarch, and therefore deny that we and our children have any part in it and that this is sealed to us by baptism. Experience has already taught us that they who come under the spell of Premillennialism finally lose their covenant conception and turn to the position of the Baptists.

Occasionally some well-meaning persons in our circles express the fear that we speak too much about the covenant and are in danger of making people averse to it. Now there may have been a time when this fear was warranted, but in our opinion it is quite unnecessary at present. There is more point to the oft repeated complaint that in our day the doctrine of the covenant is not stressed as it ought to be. And even if the fear expressed were perfectly justified, that would be no reason why we should refrain from discussing this subject. It is a striking fact that, while the advocates of Christian education always insisted on the close relation between the covenant idea and the Christian school, I have not been able to lay my hand on a single book or pamphlet, either in the Holland or in the English language, devoted to a discussion of the subject in question.

The fact is that in our struggle for Christian schools the doctrine of the covenant was always the great presupposition. The relation in which the covenant idea stands to the Christian school may have been discussed time and again in sermons and lectures that did not appear in print. On the printed page we find an occasional reference to the fact that the children of Christian parents should be religiously educated in view of the fact that they are covenant children, and that, when they were brought to baptism, their parents promised to provide such an education for them. But nowhere do we find this idea worked out. Hence it can hardly be regarded as superfluous that a paper be devoted to the relation of the covenant idea and the Christian education which we desire for our children. Even so the presentation of it can hardly be commensurate with its great importance.

* * *

For a proper understanding of the covenant of grace it is quite essential that we have some conception of the covenant idea in general. It can hardly escape the attention of Bible students that, while the essential elements of the covenant of grace are already present in the Protevangelium, its formal establishment is introduced comparatively late in the history of revelation. It was nearly twenty centuries after the creation of the world that God formally entered into covenant relationship with Abraham and his seed. And there was a perfectly good reason for this delay in the general method of divine relation, in which the natural precedes the spiritual and spiritual realities are presented in forms derived from the natural world. Under the providence of God the various forms of life, of the interactions of the social groups, and of the associations among men, were first brought to development in the natural life of men, and were then used by God as the vehicles of his special revelation.

Thus people had to grow accustomed to the idea of covenant agreements first, before God could utilize such an idea in the revelation of the eternal verities of the covenant of grace. And then He employed it, first of all, in the revelation of the so-called covenant of nature with Noah, and only after that in revealing the covenant of grace with believers and their seed.

The necessity of entering into covenant agreements was felt first of all by individuals and tribes that were brought into close relation with each other and had no authority above them to secure their mutual rights and privileges. They sought the coveted security by entering into a voluntary agreement in which the mutual obligations and rights of both parties were clearly set forth and fully secured. A covenant so made, and often ratified by drinking sacrificial blood, eating a sacrificial meal, or eating salt together, was held to be most sacred and binding. It was not, as a rule, an expression of that self-seeking spirit that is so characteristic of modern international covenants or agreements, but generally resulted from a genuine desire for closer union, more intimate relationship, lasting friendship and mutual devotion.

But though the covenant idea first found expression in the natural life of man, and was only after that embodied in the divine revelation, it should not be thought that the human covenants were the original and real covenants, and that the covenant of God with believers and their seed is only a copy of these, or that this idea is merely a figure used to express the close relation between God and his people. If we turn this right around, we are nearer to the truth. God's covenant is the divine original, and all covenants among men are but faint reflections of it; it is not a mere figure of speech but a blessed reality rich in promises and full of heavenly comfort.

If we reflect for a moment on the covenants that were so frequently established among men, especially in the early patriarchal times, we cannot but notice that they are marked by certain definite characteristics. There are always two parties in such a covenant (in fact, a covenant of one party would be a contradiction in terms), and these parties are of such a kind that they can meet on a footing of equality. There are also two parts in every covenant; each party solemnly pledges himself to the performance of certain duties and in turn is assured of the fulfillment of certain promises. And the guarantee that the covenant requirements will be met and that the covenant promises will be fulfilled does not lie in any superior power that can and will force the parties to meet their mutual obligations, if need be, but only in the sacred character of the agreement and in the honor and faithfulness of the covenanting parties.

* * *

Now let us take a closer view of the covenant of grace. We do not intend — and in fact, it would be quite impossible — to discuss this in all its details, but will only stress the points that need elucidation in an intelligent discussion of this subject. We generally speak of the covenant of grace as being that gracious compact or agreement between the offended God and the offending sinner, in which God promises salvation through faith in Christ and the sinner accepts this believingly. It may be well to use an illustration that will serve to bring out just what the covenant of grace involves, before we stress some of the more important particulars of the covenant relation. We should bear in mind, however, that the illustration conveys to us only an imperfect approximation of the truth.

Let us imagine a rich and beneficent slave-holder with a thousand slaves, who are in duty bound to labor faithfully for their master, without any claim to reward, it is true, but with the assurance that, after a period of faithful labor, they will obtain their freedom. After a period of scrupulous attention to duty the slaves gradually grow restive under the yoke, begin plotting against their master, vent their dissatisfaction in murmurings and grumbling and muttered curses, which like the distant thunder announce the coming storm, and finally break into an open revolt in which they seek to shake off their fetters and to overthrow once for all the regime of their landlord. But the latter is well disposed toward his mutinous bond-servants and is anxious to raise them to a higher level. So he himself opens the way to a full and free pardon, though it involves a great deal of self-sacrifice, and resorts to all possible means to insure their future obedience. He even condescends to come down to their level and to deal with them as on a footing of equality. He makes a compact with them, in which he promises to pardon their insurrection, to adopt them and their children into his own family with the full rights and privileges of children, and to make them and their descendants heirs of his extensive possessions; and they, in turn, accept his pardon on the stipulated conditions, vow obedience to him as their lord, and pledge themselves to his service. Naturally they, as bond-servants were in duty bound to accept whatever arrangement their master might make, and after the compact was closed they were doubly obliged to honor its provisions. Moreover, it was in their interest that they should live up to the terms of the agreement, since it opened up the brightest prospects for them and their children, and brought to them what they could in no way hope to merit by their labors — a congenial home, the precious gift of liberty, untold riches, the pleasure of life, and a choice society in which to move.

Now if we reflect on this covenant arrangement which may, at least in a measure, serve to illustrate the agreement between God and the sinner in the covenant of grace, we shall notice that, while it certainly has all the essential characteristics of a covenant, it is yet marked by certain peculiarities. There are in this, as in every other covenant, two parties; but the parties are not of such a nature that they can meet on a footing of equality. This is something unusual. We do not ordinarily find a slave-holder making a covenant with his slaves. In his estimation they have no rights that would entitle them to such consideration. He simply issues his commands, and expects them to obey.

Thus our attention is directed at once to a very important feature of the covenant of grace. The distance between God and man is infinitely greater than that between a landlord and his slave, for the latter does not transcend the measure of the purely human. However different their social standing may be, the master and the bond-servants are all men and in so far equals, and even the latter have certain rights which the former may not disregard. But God is far greater than man; He gives no account of his doings; He is not under obligation to any of his creatures. To the sorely afflicted Job, crushed and perplexed, who had shown an inclination to question the doings of the Almighty, He says: "Who then is he that can stand before me? Who hath first given unto me, that I should repay him? Whatsoever is under the whole heaven is mine" (Job 41:10, 11). Man has absolutely no rights in relation to God. God has but to command, and man is in duty bound to obey. And not only that, but sinful man has actually forfeited his life, and forfeited whatever rights he might have had in virtue of an original divine grant.

In the covenant of grace, therefore, we find two very unequal parties: the infinite God, the Creator of the universe, "glorious in holiness, fearful in praises, doing wonders," and finite man, a transient creature of the dust, sinful and polluted. The one is the rich possessor of all things, man included, and the other merely a steward of treasures entrusted to his care; the one has rightful claims on the life, the possessions, the time, and the service of his creatures, and is under no obligation to them, and the other is in duty bound to render all to God and yet obtains no claim to any reward; the one can offer riches and honor and joys beyond compare, and the other can offer nothing, not even the bankrupt life which he sometimes calls his own.

In view of this fact it is no wonder that some theologians do not regard what we usually call "the covenant of grace" as a covenant at all, but prefer to speak of it simply as a divine arrangement, a gracious disposition, or a testament, thus stressing the one-sided character of the transaction. And undoubtedly, in its origin and in its effective operation, the covenant is one-sided. At the same time it is clearly represented as a covenant in Scripture, and being essentially a covenant, it is necessarily of the nature of an agreement between two parties. God condescended to come down to the level of man in the covenant of works, and promised to reward a temporary obedience with life eternal. Again, He condescended to come down to the level of *sinful* man in Christ, and now in the covenant of grace offers eternal life to all that accept Christ by faith. The gracious element that was present even in the first covenant is far more pronounced in the second. What condescending love in God to enter into covenant relationship with sinners in Christ! Well may we be grateful for the dignity thus bestowed upon us, sinful creatures.

In the illustration used I pointed out that it involved a great deal of self-sacrifice on the part of the landlord to enter into covenant relation with his bond-servants. The same thing applies where God enters into a covenant of grace with sinners. He could not simply come down to the level of wilful transgressors and make a covenant with them without maintaining his justice and safeguarding his holiness. He could deal with sinners only in the person of someone who undertook it voluntarily to be their surety and who guaranteed that the demands of justice would be met both objectively and subjectively, i.e., that the inflexible justice of God would be satisfied by a sacrificial death, that the original demand of the law would be met by a life of obedience, and that they who would share in the blessings of forgiveness would also consecrate their lives to God. Now there is nothing peculiar in the fact that there should be a surety in the covenant of grace. This is a rather common occurrence in covenants. The moral or financial standing of one of the parties to a transaction may be of a rather dubious character thus making a surety or guarantor quite essential. In our day great companies exist for the purpose of supplying the necessary bonds. But in the covenant of grace the striking thing is this, that the party known to be absolutely reliable itself supplies a surety for the bankrupt party with which it is dealing. God gives His only-begotten Son, and the Son voluntarily takes it upon Himself to become a Surety for lost and helpless sinners. Here too the gracious nature of the covenant shines forth.

> Wouldst thou learn the depth of sin,
> All its bitterness and pain?
> What it cost thy God to win
> Sinners to Himself again?
> Come, poor sinner, come with me;
> Visit sad Gethsemane.

Wouldst thou know God's wondrous love?
Seek it not beside the throne;
List not angels' praise above,
But come and hear the heavy groan
By the Godhead heaved for thee,
Sinner, in Gethsemane.

The gracious nature of the covenant also appears very clearly from another point of view. In every covenant there are two elements, viz., promises and requirements, and this also applies to the covenant of grace. These elements find expression in the oft-repeated words: "I will be their God; and they shall be my people." But though there are also requirements in the covenant of grace, the promises are very much in the foreground; in fact, all the requirements are also covered by divine promises. It was in the consciousness of that blessed fact that Augustine prayed: "Lord give what Thou commandest, and then command what Thou wilt."

The promises of the covenant are exceedingly comprehensive. The basic promise is that of the foregiveness of sins. Sin raised a barrier between God and man which must first of all be removed. As long as it is not taken out of the way, the sinner lies under a sentence of condemnation; he has no approach to God, cannot ascend His holy hill, and cannot stand in His presence. Fellowship with God is entirely out of the question. But when sin is pardoned, the sentence of condemnation is lifted, the way to the tree of life is opened, and the sinner can again find rest at the bosom of his heavenly Father.

Inseparably connected with the pardoning grace of God is the grace of adoption. God adopts sinners into his own family. This implies, of course, that they are not children of God by nature. If they were, this adoption would be entirely out of the question. Parents can adopt a child, but they cannot adopt their own children. This is the blessing of which John speaks when he says, "But as many as received him, to them gave He the right to become children of God, even to them that believe on His name" (John 1:12). It is the blessing in which Paul rejoices, "For ye received not the spirit of bondage again unto fear; but ye received the spirit of adoption, whereby we cry, Abba, Father."

With the blessing of adoption another blessing goes hand in hand. Sinners are made children of God, not merely in a legal sense by means of adoption, but also in a spiritual sense of regeneration and sanctification. God does much more than man can ever hope to do when he takes a child into his family. Parents can adopt a child, but cannot transform it. They cannot change the inner nature of the child, cannot impart to it their characteristic traits, and cannot make it resemble them. God is not only abundantly able to accomplish this, but actually brings it to pass. He sends forth the Spirit of his Son into the hearts of sinners, crying, "Abba, Father." He restores in them the image of God, renews their lives, and creates within them a new spirit of obedience, so that as true children they become desirous and even anxious to do the Father's will.

But there is still more. Sonship includes heirship with all its privileges. Unworthy sinners, who have forfeited the least of the blessings of God, fall heir to ethical and spiritual perfections, to the most intimate and loving communion with God in Christ Jesus, and to the eternal glories of their heavenly King. They receive an inheritance incorruptible and undefiled and that fadeth not away in the city of the living God, the heavenly Jerusalem, where they as the church of the firstborn in the company of innumerable hosts of angels will walk in the light of the Lamb and will enjoy perfect peace and happiness in endless life.

We have given only the barest indications of what is included in the promises of the covenant. There are promises for the present and for the future, promises for days of prosperity and for seasons of adversity, promises for the living and for the dying. There are promises of renewed strength for those whose strength seems to fail, promises of courage for the faint-hearted and of rest for the weary. There are promises of guidance through life and of deliverance out of temptations, promises of the support of the everlasting arms and of good cheer for the afflicted and the discouraged, promises of security for storm-tossed souls, promises, too, of an everlasting home for weary pilgrims.

> Oh, wonderful story of deathless love,
> Each child is dear to that heart above!
> He fights for me when I cannot fight;
> He comforts me in the gloom of night;
> He lifts the burden, for He is strong;
> He stills the sigh and wakes the song;
> The sorrows that bear me down, He shares,
> And loves and pardons because He cares.
>
> Let all who are sad take heart again,
> We are not alone in our hours of pain;
> Our Father looks from his throne above
> To soothe and comfort us with His love.

> He leaves us not when the storms are high;
> And we have safety, for He is nigh.
> Can that be trouble, which He doth share?
> Oh, rest in peace, for the Lord will care!

And the promises, all the promises, as many promises as there are and that are yea and amen in Christ Jesus — are for us *and for our children.* That is the glad assurance we have in the covenant of grace. Hence Christian parents who take their baptismal vows seriously may always plead these promises for their offspring.

*   *   *

But now it is time to remind ourselves once more of the fact that there are two elements in the covenant, promises and requirements. This is all the more necessary because there are some really pious people who are inclined to deny that there are any requirements in the covenant of grace. They regard this denial necessary in order to avoid the errors of Pelagianism and of Arminianism. They are anxious to maintain the position that the work of salvation is a work of the grace of God from the beginning to the end, and that man contributes absolutely nothing to it. Hence they are averse to the idea that the covenant of grace is in any sense conditional. Let us consider this question for a moment. Is the covenant of grace conditional or is it not? This question cannot be answered by a simple negative or affirmative, but must be answered with careful discrimination.

If we consider the foundation of the covenant, we find it to be just as conditional as the covenant of works. Just as the covenant of works was conditioned on the obedience of Adam, so the covenant of grace is conditioned on the suffering and obedience, in short, on the merits of Jesus Christ. It is only on the basis of his atoning work that we can share in the blessings of the covenant of grace. But since all are agreed here, it is quite evident that this is not the exact point at issue. The real question is whether there is any condition with which man must comply, in order to enter the covenant and to obtain the covenant blessings and the covenant end for himself and for his children.

Now it is implied in the very idea of a covenant that there should be conditions; if there were none, there would be no covenant. Moreover, the Bible clearly teaches us that there are certain conditions. But the word conditions is not always used in the same sense, and it is possible to use it in a sense which does not apply in the covenant of grace. There is no condition attached to the covenant of grace which includes the idea of merit on the part of man. Because Christ has merited all the blessings of the covenant, the idea that man should merit anything is absolutely excluded. Moreover, there is no condition which man must fulfill in his own strength. He is constantly reminded of the fact that he needs strength from above in order that he may answer to the requirements of the covenant. Bearing these things in mind, however, we undoubtedly can speak of certain prerequisites for entering the covenant, for sharing the life of the covenant, and for obtaining the full covenant blessings.

Men enter the covenant relationship either by birth from Christian parents, or, if they are not born within the pale of the Church, by a profession of faith in Christ. They become conscious partakers of the covenant life only by a saving faith in Jesus Christ that is wrought in their hearts by the Holy Spirit, a faith by which they merit nothing but simply appropriate Christ as the fountain of all spiritual blessings. And they obtain the full possession and enjoyment of the covenant blessings and of the glorious covenant inheritance only by faith and sanctification, by separation from the world in consecration to God, and by a life of childlike and loving obedience. In the case of Christian parents this naturally involves the duty that they be diligent in training their children in the fear and admonition of the Lord, in order that these children, when they come to maturity, may willingly take upon themselves their covenant obligations and may, with their parents, enjoy the rich covenant blessings.

In this connection it is highly necessary to bear in mind that living in the covenant relationship is something more than living under the Gospel, under the free offer of salvation. There is here something more than an offer, something more than a promise; there is an agreement. The covenant is an *established covenant, a covenant agreed to,* agreed to by parents *also for their children.* When they sought the seal of baptism for their offspring, they promised, as Joshua did in the days of old: "as for me *and my house,* we will serve Jehovah." This means that, for the children of the covenant, the covenant is not merely an offer which they can accept or reject, but an agreement which they entered; and that, if they do not live up to the terms of the agreement, they are covenant-breakers. Even as creatures of God they were already in duty bound to accept whatever arrangement He made for them. But in virtue of the agreement entered by their parents also in their behalf, they have an added responsibility. They are now doubly obliged to honor the covenant, to live into it, and to meet its requirements with a grateful heart.

It may be said that when Christian parents make such a promise they promise more than they can accomplish, for they cannot impart the

new life to their children, cannot create within them the spirit of obedience. Now it is perfectly true that the parents cannot guarantee spiritual
renewal; nor does God expect or require it of them. They make their
promise entirely on the strength of the promises of God. If they
promise to intercede for their children, to educate them in the fear
of the Lord, and to set them an example of true Christian piety, they
simply promise to utilize the means which God has ordained for the
realization of the covenant life in their children; and they have the
blessed assurance that God will enable them to meet these covenant
requirements.   And if they promise that they with their children
will fear the Lord, they do it in trustful reliance on the never failing
promises of God that He will work in those children and create within
them a clean heart and a willing spirit.

Occasionally we meet with people who consider it reprehensible that
parents make such a promise for their children. They claim that the
parents have absolutely no right to enter into such an agreement for
their offspring. The children should be allowed to choose for themselves when they come to maturity. But suppose that some beneficent
capitalist offered poor parents untold riches, and offered to extend
his munificence also to their children provided the parents would educate them into a right appreciation and a grateful acceptance of that
wealth and the children would show themselves worthy of it by a
good moral conduct — and suppose that the parents accepted the offer
and entered the agreement for themselves and for their children,
promising to do all that lay in their power to meet the conditions,
could that rightly be considered as an injustice to the children? And
would it not be utter folly on the part of the children to break the
agreement? Children of Christian parents have every reason to be
thankful that, along with their parents, they stand in a blessed covenant
relation.

*   *   *

Now the question arises, How does the covenant relationship furnish a basis for Christian education? Our form of baptism clearly
implies that there is a close connection between the two. Only three
questions are put to the parents, and of these three one concerns itself
entirely with the matter of Christian education. The first question
seeks recognition of the fact that, though our children are born in sin
and therefore subject to condemnation, they are nevertheless sanctified
in Christ and as such entitled to baptism. The second requires a
renewed confession of the parents that the doctrine contained in Scripture and taught in our church is the true and perfect doctrine of salvation. And the third exacts of them the promise that they will

be faithful and diligent in teaching their children that glorious saving truth. The first is expressive of the title which the children of Christian parents have to baptism; the second, of the parents' right to seek baptism for their children; and the third, of the obligation that is involved in the privilege.

It is deserving of notice that the promise is a very comprehensive one. The parents publicly assume the responsibility of instructing their children in the "aforesaid doctrine"; and this is not merely the doctrine of the covenant, as some have asserted, but the doctrine contained in the Old and New Testament, the whole round of Christian truth with its broad sweep, touching every realm, every sphere, and every relation of Christian life. Thus we have a very clear indication of the spirit that ought to permeate the instruction of covenant children.

And now we repeat the question: In what way does the covenant relation involve the duty to give the children of the covenant a truly Christian education? There are especially three lines of thought that suggest themselves here. Let us consider these for a few moments.

In the *first* place this necessity is involved in the fact that the children of Christian parents are, with their parents, adopted into the family of God. Think for a moment of the illustration that was used at the beginning of our discussion. The generous landlord adopted his bond-servants and their children into his family. But in doing this he at once encountered the problem of their education. The privilege which he bestowed upon them made it incumbent on them to live on a higher cultural level, to move about in refined company from day to day, and to reflect their high station in life in their habits and customs and general manner of living; all of which would be quite impossible for them unless they were educated and trained for that new life of culture and refinement. It would be but natural, therefore, that the landlord should make provision for the necessary education of his bond-servants and should make arrangements which would insure a corresponding education for their children. He naturally could not permit them to degrade, but would want them to be an honor to his name.

Now the children of the covenant are adopted into a family that is infinitely higher than the family of any man of rank or nobility. They are adopted into the family of the covenant God Himself. Even while on earth they are privileged to join the company of the redeemed, the saints of God. They take their place in the Church of Jesus Christ, which is the heavenly Jerusalem. Moreover, they are destined to live and move about eternally in the company of just men made perfect, of the innumerable hosts of the angels of God, and of Jesus Christ, the King all-glorious. Perfect life in the most intimate communion with the triune God is their grand ideal; heaven with all its glories is their eternal home. Can we at all doubt whether this calls for Christian education? Can we really suggest in all seriousness that in a world such as we are living in Christian education in the home, in the Church, and in the Sunday-School is quite adequate? Ought we not rather to ask: Is the best religious education we can give our children, no matter how comprehensive and how thorough, really commensurate with the high dignity to which our children are called? Should we not bend all our efforts to make it richer and fuller, and to bring it more into harmony with their high calling and their exalted duties? Would we want our children to be a dishonor to the household of God? Let us ever be mindful of the fact that the King's children must have a royal education.

The necessity of Christian education follows, in the *second* place, also from the fact that the children of Christian parents fall heir to the covenant promises. The master making a covenant with his slaves pardoned their insurrection, endowed them with material riches, and made them co-heirs with his own children. This is the very thing that God does in the covenant of grace. Now suppose that our children had been robbing some wealthy land-owner and were caught in the act, and that this land-owner did not prosecute them, but instead heaped coals of fire upon their head by making them the heirs of untold riches. Would not this at once suggest a new duty to us, the duty to impress upon our children their utter unworthiness and the munificence of him whom they sought to deprive of his possessions, and to make them fully conscious of the immense wealth so magnanimously bestowed upon them and of the responsibility which it involved? It is quite evident that this would appear desirable for more than one reason. We would naturally feel it incumbent on us to engender in our children a spirit of true gratitude, to promote their happiness by helping them to obtain a proper realization of their great riches, and teach them the right use of their sudden wealth.

Children of Christian parents, in spite of their unworthiness, fall heir to the blessed promises of the covenant, and these promises cover the whole range of life, natural and spiritual, temporal and eternal, and as such guarantee them all the riches of grace and glory that are in Christ Jesus. These bounties naturally call for gratitude. God expects his covenant children to praise Him with thankful hearts. The unthankful are classed with the notoriously wicked (II Tim. 3:2). After Moses had reminded the children of Israel of their covenant privileges and had pointed to the blessings which they were about to receive in Palestine, he said unto them, "And thou shalt eat and be full, and thou shalt bless Jehovah thy God for the good land which He hath given thee" (Deut. 8:10). Our children too must bring their thank-offerings to the Lord. But how can they be adequately thankful unless they are taught to see how much they have received? They should be brought to a realization of the fact that never ending thanks are due and that even the best they can bring to the Lord is but an inadequate expression of the gratefulness they owe their covenant God. If the question of the poet finds an echo in their heart:

> What shall I render to the Lord
> For all His benefits to me?
> How shall my soul by grace restored
> Give worthy thanks, O Lord, to Thee?

— then Christian education must help them to find an appropriate answer.

It may be shown also from another angle that the rich promises of the covenant naturally call for Christian education. If the promises of God, which constitute the true riches of all the children of God, are to promote the real happiness and blessedness of their recipients, these must learn to understand the wide bearing of these promises and to know what treasures they include. Let us remember that, subjectively, we are no richer than our comprehension of what we possess, and that it is the true appreciation of our wealth which determines the measure of enjoyment derived from it. New Testament believers are more blessed than those of the Old Testament because they have a clearer conception of their covenanted riches. Jesus said to his disciples, "Blessed are your eyes, for they see; and your ears, for they hear. For verily I say unto you, that many prophets and righteous men desired to see the things which ye see, and saw them not; and to hear the things which ye hear, and heard them not" (Matt. 13:16, 17). Many children of God are even today living in spiritual poverty, though they are rich in Christ and heirs of the world, because they have not been taught to see the greatness and splendor of their spiritual heritage. If we do not want our children to live as paupers in spiritual penury and want while untold riches of grace and mercy are at their disposal, we must employ all the means at our command to unfold before their very eyes the treasures of divine grace of which they are heirs in Christ Jesus.

Once again, the promises of the covenant necessitate Christian education, because they inevitably impose upon our children a heavy responsibility. If all other things are equal, the affluent man has a far greater responsibility than the man of small means. He may not squander his wealth; on the contrary, he must invest it to the best advantage. And if he is not a born financier, he will need careful training for the proper administration of his wealth. Inherited riches often become a curse for the recipient because he has not been trained in the proper administration and use of money. Through lack of training the whole inheritance is sometimes lost. And may we not say of our children, to whom God entrusts great wealth in his covenant promises, that they are not all born stewards in the household of God? Yet stewards they must be, for God has enriched them with spiritual treasures in order that they should administer this wealth for the honor of His name and for the extension of His kingdom. Are we warranted in assuming that they will naturally be faithful to their trust and will make the best possible use of their God-given possessions? Are there no reasons to fear, in view of the natural tendencies of their hearts and of their lack of spiritual discernment and spiritual understanding, that like the unprofitable servant they will hide their "pound" and let it lie idle, that they will apply their wealth in the wrong direction, or that they will squander it, unless they are taught to see their responsibility and are carefully taught the proper use of the wealth which God has placed at their disposal? Surely, we cannot be too careful nor too diligent in training our children for their responsible duties in life.

This idea very naturally leads on to our *third* consideration. The necessity of Christian education also follows from the requirements of the covenant. God requires of covenant children that they believe in Jesus Christ unto salvation and that they turn from sin to holiness, i. e., follow the highway of sanctification through life. It is a very comprehensive requirement, the nature of which ought to be well understood. Hence the need of Christian education.

Faith is required in the children of the covenant. Faith, first of all, as a receptive organ by which they lay hold on Christ and all the blessings of salvation. This faith may not be a bare intellectual assent to the claims of Christ nor a mere stirring of the emotions resulting from an impassioned plea nor, finally, a momentary impulsive choice under high psychological pressure. It must be the deliberate response of a heart that is deeply conscious of sin to the glorious offer of salvation in Christ; the "amen" of the soul, elicited by the Holy Spirit, to all the blessed promises of the Gospel; the hearty and unqualified acceptance of all the covenant obligations. It is not something of a momentary or evanescent character, but an abiding attitude of the soul in which it recognizes its own sinfulness and lost condition and ever anew embraces the righteousness of Jesus Christ. But the faith that is required of covenant children is not merely passive, is not only a receptive organ; it is also active as the principle of a new obedience. From this faith must spring love to God, to Jesus Christ, and to the people of God. And all the thoughts and words and actions of covenant children must be motivated by that divinely wrought love. Then only will their lives be well pleasing to God.

But this already points to the second requirement of the covenant. Faith is the only condition for *entrance* into the life of the covenant; but for the *full realization* of that relation of friendship between God and man for which the covenant stands, faith must be complemented by a life of sanctification. The covenant child belongs to a peculiar people, a people that is separated from the world in consecration to God; separated, not like Israel of old by towering mountains, vast waters, and arid deserts, but by a far more effective line of cleavage wrought by the Spirit of God. And what does the Lord require in that capacity? With Micah we may say, "to do justly and to love kindness, and to walk humbly with thy God"; or with Paul that, "denying ungodliness and worldly lusts," they should "live soberly and righteously and godly in this present world." The life of the covenant child should ever increasingly become a true inflection of the life of Christ that is born within the heart. Nothing short of the perfect life is its grand ideal.

Now surely it needs no argument that children of whom such great, such spiritual, such heavenly things are required must be educated in the fear of the Lord. Christian education is one of the means which God is pleased to use for working faith in the heart of the child, for calling an incipient faith into action, and for guiding the first faltering steps of faith. It teaches the child to flee from sin and to strive after holiness, without which no one will see the Lord. It takes the child by the hand, and leads it step by step on the highway of sanctification to the city of the eternal King. What a blessed task, this task of Christian educators; but also, what a responsible duty! Oh, for hearts aflame with the love of God, for men and women filled with the Spirit of Christ, for teachers that speak with the tongues of angels, to perform the well-nigh staggering task of helping to qualify covenant children for their covenant responsibilities!

We sought to give an answer to the important question how the covenant of grace naturally calls for Christian education. In answer to the query why Christian parents are in duty bound to give their covenant children a specifically Christian education, we are usually referred to their baptismal promise. And rightly so. But this answer is apt to lead a reflective mind on to the further question, Why does the form of baptism insist on it, as it does, that covenant children be given such an education? We have made an attempt to point out that the covenant relation itself naturally and necessarily calls for this. May our feeble efforts contribute something to a better understanding of this important subject. May our eyes be opened ever increasingly to the glorious heritage that is ours and our children's in the covenant of grace. And may the interest in our schools grow apace, for we have in them the most effective agency to train our children for their high dignity as members of the household of God, to teach them a due appreciation and the right use of the covenant blessings, and to qualify them for their covenant responsibilities. Then God will receive all the honor; we and our children will sing unending praises to His glorious name.

Louis Berkhof

Address before the National Union of
Christian Schools Convention, Kalamazoo,
Michigan, August 27, 1929.

Key Thoughts:

1. In the struggle for Christian schools the doctrine of the covenant has always been the great presupposition.

2. In the providence of God the covenant idea first found expression in the natural life of man, and was only afterward embodied in divine revelation. However, God's covenant is the divine original, and all covenants among men are but faint reflections of it.

3. The covenant of grace is "that gracious compact or agreement between the offended God and the offending sinner in which God promises salvation through faith in Christ, and the sinner accepts believingly."

4. In origin and in effective operation the covenant is one-sided. It is of God and through God. But in Scripture it is clearly presented as a covenant, and is necessarily of the nature of an agreement between two parties. "God condescended to come down to the level of man in the covenant of works, and promised to reward a temporary obedience with life eternal. Again, He condescended to come down to the level of *sinful* man in Christ, and now in the covenant of grace offers eternal life to all that accept Christ by faith."

5. In the covenant of grace God gives His only-begotten Son, and the Son voluntarily takes upon Himself to become surety for lost and helpless sinners.

6. The promises in the covenant are for us and for our children. These promises are comprehensive: forgiveness of sins, adoption into the family of God, transformed lives, and heirship with all its privileges.

7. The covenant of grace is conditional. In the first place, as the covenant of works was conditioned on the obedience of Adam, so the covenant of grace is conditioned on the suffering and obedience of Christ. Christ has merited all the blessings of the covenant of grace. There is no condition which man must fulfill in his own strength. But there are prerequisites for entering the covenant, for sharing the life of the covenant, and for obtaining the full blessings of the covenant. Men enter the covenant relationship either by birth from Christian parents or by a profession of faith in Christ. They become conscious partakers of the covenant life by a saving faith in Christ Jesus, wrought in their hearts by the Holy Spirit. They obtain the full possession and enjoyment of the blessings of the covenant by faith and sanctification, a life of childlike obedience.

8. The covenant is an established covenant, a covenant agreed to by parents *also for their children.* The covenant is an agreement which the children of Christian parents entered by commitment on the part of their parents.

9. Our form of baptism implies that there is a close relationship between the covenant relationship and Christian education. The parents publicly assume the responsibility of instructing their children in the "aforesaid doctrine." This is the doctrine contained in the Old and New Testament, "the whole round of Christian truth with its broad sweep, touching every realm, every sphere, and every relation of Christian life." This indicates the spirit that should promote the instruction of covenant children.

10. In essentially three ways the covenant relation involves the duty to give the covenant children a Christian education:

    a. The children are with their parents adopted into the family of God.

    b. Children of Christian parents fall heir to covenant promises. Only a fuller apprehension of these promises enriches our enjoyment of them.

    c. The covenant promises impose upon our children a heavy responsibility.

Comment:

The Christian school follows from the covenant promises to and covenant obligations of Christian parents. This scriptural principle controls the entire Christian school idea. Everything we say about schooling or education in the school follows from this principle. Only the Christian school can relate this principle to the facts of education.

Sometimes we hear other grounds given to justify the Christian school. While many of these grounds have merit as a reason for establishing and maintaining schools founded on the Bible, they generally do not point primarily to the covenant obligation of parents. Hence, they are at best secondary considerations. In a sense they follow from the covenant idea.

5

The Education of Man — A Divinely Ordained Need

There is perhaps no concept underlying our system of education better fitted to bring out the distinctive character of Christian education than the concept of creation. Not as though our concept of creation is the most basic concept of our system of education; the most basic concept of all is our concept of God. But our notion of creation affords a more readily available testing point than the notion of God. Creation has more directly to do with ourselves. It has to do with the universe that is visible. And as such it offers a ready target of attack for the enemy. The attacks on creation have been more direct and more self-conscious than the attacks on God. If one defends the notion of creation he is directly regarded as defending something that very few will defend today.

Again, the creation idea when seen to be the presupposition of the covenant idea brings out the distinctiveness of the *Reformed* view of education. There are many who, believing the Bible from cover to cover, also believe in creation. They are even quite ready to defend the creation idea against the evolution idea. Yet their fight is ofttimes in the interest of soteriology only. They know that salvation through Christ presupposes creation by God. But they see no need of fighting for the creation concept in order to assure a foundation for a genuine Christian culture. Since they have no eye for the meaning of the covenant, their interest in maintaining the Biblical idea of creation is unbiblically narrow. Accordingly, as a corrective to this narrowly evangelical tendency we must defend creation as the very presupposition of the covenant. Then only will it bring out and give a foundation to the distinctiveness of our Reformed system of covenant education.

Now we are to find in the idea of creation a divine ordinance for education. An ordinance for Christian education we usually seek and find in direct commandments of God to his people as they are recorded in the Scriptures. Or, more basically, we see such an ordinance to be involved in the covenant idea. Now, if possible more basically again, we are to find such an ordinance in the very notion of creation. And this is the right order of seeking for an ordinance of God for education.

39

Direct commandments of God with respect to education are really no more than explications of the covenant idea. And the covenant idea is but a compressed statement of the educational principle involved in the idea of creation. When thus the direct commands of God are seen to be based upon the covenant and the covenant is seen to be based upon creation there will be a proportionate increase in the conviction of the justice and necessity of our educational program.

But what, then, do we mean by education? *Education is implication into God's interpretation.* No narrow intellectualism is implied in this definition. To think God's thoughts after him, to dedicate the universe to its Maker, and to be the vice-regent of the Ruler of all things; this is man's task. Man is prophet, priest, and king. It is this view of education that is involved in and demanded by the idea of creation.

It may be charged that we are at the outset arbitrarily setting up a certain theory of education and a certain theory of creation and then mechanically patching them together. Now we would grant not only but strongly affirm that certain theories of creation and certain theories of education stand or fall together. One of our chief interests is to see clearly this very fact. All too loosely are the terms creation and education bandied about. In the mouths of different men these terms may have any of several mutually exclusive connotations. We must know definitely what we mean by creation, what we mean by education, and why a certain view of education is involved in a certain view of creation. And then as to the charge of starting dogmatically we would only urge that this charge itself is based upon the dogmatically assumed position of neutrality. If the charge of dogmatism is to be hurled at us before we fairly get under way we reserve the school-boy's right to say, "You did it, too." Perhaps neither of us can be neutral. At any rate, we state baldly first and defend afterwards.

Our method will, in fact, be purposely apologetic. That Christian instruction is based upon the Scriptures we know. That Christian instruction is involved in the covenant idea we also know. That Christian instruction is involved in the idea of creation we also, though perhaps less clearly, understand. But to defend Christian instruction against those of the contrary part is no easy task. Perhaps it will be a somewhat easier task if we see more clearly the relation between Christian education and the notion of creation. Perhaps we have tried to justify our educational policy by pointing to its fruits. But these fruits are not always of the best. Moreover, you can point to external things and things for this life only. Perhaps we are hastily trying to improve our buildings and general technique in order to come up to public educational standards. But that race is hopeless and again pertains to externals alone. The final apologetic for Christian education must show that Christian education is involved in the covenant, that the covenant is involved in creation, that creation is involved in the idea of God and that without God man's life and experience would be entirely meaningless. In the last analysis we need more than anything else an immovable assurance of the truth of the principle on which we base our educational policy. With this in mind we try to prove that whatever difficulties may be involved in our view of education it is the only view that is reasonable for man to take.

We shall, in order to establish our position that in creation there is a divine ordinance for education, spend a large part of our time in reviewing the various philosophies of education in order to show that none of them, save the Christian theistic philosophy of education, has any divine ordinance, in fact, any ordinance, any reason for its educational policy at all. Our contention will not be that there are no intellectual difficulties in our philosophy of education. There most surely are such difficulties. These difficulties are many and great. But there is no philosophy of education that has no difficulties. Hence it will not do, as was the easy custom of the rationalism of the eighteenth century, to cast the Christian theistic philosophy overboard because there were very patent intellectual difficulties involved in it. Nor, on the other hand, is it sufficient in order to defend the Christian theistic philosophy of education to show that it has less, or at least, no more difficulties with which to contend than other philosophies of education. It is too late in the day of speculative thought for any one to attempt to present a philosophy of education not well loaded with intellectual difficulties. The question is now one of to be or not to be. Is there any philosophy of education that can stand at all? Is there any such philosophy that does not reduce the whole of educational policy and procedure to a meaningless march from the inane to the void? We believe there is one and one only, namely, the Christian theistic philosophy of education. We do not now discuss how we have pedagogically received our view of education. Of course we have received it from parents and teachers, just as every human being receives his general philosophy from his forebears. But the question is, now that we have to assume the responsibility of educators, whether we would still continue to hold to that which we have received on authority when we were children. We would have to reject our views if the criticisms of others would make it clear to us that our views are unreasonable for a human being to hold. But if our investigation proves to us that it is unreasonable to hold to any other view, we are strengthened in the conviction of the reasonableness of our own.

Our apologetic can, accordingly, afford to use no time for details. There is ofttimes need for detail apologetic, but detail apologetic must always be fully conscious of its subordinate position. In the argument for and against organic evolution this is sometimes forgotten. The fight on this sector of the front is sometimes waged in such a manner as though the issue could be settled at this place alone and once for all. So also men sometimes fight about the trustworthiness of the Scripture as though the next move of someone's spade in Palestine could determine everything. Facts, to be sure, are stubborn things, but facts must be interpreted. The philosophy assumed by evolutionists is a far more dangerous thing than the evidence that they bring. So also with the so-called facts of psychology and anthropology that have a bearing upon education. These facts, too, must be interpreted. And interpreted they are. Now all facts are interpreted in either of two ways. Men are either Theists or Anti-theists. The whole battle about facts is a mad scramble between these two kinds of philosophers. So every philosophy of education, too, is theistic or anti-theistic. It is on the major issue between Theism and Anti-theism that educational philosophies should meet.

The anti-theistic philosophy assumes a myriad forms. Yet this multiformity should not deceive us. All forms of Anti-theism reveal a common hatred for the theistic doctrine of creation. If a Theism is Theism indeed, with the notion of God as an absolute self-conscious personality as its determining concept, it can depend upon firm and persistent opposition from all varieties of Anti-theism, however much they may propose organic union.

Thus the range and sweep of our apologetic for Christian education begins to assume form and shape. To show that Christian education is based upon the notion of creation, that this notion of creation in turn is an inseparable part of the whole theistic philosophy of life and that this philosophy of life is the most reasonable for man to take because all others reduce experience to something void of significance, such will be our effort.

*   *   *

Our Christian education is based upon the notion of a temporal creation. There are many who incorporate the concept of creation into their system of thought but who mean by creation nothing more than logical dependence. Now, whatever creation may mean for someone else, for the Christian educator creation definitely implies that time and space do not exist in the same way for God as they exist for man. This fact will appear more clearly later. Suffice it here to indicate that here lies the pivotal point of difference between Theists and Anti-theists. Theism says that man is subject to the categories of space and time while God is not. Every variety of Anti-theism says that space and time, if they are real, exist for God, if God is real, in the same way that they exist for man.

In the literature that deals with the problem of creation at all, such phrases as "the nature of thought" and "the nature of Reality" recur again and again. The assumption of such statements is that *all* thought and *all* reality, whether divine or human, is subject to the same laws and limitations. Whether or not God can be personal is determined, for example, by asking whether thought, that is, thought *per se,* can allow for the conception of absolute personality. That God cannot be absolute is sometimes deduced from the "fact" that all thought is relative. The only thing really known is that human thought is relative, but the assumption is made that divine thought must also be.

It is all-important to see that the opposition to the doctrine of creation and to Theism in general is based upon this colossal assumption. If this assumption stands, the Christian schools must fall, but if this assumption falls, the Christian schools can stand.

If now one keeps clearly in mind this assumption of the identity of nature between human and divine thought, it will readily be understood why the idea of temporal creation must bear so much of the brunt of anti-theistic attack. Temporal creation implies the very denial of that assumption. Creation implies that God's thought alone is original and absolute, while human thought is derivative and finite. Creation implies that finite personality has been brought forth by absolute personality. Hence absolute personality could and did eternally exist in self-dependence with absolute self-interpretative power. Hence finite personality would have to look up to absolute personality as its pattern but could never set the ideal of absolute comprehension for itself. Finite personality must believe that complete comprehensive interpretation exists in absolute personality and that this comprehensive interpretation of God furnishes the only basis for man's interpretation as far as that interpretation goes. If one denies temporal creation, one must deny all that is implied in it.

The chief implication of temporal creation, the one most obnoxious to the anti-theistic assumption of the identity of the nature of all thought, is the implication that man can never claim intellectual comprehension as an ideal for himself. It is plain that if there is to be rationality anywhere there must be absolute rationality somewhere. If this were not so, rationality would float upon irrationality. If, then, human thought is identical in nature with divine thought, man must hold that complete comprehension of interpretation is a reasonable demand for him to make. If man's thoughts are not subject to greater limitations than God's thoughts, there is no reason why man should not eventually, if not now, understand all things; the unknowable is for him reduced to the unknown. Unless man makes the bold claim of essential comprehensibility for himself, he cannot be certain but that somewhere in the Universe a God exists whose thoughts are self-dependent or absolute, and who will therefore shatter the very assumption on which man had made his claims. No god must be left who will be able to tell of the slaughter of the gods.

Accordingly man *must* reject every view of creation that is not comprehensible to him. He must reject any view of creation that involves a qualitative difference between God and man. It is not the evidence of modern evolutionary theory that has made the notion of special creation disrespectful, but it is the colossal assumption of all anti-theistic thought that has forced men, irrespective of facts, to deny the possibility of creation.

* * *

The argument most frequently used against the possibility of creation readily betrays itself to be but the explication of the anti-theistic assumption spoken of. We are told that a God who was absolute or self-sufficient would not create the universe we are familiar with because he would have no need of it and it could have no meaning of its own. The only God that can possibly exist, now that this universe is here, is a finite God and a finite God could not create the whole spatial-temporal universe. The argument restated runs thus: We cannot understand how a universe created by an absolute God can have meaning at all, and therefore no absolute God has created it. Or, our thought cannot exist independently of the spatial-temporal universe, hence an absolute God has created it. The assumption of the argument clearly is that since our thought is not absolute, God's thought cannot be; God's thought must be identical in nature with ours.

But the attack on the creation doctrine has not always been so explicit. The conflict between Theism and Anti-theism has gradually become more self-conscious and outspoken. And an outspoken enemy is not the most dangerous enemy. It is the mask of friendliness toward the creation idea assumed by many anti-theistic philosophies that has always been and is now most dangerous of all. We must therefore trace some of the forms anti-theistic educational philosophy has taken in order to learn to recognize it even under cover.

Plato's *Republic* is even today considered to be a classic of educational philosophy. No better illustration of anti-theistic education could be taken. His philosophy is typical. In his philosophy no attempt could yet be made to intertwine Christian and pagan motifs.

In Plato's philosophy there is, strange to say, an overemphasis on the timeless or eternal. Is this possible judging from the theistic point of view? Yes, it is. Overemphasis on the eternity of God is impossible. But the overemphasis appears when man is made eternal as well as God. So modernism today speaks much of the divinity of Christ, but also speaks of the divinity of man without realizing, unless dishonest, that it has thus necessarily changed the meaning of the term divinity when applied to Christ.

For Plato nothing is truly real unless it be eternal. The whole visible world is only faintly real in so far as it, somehow, partakes of the eternity of the invisible world of ideas. Man's soul is more real than his body because more of eternity dwells in the immaterial soul than possibly could dwell in the material body. Time itself is real in so far as it is a "moving image of eternity." And space as the matrix from which all visible things derive is itself somehow eternal.

It will appear that Plato has begun with the anti-theistic assumption of the identity of nature of all thought, human and divine. His standard of Reality is an abstract principle, a principle of thought *per se,* that is assumed to exist apart from God. God is real in so far as he can live up to this principle. The Universe, at least the Ideal Universe, exists apart from God. God falls within the universe. Man, because somehow he partakes of this eternal principle, can determine all this with respect to God. It is this assumed rationalism that determines all of Plato's thought.

Some corrolaries following from Plato's chief assumption we must note. In the first place principle is raised to a metaphysical status higher than that of personality. This elevation of principle above personality in the realm of reality must follow if one starts with an abstract principle in the field of thought or knowledge. God *must* be a dependent personality once the Platonic rationalism be one's starting point. Once abstract thought as a principle is accepted as the Umpire between God and man, God must be dependent because the Umpire must be higher than both God and man. Secondly, on the basis of the Platonic assumption one cannot speak of a temporal creation. God is within the Universe, and the Universe to be real must be eternal. It is this Platonic rationalism that has constantly been and is today the real source of opposition to the idea of temporal creation.

It is well that we see just what the Platonic conception of knowledge and reality implies for the interpretation of reality. In the Platonic philosophy interpretation becomes a cooperative enterprise between God and man. It is true that Plato honors God by lifting him to a rather high place in the Universe. It is also true that Plato sometimes seeks in revelation for a solution of the problems with which he wrestles. But these facts do not qualify our statement that interpretation is for Plato no more than a cooperative affair. Man, though said to be created by God, had to be fashioned according to principles of goodness, truth and beauty existing independently of God, out of material once more existing independently of God. Accordingly, man was really more dependent upon these abstract principles and the independent material than upon God. Thus man did not need to live by revelation only. He could live first of all by the embodiment of the principles of goodness, truth and beauty; he could be a rationalist. He could, when unsuccessful in interpretation, ask God whether he, embracing somehow somewhat more of these principles, had any information on the matter in hand. But both God and man were dependent upon principles higher than themselves. Neither of them was the source of principle; both were embodiments of principle. There were areas of the unknown and unknowable for both God and man; they were wrestlers with Truth, both of them. Of course there could, on such a basis, be no divine ordinance for anything in the absolute sense of the term. There was no real authority of God over man. Both God and man needed education. One could really speak as well of a human ordinance for divine education as of a divine ordinance for human education.

Then, further, the cooperation between God and man may not be permanent. Cooperation of equals presupposes the independence of each member of the corporation. As long as all things go harmoniously, cooperation may continue. But is harmony, continued harmony, possible when there is a plurality of minds? It might be, we shall say, if both God and man were fully controlled by (because complete embodiments of the principles of goodness) truth and beauty. Sorry to say, these principles were not all-pervasive in the Universe. They could not be in a world of space and time. Plurality itself involves evil for Plato because no member of the purality can be comprehensive. There must be identity if there is to be harmony. Accordingly it could not be otherwise than that man must ofttimes differ from God on the matter of interpretation. And what could man do otherwise in such a case than follow his own honest convictions? Man, if rationalistic at the outset, must remain so to the end. Cooperative interpretation is really independent interpretation.

So man interprets Reality for himself. He must even determine just what place God occupies in the Universe. We will observe that Plato's view is identical with that of Eve in Paradise. Eve also elevated principles of right above God, and proceeded to determine for herself according to these principles what God's place was in the Universe and what He could or could not do. Thus we learn to identify the Platonic assumption with the sin of man, the original and controlling sin of man.   Thus we also understand what is meant by anti-theistic thought.

Anti-theistic thought, because of its initial assumption, *must* deny God.   It *must* deny the possibility of the creation of perfect though finite beings.   It *must* deny creation *per se*.   It *must* deny the meaning of history if God exists.   Not because of difficulties involved in the theistic view of God — and creation is Theism rejected — but because it is at the outset assumed to be wrong.

Once this fact, that all of anti-theistic thought is based upon one colossal assumption, is clearly seen we are not so easily tempted to yield to its siren song of open-mindedness, neutrality and progress. Especially if we see in addition that of all men Anti-theists have no right to make any assumptions at all.   They have left the theistic camp for the very reason that Theism was altogether based upon the assumption or presupposition of an absolute self-conscious God.   They would have none of such presuppositions but begin to investigate for themselves.   Thus we must needs ask them to be true to their starting point and we are not so ready to accept their conclusions once we see that the whole fabric of their thought is built upon one great assumption.   We simply ask the Anti-theist which assumption seems more reasonable to make for finite time-dependent man, the assumption of an absolute God or the assumption of an absolute man.

Which assumption is more reasonable?   By their fruits ye shall know them.   Theism was rejected, according to those who rejected it, because of great intellectual difficulties involved in its concepts. We would reject Anti-theism in turn because it reduces all human experience and the whole of history to a meaningless something.   If there be no absolute God, Himself the ultimate, eternal Reality and as such the creator of the space-time Universe, there will not be any interpretation at all.   There is then no unity to furnish any meaning to plurality.   An ultimate plurality without an equally ultimate unity shatters all interpretation.   The only basis of unity offered by Anti-theism is that of a principle apart from personality, and a principle apart from personality can be no more than an abstract universal. Such an abstract universal has no comprehension because it has no existence of itself and therefore can furnish no basis of comprehension and interpretation for others.   Anti-theism is based upon an assumption to which it has no right and which leads it to self-annihilation.

We have dwelt thus long upon Plato because his thought as a whole and his philosophy of education in particular is typical of all that we see and hear round about us today.   Modern philosophy has often tried the impossible in seeking to combine Christian Theism with Platonic thought.   Consequently we have with us many hybrid philosophies that easily deceive by their apparent similarity to Theism. On the other hand the opposition to Theism that was chiefly implicit in ancient times has become more explicit now. What were assumptions then are raised to first principles now.

This increase in self-consciousness in general is particularly true with the Platonic assumption of the identity of nature of all thought divine and human. Kant has raised this assumption to the position of the master principle of modern philosophy. Herein lay his Copernican revolution, although the really Copernican revolution was originally accomplished by Eve. According to Kant thought is *creatively constructive*. That is, *all* thought is creatively constructive, human as well as divine. That is real and is true which is in accordance with the laws of thought, and that is unreal and untrue which is not in accordance with the laws of thought. Such is Kant's contention. We see the same elevation of the abstract principle of thought to the highest possible metaphysical and epistemological status that we observed in Plato. We see now a more clearly avowed emphasis on man's equal originality with God. We see now a greater stress upon comprehensibility to man as a test of truth. Plato would, when pressed, make a desperate, can-do-no-harm appeal to Revelation, but Kant has put away such childish things. He cannot accept anything from a Beyond. Nothing that finds no immediate response in and recognition by the laws of thought working in man's mind can be accepted. To do so would be to deny that human thought is creative. It is not only in the field of morality that Kant has declared man's independence. His independent morality is but the logical conclusion in one direction of the principle of the creativity of thought. This principle must work in every direction. Man, if creative, is altogether independent.

We do not expect that creation shall receive honorable mention from Kant, if human thought itself is essentially creative how could it be created? Human thought, if created, would be primarily receptive and only secondarily creative. But for Kant human thought is primarily creative and therefore not created. Again, creation implies that God's thought alone is absolutely and originally creative. This original and exclusive creativity on the part of God is denied by Kant. God is creative to be sure, but so is man. And, really, God's creativity is not only limited by man's equal creativity but by law's independence. The God of Thesim is bowed out with thanks for past services and another god is ushered in to do watchdog duty by the side of law.

It is this master principle of the creativity of human thought that holds in its grip with unquestioned predominance all modern philosophy in general and all modern philosophy of education in particular. It is against this master principle as the heart of anti-theistic educational policy that alone we fight. Fight not against anyone great nor small but against this king alone. Unmask this king! Take away his royal robe of boasted neutrality! Remove the plumes of principle and but an ugly assumption remains. Once this is done the theistic hosts need fear no longer.

But this exposure is not always easy. By skilful manipulation modern Idealism has taken Christian theistic phraseology into its system though loading down each term with a content utterly foreign to its habits. Modern Idealism is the elder son of the parable professing faithfulness to the father but alienated from the father in his heart. Idealism speaks much of "creation," but by "creation" it means no more than logical dependence. And God is logically dependent upon man as well as man is logically dependent upon God. Hence one could speak of the creation of God about as well as of the creation of man. It is this that makes modern Idealism so dangerous to Christian Theism. It has taught modernism the art of putting new wine into old bottles without changing the labels. When Modernism speaks much of the beautiful Ideals to which Jesus devoted his life, it conceives of these Ideals as existing independently of God as well as of existing independently of Jesus and as such Modernism is not only anti-Christian, but anti-theistic as well. As long as Idealism and Modernism will not forsake the Kantian-Platonic assumption of the essential creativity of human thought no Theist can afford to raise the flag of peace.

*   *   *

But we must bring the action of the Platonic-Kantian somewhat more definitely down to date and in direct contact with educational policy today. "Pragmatism" is in the air. John Dewey controls education today. It is evolution with which we struggle. Why not speak of them instead of spending so much time on Plato of pre-Christian times? So you might say. Yet I am persuaded that one can in no way deal satisfactorily with J. Dewey, with Pragmatism and with Evolution unless one has dealt with Plato and Kant. All that Pragmatism has done is to work out the Platonic-Kantian assumption in a particular and perhaps most logically consistent direction.

We have already seen that since anti-theistic rationalism had to deny creation, two and only two possible ways were open to it. The first was that of making all reality eternal, the second was that of making all reality temporal. Plato and modern Idealism have tried the former and modern Idealism has perforce begun to admit that it has run into a *cul de sac*. Time is too real, at least the illusion of time is too real to be long denied. And since, by hypothesis, God and man are subject to the same laws in the same way, it follows that if man can no longer breath in the rarified air of the eternal and must come down to the valleys of time and space, God will have to come down with him. Pragmatism has therefore followed the second road as the only alternative to making all reality eternal; it has said that all reality is temporal. It has said, and said logically, that if Kant was right in saying that human thought is essentially creative, and man is a temporally conditioned being, then all reality is on the move. Orthodox Idealism has tried to exercise this Galileo of Pragmatism, but under his breath he said, "It does move, nevertheless." Nothing could stop the force of logic. If Eve was right Plato was right, if Plato was right Kant was right, and if Kant was right John Dewey is right, and if John Dewey is right the anti-Christian, anti-theistic system of education is right.

Strange to say, however, even Pragmatism has not altogether rejected theistic-Christian terminology. The "creation" idea in particular, has not been discarded. Bergson speaks of "creative evolution." He thinks that he has made genuine room for creation once he has opposed mechanism and materialism, just as Kant thought he had made genuine room for religion and God just because he opposed a particular excrescence of Rationalism. But what can "creation" mean apart from God? For Bergson the Void is God. Bare possibility as a shoreless and bottomless ocean envelopes the little speck of reality under our feet. Similarly S. Alexander speaks of Space, Time and Deity. Deity is for him an ideal that a space-time originated humanity has somehow cast out as an anchor to an invisible sky. God is created as well as man and of the two man appears earlier upon the screen. Here is the climax of the Platonic-Kantian principle. God has completely made the rounds. Instead of the creator of the universe, he is created by the Universe. He is to be an Omega without an Alpha.

Can education or interpretation on this basis appeal to God for its ordinance for a *raison d'etre*? Very clearly not. Man will not implicate himself into God's interpretation. Such interpretation no longer exists. If there is to be any warrant, ordinance or reason for man's educational policy it must lie in man himself. It is the apotheosis, the number of man.

But just here comes the difficulty. We have already seen that by its fruits ye shall know anti-theism. A basic pluralism without an equally basic unity, we saw, reduced experience to a meaningless something. This reduction to the meaningless of all experience as inherent in the Platonic-Kantian principle becomes most apparent in the case of Pragmatism. An avowed original pluralism with man as charter member has now become pluralism in flux. Time is made an inherent ingredient of all reality and herewith rationality as we see it in man is made to drift on the void. The bold demand for complete comprehension found this universe too narrow if God were back of it. It has made room by removing God, but it has made too much room for itself. Man would not implicate itself into God's interpretation, but the removal of God's interpretation has also effected the removal of all interpretation. There is no longer a coherent universe into which man can implicate himself. The Platonic-Kantian principle has elevated law, above God, above personality, but law is turned to license when thus elevated. Not one bit of reality can be said to be related to another bit; judgment, reason itself is destroyed. There is no rationality in anything. Pragmatism is the younger son, the prodigal, realizing that his substance is being devoured, but the more loudly proclaiming the wisdom of his leaving the father's house.

When the Pragmatism, Evolution and Neutralism largely in control of modern educational theory are thus seen to rest their whole program upon one assumption which leads to the destruction of every bit of reason for education itself, we ourselves take new courage. Whatever the intellectual difficulties involved in our view we are not ready to accept the only substitute that is offered us. Is it poor advertising ethics to "run down" our competitor's product in order to sell our own? Nay, our business is not commercial. The analogy does not hold. We employ the ethics of Solomon when he pictured the consequences for those who loved the "strange woman," who appeared so fair and offered allurement — the emptiness of which was hard for healthful youth to see.

Only in passing would we call attention to the fact that our survey, however rapid, claims to be exhaustive. There is and can be no educational policy and practice not based upon the Platonic-Kantian rationalism except that of Christian theistic education. There are and recently have been philosophers of education who reject Pragmatism and even reject Idealism to some extent. They want to be called Theists. "Creation" is much in vogue with them. They speak of the will of God as the source of this world. They maintain the necessity of the transcendence of God. The reference is to A. S. Pringle-Pattison, C. C. J. Webb, H. Rashdall, J. Lindsay and E. Hocking as philosophers, and K. Barth and E. Brunner as theologians. We most surely rejoice in their reaction against the immanentism of modern Idealism, but as long as avowedly or implicitly they still build upon the Platonic-Kantian principle of the creativity of human thought we cannot accept their overtures of peace. A Theism they may proclaim, but a Theism that is at bottom hostile to the Theism we desire.

Now, if the analysis we have sought to give of anti-theistic educational philosophy is true and exhaustive it follows that our defense against or attack upon any particular educational policy should always keep this central principle in mind. The most important thing is not what particular form an anti-theistic educational philosophy assumes, but the important thing is and remains that it is anti-theistic. Pragmatism may be the most popular opponent of our educational policy today. Pragmatism may be the most outspokenly hostile to our views. Natural it is that we should fight Pragmatism most. But let us beware lest fighting Pragmatism we make subtle entangling alliance with any idealistic or would-be theistic philosophy that may chance to have a minor quarrel with Pragmatism, too. Their quarrels are after all family quarrels and since we fight against the family as such we must take good care lest we harbor scorpions in our bosom. To play off the Assyrian against the Egyptian, or the Egyptian against the Assyrian may be wise and legitimate, but an entangling alliance with either is everlastingly forbidden for a covenant people.

*   *   *

We have said that Idealism was as the elder son and Pragmatism as the younger son of the parable when he refused to return though he already knew something of his folly. Now, to carry forth the analogy, we may call Theism in general and our theistic-Christian philosophy of education in particular, the prodigal returned to the father's house because drawn by the father's love. In hot-headed haste we had denied creation and therewith our dependence upon the father's interpretation. In "riotous living" we had spent our substance, unwilling to admit that the land in which we dwelt was still the father's land. We had made the antithesis to God so great and final that no natural pendulum swing could, Hegelian-like, bring us to synthesis with God again. Only God Himself could effect a synthesis between ourselves and Him.   Hence we do not wonder that others build upon and will not forsake an altogether unreasonable assumption. We do not expect men to be reasonable unless God has once more made them so. But this does not vitiate the usefulness of reasoning with unreasonable men. Such reasoning strengthens our faith, and who knows, may be used by the Spirit to make men reasonable.

It is thus that we return to the once discarded doctrine of creation. We do not accept it now because we no longer see or have solved all intellectual difficulties involved in it. But we have learned of the unreasonableness of the Platonic-Kantian assumption. We have learned that comprehension is no reasonable demand for man to make. We now experience that to seek for interpretation by ourselves apart from God leads to a fiasco, to self-stultification and complete destruction. We now realize that we need a God who is himself and alone complete self-conscious rationality. If there is to be reason in anything under the sun God must be absolute. He alone must be external since no externity of ours could furnish comprehensive rationality. If we are made eternal with Him the case is hopeless because God is then reduced to one of us; if He is temporal with us the case is, if possible, more hopeless still because then we have wilfully cast all hope of coherence in experience overboard.

St. Augustine has already taught us this. His thought is at bottom the polar opposite of Plato's. For Plato the Ideas or laws are next to or higher than God; for Augustine the ideas or laws are expressive of God's nature. No more radical difference is conceivable. For Plato God wants the good because it is good in itself; for Augustine the good is good because God wants it and God wants it because it is expressive of His nature. For Augustine God's interpretation is prior even to the existence of the spatio-temporal universe. It is made according to God's plan. Would one interpret reality, would one interpret anything, one must find in it the plan of God. Once this plan is found, truth is found. Whether this truth be fully comprehensible to man or not, it is the truth nevertheless.

For St. Augustine human thought is primarily receptive and thereupon reconstructive. Man as a finite rational personality must live by revelation alone. His thought is not passive or inactive. In fact, true and fruitful activity exists only where true receptivity is found. No one but the Theist finds sufficient friction to make advance in the slippery highways of interpretation. He alone does not jump from one ice lump to another in the midst of a torrential stream. He alone does not try to breathe in a vacuum. God must be external and man must be temporal or there is no interpretation at all. And since only the notion of temporal creation provides for this distinction between God and man it will now be clear that only the creation of man by God gives divine ordinance for education. Ours is a theistic system of education. If our policy of education is reasonable, is necessary, is the only reasonable system of education, it is because Theism is reasonable, is necessary, is the only reasonable philosophy for man. Our system of education is as strong as Theism is; therefore be not afraid but of good courage.

*   *   *

We have thus far purposely spoken of theistic instead of Christian education in order to call particular attention to the fact that those who reject our educational philosophy reject no "oddity" but reason itself. We have in this way already indicated that Christian education and theistic education are identical. It would seem to be useful to emphasize this fact. When sometimes we are tempted to doubt the worth-whileness of our efforts, especially if we live in a community where the Bible is still read in the public schools and dancing is not permitted, and we are asked, nevertheless, to give freely of our hard-earned dollars for Christian education, the most helpful thing would seem to be to realize that, whatever the details may be the whole of so-called neutral education is based upon the Platonic-Kantian principle of the independence of human thought and as such is diametrically opposed to Christianity not only but to God. When this is clearly perceived, Christian education means to us more than a soteriological lifeboat, an institute of conversion. Christian education then becomes the *sine qua non* of human life itself; a true humanism and a genuinely human culture presupposes a temporal creation. Thus, the education not only of the Christian, but of the human being, of man as created, is a divinely ordained necessity.

What now remains to be done is to relate more definitely the super-structure of Christian or Reformed education to the theistic foundation we have sought to lay. Or rather, since theistic education has been identified with Christian education instead of made the foundation of Christian education, we must speak of our reasons for this identifi-cation. These reasons would not seem to be so immediately available. We ordinarily tend to think of theism as a philosophy only incidentally related to the Scriptures. And we are very shy lest our seeking a theistic foundation for Christianity and our making a good deal of a theistic defense of Christian education should weaken our firm belief in the testimony of the Spirit as the only real source of faith in Chris-tianity. Yet I am firmly convinced that we must hold to the one and not leave the other undone. A theistic defense of Christian education is not unnecessary because of, nor does it in the least affect our belief in, the all-determinative work of the Holy Spirit.

In the first place Christianity is a restorative religion. Christianity is Theism restored and brought to its own. Christ came to bring man and his cosmos back to the God of creation. Those that accept salvation become true Theists once more. They and they only are Theists inasmuch as those that are not for the Christ are against Him. The line of separation between Theist and non-Theist is just as clear as the line of separation between Christian and non-Christian because the one line carves more deeply the other line. Of course there are thousands that resent this way of putting things. Modernism wants to be called Christian. We can only answer that it is not only anti-Christian but anti-theistic as well. At least the Christianity and the

Theism it professes to hold are just as deadly hostile to the Christianity and the Theism we profess to hold as could conceivably be. What then is there in the name?

As Christians we believe in the absoluteness of Christ. He said of Himself, "I am the Way, the Truth and the Life." That is, from him proceeds the Truth. He, because of God, does not testify to an independently existing principle of truth, but posits truth itself. This were impossible unless Christ, as well as God, be absolute eternally self-sufficient personality. The alternative is once more clear and exhaustive. If you would accept the Christ as He wants to be accepted, you must accept His identity with God not only but His identity with an absolute, comprehensively self-interpretative God. I cannot in any genuine sense be a Christian unless I believe in a God who alone interprets to me.

Accordingly Christ said that we must make His words the standard of belief and life. So Paul also says that every thought must be brought captive to the obedience of Christ. Obedience is not the subjective correspondent to an Old Testament arbitrary God alone. Obedience to Christ is simply the receptively reconstructive attitude of the human being once more. It is this that Christ came to restore. Whether this receptivity reveal itself in the direction of matters pertaining immediately to salvation or not makes no difference. Christian or theistic culture as well as immediate salvation is controlled by the same receptivity principle of thought. Those that have not this receptivity have no salvation, but neither have they human culture.

What then becomes of all attempts to harmonize evolutionistic philosophy with Christianity? We speak now of evolutionistic philosophy as based upon the Platonic-Kantian principle of the open universe. Such philosophy, in all its forms, materialistic or vitalistic, Spencerian or Bergsonian denies creation. And this is no detail. If creation be denied, the restorative character of Christianity is denied. How could Christ restore to man the receptively reconstructive attitude of mind if because not created man never had such an attitude? Or, how could Christ restore anything if, because there is no creation, man could not be restored to anyone? Or again, how could Christ restore when, because there is no creation, He himself is but a prodigy with no possible significance for any human being? It is as impossible to deny Christianity and preserve Theism as it is impossible to deny Theism and preserve Christianity. It is as impossible to oppose Christian education and be genuinely interested in human culture as it is to deny human culture and be interested in Christian education; a foundation without a roof affords no shelter and a roof without a foundation affords no room.

But the charge will finally be made that I accept all this because the Bible tells me. The Bible tells me that its God and its Christ are absolute and the sole source of interpretation. The Bible tells me that obedience is a covenant obligation because a creation-implication. But whence my belief in the Bible? If my reply is that an absolute God and an absolute Christ need an absolutely authoritative Bible in a sinful world, the logic is granted. Such is surely the case. If sin is what Scripture says it is, a denial of man's receptivity of heart and mind, if God is what Scripture says He is, an absolute God, and if Christ is what Scripture says He is, the restorer of man to God, then only an infallibly inspired Scripture can help make men Theists again. But how do I know that what the Bible says is true? If I say that it accords with my experience, I do not escape the charge of circle-reasoning, because admittedly my experience has been moulded under the influence of the Scriptures. If I say that Scripture accords with a Theism that I find more satisfactory than any other philosophy, I again do not escape the charge of circle-reasoning because I have just stated that my Theism, too, comes from the Scriptures. How then shall I escape the charge of circle-reasoning when men ridicule me because as an educator I assume the authority of Scripture?

The answer is that I shall in no wise seek to escape it but boldly affirm it as the only alternative to self-destruction. What I shall do is first show clearly on the one hand that an absolute God, creation, and man's original receptivity of thought that is Theism is indissolubly connected with and restored by Christ and Scripture, that is, by Christianity; and on the other hand that a finite-God, an uncreated universe and the essential creativity of human thought, that is Anti-theism is indissolubly connected with a denial of Christ's divinity and the authority of Scripture, that is with Anti-Christianity. Then, when I have done this, I gladly admit and avow that I am a Theist and a Christian because the Holy Spirit has made me so, but I equally maintain that all men should be Theists and Christians because only Theism and Christianity can offer meaning to experience at all. Circular reasoning is the most reasonable form of reasoning for a finite personality. No other form of reasoning is possible.

When as Christian educators we have thus seen things as a whole and have seen them through, we make no mean apologies for teaching children with authority. Nor do we fear that Biblical criticism and evolutionism may tomorrow make our position untenable. Nor yet do we wildly dash for a would-be-up-to-dateness in methods of pedagogy and psychology. What shall we teach and how can we teach at all if not with the authority of God and Christ? How shall the facts of Scripture or nature ever disprove the existence of an absolute

God if only an absolute God could make such facts? Or how can modern psychology tell us of the needs of the human being unless it ask of Christ and God what these needs may be? A certain independence of spirit we need in our Christian education. Not, of course, the independence of those who ridicule us. That is the independence of pride. And such independence of spirit is the denial of our whole position. But yet, an independence we need. An independence we need that has cast out crouching fear. We are right, not by our wisdom but through God. And because we are right through the work of the Spirit it behooves us to be humbly bold. If God is for us who can be against us?

Would that all Christians saw the logic of their Christianity! They would not then seek by haphazard, nervous methods of revivalism, of individualistic preaching and teaching think of the salvation for eternity alone and thus fail in large part to accomplish what they set out to do. In covenant education we seek not to extract the human being from his natural milieu as a creature of God, but rather seek to restore the creature with his milieu to God. Incomparably the wiser is this method since it transplants the plant with, instead of without its soil. Incomparably the more consistent is this method because Christianity itself claims to be restorative and supplementative of Theism. Obedience is the subjective principle of the covenant. Obedience is also the subjective principle of a creature. A Christian is a true human being once more.

Once we have seen this whole and have seen it through, the argument that the Sunday-School, the catechism and the church are sufficient for our educational purposes loses all its plausibility and charm. Such an argument denies that Christianity is a true Theism. Such an argument denies the restorative character of Christianity. Such an argument would seek to patch Christianity upon an anti-theistic foundation and thus eventually destroy Christianity itself. There is an element of anti-theism in every form of inconsistent Christianity. Only a Reformed philosophy of education is a consistently Christian philosophy of education, and it alone is free from self-destructive germs. Only it should be added that we are far from boasting that we are actually to the full extent Reformed in all our educational efforts; we are striving for the ideal.

If we would be polemically self-conscious as well as apologetically self-conscious — and the one is scarcely possible without the other — we must briefly note how in distinction from Romanism and Lutheranism the Reformed principle of education is alone consistently Christian and theistic.

It is not necessary to point out in detail the anti-theistic elements in Roman theology and philosophy. We would note something of them in so far as they have bearing upon education. We sometimes say that Rome is following a consistent policy of authority in education. Yet Rome has always tried in vain to harmonize something of the Platonic-Kantian principle of the creativity of human thought with the receptivity-theory of Christianity. Hence its strange coördination of Scripture and tradition. Hence its strange doctrine of gradation of priest above "layman" in general, and its strangest possible doctrine of papal infallibility in particular. Hence also the necessity of enforcing authority by external means. Rome's principle is weak because inconsistent. Rome's apparent strength is due to the element of truth in her principle and in addition to this upon extraneous circumstances. Rome cannot make a consistent stand against unbelief today nor in the future; it maintains itself by compromise. It is well that we emphasize the fact that we have much in common with Rome, but never should we forget that it is up to those that are Reformed to furnish the only consistent and therefore the only finally effective apologetic against unbelief.

Then as to Lutheranism, it may with joy be said that it harbors less of anti-theism in its bosom than does Romanism. Yet even Lutheranism has its pantheistic elements. Lutheranism has not clearly grasped the significance of the creation idea. It has not always firmly maintained that God is external and man is temporal. By ascribing omnipresence to the human nature of Christ, Lutheranism toned down the distinction between the temporal and the external. And the reason for this was that there is even in Lutheranism a remnant of Platonic rationalism. Man is given some independent power of interpretation. Principle is not always clearly maintained to be subordinate to the absolute personality of God. Man's thoughts need not in every respect be led captive to the obedience of Christ. The meaning of obedience is not fully understood; the whole covenant idea practically ignored. Consequently culture is but loosely related to Christianity. What then can the Lutheran system of education accomplish? Very much indeed, but not enough. Lutheran educational policy must eventually tolerate an unbiblical rift between Christianity and Theism; the natural will not be sanctified by the supernatural. Lutheran educational philosophy cannot meet the enemy of Christianity and Theism at every sector of the front.

*   *   *

Our conclusion can be none other than that in the Reformed philosophy of education we have Christian education come to its own and in the Christian philosophy of education we have theistic education come to its own. The ordinances for divine education as we find them numerous in the Scriptures are expressions of one grand covenant principle, and this grand covenant principle rests upon the idea of temporal creation as its presupposition and back of the created universe an absolute God. Not one of these ideas can one retain unless he retains them all. Together they stand or together they fall. This we would fain have our enemies see. How seldom do we find an enemy challenging our concatenation of ideas or attacking our philosophy of education in its central principle of the essential receptivity of the human mind! Ready we are to avow this principle unabashed. As Luther stood in the Diet of Worms, surrounded by an overwhelmingly powerful enemy, saying that he could not possibly retract his faith, so we stand before the bar of the educational philosophy of the day. That philosophy must condemn us. That philosophy is based upon the denial of what it has to prove, namely that an absolute God has created this temporal-spatial universe. Hence we are not afraid nor ashamed. Mighty is the truth and it will conquer at last.

CORNELIUS VAN TIL
Address before the National Union of
Christian Schools Convention, Holland,
Michigan, August, 1930.

Key Thoughts:

1. "Education is implication into God's interpretation." God as absolute, personal Creator has interpreted all facts. Education is the process by which man involves himself in God's interpretation as He makes this known in revelation.

2. At the center of this view of education stands the "essential receptivity" of the human mind. This does not mean that the human mind passively absorbs the facts and their interpretations, but that man actively accepts them before he becomes creatively productive with them.

3. At the basis of this view of education lies a temporal creation. God has called all things into being. Principles of truth, goodness, and beauty are of His making and expressive of His nature. Creation, including human thinking, is of a derived nature. God and Christ through the Spirit are the sole source of interpretation.

4. The Scripture we accept as absolute authority on these matters, for the "Holy Spirit made me so" and only on this ground can experience mean anything at all.

5. We teach, therefore, with authority, for we have in God's Word the authority of God and Christ.

Comment:

The education of the immature is a divinely ordained need to be met in a divinely ordained way.

Man's greatest need, so the Scripture teaches us, is the security attained in the fellowship with God, and through this fellowship the communion of the saints. It is by communication that this fellowship is attained. God communicates to us in Christ through His Spirit that we may communicate with Him and each other.

Christian education seeks to understand this divinely ordained need and the divinely ordained way of meeting this need. This is the basic principle of all educational research.

6

The Christian School a Prerequisite for and an Outgrowth of the Calvinistic World and Life View

Does a world and life view really have "outgrowths"? Does a world and life view after all make any difference in practical life? Does a world and life view ever determine or even influence human action?

This subject assumes that the Calvinistic world and life view will have as one of its natural and inevitable outgrowths the Christian school. And in expressing this assumption our subject compactly expresses a fundamental conviction of us of Reformed faith who believe in and maintain what we mean by Christian schools. That this assumption is very commonly made in our argumentation for Christian schools and in our feelings on the matter hardly needs proof. We often, for example, voice our amazement at the fact that many share our Reformed faith and profess to be Calvinists and yet are not to be won to active support of our distinctive educational system. May we not expect the Calvinistic world and life view to grow into enthusiasm for Christian schools? we exclaim. Well, so we might; provided the assumption is correct that world and life views ever do have outgrowths. But do they?

There are, as you know, many who would answer in the negative. World and life views, they say, are purely theoretical abstractions. They are painted pictures that neither produce nor change anything. Life goes its own way, both in nature and in man himself, indifferent to all our theorizing, unaffected by our pretentious "views." Does it make a particle of difference in their motions, for example, whether I believe the sun turns about the earth or the other way around? Did not men's blood circulate long before Harvey discovered its theory? Are not the facts of history facts quite independent of the fashion in which they are construed? Do not the natural forces of supply and demand mock all our economic theories? What is the whole history of philosophy but a series of just such ineffective "world and life views" to which the stream of life was blindly indifferent? And, once more, is the fact that many professed Calvinists are indifferent to Christian schools not itself proof that theory has nothing to do with life and its outgrowths? We are to understand that only life itself lives; only the forces of life itself are productive. Theory is bloodless; it is in itself dead and has no outgrowths. Man, too, acts as life forces him to act; he is driven by all sorts of instincts and impulses and circumstances; by these his practical conduct is determined. And if a man thinks that his world and life view has in it the power to alter either himself or the world he is as foolish as the courtiers of King Canute who suggested that the king's command could stop the ocean's tide.

This negative contention one can, of course, airily wave aside. As a matter of fact, most of us are in the habit of making short shrift of it. Aside from calling attention to its obvious confusion of natural and human behavior, there are especially two ways which we have of summarily dismissing the unwelcome thesis.

One way is very simple: to charge the contention to the ignorance and ill will and bias of opponents; to label them materialists and pragmatists and to suppose that in some mysterious fashion you have thus justified yourself. But this is hardly the way of honesty. For with many of the statements alleged by your opponents as evidence you will find yourself agreeing; some of them — let us say the statement concerning the futility of philosophical systems — you have yourself on occasion made. We all have our moments when, skeptical of its vital effectiveness, we strongly discount theory. And it is fair to expect of a man who agrees with much of the alleged evidence but refuses to adopt the conclusion that he give some account of himself.

The other way may seem more ingenious. It is to make an exception of our Calvinism. It is to admit that all philosophies are abstractions, but that the Calvinistic world and life view is not. But this way, too, offers no thoroughfare. If all philosophical systems, all systems that give fairly coherent answers to the basic questions which man cannot help asking, if all such are fruitless abstractions, then the Calvinistic world and life view is by its very pretense also a fruitless abstraction.

If then we are to be consistent and honest, we especially who insist on the practical importance of a world and life view, the negative contention is not to be dismissed superficially.

Nor is this issue a purely academic one; the issue has important bearing on our activity in behalf of Christian schools.

We shall, in consequence, have to devote some attention to the question whether a world and life view can and does have vitality, whether it can and does actually have "outgrowths" in practical life. If it cannot, if the assumption implied in the wording of our subject is false, then certainly much of our argumentation for Christian schools has been mere beating of the wind, much of our activity has proceeded on premises that were mistaken. Most of us have fundamentally, but then falsely, supposed that if we built up a truly Calvinistic world and life view the Christian school would follow naturally; or, otherwise put, we have supposed, but falsely, that the surest guarantee of the maintenance of Christian schools is a Calvinistic world and life view. If on the other hand a world and life view can and does have issues in practical life, then we should have some knowledge of the conditions under which it does, lest confusion make our activity ineffective or even paralyze it.

* * *

Does a world and life view possess vitality? Does it make any difference in practical life? Can we actually trace to its productivity such an institution as a school, for example? Life itself, we all agree, is productive; but is there anything of life in a world and life view? anything that will in any sense determine human behavior?

In attempting an answer to this question we shall proceed most profitably if we seek some clearer formulation of that on which we all agree. What do we mean by this "life" which is by common agreement productive of practical outgrowths? What factors, more particularly what inner factors, what factors actually live within me, determine my behavior?

Though it is of course impossible to split up human living into separate adjustments, yet we do use the term life in more than one meaning; and if we are to dispel some of the confusion about world and life views and their vitality, we must distinguish the main senses in which we use the term. In thus distinguishing the main levels or ranks of human living we shall unavoidably also be making distinctions within the objective world to which man adjusts himself. Our concern is primarily, however, with the levels or kinds of living that make up the "life" which a world and life view does or does not have. Recognizing that human life is always some kind of unified process, we want nevertheless to consider whether among the inner factors influencing behavior on each of its levels we also find world and life views, or whether a world and life view must remain on each level or in each meaning of life an otiose abstraction, a system of propositions as dead as the multiplication table.

The term life may have, first of all, a meaning which is very obvious. Life may mean a process of adjustment which is biological, which is not essentially rational, which is much like that of the animals. Eating, breathing, fighting the forces of disease within our bodies, even sensing lights and sounds and pleasures and pains, and being impelled by instincts and urges, and manifesting what look like rudimentary forms of judgment — all this may be called living. Here we all live; here there is vitality and productivity; here there are "outgrowths." But so long as we remain here the decisive inner factor is instinct; if the term life could never mean more than biological living, world and life views would not only be unproductive, they would not even exist. Animals live and act, but never because some world and life view is productive in and through them; and if human behavior were purely biological we should have to concede that the assumption of our subject is false.

But there is another level or type of life, one of which only human beings are capable. Here life means our production of and individual reaction to the social institutions about us — the family, the state and its laws, society's conventions, group habits and customs. This is what living means when I play my part in buying and selling, in banking, in owning property, in voting, in shaking hands, in driving an automobile through traffic, in establishing a system of currency, in practising medicine or law, in maintaining school. On this level we all live. And how vitally we all live here! No mere abstract theory, this social adjustment, but vigorous, productive, practical life.

Such social life is not found among the animals. To create such a social environment and for the individual to live a life of such social adjustment is characteristic only of man with his rational and moral nature. Such living requires reason, it requires symbols — a ten dollar bill is a symbol; so is a word; so our gestures — it requires intelligence; it requires some insight into causes and consequences. And such living also requires morality; man must inhibit his biological instincts; he must make choices; he is under obligation to adjust himself this way rather than that; he is under law. In short, here is not only living; but in contrast to life in its merely biological sense, here is rational moral living. Here appears a new determinant of behavior — not instinct, but moral reason. And (we should be disposed immediately to add) that proves the assumption that world and life views have "outgrowths." For if social living is rational, if it requires reason to live socially, then surely it requires a world and life view; and then surely the different modes of social behavior are the "outgrowths" of differing world and life views.

But can the assumption be proved quite so easily and superficially? The conductor who punches your ticket, the grocer who sells you food, the banker who loans you money on a note, the man who reads your gas meter — these are all people to whom you adjust yourself, people with whom you live socially. Do you need a world and life view to do it? The state legislature, the traffic courts, the English language, the United States postoffice, the schools, the newspapers, private property — these are all institutions or traditions, adjustment to which makes part of what you mean by social living. But do you need a world and life view for that?

Suppose we answer in the affirmative. Suppose we contend that social behavior in response to all these does in the final analysis imply at least some kind of life view. The contention could probably be established. The question is still whether we have now proved that a world and life view in the sense in which our subject intends the phrase is actually a moving factor, does actually make any practical difference. For, even leaving to one side as of lesser consequence the objection that the tracing of direct and conscious connection between a specific act and a life view is often well-nigh impossible both for the actor himself and for the observer, there is the consideration that the "reason" in social life may be no more than group reason; in other words, that what we think is a "world and life view" may be no more than mere group custom. And this consideration is of definite importance to our subject.

It cannot be denied that the "reason" involved in social institutions and in socialized adjustments of the individual is to a great extent the implicit reason of historical processes. Language, for example, is rational, yet it is not consciously and deliberately sought. Language is the product not of world and life views but of the forces of social life that seem to go their own way within us as individuals, the product of life that seems to live itself in spite of us, the product of a rationality that seems to be at best a group rationality acting through me. And so with our choices. They seem controlled by custom and convention. Even my choice of group seems controlled by the group in the training it gives me. Both reason and morality seem conventionalized; group pressure would seem to be the determining factor in social behavior. There are "outgrowths" on the level of social living; and hence there are, of course, changes. But these changes are not brought about by world and life views; rather, the basic life force assumes a variety of group forms — racial, economic, vocational, and so on; and the constant interaction and conflict of these various groups prompts social changes. All "outgrowths" are the result of the slow pressure of group life, of group rationality; it produced the institutions and groups, and acting within us the same force determines our behavior. World and life views even on the rational moral level are not causative and motivating factors; they are implied if at all only as grammar is implied by language. Grammar did not produce language — neither do world and life views produce behavior; when we assume they do, the superficiality and ignorance and bias are all on our side.

I have sought to state an ancient position which is maintained today not only by economic and other determinists, by some evolutionists, and by a certain school of historians but which seems to find a good deal of support from an unprejudiced analysis of our actual behavior.

Have we who maintain the assumption basic to our subject anything further to say?

First of all, I think, we shall concede that group pressure is a factor in behavior — just as we concede the biological. We shall have to concede more. We shall have to admit that this factor is one of a strength and of an importance we all usually fail to recognize; we shall admit that the conflict of group pressures determines practical "outgrowths" in every man's life to a far greater degree than individualists and radicals and all of us like to acknowledge. Take, for example, our attitude toward private property, or toward bankers; or take our notion of what "success" means.

Further, from the admission we shall draw a lesson of great importance to our Christian school movement. It is this. To the extent that the Christian school is the outgrowth of the pressure of group forces, to that extent the Christian school cause will have vitality only while the custom from which it issues has vitality. As long as we remain Dutch or middle-class or immigrant, or whatever the right word to characterize the inner vitality of our group life, as long in other words as a specific custom can retain its hold on coming generations, so long the Christian school may continue. And though we meanwhile flatter ourselves and each other that the Christian school is the "outgrowth" of a world and life view, we shall some day awaken to the fact that we were mistaken. When the vitality lent by life to our group custom is spent, the world and life view will appear in all its native though gilded poverty. My world and life was spending borrowed money. And while it is going bankrupt I shall have to twist and squirm and resort to intellectual contortions and be obsessed by fear and attempt coercion — in short, behave as I usually behave in analogous situations in the financial world — only to find that the collateral has lost all value. Or shall we be more literal. If such is the status of our world and life view and of the Christian school, if they are no more than the "outgrowths" of the vitality of a group custom, then when group or individual encounters other groups and customs, the world and life view will lose even its false appearance of inherent vitality and the Christian school will cease to be. If one adds that as time goes on such group conflict is inevitable for our people, but little foresight is needed to predict the inevitable outcome.

And now, the concession made, and its lesson drawn, what we defenders of the assumption have still to say stands out the clearer: The term life has a third and hitherto unmentioned meaning; thus far we have treated life as though nowhere in it is there freedom, responsibility. But socialized living is not the only grade possible only to men. Man's rational moral nature is not limited to it. There is a form of life beyond, and there is probably no man who does not in the inner recesses of his own soul experience something of it also; who does not, shall we say, on some occasion hear the voice of transcendent duty, in some measure respond loyally to the universals of science, sometimes sense the pain of accusing conscience, sometimes glimpse the eternal depths of love, sometimes yearn after a beauty not of this world, and who does not on such occasion recognize and in some way adjust himself to a reality beyond nature and beyond society? He does not question its control over him; he borrows life from it; he finds responsibility for and life in yielding and sacrificing self to it. Such life is life beyond group and custom though not necessarily subversive of them.

In short, if we remember that the forms of false religion are legion, we shall insist that there is besides biological and social life a third type or meaning of life which is always implicitly religious. We need not here attempt a complete definition of religion. Sufficient to our present purpose is the fact that man on this level finds his god. That fact makes this living religious. It is personal and selfconscious. It is, of course, a life in and of faith. And every man has in this sense a faith of some sort, a faith in some god.

And in finding his god, man finds his perspective for judging all of reality and finds his absolute value for all living. In other words, in finding his god man finds the germinal principles of his real world and life view. Your world and life view is here alive with the personal vitality of your religion; alive with what for you — be it falsely, even — is life from and with God. And because the two, religion, and personal germinal world and life view, are bound inseparably, your personal world and life view will necessarily be vital, cause changes, have "outgrowths" in behavior. Once more, that holds of false religions as well as of the true. If Socialism or Naturalism or Modernity or Art or Science is your religion, if in any one of these you find your god and your basic perspective, then it will have "outgrowths" as well as will any of the forms of what we popularly mean by false religions.

A world and life view is productive if it be one's personal, one's religious world and life view, germinal or embryonic as this may be.

But will the vitality of such a view extend to social living? Or is it not perhaps a vitality manifesting itself only in our individual consciousness? When we say that this level is personal, do we not limit its scope to just the individual's heart? Have we not implicitly admitted that it has no effect on education and schools, for example, and on institutional and social behavior generally? Must we not still leave the determination of the latter to the pressure of group rationality and group life?

To many an interpreter such practical ineffectiveness not only is in fact characteristic of religion, but is actually the boast of Protestantism. The Reformation and Protestantism generally are to be construed as an insistence that religion belongs wholly to man's inner consciousness.

A little reflection, however, will show that religion as the revelation of my absolute interest and value will and does necessarily affect social life. It will do so either by adding interest and value to social life or by detracting value and interest from social life. If Art is my religion, for example, the result may well be that socialized living loses value; if so, my practical behavior will be affected not only through but also in spite of group pressures. Likewise if Science is my religion. Likewise in certain periods of the Middle Ages; man's interpretation of Christianity and of the social corruption of the day being what it was. If on the other hand, Socialism or Nationalism, for example, should be my religion, or any other that makes of an institution or custom its god, then socialized living will have increased value and religious life will flow into social channels. Personal world and life view affects social behavior either negatively or positively — which, depends on the religion — but necessarily in some way.

You will recall that our analysis was to be interested primarily in the inner factors determining behavior in order to discover whether among these we could find a world and life view. If the analysis is correct, a world and life view borrows an apparent vitality from social living, and this vitality is vigorous while the custom or tradition or institution lives; no longer. A world and life view obtains real vitality from religious faith.

To this point we have left out of consideration the objective truth of the world and life view in question. I wish now to turn to the view I believe the best presentation of objective truth.

Our previous general conclusions apply also to it. The Calvinistic world and life view is a view with group pressure behind it and to that extent shares whatever vigor our social custom still has. But happily it is more. It is rooted in the Christian religion, in God's having revealed Himself to you and me through Christ. Here, in this life from God, lies the real spring of its vitality. And only in the measure that in your case or mine what is called the Calvinistic world and life view roots here will it necessarily have "outgrowths" and is there any guarantee that it will continue to bear fruit. And only as it is rooted here is it rooted in true liberty, is it free from narrowness and tortuous intellectual twistings — as no mere institutional rooting ever is — is it free from the obsessions and phobias of mere group psychology, is it free to grow by all truth and to nourish itself on all truly human experience, is it aggressive and forceful and the transmitter of conviction also to the next generation. This, I submit, is another important lesson.

*   *   *

And will the Calvinistic world and life view, even when religiously rooted and necessarily affecting practical behavior, also of necessity issue in the Christian school?

Calvinism is, of course, a specific world and life view, even within the group of Christian world and life views. I shall select aspects of Calvinism pertinent to our present subject. Two important facts should be borne in mind, however. The first is that an organic world and life view cannot be split up into separated propositions — no more than life can be split; the other, closely related, that the further we get away from the center and from the germinal principles of a personal world and life view, the less apodeictic and categorical we can be. The following statements lose significance except they be taken together as a living unit in a vital organism.

The Calvinistic world and life view characteristically insists on the indispensability to right living of a life view — a view of what man's duties and obligations are, of what are the true values of living, a view of what man's life ought to be. This emphasis places us in opposition to a popular attitude which, in its reaction to hypocrisy, would minimize all theory or view and would onesidedly emphasize mere conduct, which may even deny that a life view can have any "outgrowths."

It insists that such a life view is personal, is religiously rooted, that its conception of duties and challenges is the result of personal loyalty to what are considered absolute standards. Life views are not only social habit.

It insists that a life view, religious as one's real life view basically is, is the result of a view of God and is therefore, at least germinally, a world view as well — a view regarding nature, man, and God in the relations.

It insists that integral to right living is the explication of this world view in as coherent and systematic fashion as possible. In other words, the development of the germinal principles is not a mere academic luxury; it is of the essence of our living in obedience to the will of God.

It insists that if such a world view is to be intelligible and coherent and morally satisfactory and true, its center must be the God who revealed Himself in the Christ of the Scriptures, the source of the ultimate principles for our world and life view. Since He is the one true God, the true world and life view is the expression of His will.

It insists — and in organic relation to the previous statements this is of prime importance to our subject — it insists that if I am to realize with intellectual assurance the truth of the Christian world and life view and if I am to live obediently to the will of God, I must hear in every contact with reality the ringing challenge: Search till you find in me also a witness to the truth of Christian world and life view; search till you find in me also a revelation of God.

No argument is needed, I take it, to show that such a world and life view rooted in the Christian faith will issue in Christian education. That it must necessarily issue in what we today mean by the Christian school is not so obvious. A personally accepted world and life view, though it always takes precedence over institutional life and if, like Calvinism, it be of the positive type seeks to express itself in social action, need not necessarily create its own social instrument. The practical situation, socially, the institutional situation to which I must adjust myself, must be pondered, evaluated.

As concerns schools, then, the practical situation is important that as a result of various modern movements American group life has issued in schools which seek to limit themselves to neutral territory, territory not affected by nor directly affecting world and life views. Schooling has become secularized. Those who defend the institution need not be people who despair of any objective truth whatever nor who are indifferent to all world and life views; every man has some "religious" world and life view. But whatever a defender may hold, the institution is an historical product. If we could conscientiously be satisfied with it, if we could express ourselves through it, we should. One must have serious reasons for resisting the pressure of one's group, for breaking with history. There is little if any glory in the mere independence of our schools.

Now our inability with our Calvinistic world and life view to be satisfied does not arise from maintaining that there is nowhere the possibility of what is meant by neutrality. Of course there are many "neutral" facts — that is to say, facts accepted by all, whatever their world and life view; indeed what are really facts must be accepted by all; thus certainly least of all a Calvinist objects to the facts of modern science, even though arrived at by an impersonal method.

Why not, then, assign such neutral facts to the school, leaving the question of their significance and other disputed points to other agencies like home and church? Here is the crucial question. There are different ways of answering, but the one basic and determining consideration is, I believe, that education to us as Christians, as Calvinists who are religiously persuaded to the truth of our world and life view — that education to us means more and something other than we can in justice expect the customary schools to give.

The pivotal difference is not that we believe education should also include training in religion; the home and the church might provide that element. Nor is it that we believe the school should supplant the home or the church or both; we accept a division of labor between the three. Nor is it that we believe theology the only science our children must learn; on the contrary, we should be nearer the truth in emphasizing our catholic acceptance of the importance of all the sciences.

The point lies rather in something more basic than any social institution — in our religious life as Christians and in our view of life and the world which is there rooted. Not to repeat all the characteristics, it lies particularly in the Calvinist's characteristic (though not novel) insistence that God is not only the object in the narrower sense of religious faith and devotion but is also the ground and end of all existence and truth and value; or, to say the same thing as it affects man subjectively, that religious faith is confirmed by and itself furnishes the ultimate explanation of and motivation for all human experience and activity; in short, that religion and reason and morality are inextricably interwoven. Now such a conviction means in the sphere of intellect and knowledge that there is to be not a mere deductive development within my head of theoretical conclusions from the germinal principles of my personal, my Christian world and life view but such a development of the germinal principles that every widening of my intellectual horizons, every deepening of my insight, testifies in its moment of existence to the absolute reality and worth of God; a development such that in every new intellectual contact I find confirmation of my Christian world and life view; a development such that there constantly grows within me the intelligent certainty that only in the light of that view can my bits of knowledge become intelligible. And in the sphere of morality and character building this conviction means that my every experience of worth strengthens and deepens my appreciation of and loyalty to God; and again that the worth of God and loyalty to Him is experienced as the value of every bit of human living. The cutting edge of our view is that intellectual or moral growth and the religious life are in each specific instance and at that moment inseparable; they are aspects of one and the same event, of one and the same step in the process of my growth.

That is what our world and life view means for our thinking and acting to us who have long left school behind; that is what it means for what we may rightly call your and my education. But that is also what it means for the education of our children. Because we are religiously persuaded of the truth of our view we want our children trained in it as a personal, as a religious view of life and the world. And if it is to be "their personal" as a Calvinist must interpret that phrase then this view must be for them one whose truth is increasingly witnessed by all that they learn as they learn it, by all with which they become acquainted as they make its acquaintance. Religion and truth and right education unite in this demand. Our children are to be trained in so knowing and so acting.

And if education is to mean that, we cannot in obvious justice expect the customary schools to give it. Just as obviously if the parent or the minister is somehow to provide this element he will not only have to be constantly present in the classroom and have the knowledge which the teacher possesses but will himself have to do the teaching.

Such I take to be the real reason why a Calvinistic world and life view demands not only Christian education but, under the circumstances, what we mean by the Christian school as an independent institution. You may state the same point in other language. I have throughout had in mind the implications of my subject.

That is why the Christian school is "outgrowth" of our world and life view. And that, too, is why the Christian school is prerequisite. Of course you will want an independent school if you want in the most efficient manner to preserve distinctive group ideals merely as such. But then you might be better off with, let us say, a Dutch school. The Christian school is prerequisite if you mean to maintain a world and life view which has vigor because based on personal living and because to its truth and value all of life and experience and contact with reality and all growth increasingly witness. If we intend our children to be strong in their possession of our world and life view, if we intend that with them too it shall be a matter not of mere custom but of living on the level of personality, if we intend that with them also it shall bind itself in with religious faith and be productive, then the Christian school is prerequisite.

To know what we mean when we state that the Christian school in our sense of the term is both "outgrowth" and prerequisite of our

Calvinism, one must on the one hand know our world and life view as germinally present in our Christian faith and one must on the other hand appreciate the strength and importance of social and institutional pressure. I have attempted to suggest something of what is involved in both these aspects.

W. HARRY JELLEMA

Address before the National Union of
Christian Schools Convention, Englewood,
Chicago, Illinois, August, 1934.

Key Thoughts:

1. Does a life and world view issue forth in living? Some deny it.

2. If we view life as biological, our answer is "No." This is the animal level of life, and animals do not live and act according to a life and world view.

3. If we view life as social, the answer is not quite so obvious, for there is "reason" in our social life. It is uniquely human. Yet our answer must be "No," for a life and world view on this level is not causative or motivating, but implied as grammar is in language.

4. When we view life as personal, however, the answer is readily forthcoming. The personal life has freedom and responsibility in it. It is basically religious. As such it is productive of a life and world view.

5. It is our religious faith that gives rise to our life and world view. It is our life and world view which demands that we lay claim upon all of life on the basis of our faith. It is in education that these meet.

6. We need the Christian school to make this education possible. The public school tries to educate without a life and world view as its reference. The Christian school is necessary to instruct in the Christian life and world view, and the Christian school is in turn "outgrowth" of the life and world view based on the Christian faith.

Comment:

Man is basically religious. Because of this he lives by faith, for faith is the new life in Christ. His faith gives rise to a life and world view. As a free and responsible person, man directs his way of life accordingly. His life and word view issues forth in living.

It is a function of the Christian school to instruct the immature in the Christian life and world view. To do this the school must cultivate the faith which gives rise to the life and world view. The faith is the new life begotten of God. It is nurtured first of all through the Word of truth as inspired by God and the Holy Spirit. This faith begins to lay hold upon all of life as it is made relevant to life in education.

In the Christian school the Word is central first of all because only it opens the way to direct communication with God. Then too the Word is central as the infallible rule for life to open up a life and world view according to which the Christian can direct his way.

Being Reformed in Our Attitude Toward the Christian School

As the years roll by and conditions change, the conviction is growing on us that we need the Christian school and need it very much. The free Christian school has been a source of inestimable blessings for the Reformed people of the Netherlands and for the nation of which they are an important constituent. It has also been a boon for the Reformed circles in our land and may by the grace of God help us to contribute something worth while to the life of our nation. Experience taught us to appreciate this school. Outsiders have frequently congratulated us on its possession, described it as one of the mainstays of our churches, and exhorted us to guard, to continue, and to develop it. And however much many may decry it as inimical to the unity of our national life, it certainly points the way to the solution of a problem that is now weighing heavily on our public school system.

It is just because we regard the Christian school as a real blessing that we are so solicitous about it. We have been willing to finance it, even though we also had to pay our share for the maintenance of the public school. We resent the expression of opinions in our circles which might dampen the ardour for the Christian school and put it in jeopardy. We are anxious to see this school continue and to bless us with its fruits in the future as it has done in the past.

If our Christian school is to continue in the future, it is absolutely essential that we be thoroughly Reformed in our attitude to that school. This means that we must have a firm grasp of the fundamental principles that are basic to our school system. It means that we must be positively convinced of the necessity of these schools of our children. It means that we must not be half-hearted in praying and giving and working for the maintenance and the improvement of those schools. It means, too, that we must convince the coming generation of the absolute necessity of our Christian schools, and must persuade them to sacrifice and to labor for their continued existence.

Let us begin by asking ourselves the question, What should determine our attitude to the Christian school, if we are truly Reformed? Shall we say that the spirit of nationalism in education, which asserted itself in many lands in the previous century, and which calls for "tax-supported, publicly controlled and directed, and non-sectarian common schools," ought to be the determining factor? If we are of that opinion, we shall reason somewhat as follows: The state is supremely interested in welding its citizenry into a unity, in developing a national spirit, a national character, a national sense of justice, etc. Its future welfare, inner strength, and prestige among the nations of the world depend on this. The development of such a truly national spirit can only be accomplished by the establishment and maintence of a national school system, a system of free schools, offering equal opportunity to the rich and the poor, and patronized by all the people. The establishment and maintenance of such schools requires taxation, and their efficiency will be commensurate with the measure in which the people are compelled to send their children to them. Only the state with its sovereign power can tax the people and can make education compulsory. Hence it follows that only the state can establish and maintain an effective free school system. Our public schools, which are schools for the state, are necessarily also schools by the state. They do not lose sight of the interests of the individual or of society in general, but they are primarily interested in the welfare of the organized community, i.e., of the state, in the training of American citizens. And as loyal citizens of the state we ought to appreciate those schools, improve the opportunity they offer for our children, and zealously oppose all partisan schools, because they make for division rather than unity.

Now it will hardly be said that this is a characteristically *Reformed* attitude. It clearly implies the adoption of a species of utilitarianism. It proceeds on the assumption that a general education of the people, permeated with a strong spirit of nationalism, is of paramount value for the state because it contributes to its unity, greatness and strength, and to the happiness of the greatest number of its citizens. It takes for granted that this is true even when the education given is divorced from religion. And because this is so, it is held that every citizen should seek this education for his children. But right at this point a good many questions clamor for answer. Is it true that a strong spirit of nationalism pure and simple is the greatest boon of the state? Is there not a great deal even in the present demand for an international consciousness that is more in harmony with the supreme religious and ethical ideal of humanity? Will not a nationalism *permeated with the spirit of true religion* prove to be the greatest blessing for the state and contribute most to the happiness of the people? Shall we say that the preferences of the state ought to determine our attitude? Would we act on that principle if the state should decide to introduce a state religion? We leave these questions for your consideration and pass on to another idea.

Shall we say with modern evolutionary pedagogy that the child is the standard and measure of all things in education, and that a study of the child ought to determine the requisite education and should also be the determining factor in our attitude towards any school that makes a bid for the education of the child? If so, then the possibility is given that we shall reason somewhat along the following lines: The child reveals great similarity with the higher brutes and is clearly a product of evolution. The brute origin of the mental make-up of the child ought to be carefully considered, for this will point the way in its further education. There are many imperfections in the life of the child, but these do not constitute sin. They are merely manifestations of the lower animal propensities which are struggling for the mastery. The child is fundamentally good, however, and under proper conditions and wise guidance will naturally develop in the right direction. It is of the utmost importance that palatial school-buildings be erected, surrounded by spacious and attractive play-grounds, that the halls be adorned with masterpieces of art, and that the classrooms be cheery and well ventilated. In any attempt to teach and guide the child, its needs, its desires, its will, and its rights should be carefully considered. It should not be taught that it is utterly corrupt and cannot in any case attain the ideal, but ought to be made conscious of the natural urge within it to soar to the loftiest ethical heights, and of the inherent power to overcome evil and to rise to a state of moral perfection. It should never be constrained to learn things which are beyond its comprehension, such as religious mysteries and profound theological truths, but only what it can fully understand and assimilate. Above all, it should be left free to develop its own religion in harmony with the teachings of science, and should not be urged to accept the myths of the Bible, however beautiful they may be, nor to believe the Hebrew conception of creation and providence, of angels and devils, of sin and atonement, of heaven and hell.

Now if we adopt that position and reason along those lines, we shall hardly be enthusiastic supporters of our Christian schools. But again we remind ourselves of the fact that it is not Reformed to say that psychology, that the study of the child, must ultimately determine our attitude to the school in which the child is educated. Moreover, the study of the child does not necessarily lead to the view indicated in the preceding, however common this may be in the present day. And even if it did, it would only represent the result to which man with his darkened understanding, subject to the power of error and deception, came in reading God's general revelation, a revelation which, while it is sufficient to leave man without excuse, is yet obscured by sin and ceased to be a perfect reflection of the truth. It is only in the light of Scripture that man can give a true interpretation of God's revelation in nature, and it is therefore to the Bible that he must turn for guidance.

* * *

If we are truly Reformed, we shall say that the will of God should determine our attitude to the Christian school, and that this will is revealed to us in his general, but above all in his special revelation.

God has made known to us whom He regards *as the responsible educators of the child.* He has indicated this in his general revelation in nature in the ordinances which He has established. In the animal world He shows us how the old provide for their young; how they protect them and train them. We see the eagle fluttering over her young, exciting them to fly, hovering over them for protection, and carrying them when they are wearied; we see the hen gathering her brood under her wings. Jeremiah even holds up the jackal as an example for Israel, when he says: "Even the jackals draw out the breast, they give suck to their young ones: the daughter of my people is become cruel, like the ostriches in the wilderness" (Lam. 4:3). The gentile world hit upon the idea of parental obligation in the work of education. It is true that Plato wanted the state to take charge of this work, but his ideal state existed only on paper. Athens placed the responsibility for the work of education squarely on the family; all its schools were private schools. And of the five rights of the Roman citizens, that of the father over his children was the very first. He took great personal interest in the education of his sons. The home rather than the school was the center of the educational system. And even with respect to the school Pliny the younger expressed the opinion that the principle, *the school belongs to the parents,* was the only sound principle. It should not surprise us that even heathen people without the light of special revelation saw that the parents were the proper responsible educators of their children, for nature itself points the way. The children are born of the parents and therefore belong to them first of all. The parents have them under their care until they set up for themselves and are prompted by their parental love to provide for their physical, mental, moral and spiritual needs; to guide them, to protect them, and to promote their best interests. There is no one that is interested in their welfare as much as the parents are. Hence it is but natural that the parents should be the responsible educators, and that, if the parents should feel constrained to call in the help of others, these others should feel that they stand in *loco parentis.*

God's special revelation teaches us the same truth with even greater clearness. Negatively, it may be said that the Bible in speaking of the duties of the state never mentions the work of educating the children of the nation (cf. Ex. 18:22-26; Deut. 1:16, 17; Matt. 22:17-21; Rom. 13:1-7; I Pet. 2:13-15). It is a striking fact that even the Old Testament, in which we find God dealing with the nation of Israel rather than with the individuals that belong to it and consequently speaking primarily in national terms, always refers to or addresses the parents as the responsible educators of the children. The book of Deuteronomy, the book of Proverbs, and the 78th Psalm are very instructive in this respect. In the New Testament it is clearly indicated that the government must guard the interests of all those that belong to its realm, must judge beween a man and his neighbor, must preserve order by punishing evil-doers, and must levy taxes for the support of its work (Rom. 13:1-7). But when it speaks of the education of the children, it turns to the parents in the words: "Ye fathers, provoke not your children to wrath: but nurture them in the chastening and admonition of the Lord" (Eph. 6:4).

The Word of God also indicates very explicitly that the education which the parents are in duty bound to provide for their children *must be fundamentally religious*. In fact, its emphasis is so exclusively on religious training that it almost seems as if it regarded this as the whole of education. This finds its explanation in the fact that it deals primarily with the religious and moral needs of man, that it regards religion as the most fundamental, the most basic thing in the life of man, and that it would not consider any education as sound and satisfactory that was not permeated with the spirit of religion. Let us notice a few passages that bear on this point. In Gen. 18:19 we find God saying with respect to Abraham: "For I have known him, to the end that he may command his children and his household after him, that they may keep the way of Jehovah to the end that Jehovah may bring upon Abraham that which He has spoken of him." In these words we are informed respecting the reason why God decided to give Abraham an insight into his counsel touching the coming destruction of the cities of the plain. Abraham was chosen by God to be the father of a mighty nation and a blessing for all the nations of the world. But in order that the promises to Abraham might be fulfilled and the Lord might really bring upon him the promised blessings, Abraham would have to teach his descendants "to keep the way of Jehovah, to do righteousness and justice." And in order that he might be a truly effective teacher of the great lesson that the blessings of Jehovah are enjoyed only in the way of obedience, and that the way of disobedience spells death, it had to be revealed to him that the cities of the plain were about to be destroyed for want of justice and righteousness. The book of Deuteronomy is shot through with exhortations to the Israelites to be diligent in reminding their children of the wonderful way in which God had led the nation in the past in order that these children might serve Jehovah with willing hearts. And we hear what may be regarded as the jubilant answer of the pious Israelite to all these exhortations in the words of the poet:

I will open my mouth in a parable:
I will utter dark sayings of old,
Which we have heard and known,
And our fathers have told us.
We will not hide them from their children,
Telling to the generation to come the praises of Jehovah,
And His strength, and His wondrous works that He hath
    done.
For He established a testimony in Jacob,
And appointed a law in Israel,
Which He commanded our fathers,
That they should make them known to their children;
That the generation to come might know them, even the
    children that should be born;
Who should arise and tell them to their children,
That they might set their hope in God,
And not forget the works of God,
But keep his commandments (Ps. 78:2-7).

It is that type of education that is pregnant with the promise of real blessings. If Abraham diligently teaches his children the way of the Lord, then the Lord will bring upon Abraham and his descendants the things which He has promised them. Listen to the words of divine wisdom: "Train up a child in the way he should go" — mark well, not "in the way he *would* go," but "in the way he *should* go," and this, according to teachings of Scripture, is the way of the covenant — "and even when he is old he will not depart from it" (Prov. 22:6). It is no wonder, therefore, that the New speaks in the same vein as the Old, exhorting the parents to educate their children religiously: "Ye fathers, provoke not your children to wrath; but nuture them in the chastening and admonition of the Lord" (Eph. 6:4).

This emphasis on religious education is exactly what we would expect in view of what the Bible reveals respecting the essential nature of the child. It is often said that man is incurably religious. Moreover, missionaries and students of comparative religion inform us that never a tribe was found without religion. The import of this is that the idea of God cannot be eradicated from the human soul. And this is impossible because man is God's offspring, the image-bearer of the Most High, everywhere and always. To separate the image of God from man is to rob him of his humanity. The image of God is the most fundamental thing in man, and consequently also in the child. And that which is most essential in the child cannot be ignored in its education without doing an injustice to both the child and its Creator and without turning its education into perversion. It is true that man by sin lost those moral and spiritual qualities that constitute the image of God in the more restricted sense, but this does not mean that he has ceased to be the image-bearer of God. He is still a rational and moral being, able to distinguish between good and evil; he still shows a certain appreciation of what is true and good and beautiful; and he still has a certain sense of the divine and an urge within him to engage in religious exercises. Moreover, we must bear in mind that the Spirit of God is operative in covenant children — I do not say, in every covenant child — and is restoring the image of God that was lost by sin. Therefore, Christian parents have an added reason to look upon their children as image-bearers of God.

Now sound psychology and pedagogy teaches us that we must take that which is most fundamental in the life of the child into consideration *in the whole of its education.* There is a strong tendency in present day psychology to emphasize the fact that the soul of man is a unit, acts as a unit, and consequently also reacts as a unit to all external influences, though it may manifest its action in a variety of ways. The old doctrine of the separate powers of the soul is not popular today. We are constantly reminded of the fact that it is the whole man that perceives and thinks, that desires and wills. Consequently, his education should also be regarded as a unitary process. It is utter folly to think that you can inform the intellect without giving direction to the will, that you store the head with knowledge without affecting the emotions, the inclinations, the desires, and the aspirations of the heart. The training of the head and of the heart go together, and in both the fundamental fact that the child is the image-bearer of God must be a determining factor. Again, in view of the fact that education is and should be a unitary process, we understand the absolute absurdity of saying that the school is concerned only with the head and should limit itself to secular education, while the home and the church make provision for the heart by adding religious education. We should never forget that the education which the child receives in the school, though divorced from religion, is nevertheless an education of the entire child and is bound to make a deep impression on the heart.

These considerations naturally lead us on to another point that deserves emphasis. The soul is a unit and education is a unitary process, aiming at the development of man's essential nature into a harmonious life, full and rich and beautiful. But this end can never be attained, if the home and the church on the one hand, and the school on the other hand do not have the same conception of the essential nature of the child, and do not agree in the fundamentals of their teachings. How can an education that proceeds in part on the assumption that the child is the image-bearer of God and in part on the supposition that it bears the image of the brute, an education that is partly religious and partly irreligious, i.e., anti-religious, ever result in a life that is truly unified? It can only lead to one thing, and that is a divided life so strongly condemned by our Saviour (Matt. 6:21, 22), a life with scattered energies and dissipated powers, swayed and torn by conflicting opinions, wanting in singleness of purpose, in stability and strength, and in that true joy that fills the soul which is consciously moving in the right direction. We are in perfect agreement with the Modernists on this point, the only difference being that, while we maintain that in the training of Christian children the education of the schools should fundamentally conform to the religious education of the home and of the church, they strenuously assert that the religious education of the home and of the church must be in conformity with the scientific teachings of the schools. To the oft-repeated complaint that many young people suffer shipwreck religiously in our colleges and universities and even seminaries, they simply answer that the Christian home and the Christian church are to blame, because they have not prepared their children and young people for the advanced views in religion that are now taught in the schools.

The Reformed man, who believes that the child is the image-bearer of God, naturally proceeds on the assumption that that most fundamental truth may not be ignored in any part of its education, *and especially not in its school education.* This fact may well be stressed in our day. In view of the fact that the influence of the Christian home is waning, and that the church can devote only a couple of hours a week to the religious training of its youth, the school is easily the most important educational agency of the present. Is it not the height of folly even from a purely educational point of view to let the most important agency in education ignore that which is most essential and most fundamental in the life of the child? And can Christian parents reasonably expect their children to be imbued with a spirit of true religion if they persist in sending them to a school where for twenty-four hours a week they are taught in a spirit that is fundamentally irreligious, if not positively anti-

Christian? The answer can only be a decided negative. And experience will bear out the correctness of this answer. America is today reaping in its churches what it has sown in its schools. It has sown through the secularized schools, and it is reaping a purely naturalistic religion.

* * *

In view of all that has been said, it ought not to be so difficult to determine what is a truly Reformed attitude to our Christian schools. We may begin by saying that a person who is really Reformed, i. e., who makes the will of God the law of his life, and who is guided in all the relations which he assumes and in all the activities in which he participates by Reformed principles, *cannot possibly assume an attitude of hostility to the Christian school without compromising his religious convictions.* It is true that we sometimes witness the strange phenomenon that persons who profess to be truly Reformed reveal a decided opposition to the Christian school. And if we inquire into the reasons for this hostility, these persons frequently resent the query and leave it for us to surmise the truth. Sometimes, however, they will answer, and then point to one of the three following reasons or to all three combined. They tell us that public opinion is down on the Christian school, and that it is foolhardy to go contrary to the prevailing ideas of the day. Public opinion is after all, as President Wilson said, "the mistress of the world." Chances are that they who speak after that fashion are more concerned about their popularity than about their religion. Very often they create the impression that the great expense entailed in the maintenance of separate schools constitutes their great objection to the Christian school, though they are generally loath to give expression to this sentiment. Their love of money plays a great part in their opposition. They seem to rate the material things higher than the spiritual. Again, we find them pleading their Americanism as a ground for their hostility to private schools. The public school is the school of the nation and every loyal American should send his children there for their education. By taking this stand they stigmatize as disloyal citizens the thousands and millions of Roman Catholics and Lutherans who maintain their own parochial schools, and also that large number of wealthy Americans who prefer and establish private schools for their children; and that in spite of the fact that the nation and the states do not require that all children shall attend the public school and have never officially taken the stand that the establishment and maintenance of parochial and private schools conflicts with true Americanism. Those who advance this argument would evidently revise the statement of Jesus respecting the necessity of seeking first the kingdom of God, and make it read: "Seek ye first America, and all other things will be added unto it." And if there were alongside of the many free churches in our land also an established church, they would undoubtedly feel conscience-bound to join the latter, irrespective of its fundamental tenets. Now, surely, such considerations as these do not warrant Christian people in opposing schools that make it their business to educate children in the fear of the Lord. It is hard to see how any child of God can make himself believe that in waging war against schools for Christian instruction he is fighting the battle of the Lord.

But let us consider a slightly different attitude. Many Christian people who send their own children to the public school grant us at once that they would not be justified in taking a hostile attitude to the Christian school. *They want to be tolerant.* While they prefer the state supported schools for their own children, they have no objection to those who insist on having their children educated in private schools. Sometimes they are even willing to contribute to the cause of the Christian school. They seem to regard it somewhat as a matter of indifference, whether they send their children to the Christian or to the public school. This is not altogether the case, however. Their attitude reflects the idea that one *ought* to send his children to the public school, but *may* send them to the Christian school. Now this is certainly not a Reformed position. The standard of duty on which this proceeds is certainly not that of the Word of God, but simply some utilitarian consideration, centering on the individual, or on society, or on the state. Before we assume any such attitude as that, we ought to prove that the Bible, which is our ultimate standard of life and practcice, explicitly or by implication favors state education for our children, whereas it also permits, but merely permits, the parents to assume the direct responsibility for the education of their children by establishing and maintaining their own private schools. We should be in a position to maintain that the Bible deems it best that the religious element be excluded from the greater part of the education of our children, though it also allows, but merely allows, that their school education should also be permeated with religion. Now I do not think that any Reformed Christian would be very keen on trying to prove either one of those propositions. No one who regards the Bible as the ultimate standards of faith and duty can proceed on the assumption that the Christian school is a matter of indifference. Much less can he entertain the notion that the secularized school, the school that is divorced from religion, deserves the preference.

But granted that all this is true, is it not possible to assume *a compromising attitude?* There are Reformed Christians who evidently proceed on the assumption that the education which their children receive in the schools may not be divorced from religion and need not necessarily be irreligious in the public school. They maintain that it is possible and permissible to include the religious element in the instruction that is given in the tax supported schools of the state. Consequently, they do not regard the Christian school as an absolute necessity, except in localities in which the last vestige of religion is excluded from the public school. We readily see that in taking that position they assume the right to yield their parental prerogative in the education of their children, to pass their responsibilities on to the state, and to leave it to the state to determine how much and what kind of religious training their children shall receive. This is certainly not in harmony with the Reformed principle that the parents are the responsible educators of their children, and consequently have the right to determine and the duty to control the religious spirit in which their children are educated.

Some are inclined, however, to waive the principle that the school belongs to the parents provided the parents can rest assured that their children will be educated religiously. Did not the government of the Netherlands in the post-Reformation period establish and maintain the schools where the children of the nation were educated? Did not the great Synod of Dort recognize and honor the government as having authority in educational matters? And then too, have we not been told repeatedly that there would have been no school struggle in the Netherlands if it had not been for the secularization of the national school? All these questions may be answered in the affirmative. But the facts implied certainly do not prove that the principle that the parents are the responsible educators of the children and should therefore be able to control the spirit of the education that is given in the schools, is not thoroughly Scriptural and Reformed. A great deal might be said in explanation of the fact that this principle did not always control the educational praxis of our Reformed forebears.

But suppose that we leave it out of consideration for the present and face the question whether the public school can give the children the religious training on which Reformed parents must insist. *A priorily,* it would seem to be entirely out of the question that a state which has no established religion but guarantees equality and religious freedom to all its citizens, a state which claims absolute neutrality in religious matters, should teach any particular religion in its educational institutions. It would even seem that such a state could consistently do only one thing, i. e., exclude all religious instruction from its schools. This is exactly the condition that obtains in France, where, according to Payne (*Contributions to the Science of Education,* p. 207), "The French Revolution made appear for the first time, in all its definiteness, the conception of the lay state, of the state neutral among all creeds, independent of all ecclesiastical authorities, and free from all theological bias." Our government has been moving in the same general direction, though it has not yet shaken off all vestiges of religion. Its Puritan traditions still make themselves felt, and in virtue of these some insist on calling the United States Christian. It is perfectly evident, however, that the term so applied is shorn of its real significance. Batten correctly remarks that "a state does not become Christian when it incorporates the name of Christ in its constitution or opens the sessions of Congress with prayer; neither is a state Christian when certain theological ideas are embodied in its legislation and certain ecclesiastical functionaries dictate the policy of cabinets. In any real sense a state is Christian when it possesses the spirit of Christ and seeks certain great Christian ends in and through its life and service." (*The Christian State,* p. 408). Because of this difference between the United States and France, the public school of our nation is not yet everywhere neutral in the sense and to the degree that the French public school is neutral. In some localities the public school has retained something of a religious character. At the same time authorities, when speaking of it in general terms, do not hesitate to speak of it as *the secularized school.*

But just how much religious teaching will be tolerated in the public school? Draper says in his work on *American Education* that religion is not barred from the schools, but sectarianism is; and this is a distinction that is met with repeatedly. The line is generally drawn at sectarianism or denominationalism. But, of course, even this is a rather uncertain line, since even the Bible has repeatedly been declared to be a sectarian book in official decisions and opinions. Payne expresses the opinion that "the genius of our institutions seems to require that our public school should be purely a lay institution, i. e., an institution divorced from religion." He quotes the authoritative work of Judge Cooley on *Constitutional Limitations* to the effect that "compulsory support, by taxation or otherwise, of religious instruction" is one of "those things which are not lawful under any of the American constitutions"; and that "not only is no one denomination to be favored at the expense of the rest, but all support of religious instruction must be entirely voluntary." From this Professor Payne concludes that "the

American public school should not only be unsectarian, but should be absolutely neutral as to religious bias." (*Contributions to the Science of Education,* p. 213 f.). Our own Michigan School Law says: "Sectarian instruction is abolished from all public schools; and, while the reading of the Bible may properly become a part of the daily program of the public school, the comment thereon by the teacher should be of such a character that pupils and parents of all religious faiths may not detect the slightest traces of sectarian prejudice."

In view of what has been said we may be sure that in the public school the teaching of the doctrine of election, of the total depravity of man, of his absolute dependence on the grace of God for salvation, of the limited nature of the atonement in Christ, etc., doctrines which are specifically Reformed, is altogether out of the question. More than that, it is impossible to teach the doctrines of the Trinity, the deity of Christ, redemption by his atoning blood, the necessity of conversion, etc. Still further, it would not even be permissible to teach that Jesus is the Christ, the Messiah promised by the prophets, and that Christianity is the only true religion. In other words, the very heart must be taken out of religious instruction before it can be permitted in the public school. And surely it ought to be out of the question for any Reformed Christian to compromise on such a basis.

But perhaps some will say that they have been able to make the public school in their locality thoroughly Christian and even Reformed. I am not able to control this contention. There may have been, and there may be today cases in which this is actually done, though I doubt it very much. In connection with this point I will only make the following remarks: (1) The laws of the land, even where they permit or even require Bible reading in the public school, forbid that sectarian or denominational teaching should be given there. (2) The decisions handed down by the courts of several states and the opinions expressed by attorneys-general are all in harmony with the fundamental position that sectarian instruction must be absolutely excluded. I have yet to see the first verdict or opinion to the contrary. (3) According to Judge Cooley, certainly no mean authority, it is unlawful under any of the American constitutions to use the money that is raised by taxation for sectarian instruction. (4) In cases in which the school-board of some country district succeeds in evading the law by introducing sectarian instruction, the complaint of a single individual will prove sufficent to put an end to its doubtful practice. And it would undoubtedly be rather embarrassing for a Christian school board to be called to time by one who is perhaps an unbeliever. (5) We may be sure that the opportunity for such an evasion of the law will also decrease in the measure in which the district school is replaced by the town school. And the tendency at present is rather strongly in that direction. In view of all this it appears that the practice of introducing sectarian instruction into the public school is very questionable, both from a legal and from a moral point of view. They who engage in it are using money, raised by taxation, for sectarian purposes, and this is contrary to the law. They introduce denominational teachings into the public school in spite of the fact that this is explicitly forbidden. They surreptitiously employ a state institution for the dissemination of specific religious doctrines. Surely, the foundation on which they are building is a questionable and a precarious one. It is a foundation that may crumble at any moment, a foundation that is "sinking sand." And one who is truly Reformed cannot consistently build on such a foundation in the important task of the religious education of his children.

Shall we then say that the home, the catechism class and the Sunday school can take care of the religious training of the child, and that the school need not be burdened with this in any way? This position has been taken by many in the past, but the fallacy of it is becoming ever increasingly apparent. Educational reformers are proclaiming from the house tops that our educational system has not provided sufficiently for the religious training of our youth. Psychologists are reminding us of the fact that education is a unitary process. And if this is so, it is sheer folly that the most important educational agency of the present should neglect the most fundamental element in education; and also that the education of the school should be diametrically opposed in spirit to that of the Christian home, because this is bound to result in a divided life. Moreover, the many plans that are devised for the injection of a larger amount of religious education into the training of youth, such as the North Dakota plan, the Colorado plan, the Gary plan, etc., all testify to the insufficiency of the religious education of the last half century. And, unfortunately, they themselves are only half-way measures, which do not help us to escape from the dualism that now exists between the education of the public school and that of the Christian home.

If we allow ourselves to be controlled by the will of our God and by thoroughly Reformed principles in providing for the education of our children, we shall seek, wherever this is at all possible, to establish and maintain schools which will consider it a sacred duty to educate our children in the spirit in which we solemnly promised to have them educated. And if we find such schools already in existence, we will thank our God for them, we will love them, we will send our children to them. We will pray for them, work for them, and be ready to sacrifice for them. If in that spirit we and our children continue to labor for the cause of Christian instruction, we shall have the satisfaction of an approving conscience; shall confer an inestimable boon upon our children, keeping them from the curse of the divided life and instilling into their hearts and minds ideas and ideals that are truly Christian; shall make an important contribution to the spiritual welfare of our community and nation by depositing a seed that may yield thirty-, sixty-, and even a hundred-fold; and shall above all reap the blessings of our covenant God, who has promised that "our sons shall be as plants grown up in their youth, and our daughters as cornerstones hewn after the fashion of a palace."

LOUIS BERKHOF

Address before the National Union of
Christian Schools Convention, Holland,
Michigan, August, 1930.

Key Thoughts:

1. In the face of nationalism in education and modern evolutionary pedagogy we reaffirm that if we are truly Reformed we say that the will of God determines our attitude to the Christian school. This will is revealed to us in his general, but above all, in his special revelation.

2. God has clearly told us that parents are the responsible educators of the child. All others who would teach the child stand in *loco parentis*. This principle has been recognized of old.

3. The Word of God also clearly teaches that the education parents provide for their children must be fundamentally religious. The Scripture makes it almost exclusively so. It is this type of education that is pregnant with the promise of real blessings.

4. The soul is a unit and education is a unitary process. It aims at the development of man's essential nature, which is fundamentally religious, into a harmonious life, full and rich and beautiful.

5. This very fundamental truth about the child may not be ignored in his education, and especially not in his schooling.

6. A genuinely Reformed person cannot possibly assume an attitude of hostility to the Christian school without compromising his religious convictions.

Comment:

The Reformed faith implicitly commits one to the Christian school idea. No other school but the Christian school can be basically religious. And it is the basically religious that the Reformed faith underscores in man and in his ways.

No less does the Christian school demand a distinctively Reformed view of Christian education. Christian education views the child in the covenant promise. He is a person organically one in his whole personality ingrafted in the organic head. This is much more than a theological doctrine. It is a basic presupposition in the understanding of child life in the Christian home and in the Christian schools.

8

The Christian School and Authority

The idea of authority does not appeal to the common mind. There has been a very persistent demand in many circles that from the marriage vows the words "and obey" be omitted. The modern woman considers it degrading that she must submit to the will of her husband in all things that are good and lawful. She craves a freedom that is more in harmony with the spirit of the age.

In view of the prevailing restiveness, even in the home circles, it is no wonder that the spirit of independence has also entered the circles of minors. They often rebel against the yoke of parental authority, even when it is exercised with the greatest love and forbearance. They complain that the parents do not understand them and violate their rights. They protest against the infringement of their liberty and the limitation of their pleasures, and often break away to follow their own sweet wills.

In the world of labor the same opposition to authority is in evidence. The laboring man resents the authority of the employer to dictate the terms of labor. He himself claims the right to determine the hours of labor, the amount of work that may be done in a day, and the wages that must be paid. The revolt against authority often assumes dangerous proportions in the industrial world.

The same tendency is becoming increasingly apparent in national life. The people have no patience with emperors or kings or even presidents that rule by the grace of God. It is assumed as a matter of course that autocracy must make place for democracy in the absolute sense of the word. The will of the people must be supreme. Those in office are merely the servants of the people, and must see to it that the popular will is carried out. Whatever the people in general may think of the first part of the French slogan or revolutionary days, "No God, no master," it admits of no doubt that they readily chime in with the last part.

My subject is not only unpopular, it is also of rather uncertain import. It may involve any one of several questions. It may call for an answer to the question whether the school, and in this case specifically the Christian school, can speak with authority and compel active concurrence with its teachings. But it is also possible that it seeks a reply to the query whether the teachings of the Christian school are or should be based on reason or on authority. Again, the implied question may be in what relation the Christian school stands to the civil authorities; in how far it should recognize the authority of the state in school matters. But the real question is still another: Is the Christian school teacher clothed with authority? And if so, what is the nature of this authority; what are its limits; and how should it be exercised?

I do not fear that I will be accused of taking too much for granted if I simply proceed on the assumption that the school teacher, whether it be of the Christian or of the public school, is undoubtedly clothed with authority. Theoretically this authority is not called in question, however much it may often be ignored in practice. Works on pedagogy and school management invariably assert the right of the teacher to make his will effective in the classroom, and to demand obedience on the part of the pupils. And even if some erratic pedagogue should call this right in question, I am sure that Christian teachers would not do so, for they are fully satisfied that they are clothed with authority when they are conducting their classes. Any attempt to prove this point would be like carrying coals to Newcastle.

The more important question is, What is the character of the authority that is vested in the school teacher? This is a point on which there is no general agreement and on which we people of Reformed persuasion are apt to differ from those who do not share our religious convictions. In order to give an intelligent answer to this question, we shall have to inquire into the nature of authority. Speaking generally, we may say that *authority is the right to command and enforce obedience, or to speak the decisive word in debatable questions.* The general in the field aserts it, when he orders his troops about and directs the movements of the army; the judge on the bench, when he imposes sentence on the criminal that is brought before him; and the expert in any line of work, when difficult questions are placed before him in connection with his field of endeavor.

The general definition given already contains an intimation of the fact that there is more than one kind of authority. There is authority in the strict sense of the word, generally called *judicial authority*. It may be defined as the right to make laws, to command, and to enforce obedience. It is sometimes called the authority of position, because it does not inhere in the person, but in the position in which he is placed. The strong may be called upon to yield to the weak. The old may be under obligation to follow the wishes of the young. The good may be in duty bound to carry out the will of the evil.

This authority is in some cases original, which means that it is not derived from someone else. In the absolute sense only God has original authority. He is the Creator of the universe, and as such has an inherent right to command His creatures. He has no superior to invest Him with authority and to limit His rights. He is a law unto himself and demands obedience to His sovereign will. His authority is absolute; none can say unto Him, What doest Thou? The believing heart will always say: "The Lord reigneth; let the people tremble."

Among men this is quite different; there are various grades of authority. Take the army, for instance. The captain derives his authority from the major, the major from the lieutenant-colonel, the lieutenant-colonel from the colonel, the colonel from the brigadier-general, the brigadier-general from the major-general, the major-general from the general, the general from the commander-in-chief, the president of the United States, the president from the government, and the government from God. Beyond this point we cannot go, because we have reached the ultimate source of authority.

In the absolute sense, therefore, there is no original authority among men. Yet it is customary, and for practical reasons also desirable, to speak of original authority in a relative sense. That authority may be called original which is not derived from any other man, but directly from God. Thus many would say that the authority of the people of the United States to govern themselves is original authority. But we as Calvinists, who do not believe in absolute popular sovereignty, would correct this and claim original authority for the government. We would refer to Rom. 13:1-4: "Let every soul be subject unto the higher powers. For there is no power but of God: the powers that be are ordained of God. Whosoever therefore resisteth the power, resisteth the ordinance of God . . . For he (the ruler) is the minister of God to thee for good." Again, the authority of the parents over their children is original. It is not derived from the Church, nor from Society, nor from the State, but is founded in the original constitution of things as ordered by God. The children are born of the parents and consequently the parents have authority over them and are responsible for their education and training.

From what has been said it is perfectly evident that this judicial authority may also be derived. In distinction from the authority of God, which is absolutely original, all authority of man is derived. There is no power but of God. But while some are clothed with an authority that is derived directly from God, others are invested with an authority that is derived from God through the mediation of men. It is, so to speak, at least doubly derived. Governments delegate a part of their authority to their consuls in various countries.

A sharp distinction must be made between this judicial authority and what is usually called moral authority. This is the power which one derives from opinion, respect or long established reputation. It is the influence that is conferred by character, specialized knowledge, or mental superiority. Says Hinsdale: "A man who has mastered a given subject becomes an authority in respect thereto, and on occasion renders expert opinions; a physician in relation to disease, a lawyer in relation to law, a merchant or banker in relation to business matters. In such testimony as this two elements blend — one of fact and one of inference or reason; and the value of the expert's opinion, supposing him to be honest, depends upon his acquaintance with the facts of the case and the soundness of his judgment." (*Jesus as a Teacher*, p. 114).

With respect to this authority the following points deserve attention. God is the ultimate source of this as well as of all judicial authority. We discover a great diversity of gifts and talents among men. The all-wise Creator distributed them as He saw fit. With respect to the Church Paul says: "For to one is given by the Spirit the word of wisdom; to another the word of knowledge by the same Spirit; to another faith by the same Spirit; to another the gifts of healing by the same Spirit; to another the working of miracles; to another prophecy; to another discerning of spirits; to another diverse kinds of tongues; to another the interpretation of tongues; but all these worketh that one and the selfsame Spirit, dividing to every man severally as He will" (I Cor. 12:8-11). The same principle holds for society in general. God is the Author of all those special gifts that make men influential in society and lend weight to their words.

In distinction from judicial authority, moral authority does not inhere in any office to which a person is appointed, but rather in the person himself, in his character and talents, his qualifications and abilities. The more his character stands out in nobility and strength, the more he towers above his fellowmen in intellectual acumen and superior learning, the greater his authority will be.

The power so acquired is no authority in the strict sense of the word though it be graced with that name. It does not carry with it the right to command, which is characteristic of authority proper. If it did, it would also include the right to enforce its dicta, a prerogative which it cannot legitimately claim. When a man of science lays down certain propositions, he may expect others to accept them implicitly, and perhaps they will. But in case they refuse, he cannot employ the strong arm to compel assent. If he wants others to agree with him, he must prove his contentions. The acceptance of his views will be dependent on the cogency of his arguments, or in other words, on moral persuasion. Hence this authority is called *moral* authority. It is not, like authority in the proper sense of the word, immediately binding on the conscience.

At the same time it should not be forgotten that this so-called authority may be of great importance. Think of the tremendous influence exercised by such men as Plato and Aristotle, Augustine and Thomas Aquinas, Luther and Calvin, Wesley and Jonathan Edwards, Kant and Hegel, Kuyper and Bavinck, most of whom have already dominated the thinking of centuries. The significance of this authority is enhanced by the fact that the great masses of the people do not think for themselves but allow others to do their thinking for them. The simple dictum of a great man is sufficient for them; they need no arguments. Hence it follows that this authority may be greatly abused; and history teaches us that it has often wrought havoc in the world. Think of the terrors of the French revolution.

Both kinds of authority may be combined in a single person. One placed in a position of authority may be a man of sterling character, of a superior intellect, of great erudition and learning, and of unquestioned ability. If all other things are equal, this will make him a better ruler. He will rule with knowledge and understanding, with wisdom and equity. The people will have confidence in him and gladly render him due obedience. Was it not something of this kind that the wise Preacher of Israel had in mind, when he said: "Blessed art thou, O land, when thy king is the son of nobles, and thy princes eat in due season, for strength and not for drunkenness!"? Surely the moral greatness of such rulers as William the Silent and William III, of Washington and Lincoln was an asset to them in the performance of their difficult task.

* * *

After this discussion of the nature of authority we now come to the question as to the character of the authority that is vested in the school teacher. It may have seemed to some that we were unnecessarily long in coming to the point in question. But I trust that on second thought it will appear that the preceding discussion was not only perfectly relevant, but also quite necessary for the intelligent treatment of the subject under consideration: What kind of authority is vested in the teacher?

Let me begin with that which is most generally believed. Rousseau practically denies the existence of authority in the schoolroom, or at least condemns its exercise. According to him the child is predetermined by his very constitution, like plants and animals, to a progressive development quite independent of artificial aid. Though Kant followed him in laying great stress on the freedom of the child, he did not go to the extreme of condemning every show of authority in the schoolroom, every attempt of the teacher to interfere with the liberty and the free movements of the child. Rousseau's absolute antagonism to discipline is not shared by later pedagogues.

It is generally agreed that the teacher is at least clothed with moral authority, and should diligently exercise it in giving direction to the lives and activities of his pupils. He is superior of the children that are entrusted to his care in moral character, in knowledge of the subjects taught, in that practical wisdom that reveals itself in the perfect adaptation of means to ends, and in the tact that is required in the direction of youthful lives. This superiority does not escape the attention of the pupils and goes very far in determining their conduct and in shaping their course of action. With the smaller children what teacher says goes, even if the parents express some doubt. They often wax eloquent in defending the opinion of the teacher, whom they regard as a marvel of learning. And if the older pupils begin to argue and to demand proofs, the teacher that is well prepared for his work as a rule does not find it difficult to satisfy their desire for a rational insight into the subject under consideration. This moral authority will, of course, be commensurate with the moral excellence, the real or supposed learning, and the practical ability of the teacher. If these are not in evidence, it will gradually wane and finally be eclipsed by contrary forces.

Though it is generally admitted that the teacher is clothed with moral authority, which is no authority in the strict sense of the word, it is frequently assumed that he has no judicial authority. Modern pedagogy, while avoiding the extremes of Rousseau, has inbibed all too much of the views of the erratic Frenchman. He proceeds on the assumption that the child is good by nature and, if allowed the gratification of its natural desires and the spontaneous development of its latent powers, will, as a matter of course, develop into a useful member of society. The source of all evil lies in the corrupt society in which the child grows up. Hence it must be guarded carefully against the extraneous influences of present-day civilization in order to preserve it in its original purity. The keynote of Rousseau's philosophy is given in the words: "Everything is good as it leaves the hands of the Creator; everything degenerates in the hands of man." Therefore he raises the cry, "Back to nature!" and sternly faces man with a "Hands off!" The less the teacher imposes, or at least seems to impose his will upon the child, the better it will be for the pupil.

Now modern pedagogy does not concur in all the extreme opinions of Rousseau, but clearly reveals the influence of his fundamental position. There is a widespread conviction that the child is good by nature and will, under favorable circumstances, develop in the right direction. Educators wax eloquent in speaking of the majesty of the child and habitually regard it as the standard of all things in education. In the past, they say, it was largely the victim of circumstances. The schoolhouses were wanting in architectural beauty. The halls were bare and uninviting. Large numbers of children were crowded into rooms of which the very atmosphere was chilling and were compelled to sit on uncomfortable seats for three hours straight. Playgrounds were few and far between, and such as there were had a repulsive appearance, so that the children naturally developed into street-urchins. During school hours the school-master paraded through the aisles with an imperious air, issued his commands right and left, and was always ready to enforce his commands with the ever present hickory stick, without any consideration for individual idiosyncracies or extenuating circumstances. He took no time for listening to pleas or hearing witnesses. His love for the children may have been genuine, but they did not realize it and did not respond to it in love. He was an offence to their sensitive natures. His regulations encroached upon their rights, and his punishments jarred their sense of justice.

Now modern pedagogy demands that the inherent goodness of the child be recognized, and that its majesty be respected. The external environment in which the child moves from day to day during its school years must be improved, in order that it may not have a degrading but an uplifting influence. Palatial schoolhouses must be built that are well heated and well ventilated. The rooms should be cheerful and inviting, the corridors wide and airy, and the walls decorated with reproductions of masterpieces. The teacher ought to interfere as little as possible with the native tendencies and desires of his pupils. He should always consult their wishes and scrupulously respect their rights. The word of command ought to be contrabanded in school; kind requests only are in place. Disciplinary measures should not be necessary, and in so far as they are required, should be of a negative and preventive character. Above all, corporal punishment must be avoided. It has no legitimate place in the schools of this enlightened age. The teacher need not concern himself primarily about training the children in obedience to external authority, but should bend all his energies in the development of independence of thought and action, and of righteous conduct. Let him reason with the children, and by appealing to the promptings of their higher nature lead them to an ever greater appreciation of what is true and good and beautiful. The time is happily past when it was thought necessary to "break the wills" of recalcitrant boys and girls. Under proper guidance their wills will inevitably move in the right direction. The sum and substance of all this reasoning is that the teacher really has no judicial authority, and even if he does have it, finds no proper field for its exercise in school.

It goes without saying, however, that one who honors the Word of God cannot share these views. We feel also in perusing pedagogical works of the present day that, however much they may seek to derogate the idea that the teacher is invested with judicial authority, they cannot escape the conclusion that he has the power to make all kinds of regulations governing the work and conduct of their pupils and to enforce these regulations, if not by the use of the hickory stick, then by means of other disciplinary measures. Now the teacher has no such right if he is not endowed with real authority. The modern teacher may pose as exclusively the friendly guide and advisor of the children; yet he feels it necessary to exact obedience by barring the unruly from certain privileges or by segregating them in separate schoolrooms or in truant schools, if it be only for the protection of the general interests of the school or to guard the other children from their baneful influence. Surely, the teacher has the power to command and to enforce obedience.

* * *

If we cannot agree with the view that the teacher has no judicial authority, but only an authority based on character, learning, and superior wisdom, neither can we endorse the ideas that the school is not the proper sphere for exercising such authority, that the children are inherently good by nature, and that, if something goes wrong, the teacher may be sure that he himself or his methods of teaching or the organization of his school or the environment in which the children move from day to day, are to blame. This whole method of reasoning proceeds on a faulty conception of the spiritual condition of the child. We find a less encouraging but far healthier view in the Word of God. The poet says: "Behold, I was shapen in iniquity; and in sin did my mother conceive me" (Ps. 51:5). In the book of Proverbs we read: "Foolishness is bound up in the heart of a child; but the rod of correction shall drive it far from him" (22:15). Paul tells us that we are "by nature children of wrath" (Eph. 2:3). And of the Corinthians he writes: ". . . else were your children unclean; but now they are holy" (I Cor. 7:14). Experience also teaches us clearly that children are not as good and pure and innocent as some modern pedagogues like to picture them. It is only when we choose to be kindly oblivious to the manifestations of evil in their lives, that we can sing:

> Innocent child and show-white flower!
> Well are ye paired in your opening hour:
> Thus should the pure and the lovely meet,
> Stainless with stainless, and sweet with sweet.
> White as those leaves just blown apart
> Are the folds of thy own young heart;
> Guilty passion and cankering care
> Never have left their traces there.

We cannot chime in with that song, and consequently do not believe that the discipline of children ought to be purely negative and aim at warding off the evil that is operative in the world round about them. The Bible teaches the necessity of positive correction and even corporal punishment so clearly that he who runs may read. It is only a sickly sentimentalism that insists on speaking of the "barbarities of the rod." The story of Eli who rested satisfied with a word of kindly reproof and did not punish his wicked sons is held up before us as a warning example. Listen to a few of the words of the wise as recorded in the book of Proverbs: "He that spareth his rod hateth his son; but he that loveth him chasteneth him betimes" (13:22, 24). "Chasten thy son while there is hope, and let not thy soul spare for his crying" (19:18). "Withhold not correction from the child: for if thou beatest him with the rod, he shall not die. Thou shalt beat him with the rod, and shalt deliver his soul from hell" (23:13, 14). "The rod and reproof give wisdom: but a child left to himself bringeth his mother to shame" (29:15). If this was true in the days of Solomon, it is just as true today, for human nature is the same whenever and where-ever you may find it.

But the teacher should bear in mind that the judicial authority with which he is invested does not inhere in his person. He may never act as an autocrat. Speaking in terms of government, we may say that he is not an absolute but a constitutional monarch. All judicial authority is derived from God and must be exercised in harmony with the will of God as revealed in His divine Word. It is of the greatest importance not only that the teacher recognize this fact and allow himself to be governed by his disciplinary principles that are found in the Word of God, but also that he convey to his pupils the important truth that he is in duty bound to exercise discipline and does it in obedience to his God. He should not rest satisfied with telling the children that he is ruling in the name of God, with His sanction, and according to His requirements, but should cause them to feel it in the way in which he punishes the unruly. This will prevent the children from accusing him in their hearts of abitrariness and will lend to his discipline a direct appeal to the conscience. At the same time he should not be over-insistent on this point, lest he seem to claim divine sanction also for his foolish and arbitrary actions and thus endanger that which is holy.

* * *

But now the question arises, whether the authority of the teacher is derived from God immediately or through the mediation of the parents. Opinions may and do differ on this point. Howland does not seem to reckon with the fact the teacher's authority is derived in any sense of the word. He claims that the teacher's "powers inhere of right in his office, whatever dicta to the contrary may be burrowed from the dusty decisions of forgotten judges"; and he adds: "We need not that any *parentis locus* should be assigned us by the hocus-pocus of legal or judicial legerdemain, nor would we extend the limits of our domain beyond their natural bounds." (*Practical Hints for Teachers*, p. 14). On the other hand Pickard in his work on *School Supervision* (p. 127 f.) recognizes the fact that the teacher stands in *loco parentis,* though with certain restrictions. Says he: "The parent alone has the divine right to control the child. . . . Certain rights of the parent, such as the right of controlling the time and movements of the child for a few hours each day, the right of directing his course of study, are surrendered to the civil authorities, not permanently nor irredeemably, but at the pleasure of the parent. The State then assumes the act for the parent, not with the authority which God has conferred upon the parent, but with the authority which the parent has transferred to the State. . . . It is a right of human origin, inferior to the parent's right, which is of divine origin."

Now we people of Reformed persuasion proceed on the assumption that the parents are the proper educators of the children and are most of all responsible to God for the faithful performance of their duty. The complexities of modern life makes it necessary, however, that they call in the help of professional teachers. And in order that these may be able to do their work effectively, the parents delegate to them a part of their authority, the right to control the time, the work, the conduct, and the movements of the children for a certain period each day. Consequently the teachers have the same right to command the children in school that the parents have at home and are also justified in enforcing their commands. But this transfer of authority does not change its character, does not transform a divine into a human authority.

It does not make the wishes and desires and demands of the parents the ultimate standard of authority for the teacher. This standard is found for him as well as for the parents only in the Word of God. The parents have a perfect right to criticise the teacher's exercise of authority, but only in so far as it does not correspond with the revealed will of God. The teacher too is responsible to God for all disciplinary action.

Moreover, the teacher's authority is in part derived directly from God. The school is not merely an "elongation" of the family, as it has often been called. It is to a certain extent an independent institution, a separate organization of social life. It is a small community with a life all its own. Now we would hardly ascribe to the parents the right to dictate the rules and regulations for the government of this small republic; the methods of teaching; of conducting recitations, reviews, and examinations; and all the different preventive and corrective measures of discipline. These are naturally controlled to a great extent by the character of the organization and by the nature of the work that is carried on in school. Among other things the teacher certainly has original power to determine what rules and regulations are necessary for school life, and to demand of the children that they comply with them. In these particulars he is directly responsible to God and to God only. He has no right to go contrary to the Word of God. The moment he does, the parents have a perfect right to protest, not because he does not cater to their wishes, but because he does not recognize the manifesto of the King.

* * *

From what has been said several things follow respecting the exercise of authority in the schoolroom. Some of these were already mentioned or at least intimated, but for the sake of clarity and emphasis it may be well to reiterate them. In calling special attention to some of them I shall limit myself to those requirements that are most fundamental.

The very first requirement is that the teacher cause the children to understand that he is ruling the school in the name of God. After all only the authority that has divine sanction is binding in the conscience. He should let them feel that he is not acting arbitrarily, and that, if they are under orders, he is likewise. He ought never to leave the impression that in school might makes right. It may prevent a repetition of the painful experience of that fond father who asked his little son, "Do you know why I whip you?" and heard in reply, "Yes, sir, because you are the biggest." Of course, the teacher should be very careful and tactful in conveying the idea that he is ruling with divine authority. In teaching certain Bible lessons he can incidentally bring out the thought that all authority is from God; also the authority of parents over their children, and of teachers over their pupils. He can draw the lesson from both nature and Scripture that God is a God of order and therefore requires this also in the schoolroom. Does not Paul say: "God is not the author of confusion, but of peace, as in all the churches of the saints"; and again: "Let all things be done decently and in order"? He can remind the children of the fact that all evil conduct is sin against God and therefore requires correction and perhaps discipline.

The second requirement is that the teacher, in the exercise of his authority, act in strict conformity with the Word of God. The right of parents and teachers over their children is not absolute but limited by the superior rights of God. These are revealed in the Bible. Hence the Bible is the standard according to which they must govern those entrusted to their care. I cannot delay to point out in particulars what the Word of God requires in the matter of discipline, but merely wish to emphasize the fact that all Christian schoolteachers should be diligent in deriving from the Word of God the principles that ought to govern them in the exercise of authority and in the scrupulous application of these principles in the government of the school and in all disciplinary action. In vain will they appeal to their responsibility to God, if the children detect that this is merely a covenient theory that is violated in practice from day to day.

The third requirement is that school discipline proceed from the right motive, to wit, from a love that does not lose sight of the ends of justice. School discipline differs from the administration of justice in the state. Justice is the moving principle of the government. It is true that the state sometimes resorts to corrective measures for the moral betterment of the offenders, but it aims primarily at the maintenance of righteousness in public life, and at the restoration of that public order that was disturbed by the criminal. To that end it administers punishment. Now the school, as a social organization, is also concerned with the maintenance of justice. But the main purpose of its positive disciplinary measures and of those in the home is the moral correction and improvement of recalcitrant children. They are chastisements rather than punishments. It should be perfectly evident that they are the expressions of the love that fills the hearts of the parents and of the teachers to the children under their care. Hence educators should always avoid punishing pupils in a fit of anger. It is better to defer punishment for a while. Let love reign supreme!

The fourth requirement is that the teacher rule with equity and justice, and maintain order with a firm hand. This follows from the ends he has in view, namely, to teach the child obedience to authority and to instil in it a love for moral purity and civic righteousness. He may be so long suffering and so indulgent that he makes a mess of the important work entrusted to him and that the fruits of his labor will prove dangerous to social and civic life. There may be something commendable in the modern ideal to train the children for independence, but, carried to an extreme, this may prove to be a source of incalculable danger. Let the teacher be firm in his government and in his discipline. We do not plead for an incessant use of the rod, but we do maintain that it has a legitimate place in the school as well as in the home. When the occasion calls for it, it ought to be used, though with discretion and wisdom. Let us not be wise above that which is written in the Word of God and which was justified by the experience of ages. Today, if ever, it is highly necessary that the child learn the lesson of obedience to the authorities by which God is pleased to rule it.

In this connection the question may be raised, what to think of the so-called pupil government. In some cases the responsibility of maintaining good order and the proper respect for authority and law has been thrown upon the students. A council of pupils has been chosen for the exercise of proper discipline. In other cases the principle of self-government has found expression in the "school city," the organization of the school into a miniature city, with mayor, board of aldermen, police courts, board of health, etc. The school city also throws the pupils largely upon their own resources for the maintenance of order and decorum in the schoolroom. We have no time now to enter upon a thorough discussion of the problem; therefore the following remarks must suffice. The parents of our children willingly delegate a part of their authority to carefully selected teachers, but it may well be questioned whether they would be as willing to do this if they surmised that ultimately the exercise of this authority would be entrusted largely to inexperienced children. The government of children is not an easy task. It often taxes the ability of judicious parents and of experienced teachers. How then can they entrust this responsible task, even in part, to children who are still in their teens, and expect that they will have a due sense of their responsibility and will be able to obtain the desired result? Partial self-government may have a legitimate place in colleges — though even there it must be carefully guarded — but is certainly of very dubious value in primary schools. Moreover, it is to be feared that the children would be trained for a false independence, for their youthful tutors have as yet no conception of true independence, rather than for that obedience to authority that will prove so invaluable in later life and will be as a crown of glory to every Christian child.

No, let the educators, who stand in *loco parentis* and represent divine authority in the schoolroom, who have a proper conception of the difficulty of their task and of their responsible position, and who are endowed with knowledge and wisdom and tact, keep their hand on the wheel and teach the children to submit to every ordinance of man for the Lord's sake: whether it be to the king as supreme; or unto governors, as unto them that are sent by him for the punishment of evildoers, and for the praise of them that do well. Then by the grace of God they may hope to train a generation that will honor the laws of God and be a blessing for society. Then Christian parents will rise up and call them blessed.

Louis Berkhof
Address before the National Union of
Christian Schools Convention, Grand
Rapids, Michigan, August 26, 1926.

Key Thoughts:

1. God is the ultimate source of all authority among men.

2. Human authority may be classified as judicial, the right to make laws, to command and to enforce obedience, and moral or expert, derived from opinion, respect in long established reputation. The teacher is clothed with both kinds of authority by virtue of his responsibility to God.

3. The teacher derives his authority through the parents who in the final analysis are the God-appointed educators.

4. However, because the school is an institution in society, there is an area of authority reserved for the teacher. He is authorized to conduct the school and enforce its regulations.

5. Some fundamental requirements in the excercise of a teacher's authority:

   a. The teacher should cause the children to understand that he is ruling the school in the name of God.

   b. The teacher, in the exercise of his authority, should act in strict conformity with the Word of God.

   c. School discipline must be motivated by a love and not lose sight of the ends of justice.

   d. The teacher must rule with equity and justice, and maintain order with a firm hand.

6. So-called pupil government is of very dubious value, especially on the elementary level of schooling.

Comment:

There is rightful authority in the Christian school. It is not merely a case of morale and social prestige which belongs to the teacher by virtue of his position in society. It is not merely a pedagogical authority which belongs to the teacher by virtue of his learning or maturity. The teacher's authority is God-given. He serves in the place of the parent to direct the child in the God-appointed way. Because he does this in the school as a social institution, he has an area of authority rightfully his.

In the exercise of his authority the teacher carries out the mandates of his Lord and Master. To carry out his authority in his own name as teacher is to violate his stewardship. The Christian teacher is always aware of his position as a humble servant of God who too errs and must be penitent. The teacher's penitence and humility is not evidence of weakness, but of strength. It is when the teacher exercises arbitrary authority, not motivated by love, that he is weak.

9

Authority a Liberating Force in Education

"Ye shall know the truth, and the truth shall make you free" (John 8:32).

On the basis of this truth, I shall attempt to demonstrate that compulsion breeds freedom, that the fruit of restraint is liberty, and that exercise of authority releases. One might well hesitate to tackle any such paradoxes. But he whose duty it has been to interpret the Scriptures has become familiar with paradoxes. He has been called upon to teach that he who would save himself must lose himself — he who would live must first die — he who desires exaltation must abase himself — he who would have freedom must submit himself to the will of God.

It is first of all imperative in meeting the challenge of a paradox to define its terms very carefully. He who discerns well learns well particularly in this field of investigation. Let us therefore begin by placing the concept of authority under the microscope immediately. And in order that we might not go too far afield we shall limit our investigation to such authority as usually is or ought to be exercised in education. We can come to an adequately clear conception of the term before us by inquiring as to its source, nature, and objective.

* * *

First, then, where does the authority of the teacher in the schoolroom come from? Where does the teacher get the right to govern the child's thinking and conduct in the school?

The most popular answer is that such authority comes from the State. As a matter of fact the State has been and is exercising such authority in our public school system. It has determined that all the children must be educated. It has set the time when they are to be educated. It controls the subject matter of their school training. It has final jurisdiction even in the method of instruction. The extention of the State's jurisdiction over school going children is very apparent in the case of delinquent children. Much of illiteracy and delinquency has been checked by the educational authority of the State.

There are a great many teachers in this land of ours who would not accede to the position that their authority comes from the State. They labor in the consciousness that their authority comes from the Church. The Church was for a long time the *sole* educator in occidental civilization. She has in her own interest, as well as in that of the State, determined the time, contents, objectives and methods of education. And when we throw these two systems or ideas of authority in education in the balances, we will find the balance on the side of the Church. She is at least not ungodly and she does not seek to limit the child's education as being for this life only. She would honor God and His Christ and recognize the pupil as a child of God.

There are a few others in this country that believe that their educational authority comes from the parents. Many parents of Reformed and Lutheran persuasion are convinced that they should have complete jurisdiction over their children's education. I am not so sure that it is a wholesome position except when it is limited to the circle of Christian parents. This principle like all of the divine precepts is calculated to serve as a guide only to Christian parents. It was Shailer Matthews who once wrote that God has no rule of living for the ungodly; He has prescriptions only for Christian living. The application of the principle of parental authority in education has proved in many cases to be very detrimental to the child's interest. Recently the police discovered that a father and a mother were teaching their children to steal and were receiving in their homes the stolen goods. The State through its courts adjudged the parents unfit to rear and train their children. Was the State wrong in waiving the principle that parents are the proper authorities in the training of their children? Indeed, it would seem that the entire system of compulsory education grew out of the failure of parents to properly exercise their authority as the educators of their offspring. And many other evidences could be adduced to show that the principle of parental authority must be circumscribed carefully before it can be adopted.

But after all, such things as civil, ecclesiastical and parental authority are but derived and secondary. In the face of what St. Paul declared this cannot be denied. Says he, "Let every soul be subject unto the higher authorities, for there is no authority but of God. The authorities that be are ordained of God" (Rom. 13:1). Some, who may be thinking of the English translation of the Bible, may wish to retort that the word is "power" not "authority." Indeed, so it has been translated, but the original word is really "authority." It is the same word that the Jews used when they said that Jesus taught not as the scribes but with authority (Matt. 7:29).

Now the consciousness that God is the sole source of all authority has been quiescent in recent years. In the days of long ago kings reigned by the grace of God. Theoretically that consciousness is still strong in England. This became very evident when the Church played such a dominant role in the abdication of the Duke of Windsor and the coronation of George VI. However, the popular reaction to this matter was more accurately reflected in the ridicule directed toward the ex-emperor, Kaizer Wilhelm II, when he maintained that he reigned by the grace of God. The popular idea today is that of people's sovereignty or state's sovereignty, and not that of divine authority.

If, however, one runs back over the course of history, he will be amazed to find how firmly the idea of divine sovereignty was imbedded in the minds of the people. Among the primitive peoples every official civil act of any significance was accompanied with religious ceremonies because it was regarded as being of divine origination and with divine approval. Civil leaders had a certain sanctity about them that set them apart from the rest. This was very apparent in the history of Israel. The cause of Israel was God's cause. Every important transaction was divinely demanded. To curse a king was as bad as to curse God.

The Bible does not teach at all that this idea of authority coming from God rests only upon religious leaders. As a matter of fact Jesus himself, when Pilate was about to deliver him, informed him, "Thou couldst have no authority over me at all, except it were given thee from above" (John 19:11). And Paul made his clear declaration about all authority being ordained of God in response to the Christians' feeling that as people of God they need not tolerate any ungodly rule over them.

And it should be added that there would be no possibility of the exercise of authority on the part of a few over the masses if the concept of higher authority above them did not motivate obedience. If the masses should rise up in arms, the authorities would be rendered helpless. Some sort of religion, some sort of conception of God, renders the exercise of authority possible. And is it not striking that in this country we still attach so much significance to the oaths that the President, the governor, and the judge must take them upon the occasion of the inauguration into office? Then, too, there is the required oath that must be taken (with few exceptions) in the case of a witness before the bar. Is this after all an indication of an acknowledgement that there be no authority except it be from God?

Now in my estimation it is here where the ultimate source of authority in the school room must be sought. It is as true here as anywhere else that there is no authority except it be ordained of God. And it makes no difference whether you place the secondary authority in the State or in the Church or in the parents, it can be traced back to God. Indeed, if it cannot be traced back to God no child is under any obligation to submit to it. It will be well for the teacher, the pupil and also the parents to be fully cognizant of that fact.

If God be the source of all authority what is its nature? The word authority (*ex-ousia* in the Greek) means "out of (or by) one's being." It is therefore neither arbitrary nor capricious, but rather a necessary manifestation of God. It has been maintained that the exercise of authority was due to sin and that it is a redemptive device. Then authority would not be "out of his being" but out of his grace and it should then be operative only in the field of redemption. But these suggested restrictions are unjustifiable. Even in the pre-redemptive period there was already evidence of the exercise of divine authority.

How does God manifest this authority?

There is first of all his sovereignty. God instructed man to have dominion over the works of his hands. That was even before the Fall of man. This sovereignty is something that is "out of God's being." He could not possibly be God without being a sovereign, and no one can possibly be a representative of God without assuming the role of a king. I am not speaking of the manner or the sphere of ruling, but merely of the fact and the necessity of ruling. Parents must rule as authorities of God. This is not left to their discretion. And it is just because of this imperative that the command of God that children honor and obey their parents is entirely in order. It is God's nature to rule and his representative must rule. The same truth is applicable in the realm of school work. All these tendencies of removing a ruling head from the schoolroom in the interest of the spirit of democracy stand condemned both by the pragmatic test and the dictates of the Bible. The method of schoolroom jurisdiction may vary but the fact stands. God must of necessity reign. It is "out of his being." So must every one that would in any way represent him. The kingly office of the Christian can be traced back to this fundamental concept.

This authority bears in its essence not only dominion but also truth. God is sovereign, but he is also truth. This truth, just as well as his sovereignty, is authoritative because it is "out of his being." Since the teacher's business centers around the matter of presenting and interpreting truth, this is an important item under the discussion. Ungodly teachers make proper use of their authority only in so far as they succeed in catching and presenting rays of truth here and there. There is no authoritative teaching except it be the truth. No one has a right to demand submission to any teaching except it be the truth. Now there can be no room for option in this matter. The teacher, by virtue of his being authorized to teach must present the truth. This is a divine requirement. And neither is it optional with the pupil whether he would receive the truth. There is no alternative for the teacher but to teach it and for the pupil but to receive it. This follows from the fact that God is truth and his delegated authority is "out of his being." This, as you will have observed, touches the prophetic office of the Christian.

God is not only sovereign, and not only truth, but he has also the attributes of love and justice. He is love. He is just. These are "out of his being." At this point we enter upon the priestly function of the representative of God. He must love not because of the lovableness of the objects, but because it follows from God's being which he represents. The statement that children are such lovable darlings has been tremendously overworked. When we speak of children being lovable, we simply mean that they manifest certain traits that are agreeable to us. But that is not the proper basis for the exercise of love. God does not love men because they are so lovable, but because his essence or his being requires it. God's love initiates from within him and not from without. And so the teacher must find the ground of his love not in the child but in God. That is where God found it. Justice, too, is divinely initiated. One does not need to be just to the child because it has merited it, but because God required it. It is not optional with the representative of God to love or to be just as he wills; these reactions are imperative. It is the imperative that grows out from his authority.

In short, to exercise authority is but to manifest God along the lines of human activity, namely, willing, thinking and feeling. In other words it is to function properly, as king, prophet and priest.

* * *

The aim of authority needs a word of elucidation. It is well to develop the proper perspective at this point. It is a question of anthropocentrism or theocentrism.

Popularly it is held that authority is exercised for the benefit of the subject or perhaps of the objects of authority. The position that it is exercised for the benefit of those in whom the authority is invested may be almost summarily dismissed. Yet it seems to be the practical position of those who are clothed with it. Kings and others reign for the benefit of themselves. Many pupils are positive that teachers reign for the benefit of the teachers, and they are not always mistaken. This position, however, is, to say the least, uncharitable. Though it may be practiced, it is quite generally condemned. And I presume it is quite generally condemned just because those who must submit to the authority are the judges.

The position that authority should be exercised for the benefit of those who are subject to the authority is apparently a very acceptable one. Kings are expected to reign for the benefit of their subjects. Parents should exercise control over their children for the benefit of the latter. Teachers must teach for the benefit of their pupils. There is something tremendously precarious about that position. It seems to represent the primary objectives of kingship, parenthood and pedagogy. That idea was essentially the one which was slipped by the Serpent into the heads of Adam and Eve, namely, that this universe is here for the benefit of man. That was the philosophy of ancient Israel, and they could not possibly understand why the nations round about and the current events did not always serve them. That was the trouble with Peter, James and John, not to forget Judas, when they conflicted with the spirit and teaching of Jesus. That is the reason, too, why many school boards receive vehement protest when some action of the board or the teacher fails to promote what the complainant claims to be the specific interest of the child. That philosophy has been the source of a great deal of friction, just because it is fundamentally false.

God clothes man with authority with a theocentric objective in mind. He reveals himself as Lord so that He may be honored as Lord. He reveals himself as the truth so that men may see it and glorify Him. He manifests love and justice so that men may respond and thank God for it. That is the reason why every ruler, parent and teacher should study to please God. He it is from whom authority comes, through whom it is exercised, and unto whom it must be directed.

*   *   *

What is it to liberate? What is liberty?

Everybody seems to know what it is. Everybody wants it. But ask those who prate enthusiastically about liberty what they mean by the term. Upon analysis their definition will most likely be found unsatisfactory both to themselves and to yourself. We might therefore profitably begin by clearing away some of the rubbish before us.

The most popular opinion is, I think, this: Liberty is the privilege of unrestricted thought and action. But there is no such thing. Even God cannot do that. God cannot do any and all conceivable things. He is restricted. Restrictions are of two kinds. There are internal, subjective restrictions and external, objective restrictions. Though God may have no external restrictions, He is subjectively restricted. He is not at liberty to lie, steal, in short, to sin. That restriction is not due to the command of anyone outside of Him. No one can say, "God, thou shalt not lie, steal, etc." He is restricted by what He is. He cannot think or do a thing that is incompatible with his sovereignty, truth, love and justice. Well, you will retort, that is self-determination, and self-determination is liberty.

Very well, if you mean by self-determination that the subject is free just because there are no external restrictions, then this idea, too, is but a figment of the imagination when applied to man. Man is rendered forever unable to think and act unaffected by himself and the world round about him. He is created to be restricted. It is within the field of restriction that liberty must be found, if it is to be found at all.

There is first of all the restriction laid upon us by the subhuman world. And our wellbeing depends upon our submission to these restrictions. We are restricted in our movements by the laws of gravitation. But without this restriction we would not be able to move at all. And surely to be able to move is a form of liberty. You are restricted in your seeing by the sun; yet without the sun you probably would not be able to see at all. And if you should think that there is no liberty in seeing, question the blind man. We are restricted in the amount and the kind of food we eat. Violate these restrictions and we experience painful bondage. The navigator in the air or on the sea finds his maximum amount of freedom in obeying with painstaking care the laws operative in his field. Even the scientist, to say nothing about the limitations of his own mind and instruments, will experience freedom only in proportion to his obedient submission to the laws operative in the field of his investigation. That is to say you have to take nature as it is and to react to it as it is in order to live in harmony with it and to enjoy a measure of liberty.

We are restricted by the presence of human beings. Equals among equals are restricted by their mutual equality. A man cannot eat, be dressed, talk, sleep or act in any way that fancy may strike him, just because of the presence of others. This is not a matter of pure conventionality, but it is a method of securing the maximum amount of freedom in the presence of others. God laid down the restrictions of the second table of the Decalogue. He then gave men liberating principles. It is within these limits that the greatest amount of freedom can be had.

Man is also restricted by the fact that there is a super-human reality. The sovereign God created men to serve and glorify him. And it is in this service that the sense of freedom reaches its greatest heights.

God restricts. Man restricts. Nature restricts. Indeed, everything restricts. Freedom, then, may be found in the glad submission to things as they are. And "things as they are" are the truth. "You shall know the truth, and the truth shall make you free" (John 8:32). The concept "know" in the Scriptures involves the idea of approval of. Know the truth. Approve of the truth. Then live accordingly. That is freedom.

* * *

The value of authority as a liberating force becomes apparent the moment that we come to some such conception of liberty as indicated above. Authority insists upon the sovereignty, the truth, the love and justice of God. These are undeniable facts. Live in harmony with them. That is what authority insists upon. And to live in harmony with them is to live freely.

Carrying our conclusions over to the specific field of education, we find that educational authorities have been at loggerheads with one another on this point. At the one extreme we have Dr. Busby of the Westminister School in the time of Charles II. He was the strictest of disciplinarians. He believed in pedagogical authority with a vengeance. Said Sir Roger De Coverly, "A great man, he caned my grandfather." Stephen Leacock, professor in the law department of McGill University, declared that he had licked no less than ten cabinet ministers, two baronets, and four British generals, to say nothing about one half the bar and the bench of Toronto. He did not venture to say whether these men would have come to front without his aid or not. It is interesting that when teachers began to tire of this method of exercising authority a schooltext appeared on the market called, *Reading Without Tears*. It was regarded by many as a pleasing innovation.

At the other extreme we have Rousseau, presenting his Emile, who was never in any form forced. He grew up among the flowers. He could do what he wanted to and received no information except in response to his request. He was never restricted nor constrained. He just grew in wisdom and stature. This was only a story by the way.

It is needless to say that the vote today is strongly in favor of moving in the direction of Rousseau's theory. But America is entirely too thoroughly pragmatic ever to surrender entirely to the wiles of such naturalism. We have, however, toyed with the idea, but juvenile delinquency increased. Teachers liked it. They merely taught their subjects, not their pupils. The effect of the idea was to release the pupils from the traditions and restraints of the past without substituting an adequate set of restraints and ideals for the future. Dr. Link sums up the results somewhat as follows, "It tended to make students to regard parents as oldfashioned and behind times, to move them to be liberal with their parents' automobile, money and property without assuming any corresponding obligations or responsibilities, to develop within them scorn for the religious, political and moral creeds of their parents, to make them repugnant toward the exacting occupation of honest work, and to deprive them of any conviction in matters of basic right and wrong" (*The Return to Religion*, p. 161). His conclusion is that children must be made, not merely born. He makes a wholesome argument for the position that authority should be exercised even if it must assume compulsive methods. There are indications of a slight trend in that direction today.

*   *   *

The teacher is clothed with regal authority. He is king and is under divine authority to exercise his kingship, because his authority is ordained of God. By the exercise of that authority he liberates the pupil, that is, he enables him to function more freely by virtue of his making greater adjustments to the facts — to truth. The method of exercising this authority is not a matter of interest to us here, but the obligation is. And this obligation proceeds not primarily from the child's interest, but from divine command.

In applying this conception let us look at the matter of class attendance. Many schools, especially those of higher learning, do not insist upon the time of class attendance, and not even upon that fact that the student should attend at all. To ignore tardiness and absence may be the easier way. But God is present in the teacher and reigns through him. Is He indifferent to this matter? Not by any means. He is a God of law and order. He insists that the heavenly bodies run with a degree of precision that enables astronomers to determine the exact locations of comets and planets thousands of years in advance. That is the reason why there is freedom and not restraining chaos above. The seasons, day and night, and indeed every aspect of the universe are controlled by so-called natural laws of time and order. That is what God insists upon, and it must be reflected in the authorized kingly function of the teacher as he controls his class. Let me repeat that the requirement is due not primarily to the child's interest but to God's will. However, my subject forces me to consider the child's interest in the matter. Will it liberate him? Of course, because it compells him to adjust himself to things as they are, and only in such adjustment can he find freedom. Even in a world where sin has marred the perfect precision of God's world it is evident that he who functions most orderly and promptly functions most successfully and therefore most freely.

Just to take another more general aspect of the teacher's work as king, he must insist upon obedience. God demanded it from the beginning. Without it his kingship would be a farce. It was demanded even before the Fall. Man experienced unsurpassed freedom until he hurled himself into bondage by his disobedience. That law is everywhere in evidence. One cannot fly through the skies unless he obeys the laws of navigation. The slightest disobedience may cast one into the bondage of death. One can freely use electricity, but let him transgress its laws and it will snuff out his life. God said in effect, "I want obedience to myself and to the laws that I have placed in my creation." That is precisely what God wants his representatives to insist upon. Does it liberate? Of course, it does. The fact of the demand of obedience is there revealed both in nature and in Scriptures. It is a matter of insisting that the child adjust itself to the fact. Disobedience always binds. Whether you look at it from the point of view of civil, natural or moral laws, it persistently means some sort of incarceration, pain and ultimately death.

Enough has been said of the exercise of the authoritative regal function of the teacher. He is also a prophet, a divinely authorized presenter of the truth. Here again if God reveals the truth, his representatives must. He presents himself as He is and not as some philosopher or would-be theologian would have Him. He presents nature as it is and not as some scientist would interpret it. And God sees them as they are. Hence one can best get at the truth by looking at them from God's angle, as presented in Scriptures. This is what God demands of those who would function properly as representatives of him who is the truth.

Take history, for instance. It may be regarded as a record of man's achievements. It is more accurately a record of God's providential activity as it operates in the lives of men and nations. Such a view liberates because it teaches men what reactions met with divine approval and disapproval and how they liberated or bound men. It is not optional with the child to take any view that it may wish. It must take a view that compells it to come face to face with truth. Only then can it be expected to make proper adjustments, and such adjustments must be made to give one freedom. The same thing is true about literature, geography and every other branch in the curriculum of the school. Never forget it, it is the truth that will make men free. The teacher may have to force the tablet down the throat of the resisting child to free it from its fever. The wise mother will never hesitate to do it, for she knows that that compulsion is a liberating force.

To complete the triad, look at the priestly function of the teacher. In the \priestly function we find the development of proper emotional attitudes and reactions. God loves and God hates. He approves and disapproves. The same must be true of him who properly represents Him who ordained the teacher's authority. He must represent a strong love for the good, right, holy and true, and an obvious hatred of the bad, wrong, and false. He must insist upon such reactions on the part of the pupils. Expressions of sorrow and apologies to the ones wronged and resentment against sin in others are not matters of indifference. The pupils should be taught to so respond. Right emotional reactions must be made compulsory by wise and tactful educational methods. To tolerate wrong reactions is to encourage bondage of a destructive and ruinous character. The child will find freedom in the love of God and his neighbor and in the rejection of everything repugnant thereto.

It is in an atmosphere where the teacher properly exercises his authority that the child will find freedom from the shackles of error and sin. It is only through divine imposition that men learn to know the truth that will make them free. Authority properly exercised liberates. Where can you expect to find authority exercised as indicated? Only where the teacher has learned the Christian view of life and of the world. Only where the teacher functions as a true representative of God.

HENRY SCHULTZE
Address before the National Union of
Christian Schools Convention, Sheboygan,
Wisconsin, August 24, 1937.

Key Thoughts:

1. The teacher's authority in the Christian school comes from the Christian parents who recognize that their authority is God-given and that they are stewards of this authority.

2. All authority is ultimately from God, for it is the necessary manifestation of God in His Being. God is Sovereign, Truth, Love and Justice.

3. The aim of all authority is theocentric, that is the subjects under authority must honor God as Lord.

4. Authority is liberating, sets free, for as the subject accepts it he is in his very nature set free to act in keeping with his being. Disobedience deprives him of such action.

5. The teacher uses the authority of truth to discipline the child by its authority.

6. The teacher exercises kingly authority under God as he insists on obedience to the truth.   He exercises prophetic authority as he presents the truth.   He exercises priestly authority as he teaches the pupil to love the truth and hate evil.

Comment:

How can a teacher teach a child to love the truth? Who has the answer ready at hand? Yet, no Christian teacher conscious of his authority and responsibility can rest till he sees the learner embracing the truth in love.

The authority of the teacher is a liberating force in the process of teaching when he in love inspires the pupil to love. Only love unites, and disciplines.

As prophet, then, the teacher should know the truth and be able to communicate it in love. As priest, he loves the truth and inspires others to love it. As king, he is disciplined by the truth because he accepts it in his life, and he helps others come to acceptance of it.

SECTION TWO

THE AIM OF CHRISTIAN EDUCATION

1

Faith and Our Program

The first step in making progress should be a deepening of our conviction that the program we have set for ourselves must be carried out. Accordingly we speak of faith in connection with our program. We must lengthen our cords but not unless we also strengthen our stakes. We deal then with our program but also with our faith in our program. Now it may be said that we are dealing with two subjects instead of one. It may be said that we should either discuss our program as such or discuss our faith in our program as such in order to avoid confusion. Yet this is not the case. We purposely wish to discuss both subjects in order to bring out the close relationships that they sustain to one another. In fact our subject really is that of the relation between our program as the objective for which we strive and our faith as the subjective power by which we seek to realize our program. We shall try to bring out something of the close relation between the depth of our faith and height and breadth of our program.

Then, too, since it is the relationship of our faith to our program and not our program as such that we are concerned about, we can conveniently take three outstanding characteristics of faith in order to discuss the significance of each of these in connection with our program. In the first section we will speak of the *obedience* of faith. In this section we shall have to go back into the past in order to see what program God set for man and how He wanted man to realize that program when he was first placed in paradise. In the second section we will speak of the *patience* of faith. In this section we shall have to live in the present in order to see how God wants man to carry through the program originally set for him in spite of the opposition of the evil one. In the third section we will speak of the *hope* of faith. In this section we shall have to look into the future in order to see that man is actually going to realize the program God originally set for him even though it does not seem so now.

A. The Obedience of Faith

When we speak of the program that we have for our Christian schools we use the term program in the most comprehensive sense.

We do not refer to activity only. We include in the idea of program the whole ideal that we have set for ourselves with Christian education. And the ideal that we have set for ourselves with Christian education is but a part of the ideal we have set for ourselves with respect to the whole of human life. We speak of the ideal of life as a whole when we speak of our program because it is in part through education that we hope to realize our ideal of life.

Yet it is true that we speak of this ideal now more from the point of view of action than from the point of view of thought. We wish to discuss what it is that we strive for, what it is that we strain our wills for. We may accordingly speak of this ideal as the *ethical* ideal for man.

1. *The Absolute Ethical Ideal*

Now if we would seek to characterize this ethical ideal for man in one word we may say that it is *absolute*. We are seeking to build the fully perfect man and the fully perfect creation. We are seeking to build the fully developed man and the fully developed creation.

In theological language we speak of these matters by saying that man was created perfect in paradise and that he was placed as God's prophet, priest and king in the midst of the world. When we have said this we have clearly indicated that according to our conception God gave man a work to do and a task to accomplish. Man was to bring out to the full all the powers and capacities that God had placed in him and in the world about him. That man was created perfect has therefore never meant to the mind of the church that he was to be static. The idea of a static perfection is not found in Scripture. If we must use the popular term *dynamic,* it is well; in Scripture only, in its idea of a created personality only, is there any dynamic at all.

But now for the sake of comprehensiveness and for the sake of putting it in psychological language that is ready to hand for pedagogical purposes, we would include all that we have said so far with respect to the task of man under the idea of the development of personality. We must show that as Christians we have a distinct psychology as well as a distinct ethics at the basis of our program of education.

We may say that the whole of man's task was that of the development of his personality. That we have not excluded anything that could possibly be thought of as man's task by putting the matter in this way is evident from the fact that man is thought of as representative of the whole creation of God. If man developed his personality he would at the same time develop the whole of the creation of God. In this way we have also woven the covenant idea into the very warp and woof of our educational program.

Particular mention should be made of the fact that in this way we have not only a distinct ethics and a distinct psychology but also a distinct sociology at the basis of our educational effort. When we speak of the development of his personality as the supreme and only task of man, we speak of man *generically.* One generation would seek to develop the personalities of the next till all those whom God would call should stand side by side as an army with banners.

Such, in general terms, is the absolute ideal which God had set for man in paradise. We may, if we wish, speak of this ideal or program as the Kingdom of God. Rather than forfeit the use of the phrase *Kingdom of God,* because it is in our day so easily interpreted in a modernist sense, we would seek to give that phrase the truly Christian connotation once more. By the Kingdom of God we would signify the objective or ideal for which God wanted man to strive with all the power of his will.

But in order to build our house upon a rock we must go back still another step. Back of our Christian pedagogy lies a Christian sociology, a Christian psychology and a Christian ethics. But back of all these lies a Christian theory of reality, a Christian metaphysics. The sum and substance of our Christian metaphysics is the creation idea, the creation of the world by an absolutely selfsufficient God. Now it is but natural that if God is, and was at the time of creation, the absolute God, that then He should set for man the ideal of the realization of an absolute kingdom on earth. By that we mean that God would naturally wish man to realize as far as this was possible for a creature in a created universe, a selfconscious reflex of His own glory. And this also sheds a further light upon what we mean by man's absolute ethical ideal. It is not absolute in the sense in which God is absolute, but it is absolute in the sense that only the highest possible development of all his powers for the glory of the absolute God could possibly be the ideal that God would set for His rational creature. The absolute ideal or program for man is the logical outcome of the theism that lies at the foundation of Christianity.

2. *Analogical Action*

So then we have before us in broad outline the ideal for which man ought to strive. We have seen that our educational objective is the logical conclusion of our most basic convictions with respect to the nature of man and the world. And all this we have regarded from the objective side. That is, we have looked at it as an ideal that lay far ahead of man, an ideal to be realized in the future. We must now add to this that just as we have a distinct ideal before us so we have *a distinct principle of action within us* by which we are to reach that ideal. Our educational program is not only based upon a Christian theory of reality but also upon a Christian theory of knowledge, a Christian epistemology, and this Christian theory of knowledge gives us insight into our Christian theory of action.

If man is a creature of God he is an analogue of God. God is the original while man is the derivative. Man's thoughts must therefore be patterned after God's thoughts. Man must, as we often express it, think God's thoughts after Him. And what is true with respect to man's thoughts is also true with respect to man's deeds. Just as man must think God's thoughts after Him so man must also do God's deeds after Him. Just as man's thought is analogical of God's thought so man's deeds must be analogical of God's deeds. We have, therefore, as Christians an *analogical theory of action.*

That it is of the utmost importance to see this point clearly will appear as we advance. For the moment we must point out a little more fully what we mean by analogical action and how it is involved in the very bedrock of our position. We have said that as an analogue of God man must do God's deeds after Him. Does that mean doing God's deeds over again? That were impossible for man. Man is not God and could not do God's deeds. Moreover to do God's deeds over again would render them meaningless; it would be doing the same thing twice, which is unthinkable in God. In theological language we therefore say that God is all-glorious and that man cannot add to His glory. Analogical action therefore signifies action on another, and in the nature of the case, a lower plane than that on which the action of God takes place. Analogical action is the only action that befits a creature of God. And it is because we as Christians recognize that we are creatures of God that we also believe in the analogical theory of action. Moreover, it is only Christians that recognize that they are creatures of God, and therefore it is only Christians who believe in analogical action. All non-Christians deny that there are two levels of existence and therefore deny that there are two levels of thought and action. All non-Christians hold to the *univocal theory of action* as they hold to the univocal theory of thought.

But it is not enough to say that as Christians we believe in two levels of being, in two levels of thought and in two levels of action. Theoretically it is possible to think of two levels of thought and action without thinking of them as related to one another. Now the very idea of analogy is relation. Man's action is definitely related to God's action.

Finally it is not even enough to say that man's action is definitely related to God's action. Theoretically it were possible to hold that God's and man's actions are definitely related to one another much as the actions of two neighbors that have recently moved into the same community will influence one another. If we thought of man's relationship to God after this manner we would still be thinking of man's acts as univocal; the deistic as well as the pantheistic varieties of non-Christian thought hold to the univocal theory.

What, then, must we think of the relationship of God's action to ours? The nearest we can come to making this plain to ourselves is to say that just as God's thoughts are the foundation of our thoughts so also God's actions are the foundation of our actions. And it is exactly this that we seek to express in the use of the word analogical. Accordingly there are no words in human language that can lead us any deeper into this mystery. The word analogical, together with the other words that we use in theological terminology can do no more than approximate a full expression of our ideas on these things, and our ideas can never comprehensively grasp the truth of the relation of God to man. But this inability to comprehend fully what we ourselves mean by analogical action or by analogical thought, so far from giving us cause for worry, should be to us a sign that we have caught the truly theistic conception of action and thought. Mystery has lost its terror for us as soon as we know that there is no mystery for God.

On the contrary it is our conception of analogical action that gives us confidence that our action has genuine significance. When man first saw the vision of the ideal that God had set before him, he was glad to think God's thoughts after Him and do God's deeds after Him. Man was glad to act analogically. Man was gladly *obedient* to God. Analogical action is action of obedience to God.

3. *The Development of Obedience*

And now that we discussed the ideal or program in general and have looked at the concept of analogical action or obedience in general, we must try to think of how God would have man reach the ideal by way of obedience. Or, we may ask how man was to develop his personality, the task given him by God to perform.

The answer to this is not far to seek. It would naturally have to be by way of the development of the powers God had given man. And since it was the power of analogical action that God had given man, it was this power that had to be developed. Man's obedience to God had to be still more spontaneous, still more stable and still more active than it already was at the beginning of creation.

In the first place man's obedience should be still more *spontaneous* than it already was. The trial given to man in paradise was calculated to bring out this greater spontaneity. Man's action with respect to the temptation should have been similar to the action of Christ when He met the tempter in the wilderness. Think for a minute with what swiftness and decisiveness Christ said to the tempter, "Get thee behind me Satan." He did not hesitate, he did not play with the temptation. His whole being was athrob with spontaneous desire to do the will of God and thus to realize the program that God had set for Him. Anything that would keep Him from realizing that program was immediately cast aside.

Here we touch upon one of modern psychology's favorite themes, namely that of the subconscious. Have we as Christians no definite theory with respect to it? We certainly have. We hold that it too, as well as man's conscious life, was originally created in spontaneous obedience to God. It is not to be thought of as something that acts as a sort of subterranean avenue from the void that surrounds us and as something for which we are scarcely, if at all, responsible. Man was created spontaneously obedient to God in the whole of his being, but he was to become even more spontaneous in his reaction to the will of God for him. And one of the ways in which this was to be accomplished, we may hold, was by getting ever larger areas of man's subconscious life above the threshold of his consciousness. This in turn would react upon the remaining subconscious aspect of man's life by making it, too, more responsive to the will of God.

In this way spontaneous obedience would become a *habit* with man. But by the term habit we do not mean what modern psychology means by that term. We can observe this when we note for instance that in James' psychology his theory of habit and his theory of the subconscious lie side by side and influence one another. The substance of the modern theory is that by developing good habits we can do something by way of reducing the constant menace of our subconscious life, much as a man may tramp small pieces of concrete into a marshy road in order to make it somewhat more passable. Habit, according to James, is to be used as a tool by which we can make our adjustment to an ultimately impersonal environment somewhat more easy. In contrast with this we would use habit as a means by which we can make our adjustment to an absolutely personal background more effective. And the Christian conception of habit works in the direction of an ever increasingly greater selfconscious reaction on the part of man to his environment, while the non-Christian conception of habit works in the direction of the depersonalization of man. True, neither James nor any other modern psychologist openly advocates the depersonalization of man through habit, but we are speaking now of the logic of the situation.

So then it is with the modern theory of habit, as it is with many other psychological and pedagogical theories, that we can learn much from it if only we place it in a Christian-theistic setting. We should certainly seek to inculcate implicit obedience to lawful authority into our children and thus make it a habit with them to obey, but we should at the same time strive to make them do all that they do out of a burning love for God. Placed in a Christian setting this is not an absurdity but only another instance of analogical action. If man became increasingly selfconscious in his reaction to the will of God for him, he would become more like God, in whom there is no difference between potentiality and actuality. Of course, all this is meant ethically and not metaphysically; we would not think of man ever in any sense outgrowing the difference between the Creator and the creature.

And now in the second place we note that man should increase not only in the spontaneity but also in the *stability* of his obedience to God. Man should become increasingly *selfdeterminate*. In other words he must develop the backbone of his will. Not as though he was created a volitive and therefore volatile amoeba which had to pass through the invertebrate stage before it could acquire a backbone. Not as though man was created only with a "capacity for God" so that he had to acquire a personality in the future. Man was created a self. Man was created a personality. We purposely use these terms and interchange them. We would not toy with modern psychology's notion of personality by saying that man was created a soul but had to accomplish a personality. We would say that man was created a self or personality and had to become more of a self and more of a personality. Man was from the beginning the creature of an absolute self and an absolute personality and could not be otherwise created than as a self or as a personality. Man's God is absolutely selfdeterminate and man will be more and more Godlike if he increases in selfdetermination. In proportion that man becomes more selfdeterminate does he develop God's determination or plan for him. We have seen with what spontaneity the perfect man Jesus withstood the temptation. Now note with what selfdeterminateness, with what sense of responsibility for the fulfilment of his task He refuses to be controlled by anything except by the will of God. He slays Satan with the words, "It is written."

Surely this is the opposite of what modern psychology understands by the idea of selfdeterminateness. To do what Christ did, to decide on a course of action on the absolute authority of another is opposed to the idea of autonomy that underlies modern psychology as well as modern ethics. The idea of selfrealization that has played so large a role in modern ethics and psychology is based upon the idea of univocal action. All non-Christian thought surrounds man with an ultimate void. If in that void a god or gods have sprung up they can only be regarded as rivals of man. To be sure they may be made allies for convenience sake, but at bottom they are always rivals in the struggle for existence. Hence man either swallows them up or is swallowed up by them. In every case the development of personality is possible only at the expense of the development of other personality. All the fine-sounding phraseology of the modernist Sunday-school literature does not outgrow this paganism. Over against it we would set the truly Christian idea of selfdevelopment by increase of selfdeterminateness accomplished by implication into the will of God.

Finally we must note that as man's spontaneity and selfdeterminateness would increase, the *momentum* of his personality would also increase. As a child walks ever more readily and ever more firmly and therefore is able to carry larger loads as time goes on, so also the personality of man increasing in the spontaneity and stability of its obedience to God would greatly increase in its capacity and power for the realization of God's Kingdom on earth. Man would have no "capacity for God" unless created with the knowledge of God, but since man was created in the knowledge of God he could also increase in his capacity for doing the will of God. Man would strive with ever increasing power to make everything on earth contribute to the great purpose for which it was created. This, as noted above, would involve the whole of mankind. The whole race of man would be as one man in its unity of purpose, in its uniformity of action and in the steady progress toward its ideal of realizing itself and therefore realizing the Kingdom of God.

Taking now these three together, the spontaneity of man's will, the stability of man's will and the increasing momentum of his will, we see that *through obedience man would become free as he was created free.* He would have the desire and the ability to accomplish the will of God for him. He would attain the liberty of being finally and fully established in his willing the will of God.

In a society thus developed there would be no dispute about altruism and egoism. What non-Christian thought has sought in vain, the harmony between the selfseeking and the otherseeking instincts, we have found in the conception of the development of human personality by doing the will of God. Again, in a society thus constituted there would be no dispute whether happiness or virtue should be the end for which man ought to strive. There would be no contrast possible between happiness and virtue; the two would always travel side by side. Once more, in a society so constituted there would be no dispute about the goods of this world: there would naturally be plenty for all since man by sin had not brought a curse upon the earth.

B. The Patience of Faith

But how terribly ridiculous all this seems in the eyes of those who differ with us on the question of man's educational ideal. To bring in all these matters that we have brought in, to dream a dream of a golden past, seems to them utterly unpractical and utterly absurd! We must now look at these charges and seek to answer them. We must now see that we have not merely been dreaming a golden dream but that our theory of an originally perfect man who was to realize the Kingdom of God in the way that we have discussed it, is of the utmost practical significance and is the only position that is not really absurd. Let us look at the charge of absurdity launched against our position and see how we must maintain our faith in spite of this charge.

1. *The Charge of Absurdity*

In what way are we charged with absurdity? The answer is that according to our opponents all the main ideas we have found to lie at the foundation of our educational program are contradictory.

First of all the idea of an absolute program or ideal for man, as we have pictured it, is said to be contradictory. One will search in vain in the pages of the ethical literature outside of Scripture for the notion of an absolute ethical ideal. There have been utopias enough; there have been mystics who have sought to escape from the present evil world; but no serious-minded non-Christian writer has ever set the ideal of complete perfection before himself and his fellow man. The reason for this is that all non-Christian thought has taken for granted that evil is an inherent ingredient of the world as we know it. Aristotle's mean as an ethical ideal gives eloquent testimony to the fact that the ancient world looked upon evil as an ineradicable element in the heart of man and in the world round about him. If we may believe ancient ethics, man should no more hope to attain perfection than a man with a soiled shirt should expect to purify it while walking on a hot day along a dusty road. The most that he can try to do is to protect himself from the big blotches of clay that fly about as those who wallow in the mire go splashing by. And what is true of ancient ethics is true of modern ethics. James' meliorism corresponds to Aristotle's mean. The hopeless pessimism of ancient times is, if possible, excelled by the dark despair of modern times. The highest that man can ever attain, according to James, is a slight improvement in himself and in his neighbors.

Now we can readily see that if evil is to be taken as an ultimate ingredient of the universe then the notion of an absolute ethical ideal is impossible and contradictory. We grant at once that the logic is correct if the assumption be granted. But can the assumption be granted? Before we answer that question let us ask further with what other contradictions we are charged. It may be that we can make one reply to them all. If that is possible it will be the best.

The second main contradiction with which we are charged concerns our conception of analogical action. This charge is expressed or implied at various points. It is often openly expressed in criticism of our concept of God as absolute. It is simply said that if God is absolute He must be *All* with the result that man is nothing and that his deeds mean nothing. Now this charge too is logically correct if the assumption that there can be only one level of existence be correct. But is the assumption correct?

The charge of contradiction appears further in the criticism of our concept of created personality. It is said that if man was a self or a personality to begin with there was nothing more for man to do and all his deeds were nothing but a farce. And note that the charge here does not merely concern the idea of growth in the degree of personality but that it concerns the idea of the origin of personality itself. The assumption of the criticism is that for a man to be responsible for his action his deeds must be wholly and exclusively his own. Now this is impossible unless personality is an achievement on the part of man himself without the help of God. And again we remark that the logic is sound if the assumption be granted.

Finally we are asked how that which is perfect can become still more perfect. We are charged with holding to the idea of a static moral existence at the beginning of man's life on earth and it is said that in this way we have made all progress impossible. The assumption of this criticism is that progress must be a change into something that has never existed in any sense. Here, too, the logic is sound if the assumption be granted.

2. *How We Cannot Meet This Charge*

Now when we think of these various charges our first desire might be to seek to reduce their number if possible. Certainly we do not wish to make our position seem any more absurd than necessary. But it does not take very long before we realize that it would be quite impossible to reduce the number of absurdities that are charged against us. Instead of reducing the number we have to add to it.

That this is the case we can readily see if we only think into the significance of the fact that according to our conception of things the absolute ideal which we have spoken of is not merely something that would have been realized if sin had not come into the world but is something *that is actually being realized in the world today.* For that is the meaning of Christianity in a word, that God's program for man is being realized in spite of sin.

Such a proposition surely seems to bring us further away from experimental fact than even a return to an "imaginary paradise" could do. To say that mankind is perfect now and is actually realizing that still higher perfection that we have spoken of seems to lay upon us the charge of outraging the facts as we look at them. And now I realize that we can offer qualifications that seem to make our position less absurd. We do not mean that every individual in this world is perfect now. We hold that only a relatively small number of mankind are perfect. But this only seems to add arrogance to absurdity.

Then I may introduce the further qualification that even those few, of whom I say that they are perfect, are perfect only in principle and not in degree. But the world can see no meaning in such a distinction. Besides, I do not myself allow a distinction between principle and degree when it comes to the forensic side of salvation. I cannot say that I am justified in principle but not in degree. A man is either justified before God or he is not, and in this sense we hold that he is either wholly perfect or wholly imperfect. We hold then that there are some in this world today who are actually perfect and we hold, moreover, that these form the heart and core of the human race so that the others can be ignored. We hold that when we are training covenant children in the school we are training perfect personalities into still greater perfection. Yes, here, too, you may come with qualifications. You may say that children are at most dormant personalities. This is true in a sense, but it is also true that before God there are no dormant personalities. Before God our children are personalities from and before their birth; we are chosen in Him before the foundation of the world. Moreover, I must regard all children of believers as children of God till the contrary appear to be true. So then we hold that those children are perfect. Could anything more purely imaginary and more obnoxious be found in the eyes of the world than the idea that our children are perfect while others are wholly imperfect?

But all this deals with the absurdity of fact, while in this section our primary concern is with the absurdity of logic. Yet this absurdity of fact brings out the absurdity of logic. For note that when we seek to bring in a still further qualification with respect to the idea that some men are actually perfect in this world today by saying that we believe this perfection to be a *substitutionary* perfection we only seek, in the eyes of our opponents, to cover up an absurdity of fact with an absurdity of logic. Surely the idea of substitute personality will seem ridiculous to those who already object to the idea of created personality. If personality must be an accomplishment in the first place without reference to God as Creator it certainly cannot be restored for us by Christ as Redeemer.

Thus instead of reducing the number of difficulties by coming down from our speculations about the original estate of man to the affairs of daily practice we have only added to that number. One thing this surely ought to teach us. It ought to teach us that we can never seek to justify our educational system by seeking to reduce the number of "absurdities" in connection with it. Every important idea that we hold to seems absurd to our enemies. And certainly the idea of substitutionary atonement which lies at the heart of our covenant concept and as such controls all our education seems, if possible, the most absurd of all. No degree of compromise will ever get a hearing for our views; we can get a hearing only if we have compromised everything, and then we no longer get a hearing for that which we wish to get a hearing for.

3. *How We Can Meet This Charge*

We shall therefore have to follow the opposite method. And that method implies first of all that we reduce all the charges of contradiction to one charge and reduce all the assumption that underlie these charges to one assumption. Now this can readily be done. It is plain at once that the idea of substitutionary personality is only another form of the objection to the idea of created personality. In short, all the objections are directed at the idea of having finite personality dependent upon an absolute, selfconscious Being. If there is such a Being, man is a creature and his personality cannot in the first place be an accomplishment. Hence the assumption that lies at the basis of all the objections or as we may now say, which lies at the basis of this one great objection, is that *the universe is a universe of Chance.*

If the universe is a universe of chance, and only if it is such must there of necessity be only one level of existence, so that our God concept and our creation concept appear absurd. In a universe of chance and only in a universe of chance will the idea of analogical action seem absurd. In such a universe no one being is brought forth by any other and so no one can act analogically to any other. In a universe of chance and only in a universe of chance personality must be wholly an accomplishment on the part of every individual. In a universe of chance and only in a universe of chance can evil be thought of as having as great an ultimacy as the good. In a rational universe the evil would be subordinate to the good because the good itself is an aspect of the rational.

Now we ask whether it is reasonable to make this assumption of a universe of chance and on the basis of it make the charge of contradiction against our position. We would ask whether the assumption of a universe of chance can furnish a foundation for a universal law of contradiction. Our opponents take for granted that they are applying to our concepts nothing but a law of contradiction that is recognized as universally valid by any one who is rational. So we would now ask whether there is any such law of contradiction that is universally valid if the universe is a universe of chance. The answer is simple. If the universe is a universe of chance there is no law of contradiction at all. In such a universe every one is master to himself. In such a universe there could be nothing but a Babel of confusion; no one would be able to speak with his neighbor.

Accordingly we hold it to be the best proof of the truth of our position that our opponents are able to make objections to it that seem to have some show of reason. This fact is the best proof that the universe is not a universe of chance. And this fact makes all the arguments of our enemies drop to the ground at one time.

In the second place we would note that when we have thus destroyed the foundation of all the arguments of our opponents against our position we have at the same time destroyed the foundation of all the positive arguments for their own position. We have shown that they cannot interpret human experience and get any meaning out of it. The whole idea of the exclusive accomplishment of personality appears to be an utter impossibility. Personality would have to come into existence by chance operating in a void. Granted that it is rational to think of such an idea, it would surely not be true that personality is a self-accomplishment. And so with the whole idea of univocal action. There would have to be a personality that was wholly a unit before it could act univocally, but it is impossible to get meaning into the idea of a unit coming by chance. Thus the only alternative to our position is that of complete irrationality.

In the third place we would note with the destruction of the enemy we have established our own position. We have established it because, as we have just seen, there is no other position that is not wholly unreasonable. We have established it still further by the fact that it has now become clear to us that it is the most natural thing that we should not be able to understand comprehensively and exhaustively the possibility of analogical action. Without the existence of a God who is wholly rational our experience would be meaningless. But there can be only one such God. If there were more they would not be wholly rational; they would depend upon one another. Now since there can be only one it follows that all other personalities must be analogical of that one God. Hence the action of all other personalities must be analogical action. It is in this way that we would modify the ancient church father's dictum, "We believe because it is absurd." It is the most reasonable position for man to hold that he cannot completely comprehend the relation of himself to God.

Now all this we would include in the idea of the *patience of faith*. We said at the first that we would have to see how the Kingdom of God is to be realized by us in the present time in spite of the opposition of the world. Now it is natural that this must be done positively by carrying through the program as we have outlined it, on the ground that it was the task given to man at the time of creation. But it is especially necessary to note that that program must now be carried out under constant opposition. We must build with our trowel in the one hand and the sword in the other. Just as we saw in the first section that God has placed an absolute ideal before man, so we have now seen that that absolute ideal cannot be realized except the enemies be destroyed. We must feel our strength in the Lord. Then we are able to maintain our faith in spite of opposition. To hold on to the faith, to carry through the absolute program though nearly all men oppose us, *that* is the patience of faith.

And when we have seen that our enemy is destroyed, we can also be patient with him in the sense of longsuffering with his stubbornness and blindness. We learn not to get angry but to pray; we learn not to use harsh words but to beseech in the name of the Lord. We learn to look upon our enemies no longer as those that are to be feared for their strength but to be pitied for their folly. We gladly learn from them in matters of detail while we differ wholly on matters of principle; we walk in the midst of a conquered city choosing from the spoils whatsoever we please, to bring it as a trophy to our King. For that will be our future joy.

C. The Hope of Faith

We have looked at the past. We saw that God gave man a program to realize. We have looked at the present. We have seen that this program is being realized in spite of the entrance of sin into the world. Now we must briefly look at the future in order to see that the program which seems to be so slow of realization now will be fully realized hereafter. We have looked at the obedience and the patience of faith; now we must look at the hope of faith. As Abraham by the obedience of faith left Ur of the Chaldees to go to a land of which he knew nothing by experience and as he lived in that promised land as a stranger in a strange land owning not a foot of ground, so we have considered our program. We have received our marching orders from God. To them we have been obedient. But experience did not bring immediate and great results. The fruits have so far been very small. Yet we carry on. Are we then indifferent to results? Not at all. But we are like Abraham, who not only manifested the obedience of faith and the patience of faith, but also the hope of faith. With him we look for the city that hath foundations.

1. *The Challenge of Immediate Results*

But someone will perhaps object to the statement just made that our results so far have been small. Someone may say that our results have been great and that we are perfectly willing to have our schools tested by the common standard expressed in the words, "By their fruits ye shall know them." Now we grant that the fruits have been great. The chief illustration of this is and remains up to this time the little country of The Netherlands. The great social and political stability of that country is to a great extent to be attributed to the people of Reformed persuasion, many of whom have enjoyed Christian instruction. But it will be granted by all that the chief fruit of our labor is internal because spiritual. And though we believe that also in this respect there has been a great blessing of God upon our little labors it remains true that these blessings are hard to measure. They are hard to measure even by those who believe in them and they will not be regarded as blessings at all by those who oppose us.

So then we find ourselves once more in a clash with our opponents. They maintain or rather simply take for granted that there is a common standard by which the results of an educational program can be judged. That standard they take to be the results in the way of things that pertain to this world alone and of things of which they can judge as well as we. But here we must take exception. We maintain, in the first place, that the fruits of our labors will not appear in their full significance till after this life. And what is more, we maintain that those fruits will suddenly appear in their fulness and beauty at the time of the judgment day. It sometimes happens that the spring is cold and wet and that in addition to all this a hailstorm sets back the crops. Yet to the great surprise of all the fall will bring an abundance of fruits. Now this is true in a much greater degree in the realm of spiritual things. In this world there is opposition from without and opposition from within while we build our program. Hailstorms descend upon us and cut all things level with the ground. There is very little in the way of fruitage that can be seen. Yet we know that when all the opposition of sin will be removed and the sunshine of the Son of Righteousness will shine upon it all the time, then there will be such fruitage as has never been seen in this world.

And as in the case of our claim for the present actual existence of a perfect humanity we made it abundantly plain that our sole reliance was upon the substitutionary work of Christ, so we must now once more emphasize that the guarantee of the future realization of our program rests upon the selfsame foundation. Paul insists that those whom Christ has justified, that is made perfect forensically, He will also glorify, that is, make perfect ethically and in full degree. And that he thinks of all this organically and comprehensively appears again and again when he speaks of those that are redeemed in terms of the body of Christ and when he speaks of the whole creation being given over by the Son to the Father so that God may be all in all. In consonance with this we have in the book of Revelation the picture of the new Jerusalem in which there is not a single discord while the glory of the nations, all that mankind has accomplished in its realization of the program given it by God to perform, is brought into it.

Then, in the second place, we maintain that because our opponents look at this life only they cannot judge of the fruit that our activity has produced even as it pertains to this life. What one thinks to be most useful in this life depends upon the configuration in which this life is set. If one regards this life as primarily a preparation for eternity, he will regard it a great fruit even for this life if through the agency of Christian education a good foundation has been laid for the life to come. If on the other hand one does not regard this life as a preparation for eternity, any effort to prepare for eternity will be regarded as that much waste of energy at best. The charge that other-worldliness makes us unfit for the tasks of this world is very common even today.

Thus we see that the final test cannot be an immediate and external one. True, Christ says, "By their fruits ye shall know them." Moreover He tells us to let our light shine before men that others may be led to Him. And all this presupposes that men can see something of this light when it shines. But this cannot mean that all men can fully judge of the fruits of our lives unless Jesus' own words, that only the regenerate can see the Kingdom of God, fall to the ground. Only a small degree of the internal perfection that we speak of ever appears unto men and even this small degree men do not easily see because of the tares that resemble the wheat. And if in spite of all this we are still warned to let our light shine before men, we have simply to obey Christ's command, trusting that God will use even our small ray of light to bring others out of darkness to Himself. No more therefore than the church of Christ should expect to be justified in the eyes of the world till the final judgment day should we expect to be justified in our educational policy till the final judgment day.

2. *Our Concept of Results*

What then do we desire for the future? We desire of course more momentum for our movement. But how shall we attain to this? Our answer to this question must be twofold. In the first place negative and in the second place positive.

Negatively we may affirm that our hope for the future cannot be found chiefly in the possibility that as time goes on men will be more readily convinced of the reasonableness of our program. In fact we may expect the very contrary to this. As time goes on we hope and expect that the idea of a separate and distinct program for Christian people and therefore a separate and distinct program for their education will come home with increasing fulness to all that name the name of Christ. The whole meaning of Christianity is already far more definite to both its adherents and its opponents than it has ever been before. Hence the battle is today more pointed than it has ever been before. Hence also we may expect the heat of the battle to increase in the future. It is now and will be even more so a fight to the death.

Our program, we have seen, is an absolute one and an absolute program can never be reached by compromise of any sort. An absolute program can only be realized if the enemy be destroyed. We have found that we would be able to maintain the faith in our program in no other way than by the destruction of the enemy. We cannot believe in our program and we do not believe in our program if we look at it merely as something that is somewhat better than the program of our enemies. What holds for the patience of our faith holds equally for the hope of our faith. Negatively our hope for the future lies in the conviction that our enemies *will be* destroyed. In the first part of our discussion we saw that by obedience only can we enter upon the fulfilment of the absolute ideal. It is by obedience only that we can have the vision of the absolute ideal. Then in the second part we saw that the choice between our program and the program of our enemies is not that of choice between two possibilities but a choice between a program that makes a farce of human experience and a program that trusts in an absolutely rational and therefore a never wholly comprehensible God. In consonance with this we now point out that the hope of our faith places us once more before an exclusive alternative. We have seen the ideal by the regenerating power of the Spirit of God. We have demonstrated that ideal to be the only rational ideal. Now we would confidently expect that that ideal will be realized because its opposite will in the nature of the case have to be destroyed.

3. *Our Confidence for the Future*

And note well that there must of necessity be a direct proportion between the obedience, the patience and the hope of our faith in this respect. Only those that are truly obedient, that is, only those who are truly spontaneous in their obedience and truly stable in their obedience will really see the "absolute otherness" of our ideal and will therefore see that this wholly other ideal must, if it be the true ideal at all, be the only rational ideal. It is only if we see that our ideal is the only rational ideal that we will be convinced that it will fully conquer in the end. It is that which gives us courage to labor on even though, as far as immediate results are concerned, we seem to make little progress. It gives us something of the courage of an Athanasius who would stand for his convictions though the whole world were against him. Who will deny that it is this sort of courage that we need more and more? We need men and women on our teaching staffs that are intelligibly unafraid. We need men and women on our teaching staffs that are confident of their own regeneration, that gladly work for the realization of an ideal that the world ridicules. We need men and women on our teaching staffs that understand the Christian and as well the anti-Christian philosophy of education that controls the pedagogy of our day. Such teachers will have the power of discrimination that is so all important for their task. They will be able to take of the spoils of Egypt without afterwards yearning for the fleshpots of that false fatherland.

And what is true of the teachers is true also of the ministers with whom the teachers must cooperate. We need ministers who believe in Christian education not only after a fashion but with all the passion of their souls. We need ministers who not only say that Christian education is a *nice* thing, a sort of luxury, but who say and show with their deeds, that they believe Christian education to be the only education that is fit for a covenant child. I speak of this with shame. Must we as ministers of the gospel lag behind in our grasp of the rationale of Christian education? Must we who preach the gospel of redemption from eternal woe be told that this gospel of redemption implies the destruction of sin along the whole front of our conscious lives? And who of us will say that there is not a great field yet to be conquered by us in the way of a deeper grasp of the truth and the power of victory in the Christian faith which we have embraced? And think not that I forget the man who is neither teacher or preacher. All of us must stand together as one man. In this day when boundaries between the believer and the unbeliever are so generally wiped away we should seek to mark those boundaries anew and mark them well. We should seek to mark these boundaries not with chalk that disappears with the first rainstorm that comes, but we should try to mark these boundaries with indelible ink on the hearts of those who believe.

And thus we have by implication also touched upon the positive aspect of the question as to how we are to gain momentum for our cause in the future. Perhaps some of you have already become impatient and have asked when we are to come to the constructive side of the matter. You do not like this emphasis upon the necessity of destroying the enemy. You would rather hear something about building the walls of Jerusalem and erecting the temple of God. Well, all we need to say about the constructive side has already been said. We mean by that that our constructive program is nothing else but carrying through, as far as we can, in this world of sin the program that God gave man to do in paradise. That program, we have seen, is the realization of the personality of man and thus the realization of all the powers that God has laid in His creation. We are only beginning to see what that implies. Eye hath not seen and ear hath not heard all the glory that is laid up for us. A glimpse of it we have tried to see. But our vision will increase only if our obedience increases. It is faith that builds our program because without faith we cannot even see it. But now within this vale of tears it is only with great difficulty that we even maintain our faith; how then shall we expect that in this life we shall see much of the turrets of the temple of God? We are building under terrible pressure. There is only now and then a Columbus in our midst who sees the vision of the shore that he has never seen, who checks our mutiny, who makes us work by glimpses of the reward that awaits us. Our chief business in this world will be to pull for the shore. Our chief energy must still be expended in fighting the waves and the billows that would swallow us up. It is not till the haven is reached and the danger fully past that the foundation will be solid and our work will stand. Through many tribulations we must enter into glory, but into glory we will enter and the works of our hands do follow after us. Such is the promise of our God.

CORNELIUS VAN TIL
Address before the National Union of Christian Schools Convention, Chicago, Illinois, August 16, 1933.

Key Thoughts:

1. The purpose of education is the development of personality, for that is the whole task of man. This task is all-inclusive, for human personality is thought of as representative of the whole of creation.

2. This purpose is the absolute ethical ideal God has set for man in paradise. It is the ideal or program of the Kingdom of God.

3. Man is a created personality, analogical to God in being, thinking, and action.

4. It is in the obedience of faith, the patience of faith and the hope of faith that men realize the development of personality.

5. We develop obedience by aquiring greater spontaneity of analogical action, by becoming increasingly self-determinate as analogical personality, and by increasing the momentum of the will in the capacity to do the will of God.

6. It is by obedience that man becomes free as he was created free.

7. The educational ideal of perfection applies only to the covenant youth as a perfect personality in the subsitutionary perfection of Christ.

8. The Kingdom of God is being realized in the present time in the perfecting of the substitutionary perfect child of God.

9. The program of the Kingdom of God is being realized negatively in the destruction of anti-Christian, univocal thought and action, and positively in the restoration of personality analogically.

Comment:

There are those who scoff at the idea that the Christian school aims at the development of personality. They would assign to the classroom teacher the limited range of knowledges and skills, the tools for higher learning.

Man as the self-expression of God in the whole of his personality constitutes a unity which permits no such limitation. The school too must honor this unity by seeking to develop it in keeping with ways of child life.

The Christian school seeks the development of the personality of the covenant youth in the medium of what the school as a social institution has to offer. It has an area and function distinct from both home and church. But together with home and church, the school seeks the cultivation of the whole child in the obedience of faith.

2

God's Image Bearer in the State of Perfection — Man's Twofold Function in Life

"When I consider thy heavens, the work of thy fingers, the moon and the stars, which thou hast ordained: What is man that thou art mindful of him? And the son of man that thou visitest Him? For thou hast made him a little lower than God, And crownest him with glory and honor. Thou madest him to have dominion over the works of thy hands; thou hast put all things under his feet: All sheep and oxen, Yea, and the beasts of the field, the birds of the heavens, and the fish of the sea, Whatsoever passeth through the paths of the seas. O Jehovah, our Lord, How excellent is thy name in all the earth!" (Ps. 8:3-9 R.V.).

The Psalmist presents an unusually high evaluation of man — an evalution to which we are not accustomed. It makes little difference whether one peruses the fields of thought among the liberals or among the orthodox, man is held cheaply. Walter Russel Bowie made the complaint that one of the sad things about modernism is that it has lost an appreciation of the value of human personality. That is not strange at all, since the liberals have adopted the conclusions of the scientists who declare that men are the sons of apes and that nothing but dust is their destiny. With such a prevailing conception of humanity, it is no wonder that the gospel of hatred can be so successfully preached, that human blood can be shed so readily on the slightest pretext, and that immorality can blow its blighting breath over the bloom of mankind. However, even in orthodox circles one becomes accustomed to deprecatory remarks of man. To say that "man is less than the worms that crawl in the dirt and are trampled under foot" is, I fear, not entirely true. At best it is only a part of the story. To declare that "man is nothing but dust and ashes that fly into the eyes of God and hurt him" is again, I think, a distorted statement. There can be little doubt but what man viewed from the moral and spiritual angles has revealed himself to be something contemptible. Words seem to fail in expressing the low levels to which man has fallen. But when he is compared not with God, but with the subhuman world of creation, a re-evaluation seems called for. It would seem to me that one would

then have to take the creature that he has classified with the worms
and has trampled into the dust, and place him on the very pinnacle of
divine creative productions.

Let us examine this creature as he was or as he ought to be. That
should indicate one of the great objectives of Christian education,
namely that to which the sinner should be restored. Let us in succes-
sion examine the characteristics and the function of man as God conceived him.

The Characteristics of Man

Man is the Masterpiece of God's Creation

A glance at the Scriptural account reveals the fact that God created
the world in the form of graded series. Each successive creation was
of a different and higher form. From the so-called inanimate world
the record passes on to the world of plants, of vegetation; from the
world of vegetation to that of fish and fowl; from here on into the
kingdom of animals; and finally as the capstone of it all man appears
on the scene. These were not merely different creations. In each
series there was an advance. There was a higher form of life, greater
mobility, dexterity, complexity and so on. When God had come, as
it were, to His supreme creative act, He seemed conscious of the fact
that it would complete His creative activity. He adopted a special
method, after special consultation, and selected the supreme pattern in
the universe. That pattern was none other than God Himself. This
was to be and was the very acme, the masterpiece of all His works
of creation.

Now God has left the imprint of His graded series of creation on all
His works. All men are able to see it. Even the ungodly have seen
it. The scientists have been able to discover it. The evolutionist has
long ago insisted upon the same series of development. It is a matter
of moving up from the inanimate world, through the plants, fish, rep-
tiles, fowl, animals, and finally man. That is precisely the order that
one finds in the Book of the Beginnings and in Psalm 8. Where
did he get that information? Why he got it from revelation, from
general revelation. What he does with that discovery of his is another
matter. But God had left the imprint of His creative steps in the
world so clearly that even the ungodly could find it. And they all
seem to believe that man is the end of this so-called evolutionistic development. There may be development within man, they aver, but
there is none beyond him. Here, too, we have a recognition of man
as the acme of the universe.

Man was Made to have Dominion

However, man is at the head of creation not only because he is the finest specimen of God's handiwork, but also in the sense that he himself is placed by God to rule over the created universe. That was one of the chief reasons why God made him. The creation account tells us that God planned to create one for just such a purpose and after the creation God approved of His product and issued the order that he should have dominion over the works of his hands. Psalm 8 verifies that position. This reign of man was not to be such that he could bid the created world at random to do his will, but in the sense that he could bid all the universe to serve him and through him to glorify God. This reign was to be absolute. It was to be over "all things," over "the works of thy hands." When the Psalmist beheld "the heavens, the work of thy fingers, the moon and the stars which thou hast ordained," he realized that they must come all the way down from their lofty position and serve man. They were put under his feet. When he considered the lofty and majestic mountain peaks, the broad and rich valleys below, and the endless expanse of the seas with their myriads of swimming and creeping things, he acknowledged that man was to have dominion over them and that they were placed under his feet. When he beheld the beasts of the field, numerous and varied, small and large, gentle and fierce, he was cognizant of the fact that they were placed under man's feet. Here, therefore, was the masterpiece of God, the head of creation. One can appreciate why the Psalmist cried out in bewonderment, "What is Man that thou art mindful of him and the Son of Man that thou visitest him?"

God Gave Man a "Plus" Something

The facts that man is God's masterpiece and that man occupies the unique position of ruler within the universe do not exhaust his distinctiveness. He is a rational, moral, free agent. One may assume, for instance, that man's relationship to the kingdom of animals is like that of the animals to the kingdom of vegetation, and like that of the plants to the kingdom of soil under them. Now it is that, but not only that. Each successive series seems dependent upon the lower one. There is a sort of mechanical, organic, instinctive, unconscious relationship between all these series. But do such adjectives exhaust the meaning or the character of the relationship between man and the subhuman world? Of course not. The inter-relationship in the subhuman world seems controlled by purely natural laws imposed upon it, but in man you will find a creative principle operating because of man's qualities of mind and will.

The Scriptures once and again speak of man exercising dominion over the creation. But one will look in vain for a statement to the effect that the plants exercise dominion over the world of the soil, and that animals exercise dominion over the world of plants. These were not created for that purpose and they were not qualified for it, but man was. Now bear in mind our conception of exercising dominion. It does not mean that man as a despot can arbitrarily demand that the stars change their course and they obey. Neither does it mean that he can demand that the seas dry up and immediately the world becomes bone-dry. Neither does it mean that he can bid the winds be still, and they at once die down. It is very fortunate that it is not that. But it does mean that he can force all nature to serve him, to give him delight, and to glorify God through him. He exercises dominion over the seas, and they surrender to him a seemingly inexhaustible supply of food and they carry him and his precious freight on an even keel to the various ports of the world. He exercises dominion over the earth, and it serves him by giving him valuable crops, minerals, and a host of other things too numerous to mention. He commands the winds and they furnish him with power and they carry him aloft to his chosen destinations. He exercises dominion over the very heavens and they stoop to guide him as he leaves his habitations and to furnish him with the quickening warmth and to offer him a record of time. We must be all agreed that these things are true. But how is it that man can do it? It is by the special equipment that God has created him with. There is the matter of a mind that can understand something of the nature, the origin, the values, and so forth of the things over which authority is to be exercised. Just a glance at the history of developments in the field of science will show that only as man begins to understand these things is he capable of utilizing them. Now it is true that the men of science have gotten these things under control and then served the force of evil with them. That is a terrible and tremendous responsibility. But it nevertheless demonstrates the fact that man is equipped by God with a unique something that enables him to function as God would have him function.

Man is a Final End within the Created Universe

It would seem that the entire universe was created to serve the purposes of man's existence, delight, and proper functioning. He is a sort of supreme end within this world. That does not exclude lower ends such as the grass for the animals, the water for the fish, the air for all breathing creatures, etc. And if we go beyond the world of nature, we may find higher ends such as the glory of God. There is even a delight which the Creator has in the perfection of His own productions. God saw the works of His hands and declared that they were good, but He did not use the phrase *very good* until man had been created. But all this does not militate against the position that the main purpose within the created universe is that things were made to serve the purposes of man's existence. That thought forces itself upon us when we contemplate the structure of the universe. The distribution of the land and sea, of the rivers and plains, and so on, would seem to be of little benefit to any other creature outside of man. The hidden resources of the earth, such as coal, oil, precious stones, and all, would seem to have been placed in the earth for the sole purpose of serving man. There are tremendous forces in nature such as electricity, ethereal waves, and so on, that no other creature can harness utilize. But man can and does. And there are other ends that really come into their own only when related to man. The beauty of it all delights man. Its sublimity awes him. Its vastness strikes him with a secret terror. It all reveals God. But for whom? For man. It is all calculated to serve the moral, religious, intellectual development of the human species.

Man a Mediator between God and the World

Man is also unique in that he is made up of body and spirit. He is the link that joins God and the world. We have long ago learned from the Heidelberg Catechism that a proper mediator should have the qualities of both of the parties to be mediated, and that therefore the perfection of Jesus for his mediatorial task lies in the fact that he is both very God and very man. Something similar to that is found in man. He is both a representative of God and of the created world. He has in the spirit side of his makeup something that enables him to be in direct communion with God and on the material side of his makeup something that contacts him directly with the material world. He is the link that joins the spiritual and material worlds together. Let us bear that in mind for a moment as we attempt to answer two related questions.

First, how can we speak of nature revealing God? In Psalm 19 we find that "the heavens declare the glory of God and the firmament showeth his handiwork." But, pray, to whom does the heaven declare the glory of God and firmament show his handiwork? Surely not to the inorganic kingdom. There is no perception there at all. Neither to the world of vegetation. That, too, is blind and deaf in the current sense of the term.   Neither to the animal kingdom, for the animals lack the reflective faculty that is necessary to detect the divine in nature.   It can hardly be a revelation of God unto Himself.   He does not need a created world in order to reveal Himself unto Himself. He has a direct knowledge of Himself, which is perfect and complete and which can only be reflected in the created universe.   Hence by the process of elimination, it would seem that man is the recipient of divine revelation.   Wonderful is the position and privilege of man!   Without man there would be no revelation of God within this created universe of which you and I are parts.   One cannot reveal himself unless there is someone to reveal himself to.   But God is a spirit and only the spirit can discern the things of the spirit.   Man is equipped, and only man on this side of the spiritual world is equipped, to read the handwriting of God in the material world.

The necessity of the kind of being that man is for divine revelation and glorification becomes apparent also when one faces the second question, to wit, How can nature glorify God?   There is no doubt about it but what it does.   The Bible speaks about it.   But how does it?   Nature could not do it of itself.   It lacks the conscious element, which brings the glorification to its greatest height.   Certainly there is a divine satisfaction in the perfection of His own created things.   But the glorification of God through nature comes to its own only when properly mediated by man.   How about the heavens, the moon and the stars, do they glorify God?   Do they in themselves declare the glory of God and show His handiwork?   Why, no.   The sun merely shines and moves, etc.   The stars twinkle, and that often with borrowed light.   The clouds go floating by after they are formed and then again they disappear.   Does the beautiful flower in the field of plants glorify God?   It merely nods its head in the breeze and gives off wonderful combinations of colors and fragrance. Go into the animal kingdom.   Do the animals that graze upon the hillside glorify God?   No, they merely graze, reproduce, and die.   But all these things do glorify God through the man that functions properly. It is man that declares that the heavens declare the glory of God and the firmament showeth His handiwork.   The very heavens had to come down and through man bring proper recognition to the vastness and glory of God's creation.   The animals of the field must leave their places on the hillside and through the channel of human interpretation and reflection bring glory to God.   The glory of God will not be thought and articulated until man does it.   The flowers of the field must come through man and bring glory to the living God.   That is the process through which the glory of God comes to its own in this world.   So man represents the entire created universe before God. And that is a reason why God has made him to have dominion over it all.

We have considered man's characteristics as he is related to the created universe. He is a marvelous creature. Human reflection cannot do justice to the beauty and the importance (in the scheme of God) of this creature known as man. He is a veritable masterpiece. However, the devil in the form of a serpent sneaks into the Garden. He snatches the masterpiece from off its pedestal. He dashes it to the ground. It is broken into a thousand pieces. It is marred, stained, and become altogether filthy. It can no longer exercise dominion properly. It no longer serves as an adequate channel through which God can be glorified. It has become fit only for the junkheap. The restoration of his masterpiece is a part of the redemptive program of God. In that process education plays a very prominent part. But only Christian education can consider itself at least in some measure equipped to be engaged in so wondrous a task. It has God's plan for that restoration at its disposal. It has therefore a noble and an exalted calling.

Man the Rational Image Bearer of God

We have up to this point discussed the characteristics of man as he is related to the created world. Let us turn now to consider him from the point of view of his relationship to God.

The Psalmist declared that God had made man "a little lower than God," and had "crowned him with glory and honor." That is an exceedingly high evaluation. But, none too high.

Man first of all bears the rational image of God. This is fundamental to any understanding or comprehension of the world on the part of man. Allow me to repeat the suggestion that the revelation of God in nature comes to its own only in so far as someone understands it and comprehends nature. In order to realize His ultimate purpose of self-glorification, God created a creature with a rationality like unto His own. The reason which we find in ourselves is of the same kind as the reason which expresses itself in the universe, and that in the universe is divine reason. If that were not true, any true science would be impossible. May I express this in a slightly different way? You would not be able to understand or comprehend the least of this universe had not God given you a mind like unto His own. Oh, I realize that there is a tremendous difference between the two. The difference between the finite and the infinite will never be eradicated. Yet God can reveal Himself in nature to man only if He had equipped man with a mind that can read His thoughts as they were written in nature. Allow me to illustrate. Suppose that you were asked to translate a Dutch book into the English language. As a translator you must have a mind similar to that of the original author, or you would be utterly unfit for the task that was assigned to you. You would have to be able to think as he thinks, to place yourself in his thought trend and invironment. If you are not so equipped, your work is doomed to failure. Precisely the same holds true of our interpretation of the world which is a product of God's mind. That God actually so created man is apparent from the way Adam in the state of rectitude could properly name the animals as they passed before him. Each animal was an expression of a divine thought. To properly name an object is to express in the name the essence of the thing named. So Adam revealed this ability to read the thoughts of God in the world only because he was in that respect created after the image of God.

Man Bears the Moral Image of God

Man also bears the moral image of God; not in that he was made in innocency and possessed what we may call righteousness, but in that he was indistructably moral in his make-up. First, he has God's moral image in that he has the power of moral knowledge. That moral knowledge you will not find in the subhuman created world. However, it can be found in God and also in man. In God the perfect moral knowledge, in man always the derived moral knowledge, but moral knowledge nevertheless. It is an aspect of his rational knowledge, I think. For even as I get the elements of knowledge through the mind, so also through that channel God gives me the laws of duty. This element would again seem necessary in man in order that God may achieve His purpose with His creation of man and universe. Suppose, for a moment, that man was non-moral, that he had no knowledge of what was right and wrong, that there would be no possibility of a conscious being choosing to glorify God by proper reaction to the universe, recognizing God back of it all, and seeing things so that he could see God in it all. Knowing man as we do, he would persist in so interpreting the natural phenomena that he would find himself reflected there. But there has been a moral *ought* created in his being and he cannot shake the conviction of his moral responsibility. Even the ungodly have such principles engraved in their conscience or in their hearts. Their very make-up tells them that they ought to see God in nature and in themselves, that they ought to do good and not bad, and that they ought to glorify God and not self.

God has also made man to be a free spiritual cause, that is to say, to have moral freedom. I am not speaking of a man as he actually is, but man in the constitutive parts of his nature. His being created in God's image also implies that he has been created morally free. Let us ask once again, why such a creature? Because God seeks in and through His creation the highest possible type of glorification. The whole created world is mute as far as the divine glorification is concerned, but it does occasion in man — the image bearer of God and because he is the image of God — concepts of sublimity, majesty, vastness, eternity, etc. Now what is man's reaction to these concepts? Is he inclined to go into a process of self-glorification in spite of the evidence of an infinite being, or is he going to cry out as the Psalmist, "I give thanks to thee, for I am fearfully and wonderfully made. Wonderful are thy works and that my soul knoweth right well"? Either is possible on the basis of man being a free moral agent. It is just in that free moral act that you find the summit of glorification would be imposed and mechanical. He would glorify God because he was morally incapable of doing anything else. There is a world-wide difference between the praise that a person receives from another when it is forced or when it comes voluntarily. And there is no praise of God that exceeds that of man who deliberately and voluntarily stands before the works of God's hand and thankfully and sincerely expresses his praise to the Most High. That is divine glorification that reaches its highest point of perfection. That is the kind of glorification that issued forth from Jesus.

Being created in the moral image of God also implies moral affections. God is love, we are told. If that is true man must have it in order to be a proper image of God. That is true of all the affections of man. He loved what God loved, he hated what God hated. He had fundamentally the same affections that God manifested. So created, man can, of course, effectively and properly represent God before the created universe.

Man has the Sovereign Aspect of God in his Being

The sovereign aspect of God is one of the most cherished doctrines in the hearts of all true Calvinists. To our minds God is first of all sovereign. That is one of the chief character manifestations of men. Men are naturally bossy, it is said. Why, of course; that is the way that men are created. What man does with that tendency to rule is entirely a different question. But he was made to have dominion. One finds nothing like that in the inorganic world, nor in the kingdom of plants, nor even in the kingdom of animals. One may find among the animals a tendency to defeat all rivals in the conquest of sex or in the search for food, but that is altogether a different matter than to exercise dominion. And to the reality of this human sovereignty all man's achievements abundantly testify. He harnesses the laws and forces of the inorganic world, and he makes them serve his purposes. He enters into the field of vegetation and it serves him, either by beautifying his parks or satisfying the pangs of hunger. He orders the desert to blossom as a rose, and it does. With all his scientific developments one can detect his gradual conquest over the various forces, good and bad. Man is a ruler, made after God's image, because he is to represent God.

The Potential Infinitude of Man

There is still an other aspect of this masterpiece of God which is seldom emphasized and which is nevertheless of prime importance in understanding that man has been created a litttle lower than God. I refer to what may be called, for the want of a better term, man's potential infinitude. Man is so created that he does not seem to be satisfied with what he is. He does not like the limitations to which he is subject. He tends to leap over the boundaries that keep him a finite creature. Do you know that it may be impossible for man to know that he is finite unless he transgresses the limits of the finite and frames some conception of the infinite! It is marvellously strange that man is finite, hedged in on all sides by his finiteness, and yet has a constant tendency to leap over the bounds of his limitations and to ally himself with God. God only is omniscient. Yet there is in man an insatiable desire to go beyond the knowledge that he has. He would penetrate the unknown. He would pierce the darkness. There seems no limit to his knowledge and he is always dissatisfied with what he knows. God only is omnipresent. Man is confined by his "six feet tall and forty inches of waist measure." And yet he refuses to be so confined. You have been sitting in a meeting and during the time someone was speaking you may have been at home, in the midst of the world struggle, at your work, and even in heaven with your thoughts. Why roam all around when you are supposed to be only here where your body is? God only is omnipotent, but in man you will find an insatiable grasping for more power. It is a natural tendency. This power may be in the world of literature, of finance, of society, etc. But it is there. We seem irked by our limitation of power. We strive to become almighty. I need not go on to present other illustrations of the tendency of man to reach out and beyond himself and to approach God. This is not bad in itself. Sometimes we seem inclined to think so. The bad element in it touches the matter of man's disposal of the powers when once they are attained, of his purposes, and of his methods of reaching out, etc.

After all, the perfection of this creature of God as he left the divine fingers is past finding out. He is marvelous beyond description. He could think God's thoughts after Him. He had the same moral qualities. He bore the sovereign image of God. And he had desires for a higher status than that in which he was made. Truly, he was marvelously made. But once more, satan entered in' and crushed to pieces that masterpiece. Man raised his eyes to read God's revelation, but he found that his ability of reading the language of God was practically gone. He regarded his moral equipment, and that was sadly broken down. He tried to exercise his sovereignty, but the whole world rebelled against man's rule. He reached out to get beyond himself and by each such act he threw himself into sin. That creature must be restored. He must reflect what is reflected in Jesus. And in this marvellous restorative program, the Christian school may have an exalted part. Man must be brought where he can again truly represent God before creation.

The Function of Man

We have discussed the characteristics of man as the masterpiece of divine creative activity. May I now invite you to reflect upon his function? First, let us examine his function as the representative of the world before God.

The Function of Man as Creation's Representative

The first function of man representing the world is that of a conscious, deliberate and rational acknowledgement of God. For the sake of practicality, I shall place this masterpiece in the presence of this world as it now is. This will help us to understand what the proper function of a present day Christian is and what the objectives of Christian education may be. There must be an acknowledgement of God even at the present time otherwise this world would not now be glorifying God. The man that is functioning properly, and he can be none other than a' redeemed and Christian trained person, will do what others are not doing. He will represent even the ungodly world round about him. He will not represent the ungodly world in a sort of substitutionary or vicarious way. This recognition of God in the world will not be to the credit of the ungodly. But it will bring glory to God through man who was made for that purpose.

The average man looks at war and reflects upon it without bringing God into the picture. He finds in it the selfishness of some ambitious monarch, or the fulfilment of a desire for revenge, or the expression of various ideologies, or a quest for Lebensraum, etc. That is as far as he goes. But there is something lacking. The man who represents this world before God will be able to see the handwriting of God in it. He will see traces of divine justice being expressed; he will find evidence of it working out together for good; and he will be brought to the point where he can thank God for His wisdom, justice, love, etc. It is only when someone somehow finds a proper place for it in God's scheme of things that it can serve to glorify God. Only he who is equipped with eyes that can see is able to read.

A few years ago we were in the throes of a depression. People starved. Industry shut down. Work was unavailable. Economists prated about underconsumption, overproduction, economic ignorance, etc. But if that is all that could be said about it, God was not receiving His due. But He in His providence furnished individuals, sufficiently restored, who could trace something of the spiritual values in it all, and who were even able to thank God for them. Such persons were functioning properly. You can yourself furnish all sorts of illustrations from history, and from your own experience and other sources, of the fact that God is being and can be and ought to be glorified and acknowledged by those whom He has created and restored for that purpose.

The man that properly represents the world before God will be filled with a proper sense of repentance and sorrow because of the sins of the world round about. There are thousands and thousands of sins committed by men and women in this world that seem to go out into history followed by no repentance. Must such sinning go on without the proper responses anywhere and without somehow, however indirectly, glorifying God? The Lord would then have no reason for continuing this sinful world; it is not realizing His purpose. But there are thousands of representatives here too that become aware of the sins and cry out, "God, this sinning is terrible. Man is in the grip of satan. He defies God and serves the devil. Thou alone art holy and perfect, and we all ought to be like thee." And as long as there are men so reacting to the sins in this world, the world even with its sin, however indirectly, is still glorifying God. It still can in the sight of God be justifiably maintained. The disapproval of the sins of Moses, Abraham, and all the other worthies in the Bible is a method by means of which God is being glorified, and perhaps suggests a reason why these sins as a matter of fact are recorded in the Bible.

The man that functions as he ought will also be the representative who gratefully receives the blessings of God. Let us limit ourselves in the interest of brevity to the gifts of salvation and redemption. God has continued to offer these throughout the ages. Men have said in effect, "God, we don't want your offers." They hurl them back at God.

They hold them cheap. They refuse to accept them. How long do you suppose God will continue to make these offers? Why does He not destroy this rebellious world that treats Him with so much contempt and disdain? Is it not because there are always representatives here that are still reaching forth eagerly and gratefully and receiving these blessings? Is it not because He is still being honored by this reception? Abraham once argued with God about sparing a certain wicked city. He pleaded whether God would not spare the city if there were still fifty righteous there. God declared that He would be willing, and that if there were fifty righteous He would spare the city. Abraham continued his "bargaining" with God until finally he received God's assurance that He spare the city if there were but ten righteous. Let me tell you that He would spare the city if there were only one righteous there. The presence of such a righteous one would guarantee that there was still divine glorification rising like delightful incense to the throne of God.

The man that functions properly as the representative of the world will exercise close communion with God. He is the one that prays for the needs of those round about him. The ungodly is not going to ask for food (and much less for salvation) from God. It would be a piece of sinful hypocrisy if he did. The only one qualified to ask God to bless this nation and to supply its needs and to thank God for the priceless blessings already received is the child of God properly trained to do so.

And, of course, the same thing is true when one contemplates man's relationship to the world at large. It makes no difference what he sees and what he experiences, it must all after it has gone through his soul be presented to God in such a way that all the honor and glory go to the divine presence. I know of no loftier work than that of preparing or training a person to so represent the world before God. It is a task that calls for a distinctive Christian interpretation of the entire field of human knowledge. It is a matter of interpreting everything in the light of God's Word and of then living and functioning in accordance with such findings. If a schoolboard or teacher wants inspiration in carrying out their various duties, right here is a rich source of it.

The Function of Man as God's Representative

The only person qualified to represent God in this world is he who is God-like. And to be God-like is to be perfect, or holy, or living in full agreement with His commandments.

There is, for instance, the matter of love which is required by the law of God. Now love will find its first object perhaps within the circle of the brethren. But one may retort, "How can I love the brethren? They are so sinful, so hypocritical, so utter unworthy of love." Now that may all be true; but you are not asked to love them because of any worthiness that they possess, but because God loves them; and the representative of God must love what God loves. The objects of love may be widened to include the poor and needy. One may protest that these poor are usually so ungrateful that they frequently lack appreciation, and so on. Once again the representative of God will love them not because of any returns in the form of appreciation, but just because they are objects of divine love. And exactly the same thing is true when you are placed face to face with the command to love your enemies.

And the high duty of representing God in the matter of love before the world simply staggers one when he begins the task of analyzing what that divine love is like. When one contemplates it in all its beauty, forgiving spirit, self-giving, comprehensiveness, and effectiveness, he is filled with awe at the high and noble calling to which he should attain.

The representative before the world should also represent God's justice in the world. That must, of course, first of all be a personal justice. God Himself is just and therefore He promotes justice. One must first cast the beam out of his own eye. It is only the just that can and that have the right to promote justice. It is right at this point that we find the weakness of reformers: They would reform others before they are thoroughly reformed themselves. Here is the weakness of parents: They would promote a genuine and deep religious spirit within their children before they themselves have become genuine and deep in their spiritual life. Here lies the weakness of God's people in the social group: They would have the spirit of Christ to permeate the social group before they themselves have become thoroughly permeated with it. One cannot represent God's justice without becoming just first of all.

Then, too, such a one will promote justice in the world of which he is a part. Passive Christianity is no Christianity. It is dead. God Himself performed a miracle in order that justice may be done. His work of redemption is a work of justice. Other schemes of salvation may have the element of mercy and love and so on in them, but God's plan promotes justice. To insist upon justice is to insist upon what God insists upon.

Let me present but one more illustration. The child of God who functions acceptably presents God's truth. Again personal truthfulness is required. God presented Himself precisely as He is. It is the duty of the child of God to present himself as he actually is, to wit, a child of God. It is a sad fact that so many of God's children present themselves as children of the world. It is a sinful form of hypocrisy which is infinitely worse than that of the Pharisees, who presented themselves as good but were full of rottenness and decay. One's value as a leaven and a light bearer depends upon his willingness to think, speak, and act truthfully.

That is what God did and does. Men may have twisted and still do twist this self-manifestation of God, but He is true to Himself. He must insist upon practical truth in the world, because truthfulness is basic to the existence of any society, and certainly of the society of God's people. The lie always disintegrates. It is of the devil. He who lies and promotes lies is a representative of the evil one. He who speaks the truth and promotes it is of Him who is the truth.

Enough has been said so as to suggest how man must represent God before the created universe. He merely puts into practice the prayer to which he gives utterance when he asks, "Thy will be done . . . on earth as in heaven."

I have given expression to man as he was made, to man as he was revealed in Christ, to the man that the child of God must develop into. It is a glorious redemptive process. It is a joy to believe that one can be engaged as co-worker with God in such a program that has been all too weakly presented. It is the challenge that is being presented to all those who have sacrificed and are willing to sacrifice for this great cause.

HENRY SCHULTZE

Address before the National Union of
Christian Schools Convention, Grand
Rapids, Michigan, August 26, 1941.

Key Thoughts:

1. Man is God's masterpiece in the graded series of creation. He is the mediator between the spiritual world and the material world in his person as spirit and body.

2. Man was created to have dominion over the sub-human world of God's creation.

3. In relation to the sub-human world, man constitutes a final end in creation.

4. As image bearer of God man is rational, moral, and free.

5. There is a potential infinitude in man that reflects God's omniscience and omnipotence. He ever seeks to reach out beyond himself and to approach God.

6. The function of man as a rational being is to acknowledge God, to represent the world before God, and to represent God in this world.

7. It is the purpose of education to restore man to his God-likeness in the world in which God places him.

Comment:

> Education is a restorative process.
>
> The organic unity of the personality in the spirit has been tragically disrupted because the life-line of the human spirit with the Spirit of God in the fellowship of love has been broken. Two things must occur. The life-line must be reestablished. God does this when He grafts the sinner into the vine which is Christ. No human effort can effectuate this change. The life-line being reestablished, the organic unity in the spirit can be achieved.
>
> In Christian education we co-labor with God in restoring the lost harmony of the person in his personality. Instruction in the Christian school must aim to achieve this end. Only when instruction is educational in this sense is it Christian instruction.

3

The Full-Orbed Life

We have found in the covenant and in the creation idea a divine ordinance for education. Our educational program as involved in the covenant idea is based upon the concept of creation, and the concept of creation is once more based upon our idea of God. And as for our idea of God, we hold to it not as to a moral or mental luxury but as to the very foundation of the structure of human experience.

Upon this basis we come to certain definite conclusions with respect to our educational program. We begin more and more to realize that we should declare our independence once for all. We should forget the house of bondage and not yearn for the fleshpots of Egypt at every turn of the way. We have resources of principle such as no other commonwealth of education has. More than that. We not only claim our rightful place among the commonwealths of education but we have a definitely imperialistic program. No mere Monroe doctrine will suffice. We are out to destroy — albeit with spiritual weapons only and always — all our competitors. We do not recognize them as equals but regard them as usurpers. Carthage must be destroyed.

But if such be the demand of the creation concept underlying our educational policy, it would be strange if we did not find a similar struggle when our opponents and we face the problem of the future. To anticipate our conclusion we may say that according to our view there is in this world and there will be in the next a full-orbed life. Our opponents hold that they do not know and that we do not know anything about the matter at all.

Now if this rough simplification of the matter in any measure betrays the true state of affairs it will appear that an argument must follow. From our side we must give an account of the faith that is in us because its reasonableness is not patent to all who look at the "facts" of life. Moreover we are attacked. We think that we see the truth, while our opponents are quite sure that we do not. A well known story may illustrate this point. "There was a country where most of the inhabitants were blind, including the philosophers. But there were a few simple people whose eyes were not sealed, and they spoke of the joy of seeing the sun. 'But,' said the philosophers, 'you must not talk in that excited metaphorical strain. There is a diffuse warmth, as we all know, but your talk about a visible luminous body is an antiquated objectivism. There is no sun.' Yet the simple people asserted all the more that they saw the sun, and a psychological committee was appointed to investigate the matter. They made many experiments and in the course of time they discovered that whenever those whose eyes were not sealed said they saw the sun, they had opened their eyes. The blind psychologists felt over the seeing faces and they made sure that there was a precise correlation between the openings of their eyes and the visions of the sun. 'Dear friends,' they said, 'you are suffering from an illusion; the image of the sun that you speak of somewhat unintelligibly is produced by this trick of opening your eyes. Be honest now and tell us if you ever behold the image of the sun except when you open your eyes.' The simple seers said 'No' and the committee was well pleased with them and hoped that they would recover from their sight. But the simple seers smiled to themselves, and went away saying, 'We see the sun.' "

This story illustrates the point that our opponents cannot make their position of doubt or negation reasonable to themselves unless they seek to show that we as well as they know nothing of the matter at all. If one should argue that airplanes are the illusions of the heated imagination while Lindbergh was flying overhead he would have to give good reasons for his faith. So our opponents are driven to appoint psychological and philosophical committees to prove that we are selfdeluded. And the woeful plight of the world gives them a lenient and a favorable jury.

As on Mt. Carmel then we meet these foes. We believe that our enemies serve the gods of the Zidonians. We believe that many of our "friends" have done what Ahab did; they have made a false alliance with our enemies. They say that it makes no difference which gods we serve because all of them are symbolic and not real. Consequently these "friends" are ready when occasion arises to harness the noble steed of religion to the dogcart of political or social exigencies, teaching in the name of the state or in the name of science that which we believe to be subversive of both state and science.

What is it then that modern man would consider to be the supreme good for himself? Will Thomas a Kempis be called upon to set forth the glories of the future life? Now it is not easy to ascertain what our opponents hold to be the full-orbed life if they believe in its existence or on the possibility of its existence at all. There is among them a great diversity of opinion on the subject. Yet on one point they all agree. All of them are equally insistent that it is not "the rest that remaineth for the people of God," that they desire. "Our matured age is restless." It "envies not the dead that rest." To modern men the occupations of the damned in Dante's poem would be pleasing pastimes in comparison with the "ennui" with which the traditional heaven has been furnished.

Reserving this point for a moment, let us observe that if it be true, as suggested, that our opponents finally maintain an uncertain or agnostic position, they at least are unanimous in their wholehearted rejection of our position.

Those given to demanding the Shylock's price in things logical will at this point wistfully ask whether such a universal negative can furnish a good foundation for an educational system unless there be a prior affirmative. Suppose that you have lost your door key. At once you search that pocket in which you usually keep it. You have searched every nook and fold of it. If so, you have every reason to say that even if you find it nowhere else you need not search that pocket again. But has modern man made such an exhaustive search of the traditional heaven as suggested by our analogy? Or is he more like a boy who in careless haste has cast one glance in a large storeroom and has decided that the key is not there. Why should not modern man take another look at that which he has rejected in careless haste inasmuch as he has not found his coveted prize elsewhere? Man cannot live by negation alone.

But let us watch the progress or at least the process of the prodigal. We have seen that modern man has started on his way with a cordial negation. He felt sure that the paternal roof was too narrow and too low, both for the individual and for the race. He must get out. He must go "out West." There were rumors of gold in California. It was the era of expansion. With the fierceness of a Mencken he forsook the benighted, bedridden, hidebound herds of tradition-driven slaves as not worth saving and trampled upon the plague stricken victims of authority.

Modern men said they knew where they were going. They claimed to have a definite objective in mind. If only the human intellect was given freedom in its exercise it would carve out for itself a marvelous estate of bliss in the unlimited and ungoverned territories of space and time. The few "Indians" that would be there could easily be subdued. Given full freedom the human intellect could educate the rising generation into complete happiness.

Thus, roughly stated, ran the slogan of the eighteenth century. It was the revolutionary war of intellectual independence that then was fought. And the battle was won. Rationalism gained control in many of the institutions of learning. There was traditionalism still, but the colony of rationalists was large enough to give their principles a fair trial. And a fair trial these principles of Rationalism had. Did they enable man to live the full-orbed life? We need but follow the course of events to find the answer.

It was soon discovered that the struggle against a common foe had furnished the only cohesive principle binding the Rationalist colonies together. When the common foe had disappeared, the principle of cohesion had also disappeared. A jolly time they had of it, these swashbucklers of the intellect, vomiting vitriol on the painting and sculpture of the ages. Cathedrals that were centuries in building trembled before the cohorts of vandalism.

Yet when the time of reconstruction came there seemed to be some difficulty. It was easy to ridicule some of the things in which St. Augustine believed but not so easy to give a better explanation of history than that given in the *City of God*. Some seemed to tremble whether the intellect of man even when untrampled and free was equal to the vastnesses and deeps of reality. Friction soon arose. A national constitution had to be adopted and no one had power or authority to do it. In desperation the drivers of the intellect when met in Constitutional Assembly exceeded all their delegated powers and provided for a government strongly centralized. The states could not secede at will of whim. Why then should they join? For the sake of life itself. To be or not to be that was the question. Thus it came about that self-contradiction based upon negation furnished the mortar for the imposing capital of Rationalism. It was a *modus-vivendi,* nothing more; the civil war was in the offing when the revolutionary war was scarcely over.

* * *

The rising generation of the nineteenth century once more found the paternal roof too narrow and too low. "Our fathers," they said, "have proclaimed the freedom of the head and they did well, but we must proclaim the freedom of the heart. How can we live the full-orbed life as long as our newly erected central government of the intellect keeps making universal laws apace? The new government is as tyrannical as the old. We cannot breathe in such a stifling atmosphere. We cannot brook the Rehoboam's message of the intellect; to your tents, O Israel!

In some such wise as this the nineteenth century cried for a new and greater freedom. And again they seemed to know their goal. They had men to lead them on. There was Bergson, that Heraclitus of the modern age, that hater of finalism and intellectualism alike. It was this apostle of the Irrational that led the new crusade. Each nation furnished a contingent of soldiers. France led under Bergson himself as the Peter the Hermit who made the general rallying cry. Germany met under Nietzsche's lead with the slogan of the "superman" to cast off the galling yoke of the mediocre and to give the individual his rights against a dominant society. Austria sent Freud to open the fountains of the deep and set at liberty the captive forces of the midnight hour; the hegemony of the intellect must be broken in the individual before it can be broken in society. Freud drilled the reserves before they went to the front. America, mindful of its Monroe Doctrine, was loathe to join the fray. Yet it was not long until William James insisted on a separate sector of the front. His drive was directed against the "Block Universe" and his battle cry was "Down with the Absolute." His method was hydraulic, that of undermining by the "stream of consciousness."

Thus the allies of the heart advanced against that Hun, the intellect, wherever he appeared. A jolly time they had of it, these swashbucklers of the troubled deep. The imposing statues of Bismarck, Hegel and Voltaire alike were crushed for macadamizing the Appian way. The soldiers were to live on pillage and plunder while fighting and were to be rewarded finally with a harem all their own.

But when once more the time for reconstruction came, the apostles of the heart had great difficulties facing them. The eighteenth century Rationalism had fought against a certain universal law, but the nineteenth century fought against all universal law. The Constitutional Assembly of Rationalism had to overstep its rights in order to frame a constitution, but the heroes of the heart were not even able to call a convention. No one would delegate any authority at all; all feared the capitalists of the intellect. The spectre of petrification stared them in the face whenever any renegade dared to speak of constructive thought. They believed in the future, not in the past. They wanted to live themselves out, not to be cramped in once more. Zola became the literary hero of the day; Walt Whitman's terrific sympathy surged in their bosom.

So no reconstruction was effected. The time of the judges was in the land. Surely that ought to be the time to live the full-orbed life! Freedom was there was it not? So it seemed. Yet there were misgivings soon. The theory had been that all the hidden forces of the heart were as so many innocent victims of the usurpers of the past. Now that these forces were unleased, this theory was put to a test. And scarcely were the prison-gates unbarred and the "innocents" escaped abroad but they appeared as a blustering band of imperialists out conquering and to conquer. Pandora's box was opened; only hope remained.

Thus we see the bold assurance with which modern man began on his way slowly yielding to uncertainty and lack of confidence. The fiery optimism of the crusade died down slowly and gave way to sullenness; some even spoke of turning back. Hence more and more discipline had to be applied to the cohorts of the faithful. The chaplains of the army received their instructions every week. More and greater sacrifices were offered to that demon logic to appease him as his canons were more universally and more ruthlessly ignored. Rationalism had placed contradiction upon negation; Cordialism now undermined them both by the "stream of consciousness." Well may the wistful once more ask whether such procedure has any meaning except upon the presupposition of a fundamental affirmation. But we will let the wistful watch and wait.

* * *

Then that Titan Time turned the hands of the century clock once more. A new generation arose that knew not its Moses who had led their fathers out of the Egypt of traditionalism into the desert freedom of Rationalism nor its Joshua who had led them into the promised land of the swampy freedom of the heart. And as their fathers before them had been unable to see the symbolism and the typology of things so these secularists in a sacred land were baffled and dismayed. Were they not the chosen people of God? Why then did the Canaanite still dwell in the land? It seems that all the resources were exhausted.

Yet that is not the case. The age of paradox has come. Dictators appeared suddenly and everywhere upon the scene. Wilson in politics and Stalin behind politics; Barth in theology and Heidegger behind theology; Dewey in education and Dewey behind education — all of them spectres suddenly appearing in the gruesome shape of the laocoon seeking in vain to escape and to help escape from the coils of the strangling serpent of despair. Never before have the eyes of men beheld such a scene. Democracy recalls the tyrants in order to accomplish its tyranicide. Theology storms the very heaven for transcendence in order to free the world from the "otiose deity" who once did rule the skies. Education begs for the shackles of the slave to set its freedom free.

As to task, the dictator must rationalize the irrational. He must show meaning in a system of politics and social life or education which by its own presuppositions has no meaning. As to program, the dictator must be inconsistently inconsistent. He must go in all directions at once in the name of strategy; he must be either wiser than all men or a greater fool than any man.

Yet the dictator is not to be blamed particularly; he is but the fruit of an epoch; the surging sea has brought him forth. In an age that feeds upon the negation of all that is called absolute you may expect the strangest combinations of freedom and tyranny. Life is then no longer as a river following a certain course but as a shoreless ocean without direction. The freedom of the swimmer suddenly becomes the anguish of the drowning man. If all reality is but a temporal mass of fluidity, there may be sharks in it unbeknown to the innocent rowboat pleasure-seeker. Hence the appearance of the huge ocean steamers, the trust, the labor union, the chain stores; hence the syncro-mesh transmission from the wildest libertinism to the most rigid standardization of the machine; hence above all, the mob spirit and the power of the demagogue such as has never been seen before.

Then hope turns into fear. Men turn hither and thither in frantic fear lest the ship will sink. Thousands flock to this man here or to that man there saying, "Be thou king over us and lead us out of this." Says Paul Elmer More, "Futility is the final word: the literature and art most characteristic of the day are criticized as chaotic, joyless, devoid of beauty, comfortless, fretfully original, or feebly conventional, impotent, futile." Intellectual defeat and spiritual dismay stalk about everywhere.

> It's all Nothing.
> It's all a world where bugs and emperors
> Go singularly back to the same dust.

The novelists offer no program of reform; as vultures they gloat over the carrion of modern life. And as for the philosophers, they too are "sicklied with the conscious depression of futility." Man is seen "as a slave of his temperament, or as a mechanism compelled by complexes and reactions, or a vortex of sensations, with no will to govern himself, no centre of stability within the flux, no direction of purpose to rise above the influences that carry him hither and thither." A la Mencken "they have come to realize that the morons whom they sweated to save do not want to be saved and are not worth saving."

* * *

The wistful will ask at this point whether the full-orbed life has now been reached. But the wistful must still watch and wait. We have not yet sounded the deepest depths of the negation of modern life. The prodigal is at the swinetrough now. He is thinking with an empty stomach and sees the husks the swine did eat. He has denied his manhood and cannot be an animal. Yet he will go to one of his friends. He goes to the home of the dictator now.

Unfortunately the dictator is a man of the same country, ridden with the same psychologism and historism as those that come to him for comfort. Yet he is not without good advice. He tells the prodigal to forget. He tells his clients that the present malaise is but a temporary depression.

And if the prodigal should then become panic-stricken and suggest that the world itself seems to provide no full-orbed stomachs he is told to feed the swine again for exercise so as to forget his hunger. All the instincts that clamor as the inmates of a menagerie for the satisfaction of their elemental wants are whipped in droves for purposes of sublimation. Psychologists are hired to teach them this noble art; hence our Y.M.C.A. and Y.W.C.A.'s; hence our Boy Scout movement and the general emphasis upon physical exercise and sport. Thus what the head failed to do in the eighteenth century and what the heart failed to do in the nineteenth century the hand is asked to do in the twentieth century. The prophet failed. The priest failed. Now comes the king.

Ye critics now stand by and let him have his hour. How well we all know that a king is a contradiction in terms in such an age as ours, but we will call him dictator now. How well we know that subordination and drilling of the most trying kind is with us again, but we call it sublimation or syncopation now. Let there be no slackers then; this is a world war. And well we know that there are no signs of a full-orbed life, but let us have patience to wait a million years.

Thus the easy victories that seemed to be in sight have receded into the far distant future. Thus also the sword has been thrust into every hand; a nation, not merely an army mobilizes now. Never before have free citizens realized "how irresistibly a modern government could impose its ideas upon the whole nation and, under a barrage of publicity, stifle dissent with declarations, assertions, official versions, and reiteration." New Espionage and Sedition Acts were passed to make any criticism of the war program illegal now. If any one will not follow the educational dictator, John Dewey, if any one dare to hold that evolution-theory is not the gospel truth to be poured down the children's throats, let him be anathema.

This renewed and heavier emphasis upon the enforcement of the Sedition acts seems to tell us something. When William Bateson gave his famous address on "Evolutionary Faiths and Modern Doubts" in which he boldly asserted that the origin of species is a question about which science knows nothing as yet, he guarded himself against any victory that the believers in special creation might draw from such a confession by saying, "When such confessions are made the enemies of science see their chance. If we cannot declare here and now how species arose, they will obligingly offer us the solutions with which obscuranticism is satisfied. Let us then proclaim in precise and unmistakable language that our faith in evolution is unshaken." Similarly Henry Fairfield Osborn tells us that his faith in evolution remains immovable though the evidence has convinced him that the earliest man of which there is any trace was just as intelligent as man is today.

And now the wistful will hasten forward again and say that all this begins to look too much like fighting a losing battle. This military display, this excessive rigor of martial law and these loud protestations of persisting faith in the absence of evidence indicate an internal hollowness. There must be great fear in the ranks. Yet we must wait and see.

* * *

The efforts in search of the full-orbed life that we have so far observed have all been characterized by a sort of individualism or separation. First the head was going to bring salvation without the aid of the heart or hand. Then the heart was going to bring salvation without the aid of the head or the hand. Finally the hand was going to bring salvation without the aid of the head or the heart. But the program now proposed seeks to join all three of them. All the reserves are to be brought out at once. All the forces of land and sky and sea are marshalled under one supreme command for this last great battle of Armageddon.

Emblazoned on the new escutcheon is a harp, as the symbol of organic union. For *Organism* is now the word in English and *Resonanz* is now the word in German. This new concept of organism appears everywhere you go. It binds together the individual first of all. The intellectualism of the old psychology and the mechanism of the new is giving way to Configurationism with its emphasis on the centrality of the human person.

Then further, this concept of the organism is to bind the individual to society, and even to the cosmos. And here the subliminal self of James, though modified, furnishes the connecting-link between the individual and the "objective" world. The conceptions of dual and multiple personality make a gentle transition from one personality to another possible. There are underground connecting ways found everywhere. Child psychology has bridged the gulf between the adult and the infant. Animal psychology has bridged the gulf between the animal and the child. How gently and easily the old wrangle about the theory of knowledge seems to be settled here. Are we really gaining knowledge of the objective world? Certainly, comes the answer, for we are part and parcel of the objective world. A new objectivism has replaced the old.

Still further, scientists are everywhere corroborating in their specific fields the concept of the organism. Driesch's vitalism is once more revived in biology. But more important it is that the physicists have realized the dream of mediaeval alchemy. The very elements are beginning to move and show signs of life. The deadness and inertness of matter is gone. Matter is electricity and electricity can be given no adequate expression but in mental constructs; so thin has the partition between matter and mind become.

And further still the emissaries of organic union go. With one grand *Entschluss* Barth has ballooned the message of organic union into heaven. Then God himself no longer dared enforce his erstwhile Monroe doctrine but joined the league of nations. Then all the former enmity between transcendence and immanence was put away because all *Sein* became *Zeit*. God can be temporalized on occasion, and when the convention is to meet in heaven man is readily eternalized.

Surely Modernism, the heir to all this patrimony, has a message to bring to us. Do not marvel that its preachers sometimes wax impatient at our recalcitrance. Why still linger over the forensic concepts of Luther and Calvin when art has replaced morality? Why not join Fosdick in preaching the holiness of beauty instead of beauty of holiness? It is all a matter of the tuned string, a matter of cosmic rhythm and resonance. If God himself has joined the union without fear of losing his creed then why do you stand back? For remember that if you do not join on your own initiative you will eventually join on the initiative of someone else. The intricacy of modern life ought to teach you that. This gospel of organic union and cosmic resonance must be taught unto the children of the nation. Suppose then that you refuse to have your children taught these doctrines; you would become dangerous to the state and would have to be dealt with accordingly. The state will have to extend its kind paternalistic hand to you to lead you gently and irrisistibly into line.

*   *   *

Surely he who does not see the full-orbed life here must give a good account of himself. He goes contrary to all the scientific and philosophical opinion of the day. If one still wishes to retain traditional views he must do it with the conviction that the traditional views have faced the the same problems that the modern man has faced. He must be convinced moreover that the traditional views have given a better answer to these problems than the modern man has given. We cannot build separate schools for the sake of a hobby. And this is so not only because they cost a deal of money but still more is this so because we would not then be giving a good account of the faith that is in us. We must therefore seek to give our reason for being out of harmony with the gospel of harmony.

Now we may perhaps sum up these reasons by saying that there is too much disharmony in this gospel of harmony. Or better still we may say that we believe there is no harmony at all in the modern theory of harmony. It is not a question of a little more or less harmony between us and our opponents but the question is where we may expect to find any harmony at all.

To begin with we may emphasize the point already alluded to, namely, that there is too much of the fanfare of war in the whole of our opponents' program of peace. No country will bring to the front all of its reserves unless it is at the end of its strength. Such a military display as we have witnessed of late should bring immediate victory, or we cannot help but think that it spells defeat.

We should say to our opponents: We know right well what measures of discipline you have used upon your troops to bring them into line. Your discipline has become more rigid at every step. Your Kaiser has threatened to turn the guns of his army upon his own people because they spoke of revolution, and men that are leading a full-orbed life do not mutiny. Your chaplains have preached in season and out of season *that war itself is the full-orbed life.* Let us prove this point from your official documents, for it is all important.

One of your leading philosophers, Edgar A. Singer, has sought to demonstrate in a paper of state that the only possible science of religion is one that is based upon the *apriori* of desire. The ancients, he tells us, thought the Danaides unfortunate because they were doomed to carrying water in sieves in Hades for the killing of their husbands. So the old-fashioned Christian too looks for a heaven of perfect rest. "But," says Singer, "it is exactly this prospect of eternal peace that troubles a matured age." "For it is Kant who first perceives the divine to be all too human, if it be not for us humans *eine reine Idee.*" There is the crux of the matter. Modern man does not wish to attain, but only to advance. "Neither for the Danaides of old nor for the humanity of today is there misery in a failure to attain; though there is hell enough for both and for all men to come in any persistent failure to advance."

But where, then, is the harmony of which you have spoken so much? Can there be any certainty of harmony if at any moment some new and totally discordant note may appear? You do not wish the "ennui" of our heaven. It is well. You care not for attainment. It is well.

Only, will you tell us how you expect to make advancement in your self-chosen hell? Is not your hell based upon the negation of the Absolute? You have stormed the very heavens to bring the eternal into the temporal. Your god is but the next higher step in the process of advancement. You have identified god with the idea of advancement. But how do you know that there has been or will be any advancement in such a shoreless sea as that in which you welter? All things are at loose ends and you cannot even know that there will be any course or direction to anything that you may do. If it be true that in grammar two negatives make an affirmative, this is not the case in logic. You cannot expect a new affirmation from the negation of negation unless there be a dialectic functioning. And there exactly comes the rub. You have provided for no atmosphere in which a dialectic could function. You start with the void and therefore you must also end with the void. And in the void there is no cancellation power. You could at best mark time and you cannot even do that. Parmenides would not allow his opponents to say anything but "being": we will not even allow you to say that much. An eternal silence and an eternal standstill is the price you must pay for your idea of advancement. You never have had and you never will have anything that looks like your idea of the full-orbed life. What you will have is a travesty on the "rest that remaineth for the people of God." According to your own words there is hell enough and to spare in a failure to advance. Refine then if you will a hundred-fold by all the intellectual tortures of modern mathematical genius the punishment of the Danaides and you will not even then approach the idea of utter self-stultification implied in your idea of progress. We do not hesitate to submit that the very presupposition of any advancement is the affirmation of an absolute selfconscious God. Without such a God there cannot even be a hell, let alone a heaven. And with such a God, given the fact of evil, there must be both.

So then if we may now turn preacher we would say that your gospel of harmony is bound to fail because it has not included God. You have included many gods, but you have not included God. Hence your circle is not large enough. Your policy of inclusiveness has after all proved to be one of exclusiveness. God has refused to meet your conditions of entrance into the league of nations. In turn He lays down His conditions for entrance into harmony with Him. It is these conditions which we have accepted. We have realized that if we are to be in harmony with an absolute God we must be in harmony with Him on His own terms. Accordingly we feel confident that we have and will have the full-orbed life.

In opposition to this you have desperately resolved that you would rather enter the barren desert hoping against hope that there will be a Canaan beyond and oases on the dreary way, than return to the father's house. Some of your leaders are beginning to confess that they do not know where they are going. We have already referred to Osborn and Bateson. Let us add the testimony of James Jeans who says that science has "no pronouncement to make." Of course we do not wonder that science has no pronouncement to make. The starting point of the modern scientific method is the negation of the absolute. That negation is involved in its so-called open-mind attitude. It follows that science, unless it changes its method, never will have any pronouncement to make. With the present method it would require someone beyond God to make a pronouncement, and even the scientists are not beyond God inasmuch as they are, according to their own view, bound up with God. And if enough of all this has come to your realization that you are willing to admit that you know nothing as yet about the nature of reality, it would seem that our position may once more have a hearing.

Yet of this we would not speak if you were content to let us alone. But that exactly you will not do. You force your agnosticism upon us and upon our children. Jeans, for example, tells us that this universe has come by accident and that we should speculate no more about the matter since accidents will happen. Then further, with respect to human life we are told that, "In the course of time, we know not how, when or why, one of these cooling fragments gave birth to life." It is thus that the humble scientist who pretends to be satisfied with searching the facts in the laboratory suddenly turns philosopher, theologian, teacher, and preacher, pouring down our throats large doses of antitheistic metaphysics in the dread name of science.

Here we reach the highwater mark of present day antitheistic thought. Our opponents maintain not only that they do not know anything about the nature of reality but that nobody else can possibly know anything about it. The present day scientist is often not the humble seeker after truth but the militant preacher of a faith, and the faith that he preaches is the faith of agnosticism. It is this point to which we have seen all things come. The face of science and philosophy today is, with rare exceptions, set squarely against Christianity and the Theism that serves it as a foundation.

*   *   *

What else, then, can we do but take the sword as well as the trowel? We are driven to a defense of our faith. The full-orbed life, that which the world has sought in vain, is in our possession. We have an absolute God in whose fellowship we have even now the full-orbed life. We have an absolute God who alone can give meaning to all our strivings for advancement. We have an absolute God who alone can guarantee that that which we have in principle now will be fully realized hereafter.

Is our position modern? If the principle of the organism is a modern one we have been modern for all these years and centuries that it took "modern thought" to become modern, for we have never separated head and heart and hand. And as to setting man in his environment we have never sought the full-orbed life by separating man either from the cosmos or from God. If then our brief review of modern aspirations has shown that our opponents themselves have felt, have admitted and have shouted from the housetops that the full-orbed life can only come in a union of man with his total environment, why should we fear to proclaim that we have the full-orbed life inasmuch as we have that total environment in our concept of God and of the world?

It is this point too that we will have to keep in mind when shaping our educational policies. Our educational ideals and those of our opponents are as the poles apart. How impossible, then, for us to inculcate our ideals in any satisfactory way unless we have the educational influence all to ourselves. The modern emphasis upon environment is itself a warning to us not to be satisfied with injecting a grain of religion here and there in cooperation with an educational program that is radically opposed to our own. Then too, the fact that the emphasis is no longer upon the liberation of the head or the heart or the hand alone but upon the liberation of the whole personality, and the boldness with which this liberation is proclaimed ought to make us realize anew the extent to which the secularism of our age has advanced. The questionnaires that indicate a decrease in references to Deity in the readers used in schools today find their explanation in the movement we have traced above.

How glorious a task it must be then to teach in a Christian school! In the educational field it is that the struggle for or against God is being decided today. Teachers fight on the most dangerous sector of the front.

CORNELIUS VAN TIL

Address before the National Union of Christian Schools Convention, Hull, Iowa, August 18, 1931.

Key Thoughts:

1. The eighteenth century sought liberation of the head.

2. The nineteenth century sought liberation of the heart, or deeper unconscious impulses of man so native to him.

3. The early twentieth century sought liberation of the hand, or freedom of action.

4. Today we hear of the liberation of the whole personality.

5. How necessary are our Christian schools that strive not for liberation of man, but for the full-orbed life centered in God which is man's freedom!

Comment:

What do we seek to liberate by education? What are we trying to set free? Christian education has but one answer. It does not change its answer from century to century. The answer of Romans 7 is the answer for us today. We are seeking to liberate the new man from the shackels that still hold him bound in the dimensions of his personality. The barriers of the soul-life that keep the mind of Christ in him from expression must be leveled. The channels of his life must be cleared of all obstructions that he may develop into maturity as a son of God.

The basis for this freedom is genuine obedience from the heart. This obedience is an achievement in the soul-life of the youth. Christian education seeks to undergird the youth in achieving this obedience of faith.

4

The Man of God Thoroughly Furnished

"That the man of God may be perfect, thoroughly furnished unto all good works" (II Tim. 3:17 A. V.).

These words, written by the great missionary educator, were addressed to Timothy, who was a faithful and loyal young man. However, young Timothy was also afflicted with many weaknesses, and he was therefore constantly in need of admonitions and encouragement. He was very far from being perfect and thoroughly furnished unto all good works.

In the third chapter of this second epistle to Timothy Paul presents a tremendous contrast. First, we are informed what we must not do in order to be a perfect and thoroughly furnished man, and then we are instructed as to what program should be followed to achieve this great goal. His program can be properly labelled as the program of Christian education.

Paul mentions at least four classes of individuals whose example must be avoided if the man of God is to be perfect and thoroughly furnished. First, there are those who are lovers of their own selves. They are proceeding along the highway of sinful selfishness. Selfishness is always sinful, and sin always is disintegrating. The road that leads to unity of personality and to integration is one of love as presented in the summary of the law. Second, one must avoid the example of those who have only the form of godliness. This means that they are not integrated. They are one thing but they manifest themselves as being something else. That is hypocrisy. Again this road will lead a person away from the Christian objective indicated in the text quoted above. Third, one should avoid the example of those who are always learning but never arriving at the truth. Their minds are filled with inconsistencies. They must unlearn as much as they learn. There can be no progress. Such learners are not "of one piece." Mentally they are disintegrated. Fourth, those who are never making any progress cannot be examples of Christian development. Christianity is always dynamic. It is never static. Few knew better than Paul that men "do not attain" in his world and that the goal of Christian living is so high that their journey is always upward and onward. All such people as depicted by the Apostle cannot present to Timothy or any one else a type of the kind of education a person needs in order to be perfect and thoroughly furnished.

But continue *thou* in the things which thou has learned and been assured of. Timothy had been trained by Christian parents. He had been trained by a Christian teacher. He had been trained in the Scriptures which can make one wise unto salvation and which are calculated to make a man perfect, thoroughly furnished unto all good works.

In recent literature on education one can find the word "integration" used frequently and variedly. By integration we may mean and do mean a process in which the subject becomes a unity, an integer, if you please. And the entire educational process may be regarded as one by means of which a person becomes a unit, relieved of all sorts of contrary thoughts, emotions and wills. A man of God who is thoroughly furnished unto every good work is an integrated personality.

The Objects of Christian Education — Disintegrated Personalities

A. Examples of Disintegrated Personalities

1. An example from Scriptures. Psychologists have long since spoken and written about a dual personality, or about a multiple personality. They simply mean that there are persons who change so much on the several occasions as to represent different types of personalities in the various situations in which they find themselves.

I know of no more striking example of such a disintegrated personality than David, who has been called a man after God's own heart. This David is so different as we meet him on the various pages of Scripture that we would not be able to recognize him had he not been named. Yesterday he appeared to be a man of humility and lowliness. He seemed to be a perfect example of contrition and meekness as he fell on his knees before the living God. But today, he appears to be a man of pride. He vaunts the number of his mighty men of valor as he parades his army before the living God. His conduct is so reprehensible that it calls forth a severe rebuke from God. Yesterday, we found him to be a man of integrity. We would have trusted him with any and all of our belongings. But today, he is a cheat and deceiver. He deceives so cunningly and adroitly that even he who had reasons to suspect him was deceived. His great benefactor Achish was not able to detect an assumed madness. Yesterday we heard that he was chivalrous. He would tolerate no humiliating defeat to be administered to his deadly enemy. But today, we hear that he pronounced an awful curse upon the head of his able general, Joab. Yesterday, we were informed that he spared the life of Saul, whom he had in his power and who was intent upon killing him. He carried his consideration for his enemy to the point where he was literally flirting with death. But today, the news comes to us that he, in a most damnable way, killed his faithful soldier, when he disposed of Uriah, the Hittite.

Now such contrasts may be sharper in David than in many others, but they are nevertheless common to mankind. The most humble may be proud. The most trustworthy may be a cheat. The most chivalrous may lack that quality on other occasions. And the one who spared a life may take it. That is to say, personalities are not of "one piece." There is war within the personality occasioned by sin, the cause of any and all war. At any rate, those are the types of personalities that we send to our Christian schools for an education.

2. An example from fiction.   Several years ago Robert Louis Stevenson wrote *The Strange Case of Dr. Jekyll and Mr. Hyde*. It is a masterful portrayal of a case of dual personality. Dr. Jekyll was a kindly man, a lovable character, and a trusted friend of everyone in his community. Dr. Jekyll concocted a potion by means of which he could change himself into a beastly character. He became brutal, cruel and hideous. In short, he became an embodiment of all that is sinful and hateful. By means of another potion he could change himself back to Dr. Jekyll. But the potion that could change Mr. Hyde back into the congenial personality of a Dr. Jekyll became weaker as time went on, until at last Mr. Hyde could not be changed back into Dr. Jekyll. The poor man ended his life by suicide. This book constitutes a striking portrayal of a dual personality and of the fact that unless some divine intervention takes place the evil personality tends to "take over." Now that is the way with men. However, men do not need a special concoction to make the change for they already have it. It is sin. That disintegrates. And one cannot hope to remove the disintegration except by the removal of the cause. Christian education in some way must be a sin-removing process.

3. An articulation from St. Paul. The Apostle Paul could see this matter of dual personality very clearly. He realized it fully in his own life. He was not always the same. He was at variance with himself at times. He knew that "the good that I would I do not: but the evil which I would not, that I do" (Rom. 7:19). This great thinker carried this thought through and realized that man was not one but at least two. He himself could and did distinguish between the old man and the new man, or between the old and the new nature. These were worlds apart, yet harbored within the same person. He did not have in mind the many variations of the manifestation of personality which

are recognized by practically all students of the human species. He had in mind that deep clevage that existed in man by virtue of the work of the Spirit. He realized that sometimes the one man manifested himself and then again the other. He saw the fact of dual personality in its sharpest contrasts. No person is consistently and altogether bad, save the devil. And no man is altogether good, save the God-man. Christian teachers must realize that they have before them individuals manifesting the disintegration that Paul articulated.

4. The recognition by Jesus. Jesus came in touch with this phenomenon again and again. He always condemned it. The hypocrisy of the Jews was condemnable in his sight. This pretense clearly revealed the fact that they were not one, but more than one. They manifested one thing and were quite another. He recognized the situation when He informed the Jews that they could not serve God and Mammon. The fact is that they were endeavoring to carry out this dual service. Jesus condemned it. The articulation of the law of God in terms of undivided love is aimed at correcting a multiplicity of loves. Jesus found it in his disciples and certainly not least of all in Peter who was so devoted to the Lord and yet could deny Him.

The Christian teacher must recognize this phenomenon also. Jesus did and he taught his disciples accordingly and by his teaching sought to make them units, serving Him with undivided devotion.

B. *Conditions that Promote Disintegrated Personalities*

1. As found in the Church and articulated by Fosdick. In sin one can find the deepest cause for the situation indicated above. Sin has thrown everything out of proper adjustment. It has disintegrated that which was integrated. But there are various secondary causes that promote this thing known as multiple personality. There is for instance a natural tendency to adjust one's self to his environment. That is the way of least resistance. It is the easiest way to avoid friction. Harry Emerson Fosdick realized this principle and found it applicable to the church and condemned the church for it. He found that a church which finds itself in a nation at peace tends to become pacifistic. That same church tends to become militaristic in times of war. It is not right that it can be both. It can be one or perhaps something else. That church, he averred, will be red when placed in a red environment, and green in one that may be labelled as green. In the midst of a CIO environment it supports the CIO. In the midst of a capitalistic environment it is capitalistic. It is simply not of "one piece." He condemns it as he ought to. The church should lead, but seems to have been satisfied by being led. And if it is to be led by a

thousand different sorts of environments, it cannot escape the process of disintegration.

2. As found in our Christian homes and schools. This problem of varied environments causing disintegration of personalities can be found right at our homes and schools. The average home in which our children find themselves does not present a uniform environment. The motives found there are varied. The spirit that serves God is there. The spirit that serves self asserts itself. The spirit that seeks money, fame, and what have you, is there. No wonder that the child appears with conflicting motives when he arrives at school. The atmosphere at home may be charged with love, or hate, or coldness, and so on. All these things will fill the child with a confusion that may not be clearly detected but is nevertheless real. One can find the same situation in our schools. The teachers and the schoolmates represent a thousand different items to which adjustment must be made. Because of physical and emotional disturbances, even the teachers fail to represent a single front. And the pupil soon learns that he can be safely funny on some occasions and quite different on others. And so the problem of fitting a varying environment intensifies in many ways the problem of integration.

3. As found in our conception of God. The only safe environment is God Himself. If one can only develop a consciousness that the great determining and constant environment to which (Whom) adjustment must be made, we could develop a strong force toward integration. He is the same. He calls for no varied reaction. And surely the Christian schools are called upon to do nothing less than that. Even at this juncture we do not escape the disintegrating forces because we are constantly molding God over to suit our own fancy. He is a God of love when that suits us. A God of justice He is when that is the kind of God we want. He is a God who is a Father, a Judge, a Redeemer, a Creator, and so on, as we would like to have Him be. We must develop a comprehensive conception of God that is constant. Varied conceptions of God tend to disintegrate further still the disintegrated students or pupils.

The Aim of Christian Education — Integrated Personalities

A. The Encyclopedic Aim

There are many people that are quite convinced that the purpose of education is to load the mind of the pupils with facts. In fact these people were quite convinced that the only real difficulty with the pupils and students that failed to make proper adjustments to their environments was that they did not have sufficient facts. They were certain that no one would transgress the laws of this country if they knew all about its history, government, and so on. And they were equally sure that immorality would no more be found among the young people if all the facts of sex life were known. And so they developed a tremendous system of fact-dispensing. But the program failed to work out. We found that the more that the criminal knew about our country and its laws, the more effective did his criminality become. The more the people knew of the facts of life, the more they were tempted to indulge in immoral practices. The idea was fundamentally defective.

Strange as it may seem that aim is precisely what many in our circles would like to see realized in our own schools. Ask the average parent what he would like to see the Christian school do for his child; he will say to get him thoroughly acquainted with the Bible. The success of a teacher is measured by his or her ability to fill the pupil with Biblical material. The pupil that comes home and quotes a few Bible texts, and repeats a few Bible stories, and sings a few sacred hymns seems to have evidences of being well taught by a good Christian school teacher.

Far be it from me to deny the value of these things. But at best the memorization of Biblical material can be but a means to an end. Some of the cleverest atheists have an enviable knowledge of the Bible. We have seen boys and girls go bad, and then we exclaim that we cannot understand it because they have been taught differently and certainly know better. We little realized that individuals that know the Scriptures well can blaspheme a bit more heinously because they have at their disposal Biblical material, and for the same reason they can mock a bit more effectively. It is well to note that Jesus placed no special value upon minds well stocked with Biblical materials. He then would have sought his disciples among the well-educated Jews from Jerusalem, who were experts in Biblical material. But he preferred the Galileans who yielded their lives to the molding influences of the Gospel and manifested the truth as a living truth.

It is clear then that the mere knowledge of the facts of the world and of the Bible will not integrate. In fact, that may make the disintegration infinitely worse.

B. *The Mental Discipline Aim*

There are a host of educators that have realized that the encyclopedic objective will not suffice. They have felt it is much better to have a well-disciplined mind than a wealth of knowledge. They have seen individuals who seem to have a wealth of material at their command but do not seem to be able to use it. They are failures. And they have seen others with no education and with but limited knowledge who forge ahead in the world. It was thought therefore that what men need is the ability to think cogently, rapidly, and profitably. Such educators placed the emphasis upon the classics, mathematics, and every other branch of study that is calculated to be a mental stimulus.

But the results were disappointing. The method did not integrate. The criminal could outwit the law enforcement agencies. His crimes became a bit more clever. Crimes became more perfect. In the field of the moral, things appeared no better. Immoral practices went apace. The moral, social, and physical consequences by clever methods seemed to be practically nil. Men of great mental ability are not necessarily good men. In fact, they may because of their very cleverness be more multiple in their personality still.

Even Christian school advocates have insisted that this was a prime objective. They wanted the children to be trained mentally so that they can stand up before any foe. They did not want them to be tossed to and fro by every wave of doctrine. They must hold their own against any and all opposition. Now, I have often wished that I had more of that ability, particularly when another fellow had me placed securely in a corner. I would like to be able to silence every one that dares to raise his voice against me. But after all the motive is not a wholesome one. And even if the objective were achieved it would not guarantee integrated personalities. It is an objective that may be thoroughly selfish and genuinely sinful.

Some of the cleverest debaters that we have had in the field of religion were atheists. If you want to hear some clever debating, contact a representative of some fanatical sect. It is indeed possible to argue quite convincingly about the truth of the Gospel and still not believe a thing of it. That has been done repeatedly.

If Jesus wanted clever men, He would have looked for his apostles among the trained men at Jerusalem who were unusually well trained in the art of debating. These people could think well and quickly, but Christ placed no special premium upon clever heads and glib tongues. If there ever was a group of disintegrated individuals in the world it was those clever Jews who had the form of religion but not its heart. They were abominable to God.

C. The Character Aim

Many a leader in the educational work soon learned the futility of striving to realize the aims suggested above. "What we want," they insisted, "is good men, men of character, who can adjust themselves to their several environments and make themselves serviceable to God and man." So they trained the pupils to be correct, especially in form. The children were taught to say, Please, Pardon, Thanks, and so on. The loser in any game was taught to congratulate the winner. It developed a race of formalists who could say and act one thing and mean the very opposite. The Japanese were past masters at this. They could sink a Panay and square everything with a few *regrets* or *so sorry's.* But they were not very far ahead of the hypocritical Jews in Jerusalem. Their form was perfect. They would be called by the patriots of the time *good* people. But Jesus got their number and cried out in indignation against their formalism and admonished them for serving God in form, with their lips, but not with their hearts. And there are few individuals that are more disintegrated than they who are good in form but bad at heart.

D. The Redemptive Aim

Christian educational forces are directed toward the restoration of the image bearer of God. The child is to be conformed to the image of Christ. It is in that process that integration can be achieved. The unity was found in the insistence upon the God-centered view of things. Everything is viewed as God would view it. Thinking the thoughts after God was and should be the great educational objective. Pupils should be trained so that they cannot look at anything without seeing God, nor hear, touch, or taste anything without coming in vital connection with God. That is the way Jesus lived and He was fully integrated, perfect, and thoroughly furnished unto all good works.

The Method of Christian Education — Integration

A. The Method of Self-denial

Selfishness lies close to the origin of sin. And sin always disintegrates. Selfishness forces an individual to react differently to every different environment, so as to extract the most of it for personal gratification. If we cannot promote the eradication of selfishness from out of our pupils and students, we cannot carry forward the integration process.

Now self-denial is not a positive reaction. In the days gone by the Christians who mutilated themselves, deprived themselves of the necessaries of life, were not engaged in self-denial. Those exercises constituted a very positive form of self-assertion. The Jews did that very thing when they fasted with long faces in hypocritical fashion.

One denies himself when he does not know it. In the context where this injunction to deny one's self is found (Matt. 16) this position is clearly indicated. In the preceding context it is clear that Peter had not exercised self-denial because he had been mindful of the things of man and not mindful of the things of God. Had he been mindful of the things of God, this self-denial would have been a matter of course. To deny yourself is to think of and to be devoted to something else. In the following context the same suggestion is made, when the disciples are urged to lose their lives for Christ's sake and the Gospel's. No one loses anything by trying to. Losses are made when the subjects are not aware of it. No one, for instance, can forget anything by trying to forget. Such trying would involve keeping in the mind the very thing which he hoped to forget. Everyone knows that the only way to forget something is to think of something else. Self-denial can be exercised therefore only by thinking of God and not of self.

It may be well for practical purposes at this juncture to analyze the concept of self. It may be taken in its broadest sense. It cannot be made so broad that it is not applicable to the text. It was William James who defined self to be the sum total of that which I can call my own. That definition will do.

One could speak of the *material self*. In that self could be placed one's body. This body is so much a part of self that we are aggrieved or elated depending upon the condition of our bodies, or upon the reactions of others to them. Our relatives may also be included. In fact, this is sensed so clearly that when anybody makes some favorable comments about our relatives we swell with pride as if it were our own compliment; and if our relatives are shamed, we hang our heads as if it were our personal shame. Our clothes belong to that material self. Indeed, many ladies feel that their own personalities are expressed in their clothes, in the selection that they have made, and in the way that they wear them. If you wish to compliment some people, compliment their clothes. The products of one's hands and brains are also considered a part of the self. We talk about being impersonal in our criticism. That is next to impossible. No one can say anything about what I do without saying something very definitely about me. Perhaps the most striking case of this material self is that of the miser with his pile of gold. His hoarding seems to have no value except the expansion of the self. No grief is more bitter than his when he discovers that half of his gold was stolen during the night. Why all the grief? He did not expect to use any of that gold to buy some of the necessaries and luxuries of life. He expected to go to his grave without that pile of gold being diminished. Why then the grief? Because he experienced a partial reduction of self, a shrinkage of self.

That self must be denied. The children must be taught that if they are to be integrated they must deny this physical self. That does not mean that they must be deliberate about it. They need not wreck their body. Proper self-denial may mean building it up. It does not mean that they must seek to get away from their relatives nor that they run about in soiled garments, nor that they destroy or think depreciatingly about the work of their fingers and their minds. It just means that all their reactions to these things must be determined by their being mindful of God. The thought of God should control every aspect of their lives, which may mean the building up of these values, and perhaps their breaking down.

Jesus clearly indicated that conception when He said that he who would not leave his relatives and possessions for His sake was not worthy of Him. And when Peter boasted that he had left all and followed Him he was told in effect that he had done no more than that which was his duty to do. True, the body was not here listed by Jesus, and it could not be because it cannot be left in the sense that the other possessions can. Yet the body is clearly included, as seen from the Sermon on the Mount. "Take no thought of your body." That is a clear injunction. And in contrast to that order comes the command to be trusting in God. That is precisely the idea that we are advocating in this section.

There is also the *social self* to be denied. We have as many social selves as we have people in whose opinion about us we are interested. One may be a pious fellow in the presence of his Sunday school teacher, but he may swear like a trooper in the presence of his tough associates. A man may be chivalrous enough in the presence of a strange lady and yet be a brute at home. We sometimes say that we like him as a man, but he is a poor preacher. We may like someone as a politician and hate him when we view him from another angle. Note how concern about these various social selves disintegrates the subject.

This sin of asserting the social self, or the sin of social selfishness was bad among the Jews. They loved the chief seat in the synagogues. They made broad their phylacteries and they enlarged the borders of their garments. They longed to be hailed as Rabbi. They were terribly selfish socially.

This according to the Scriptures must also be denied. Jesus taught so clearly. One may pray in public, but not to be seen of men. That would make it social selfishness. Hence one is advised to go into the inner chamber so that he may be only seen of God. It is all right to give gifts in public, but it is social selfishness when it is done to be seen of men. That is condemned by the Christ. It may be advisable to fast but not merely to be seen of men. That again is selfishness from a social angle. All these things must be done only to be seen of God. That makes a person of "one piece."

There is such a thing as a *psychological self*. Men have since time immemorial been divided into a thinking, emotional and volitional being. To get an inkling of how much the thinking ability of a person is a part of himself, one needs but to say of another that he does not know very much, or that he is a bit off. Nothing seems to cut quite so deeply into the self, and nothing hurts the person more severely. That intellectual self must be denied. That does not mean that one must quit thinking, but that he must think being mindful of God. And deeper thinking is required of none other than of him who tries to follow the deep thoughts of God. The emotional self is also real. Men do not care to be criticized about their lack of love, hope, and other emotional qualities. This side of self need not be crushed so that the self becomes a sort of Stoic self. Nowhere is greater emotion required than in the Christian religion where a person is asked to love God with all that he has, and when he is asked to fear the righteousness of God with the most intense fear. To deny one's volitional self does not mean at all that the Christian is to have no will, but that he is to will the will of God. And that in a world of sin, within and without, calls for a tremendous volitional effort.

So one could continue deciphering the self. But it makes no difference how you tear the man apart, at every step this same fundamental requirement holds. One cannot be integrated until he has learned to regard all that he has and is and knows in the light of God's will.

B. A Positive Definition of Aim

Of course, it is not necessary to tell the pupils what the objective is. But the teacher must be clear on it. One cannot merely teach. One must teach towards something. One must answer the question, What shall I teach my pupils to be like? There are a thousand answers to that question. One may have lesser objectives, such as training lawyers, doctors, instructors, builders, and so on. But there is nothing distinctive about it. In fact, if that is all that is wanted, there is no excuse for the expenditure of Christian education. I know of no higher objective than that of developing integrated personalities. The purpose is then to promote lives entirely free of duplicity, minds free of confusion, and desires free of contrary directions. An integrated personality is one which finds all things centered in God, coming from

God, evaluated by God, existing for God. It is a matter of making Christlike individuals. And Christ was a fully integrated person.

C. Maintaining of Consistency

There is no surer way of developing disintegrated personalities than that of permitting the various educational forces to be pulling in opposite directions. When the home by the conduct of the members or by the literature found there or by the radio programs that enter directs the child into the field of the secular and the Church draws the child into the field of the sacred, it cannot but develop lack of integrity. If the school pulls the child into still a third direction, one can expect nothing but hopeless confusion. It is therefore of the greatest importance that the various forces that train the child pull in the same direction. It may not at all be amiss that the educating authorities of the home, the school, and the church get together so as to assure each other that they are all striving toward the same goal.

Even within the school it is possible that the various teachers having the same child in the same term or in successive terms may unbeknown to each other be promoting disintegration in the child's life. Christian school teachers should have many conferences, and rechecking of their methods and aims.

D. A Controlled Atmosphere

It is, of course, well known to all that it is beyond the competency of any teacher to inject the Christ-life into the veins of the child. No sane person expects that of the teacher of his child. But what the teacher can do is to surround that child with a spiritual atmosphere so that he cannot reach out without touching God from some angle. Even misdemeanors on the playground or in the classroom can be converted into a situation where God appears on the scene. Let all the branches of learning bring God into the life of the child. This atmosphere should also be controlled in the home. It can be done by the attitudes, the words, the discussions, the spirit, the placards on the wall and so on. One will not have to change the world to effect this controlled atmosphere. They need not be in a sinless place. Proper reaction to sin brings God immediately into the situation. And that is true of every possible condition. God is always there and needs but to be brought into the consciousness. That makes for integrated personalities.

There is no greater task for man than to unite what sin has torn apart. There is no nobler calling than to integrate what sin has disintegrated. To that task the Christian school teacher is called. And by pursuing such a task the Christian teacher is cooperating with God toward developing men and women thoroughly furnished unto all good works.

HENRY SCHULTZE

Address before the National Union of Christian Schools Convention, Orange City, Iowa, August 18, 1942.

Key Thoughts:

1. The child is by nature a disintegrated personality.

2. This disintegration originates both from within and from without the child.

3. The aim of Christian education is the development of integrated personalities.

4. Integration of one's personality can be achieved only by learning to regard all he is, has, and knows in the light of God's will. This requires self-denial.

5. The aim of personality integration must be consistently followed in home, school, and church on the same basis if integration is to be effected at all.

6. Integration cannot be imposed upon the child, but we can surround the child with a spiritual atmosphere so that he cannot reach out without touching God.

7. The Christian school is to seek integration of what sin has disintegrated.

Comment:

When we begin to take the integration of the child's personality in the classroom seriously, something will happen to our educational program in the nature of a reform. The implications of this overall purpose for the school reach into the whole of the child's schooling.

In a sense good teachers have always made this their aim. They seek to understand children because they love them for Christ's sake. They employ the subject matter as a medium and try to make the child secure in the understanding and mastery of it. They discipline children in love. The children constantly feel the loving embrace of a teacher who loves from the heart.

The Christian school will begin to take the integration of personality seriously when its entire program is organized to accomplish what these good teachers spontaneously do from the heart. When so organized, Christian schools give good teachers a fuller opportunity to employ their resources for teaching.

5

The Social Aim in Christian Education

Teachers have no doubt frequently wondered how much of his education the child gets through the agency of the school. Answers to such a query are sure to be different. Still I think all will agree that the child gets at least half of his education outside of the very place intended for that purpose. I am convinced that in many cases he gets by far the greater part of his education not in the school room but on the street, on the playground, at the swimming hole, at home, and where not.

For the average boy the eight years of primary education used to be (and perhaps still is) a rather unnatural process through which he was forced to pass, from which he was ever eager to escape, and compared with which holidays and vacations were oases in a varitable desert of weariness (unless perchance he was a character forcible enough to contribute to his own and others' education by his unlawful antics in the schoolroom). After eight years of such training it would indeed be strange if he did not develop a wrong "slant" on life.

You may reply that real education is after all something intangible and that one does not have to recall the tangible side of education. I agree and this is exactly my contention, that it is the intangible that counts in education. But I would immediately add, and of this I am convinced, that the school has not been as much of a positive force in this intangible way as it should have been, that the real education of many a child for good or evil has not come from the school but from other influences. In other words it was life (not only school life) that did the educating while the school was supposedly preparing the child for life.

Apart from any other possible aims that it may be serving, education does not today realize the social aim. Quite obviously the social purpose of education may be considered to be the attainment of better organization in society. Organization is however something external and can continue only if it is the product of something in the lives of men that calls for better organization. In other words society cannot be bettered unless there is a living desire for better society, unless civilization becomes something full of meaning and of desire for the individuals who make up society. And civilization as a living force cannot be attained unless individuals are brought to an understanding of and a desire to realize the real meaning, the real fulness of life. Education is the process by means of which this understanding of life is brought to men and by means of which the idea of civilization, of living together for the best interests of men, is nourished and developed in the lives of men.

* * *

The social purpose of education is the helping of the individual to an understanding of the wholeness, the unity of all of life, to an understanding of the beauty of that unity, and to an ordering of his own life so that in it he may achieve organic oneness of body, mind, and soul and organic oneness of himself with his fellow men and with his God. The end of education in this sense is a world of men and women sound in body and mind, beautiful and accomplished, intelligent and reverent, devoted to the task of becoming perfect followers of God. The real end is the "largest attainable measure of perfection." Education is immoral if it does not help us to achieve this end.

In a large sense all education is social as well as individual. In fact it is a truism today that one cannot really speak of the one of these terms without speaking of the other. Real education of the individual ought to mean social development; social betterment implies the highest development of the individual. In other words, the social purpose is real human living resting on a rounded development of the individual; it is real unity and harmony of the individual with his fellows, harmony of the individual with all of the universe.

To realize the social purpose of education involves the understanding of social life, of all life in fact, involves in short a philosophy of life. This should be evident from the little we have said so far — you cannot work toward the achieving of a social purpose unless you have one, and you cannot have one without having a view of life of your own. We have really proceeded on the basis of one in assuming the organic oneness of all life, of all creation.

Hence the Christian who insists upon Christian education is quite consistent. He has a view of life on the basis of which he can develop a social aim, and toward the accomplishment of that aim he can organize his educational efforts.

Our leaders agree that the essence of Calvinism is this: "that God is in immediate communion with His own who in turn, bowing before the sovereignty of High God, live their whole lives in His presence." (T. Van der Kooy, *The Distinctive Features of the Christian School*, p. 22).

The unity of man with his Creator could not be better expressed than it is here. This is the central thought of the Christian's view of life. It is God-centered — everything in life has its origin, its life, its existence in Him, and all things function together and severally to attain His purpose. Every part of creation has its purpose and everything in creation stands in definite relation to and in dependence upon everything else. The Christian believes in the fullest development of every side of man's nature, the development of his relation to nature, to the animal world, to his fellow men, and to his God. The Christian believes in the organic nature of all creation and must consistently stress this in his ideal of education as Johann Sturm does in his expression of the purpose of education: "True piety in organic relation with thorough knowledge and genuine culture" (Van der Kooy, *op. cit.,* p. 40). Professor B. K. Kuiper stresses this in his *Ons Opmaken en Bouwen* (p. 183) when he insists that everything in this world is organic, that therefore all the factors in education must be emphasized and that none of the factors can be educative if they do not fulfill their purpose.

It is man who must see to the realization of this organic relationship in all its possibilities. He must see to it that education accomplishes this: that man as an individual may live most fully, richly, abundantly, beautifully in and in relation to his natural environment, that he may grow into beautiful fellowship with his fellow men, that, as an individual and as a social whole he may glorify God. The stumbling of one side of life makes an inroad upon another.

The primary end of education is perfection, the attainment of consistency in all of life so that man may truly become a companion of God. In order that this fundamental ideal may be fulfilled each individual must develop the highest possible degree of social serviceability and the highest possible degree of personality. These two are inseparable although frequently stressed as if they could be separated.

This is too idealistic you say. I grant that it is idealistic but I contend that your success in attaining the real purpose of education will depend upon your really seeing and knowing the ideal. One may readily fall into error by failing to see the ideal in all its fulness. Let me illustrate by means of lessens which the splendid little book of Van der Kooy brings home to us.

Van der Kooy believes that the central thought of Calvinism is this, that God is in immediate communion with His own who in turn live their whole life in His presence. From this central idea there follows (according to him) first, a strong sense of the absolute character of truth and of goodness, and secondly, a belief in the objectivity of truth. He insists that the Calvinist is opposed to subjectivity and is certainly right when he says that the Calvinist is opposed to a "subjectivism in which man is the criterion of all things, his own King and Lawgiver" (p. 25). He insists that submission to the absolute, submission to the objective is one of the principal characteristics of the Christian school and that "the Christian school is marked in general by a certain tranquility, a calm objectivity" (p. 25).

Here however is a real danger, a danger that our schools may be marked by more than tranquility, by mere complacency because of a cold subjection to objective authority. Van der Kooy himself does not want complacency — what he wants is "the calm of innate power and strength which is the result of being rooted in a life view," "the tranquility of the oak, the king of trees, firmly rooted." He insists, as Bavinck does, that "He who is instructed in the Scriptures rises to a height from which he surveys the great totality of things" (p. 26). But there is a danger (perhaps even the result of our insisting upon the objective) that we may leave everything to God as if we had nothing to do with the matter. We should be the most ardent subjectivists of all those who believe in any subjectivity whatsoever. In fact we should be so extremely and continuously objective as to be subjective. We must truly live our whole life *in God's presence;* then we shall be both objective and subjective at the same time. This Van der Kooy admits when he speaks of innate power and when he speaks of the covenant child as "already included in the ranks of King Jesus, whose insignia he bears" (p. 69). To repeat, there is a danger of our education being one sided, cold, apart because of its insistence on the objective. This need not be the result if we but become so objective as to be in fact subjective, if we but serve Christ so intensely as to be one with Him. We need to envisage the whole of the ideal, to see every aspect of it.

There is danger also of a certain amount of asceticism, of a cutting off of certain interests in the life of the Christian. If any individual should live a well rounded life the Christian should. Those who urge resignation, renunciation, contentment have hardly caught sight of the real splendor of life, of the fulness of the purpose of education. Contentment is likely to be a coward's doctrine — we must live fully, abundantly. True, we must accept life as God has intended it, we must accept the universe as it is, we must accept the life that God has given us, but we may not accept the present moment, the present situation as the one intended for all time. We may not be contented with our present individual status, religiously, for example, nor may we be contented with the present social order.

The Christian's ideal of education is something beyond this life. Very good, but what does that mean for this life? It has no meaning apart from this life — does it not mean a fulfillment, a perfecting of this life? If it is to be attained hereafter, it is to be attained here and now. We are in danger of making the same kind of distinction between the present and the beyond that we make between the objective and subjective, and we are, therefore, in danger of not seeing things whole.

Van der Kooy rightly insists that the ideal must be the organic relation of the pupil's capacities as of one created in the image of God (p. 41). This is the ideal of education, but to what extent do we insist on it? Even Van der Kooy after insisting on this beautiful purpose refers to the training of the body as if it were but an after thought.

*   *   *

Let us turn now to some weaknesses of education in general. It is a matter of common knowledge that the child is eager to think, is desirous of activity mental as well as physical. Education is, however, a matter of strain for the child, something that he ever enjoys getting away from — and we ourselves contribute to this very tendency by our emphasis on vacations, etc. Children come to look forward to respite instead of mingled work and pleasure. They get a wrong view of life.

What is wrong? Why so much of partial death in education?

Undoubtedly one of the reasons is the fact that we do not succeed in getting the child interested in school life. The school should develop the child's interest, it should develop his will power — instead it forces him to do what he is not interested in until his will power is broken (unless strengthened by the ordeal). Education should guide the development of the child's innate capacities, better still it should get him interested in that which will develop them, or make him want to develop them himself. One of the tragic commentaries on the school is this, that instead of taking the child's fears and turning them with love into wisdom and strength it frequently turns them into torment and leaves the child — a broken vessel. The weakness especially of public education is that, having all the modern opportunities for education, it does not give the child sufficient motive to go on with it all, it does not get the child to care. Our public education lacks one thing necessary to any real education, a foundation, a life view which will give real motive power to those educating and those being educated.

Another weakness of general education is this, that it is planned for the superior scholar, not the inferior. It is not (at any rate was not formerly) educational at all in the sense of developing something that is not yet there. It merely uses the best of the students and the others tag along, education for them being a very negative something. Education, as C. H. Henderson says, does not make for power, it merely uses it. It is selective of the best and virtually throws overboard the others; worse still, we are usually proud that we can eliminate them. If there is any truth in the theory of the organic relation of all things that we profess, we will have to (and do in fact today) pay for our neglect of the inferior.

Another weakness is this, that we attempt to teach too much. Let us seriously ask ourselves the question, what is the real end of education, and if it is what the Calvinist professes, the organic development of all the capacities of man as the image bearer of God, let us review all that we try to pump in and measure our degree of success. We do not like to hear the selfmade man speak of his success, but his success is a commentary on the real purpose and success of all that we try to teach. Less of actual drilling in of lessons and more of the living out of them even in the schools will help us nearer to our ideal.

This suggests another weakness that we are becoming aware of. Education was until recently a rather mechanical drilling of the mind as if the mind could be separated from the body and as if the individual mind could be successfully drilled apart from the association of real life. "Any attempt to separate our work, to cultivate the heart, or the mind, or the body quite alone is doomed to failure, for the organism does not so act" (C. H. Henderson, *Education and the Higher Life,* p. 116). We must deal with every detail of daily life; education must grow out of life, must grow naturally out of the life of the child. The school must furnish the child with "growth-situations" as Van Der Kooy has it.

It is the fundamental aim of all education then to help children to find their places in life, to give them an idea of their responsibility for the life they live as well as an idea of the worthwhileness of the life they can live; in other words, to teach them to know God's will and to do it. More particularly, the social aim, as we have intimated before, is the training of the child to take his place in society and to work there for himself and his fellows so that the social relationships they form may conform to the ideal of education just mentioned. And all of this necessarily involves the highest possible development of personality on the part of the individual. Since the child cannot be of social service unless he develops personality and since the development of personality is impossible apart from social relationships, education which is to give both must from the beginning be social as well as individual.

Organic education means the training of the body and the mind and the training of the two together as dependent on each other. Writers tell us today that one of the finest ways to train the brain is to train the senses. What are we doing to enrich the sense perceptions of the child? In the case of Swedish gymnastics the end is not so much the developing of a certain set of muscles as the training of the body and the mind at the same time. The end is a body responsive to the calls of the mind and a mind that is made alert and kept alert by the very drills that develop the body. Organic education means training the individual as an entity, all the parts of which must function together. So also it means education of individuals in the very midst of society in order that they may function together naturally, harmoniously, that each may carry on his own work of his own accord.

*   *   *

How shall we accomplish this aim? I would rather leave the answer to the teachers themselves. Still I should like to make a few suggestions. We want to overcome the narrowness that characterizes much of our teaching, the peddling out of knowledge in the class room, in laboratory explanations, in lectures, etc. We want to get away from the catechetical method of imparting knowledge. We want to get away from teaching that gives the pupil the idea that education is a sort of guessing game in which the pupils do the questioning and the teacher knows the answer. We want children to begin reasoning for themselves as soon as possible. We want them to study the facts for themselves, we do not want them to rely always on the teacher or the textbook. We want them prepared in school for life in the richest possible way, not necessarily in the way of receiving knowledge of the manual arts but in the way of receiving real culture that will enable them to fit into industrial, social and religious life without painfully having to make their way for themselves after they get out of school.

As a step in this direction the kindergarten has come to be very generally accepted. In fact we realize that it is in the kindergartens that we need the best teachers. But having admitted that, we rather thoughtlessly send the kindergartners out into the mechanical routine of the grades. We must introduce the naturalness, the group work, and the group play aspect of the kindergarten into the rest of the grades. The child likes to reason and it is by reasoning that he develops, but it is social organization that greatly stimulates the process by giving the individual reasoner both the help of criticism and the sense of social serviceableness in the case of success. In the same way all of education is social and individual.

It is up to us as teachers whether we wish to let little groups become interested in projects of their own or whether we wish to introduce other and better methods of achieving the social aim. It is necessary that we do find some way of making primary and high school work as human as that of the kindergarten. If accumulating a little knowledge is not the chief end of education it is high time that we begin to consider how the child may in the school be prepared to take his place in the world outside. Get the child to get what he does through his own efforts, and enlist every child in the effort of the whole group. The purpose is the inculcation of "creative responsibility." What educators want and what we should want as Christian teachers is a type of education that will enable each child to realize his possibilities and that will get him of his own accord, on his own initiative, to throw himself into the social relationships of later life. We want to give him a motive for that participation so that impelled by that motive he will find himself and thus work for his fellows and his God. Our desire for the child should be that he live simply, that he care deeply, that he live energetically, that he live passionately in order that living thus he may develop every capacity and live fully in every relation of life.

Henry J. Ryskamp

Address before the National Union of
Christian Schools Convention, Grand
Rapids, Michigan, August 25, 1926.

Key Thoughts:

1. Education in school has lacked the unity of life. The organic unity of life has been broken up by the one-sided emphasis upon knowledge-getting.

2. The Christian views the individual and life in their unity. The primary aim of education is to realize this unity in the life of the child.

3. We see, however, that education is often as divisive in the child's life as it is unifying. Four reasons, from among others, might be given:

    a. We fail to stimulate real child interest.

    b. Only the superior children have a real chance.

    c. We attempt to teach too much.

    d. We attempt to train the mind in isolation from the whole of the child.

Comment:

The Dutch have an expression which says, "Alle onderwys moet opyoedkundig zyn." Freely translated this means that all instruction must nurture, bring up a child to maturity. Knowledge-getting apart from the unity of life fails to nurture, bring up the child. It acts as a divisive force. Real education, when present, takes place in spite of it because the child has hold on the unity of life from some other source.

When the school retains the unity of the individual and life that the child experiences before entering school and enriches and enlarges that unity, it nurtures and matures him in his total personality. There can be no genuine Christian education without this unity. Developing the curriculum and the learning process to promote this unity in the school is one of the challenges that comes to the Christian school today.

6

Our Urgent Mission

When we consider a task to be done or a mission to be performed our thoughts naturally break up into two main streams. We rather naturally think of the setting in which the mission must be carried out and the mission as such. First of all then we shall turn to the setting in which our urgent mission must be performed.

The Setting

We can gain a clearer understanding of this setting if I introduce to you a person whom we frequently meet today. I shall not tell you his name. Rather let me introduce him to you by telling you some significant things about him.

The first thing we must say about this man is that he is not a deeply and truly religious man. He has little use for the church. If he does attend occasionally it is as a matter of social respectability or as an escape from certain tensions. The spirit of worship and adoration of God Almighty does not characterize his life. God's name is often freely used in profanity, hardly at all in reverence and awe.

What about this man's morals? They are much like his "religion." No great moral law controls him. His morals are no more than the most convenient thing for him to do on a particular occasion. He will promise you that he will do so and so. He may do it, he may not do it. He will do what meets his convenience regardless of his commitment.

His intellectual life is in a sorry state. It is just about as bare as Old Mother Hubbard's cupboard. Very often his highest intellectual achievement is the wisecrack, which he probably picked up by listening for long periods to inane radio programs. If you present him a carefully formulated opinion he will probably say, "Nuts to you, I have just as much right to my opinion as you have to yours." His reading matter is largely limited to propaganda stuff that suits his prejudices. Critical books or articles written on the high level of principle are the "bunk" to him.

This person's taste in music and art is largely wretched — if it can be called taste at all. He listens to outlandish noises and he calls these noises music. He finds his art in pin-ups and magazine covers. If he reads books he finds them on the drug store book shelf.

This man is, of course, a part of the whole social pattern. How about his sense of social responsibility and justice? His social sense is generally low. It is largely governed by a desire to gain all the advantages for self and to avoid the responsibilities of social, political and economic inter-relationships. If you should try to point out to him that his desire to gain certain advantages should be governed by more regard for his neighbor he may reply, "We're gettin' ours while the gettin's good; now's our chance."

Who is this man I am speaking about?. His name is legion. There are many of him. There is a whole mass of him. He has become a dominant force in the political and cultural life of our times. Possibly he has become the dominant force in our times.

Where does this man come from? What has produced him?

To understand this man about whom I have been speaking there are, it seems to me, three important factors in our present cultural situation which we must reckon with. A knowledge of these three factors is indispensable if we would become thoroughly acquainted with this person I have introduced to you. Permit me to present to you a sociological factor, an intellectual factor and a psychological factor.

The Sociological Factor

Of utmost importance in analyzing the cultural situation of our time is the fact of the tremendous growth in the political power of the common man. Political power used to be in the hands of a select group. By and large those wielding this power were trained to exercise it. And the masses were largely content to accept this rule by the few with its sharply varying degrees of perfection and imperfection.

You and I know what has happened to this select group that once held the political power. In the course of the last century or more kings and princes have been toppled from their places of special power. Or, they have been reduced to places of relative impotence compared to the power they once held. Liberal democracy has swept across the west and the common man possesses a power that he never dreamed of before. Furthermore, this power has taken on the proportion it has also because of the benefits that technical science has brought to mankind in general.

Some may ask, is not this development a good thing? Is it not a good thing that the common man has been rescued from the oppression of the intrenched political power of kings and czars?

Of course we believe that this development has in the main been a good thing. We believe in democracy. We are happy that the common man has achieved a liberty and a position he did not have before.

It is at this point, however, that we have to be careful. The wider distribution of political power may or may not be a good thing. It all depends on who wields this power. In our discussion it depends upon what we mean by the "common man" or the "mass-man."

The distinction between the common man and the mass-man on the one hand and the special man or the non-mass-man on the other hand is not a distinction of wealth. Nor is it a distinction of social position. The difference between these two is a cultural distinction, yes, a spiritual distinction. For this reason one finds the mass-man among rich and poor alike, among those occupying a socially privileged position as well as among those on a "lower" social stratum.

In describing the difference between the mass-man and the non-mass man I follow the fine discussion in Jose Ortega y Gasset's book, *The Revolt of the Masses,* a book that persists in holding a respectable place among students of modern culture. Ortega states, correctly I think, that the mass-man is a man who recognizes no real standards. There are no significant spiritual, moral or cultural standards that govern his driving desire and will. He wants to be a law unto himself. On the other hand the special type of man, the non-mass-man recognizes the existence of standards which he regards and honors in the control and expression of his life.

It is the common man as thus described that has come to power in modern times. He is governed by no real spiritual, moral or cultural standards. His life moves on the level of what he wants or what he thinks he ought to have. And since that is the case, he does not hesitate to use whatever means he deems necessary in order to gain the ends he seeks. We have seen again and again that the mass-man will invest everything in an all-powerful government in order to gain the advantages he seeks, advantages not determined by high standards and not counter-balanced by accompanying responsibilities.

In my judgment it is not hard to trace this movement of the mass-man and his new political power in recent history. Communism and socialism are definitely mass-man movements. They operate somewhat differently to be sure. Yet they are one in that in one form or another they are expressions of the political power of the mass-man. The fascist movements were such too. Italy's fascism under the fatuous Mussolini was a popular movement of the common man. Hitler's nazism was also such a movement, a movement in which the common man surrendered all to those who promised security. Although lacking in the matter of popular assent Russian communism is also a movement in which the common man is seeking to give to the mass of men a certain kind of security, a security quite contemptible in the eyes of the non-mass-man.

There seems to be sufficient evidence by which to declare that the socialist movement in England is basically of the same character. Reports of the decline of standards in the nationalized medical profession are too frequent to ignore. On this count and on others we see in Britain too the characteristic decay of standards of the mass-man in power.

Furthermore (there are those who will disagree with me violently at this point), it is my considered opinion that the type of political and social movement that has dominated the American scene for these past twenty or more years is also basically a movement of the common man as we have described him. With persistent pre-occupation with physical things the mass-man in our land has demonstrated his essential character by seeking advantages continually and not wishing to accept the accompanying responsibilities. We have become a nation of people who seek more and more good *things,* more and more security, more and more creature comforts, but we have become increasingly irresponsible, undisciplined, a nation of people showing little respect for genuine spiritual, moral and cultural standards. To be sure I am grateful for the improved position of certain elements in our population today. I am glad, for instance, that the labor group has achieved a self-respecting position from which they can seek to gain just objectives for themselves as free men. But in many instances the predominant political and social movement in America in recent years has shown little respect for those high standards that must govern all human effort and striving if true freedom and true human blessedness are to be achieved.

The Intellectual Factor

The second factor which we must appreciate if we would understand the modern cultural situation is of an intellectual character. In getting at this important matter I will simply say that essentially the most important influence in the thought life of our times is the development of the natural sciences. This development with its roots in the history of philosophy in thinkers like Descartes and John Locke has had a tremendous bearing on our way of life and thinking. With mathematics as its instrument the natural scientist has great accomplishments to his credit. So impressive were these achievements that the scientist began to feel that he could include every aspect of life and experience in his tight world of natural laws. Even man, complex and troublesome creature that he is, could be brought into the compass of the natural scientist's scheme. This was particularly the case after the work of Darwin in the field of evolution and the work of Wilhelm Wundt in psychology in the nineteenth century.

In this highly important development of the method and scope of the natural sciences two things must be carefully noted. In the first place, the scientist assumed that he could carry out his method and program without reference to God or to absolute truth. All metaphysics and all absolutes had to take their places on the discard pile with ghosts and witches and myths. The scientist could conquer the universe and usher in the millennium without such leftovers from the pre-scientific past. Natural law would be his absolute.

The second matter of note in this development of the natural sciences is the important place given to the natural laws that are supposed to govern the development of life. I refer to the theory of evolution. If man is the resultant of a process of natural laws working in an evolutionary development, then the thought structure that man may develop is also the result of such a process. If that is the case then it does not make any real difference what a man thinks. It is all the result of the working of natural laws anyway. It is obvious that a complete relativism results from such thinking. For this reason we have often heard in modern times that it does not make any real difference what a man believes. All that matters is that he be sincere and that he gain some spiritual enrichment and support out of what he believes. Therefore, all questions of truth and value are approached from the pragmatic point of view. Whatever ideas and concepts prove useful and helpful to man are the proper ideas at the time. The test of truth no longer exists. All sense of truth is lost in the wilderness of relativism.

To be wholly up to date we should point out that the intellectual situation has undergone a change from the position just now described. The change is a rather subtle one. The scientist used to think of natural laws in absolute terms. Natural law was his god. Today the scientist no longer regards natural laws as ironclad and fixed. Today the law of the scientist is a matter of probability, not a matter of certainty. The natural law is today a statistical average. The scientist used to say B always follows A. Today the scientist says that B usually follows A; so far as he knows it has always followed A, but that is no guarantee that it always will. The natural law today is simply a matter of statistics. As a result the sense of absoluteness and stability once gained from natural law is gone and the relativism referred to above is even more of a void than it was before. So much is this the case that intellectuals like Bertrand Russell and W. T. Stace frankly tell us that the thinking man today must be satisfied with a universe of hopelessness and despair.

The Psychological Factor

So far we see the modern picture as follows: the common man, that is, the man without moral and cultural standards, has a pattern of thought and life that rules out regard for fixed truth. He lives in the world of utter relativism, a world where there is no framework of truth in which standards may be fixed.

Now we turn to the third important factor in the modern situation. This third factor has to do with the nature of man himself. A rather fundamental change in man's understanding of the nature of his own being has taken place as the science of psychology has developed. Up to rather recent times the idea has held sway in a rather uncritical fashion that the intellect was supreme in man's make-up. For centuries the idea of the Greeks in this regard has prevailed. The Greeks had the idea that the intellect ruled supreme in man, that it was the mark of divinity in man.

As Heidbreder points out in her book entitled *Seven Psychologies,* there is almost universal agreement among psychologists today that the intellect is not the master that men had thought. In fact we have found that there are forces, drives in man that are far more powerful than the intellect. That careful theologian Bavinck saw this point too as he told us that "the emotions and passions play a much greater role in the life of the individual person and in the history of people in general than does the pure (*gezond*) understanding. They are the most weighty factors and the most powerful forces that we know in the world of men." These powerful energies in man take the form of a yearning for affection, a will to power, a drive for prestige. In short, psychology today thinks of man in terms of energy — driving, pushing energy.

These, then, are the three important factors we would say one must understand if he would get a clear picture of the situation in which we must perform our urgent mission. What do these factors mean? We can summarize their thrust in just a few words. Today we have to consider a tremendous mass of human energy driving onward relentlessly without the controls that are formulated by standards of truth and right and cultural worth. A tremendous mass of mankind is surging in a relativistic chaos.

What is the end of such a process? What happens when energy is allowed to spend itself without adequate controls? What happens when you start a car and then let that quantity of energy bound ahead without proper controls? What happens when a child is allowed to develop without controls? The end of such a process is always and simply destruction. And that we dare say is precisely what the cultural situation adds up to today. There are in this situation dynamic factors which, if unchecked and uncontrolled, can end only in the destruction of all that is precious and beautiful and rich in the world in which God has placed us, placed us for the purpose of developing all things in this world for His praise and glory.

The Mission

How can we meet the critical situation we have just outlined? What is the answer? What is our urgent mission?

Obviously the answer lies in the area of human personality. Our problem is not so much with things, not with machines, not even with atomic bombs. Our problem, as has ever been the case, lies with men.

The situation requires that kind of personality that will so express the energies within himself that they are freely directed toward the proper ends and subjected to the proper controls.

How shall we develop such centers of human energy so directed and controlled? The answer that will quickly come to the mind of many is "Evangelism." And in that suggestion I can readily concur. Certainly personality can be re-made only by the grace which resides in the gospel of redemption in Christ Jesus.

However, I cannot concur in the suggestion without reservation in view of what is commonly understood and practiced as evangelism today. In the first place it must be said that much of what is called evangelism is not thoroughgoing enough. It is too commonly assumed that a decision after a stirring appeal, possibly under the pressure of mass excitement, means that the issue of that person's spiritual condition has been settled. The making of a "new creature" for whom "all things are of God" is too profound a process to be sought by the often flimsy methods and appeals of much "evangelistic" effort. Furthermore this type of evangelism tends to develop a cleavage between the spiritual life of the individual concerned and the world in which he is expected to develop his Christian personality and which he must subdue for the glory of God the creator of all.

How shall we meet the situation we have outlined above? With some reluctance we have criticized much of modern evangelism as inadequate for the task. What is our urgent mission? Is it the typical

American popular education of today? Does the contemporary public school meet the situation? Decidedly not. Public school education is caught in the very process we have been describing. Just one fact will bear that out. Has not John Dewey stressed again and again that there must be no absolute standards that are superimposed upon the educational process? The standards are to be set by the process itself. Hence, public school education is caught in this deteriorative process and is therefore being subjected to vigorous criticism from many sources. Particularly vigorous are the writings of Bernard Iddings Bell, who in his book *Crisis in Education* has charged that popular American education is betraying the common man's children by giving them a standardless education that does not educate.

What then is our urgent mission in the light of our present cultural situation? Our urgent mission is simply Christian education, genuine Christian education. In saying this we are not setting Christian education and evangelism over against each other. Rather we would think of true Christian education as including evangelism and evangelism as demanding Christian education.

When we say that Christian education is our urgent mission, there are particularly three things which we would stress with regard to this thoroughgoing training of the personalities of men. These three matters are to be related to the three major factors that we have described as making up the setting in which our urgent mission is to be performed.

True Education for the Common Man

The education which is called for must first of all be an education for the common people. Our schools may not become schools for the privileged, for the so-called rich as over against the poor. They may not cater to any special group in the social order. The common man is here in large numbers and he has received a new place in the sun. We must reckon with that fact.

However, we too would be betraying the common man and his children if we left the matter there. To be sure, this is the "century of the common man," to use Henry A. Wallace's phrase. But just because a man is common and just because there may be many of them does not mean that we must accept that fact as our starting point in the educational process. Yes, Abraham Kuyper spoke about the "kleine luiden." But I dare say that his "kleine luiden" were not the same as the common man that we have been talking about.

What do we mean? Just this. Our education must be truly Christian in that the people who are its subjects will not only be common

but they will be more than common.   In Christian education we deal
with people who are re-made by the grace of God.   We teach children
who are in the covenant of grace.   We work with people re-made by
God's redemptive process into princes in the earth.   We deal with
those in whom a new principle of life and action is operative.   This
new principle makes these people more than common.   It makes them
God's aristocracy.   It makes them kings and princes among men.   It
places them and their children in that setting where true education
becomes a possibility and a reality.   Here is the setting in which
standards — the mark of the special man as over against the common
man — become meaningful and real.

An Education of Truth

In the earlier part of our discussion we dwelt on the relativism
which marks the life of the common man today.   Absolute truth does
not exist in his life.   He lives largely without cultural, moral or
spiritual standards.   He lives by what is useful or convenient for him.
Pragmatism is not a conceptual system for him; it is a work-a-day
pattern of life.

A most thoroughgoing answer is required to meet this destructive
relativism.   The answer must be the opposite of this relativism.   It
must be in the form of a comprehensive program of training and education in which every experience is set in a framework of absolute
truth.   We must insist that only this type of training can satisfy a
basic need of man, namely, the thirst for meaning.   We must declare
by word and by educational deed what Professor Sorokin has so
plainly said in his *The Crisis of Our Age,* namely, that a culture that
has no regard for absolute truth cannot long endure.   Our urgent
mission is to demonstrate to our generation, for the glory of God,
that every step in the process of nurture must be a step with the living
and redeeming God.   In order that the whole of experience may have
meaning, may have eternal meaning, we must carry on our educational
program in the light of and under the direction of culture's first and
final dictum, "Thus saith the Lord."   This is the education that makes
for order in the individual life and in society.   This is the education
that educates image-bearers of God.   Education not so governed must
ultimately lead to chaos.   When God's eternal truth does not rule,
the end can be nothing other than chaos.

Educating the Total Man

We have previously seen that modern psychology does not give to
the intellect the place of complete authority once accorded this aspect
of man's personality. There are energies and drives in man that require

a revamping of notions of man's being that owe more to Greek philosophy than to biblical revelation.

In the light of this psychological factor in the modern picture we must insist that this truth-controlled education for the God-related common man must be an *education for the total man.* That is the third consideration we would seek to emphasize as we describe our urgent mission. The education for this day of decadence cannot be geared to a falsely simple notion of man as largely and narrowly an intellectual being. There are springs of life deeper than intellect. It is these deeper springs that true education must seek to influence and direct to rich spiritual and cultural productivity in all areas of human life and interest.

How shall we reach the total man in education? How may we be sure that our educational program will not leave man disintegrated and at odds with himself and with the universe in which he must live — and at odds with the sovereign Judge of men?

It seems to me that we can educate the total man if we continually insist on two things. In the first place education must be religious at its very core if it is to educate the total man. It is in the God of all the earth and in his Son that history in whole or in part finds its meaning. That is the point at which that part of history that you and I are finds its meaning. All of life must be related to that great God who in compelling glory transcends all and yet rules all. Relation to him must not be a narrowly religious matter. Life in its totality — in its chemical, biological, mental, moral, spiritual, social totality — must be lived in his fellowship, to his praise. In other words, education must be in harmony with the fact that experience centers in what the Bible calls the "heart." An education that ignores this dynamic center of man's being must in the end fail to gain that order and that integration which a true education should achieve. It is no accident that many of the books and articles that examine education critically and candidly today give prominence to this very matter of the central place of religion in education.

The second point we must insist upon if we are to educate the total man is that all of man's experience must be brought within the sweep of this religiously centered, God-centered education. It seems apparent that to gain this end it would be most wise to capture the individual's experience at the highest point of its impressionability. That point is definitely childhood.

We would press that point a bit further. There is a large body of opinion among psychologists today that the most meaningful experience in life's most impressionable years is the relationship between parent and child. It is safe to say that for the personality's whole history and development there is no more significant human relationship than this. It is a relationship of unquestioning love and total dependence. It is the one epoch of earthly experience when the individual's experience is truly simple, yes, is one. If this is true — and I think abundant evidence points to its truth — then a rather obvious application should follow. We have insisted that it is religion, fellowship with the God of all the earth, that integrates human experience, that brings unity into life's confusion. Why not correlate this final unity of human experience with that unity of experience that is the child's in his most impressionable years? Let God, "in whom we live and move and have our being," be a living partner in this all-important parent-child relationship. Let that be the starting point in education. Then as the child develops, the total love and dependence and obedience that were directed toward the parents are transferred to the Lord of all. Then quite naturally under wise and godly training the child's experience will grow into a deeper oneness in the obedience of love to life's first and final law: "Thou shalt love the Lord thy God with all thy heart, and with all thy soul, and with all thy mind." As the child develops under this kind of education every new experience and every new interest in home or church or school or playground takes its place in this simple but rich framework of true Godliness with its roots deep in life's first unified experience where natural and spiritual factors are beautifully fused.

That is simply another way of describing covenant education. This is education that makes for effective integration. This is true education. It is the rich development and propagation of this education that constitutes our urgent mission today. Our urgent mission in this day of educational, spiritual and intellectual decadence is to press relentlessly forward with an education that educates people within the framework of God's program of grace, that educates them under the direction and control of God's absolute truth, and that educates them in the totality of their being. We must press forward with that education that educates the *heart* from the very beginning of life in fellowship with that God whom to know is life, yes, life eternal. This is our particular urgent mission — a mission in which we may not fail to be faithful and zealous.

There are those who will say, "What can we do? We are so few." That is the language of those who are faint-hearted, who are lacking in vigorous faith. Such sentiments should always annoy us. Such attitudes are really not Christian. And such attitudes fly into the face of a fact demonstrated many times in history. This fact is simply that a minority wholeheartedly committed to a great faith can move mountains

— mountains of lethargy, mountains of fear, mountains of opposition. In the providence of God a faith rich in spiritual grandeur and strong in driving power has been committed to us. It is a faith centering in nothing less than the sovereign head of this universe. It is a faith of pure grace, unspoiled by human frailties and sin. This great faith has shone with particular splendor in the Christian school movement. May we, dare we be faint-hearted before our urgent mission? God forbid.

There are those who reason that positive Christian textbooks will make the student dull toward cultural influences that he should be conversant with if he is to be an educated man. I am not insensitive to that line of reasoning. Its thrust is not lost upon me. But this matter of cultural impact is a two-way highway. To be sure, we must so teach our children that they will become intelligently conversant with the main streams of learning and culture, even those that differ from the stream of thought and life in which we move. But, how about the cultural influence that flows from Christians? Shall we fail in that? If our appraisal of the cultural situation is at all correct, then it seems to me we are at a stage in history when we with our dynamic faith centering in the absolute God must pour our very best energies into the bloodstream of modern life. And it seems to me that the production of high-quality, scholarly, culturally sensitive, and doctrinally correct Christian educational materials is one of the very best ways for us to influence the cultural situation for good. Shall we be the salt of the earth, or shall we not?

In conclusion I think of the frontispiece of Van Loon's *Story of Mankind*. This picture as I recall it is done in the scrawny pen sketches that Van Loon used to illustrate his writings. This sketch showed uncivilized man walking fearfully and unclad and alone with mountains of superstition and dread rising on either side of his path. I am not so sure that sketch should be applied to uncivilized man alone. If certain destructive forces at work in modern civilization continue as they are going, it may not be too long before men will again be plodding that dismal road of dread and superstition. Not a few people are doing so already, even in nations that have known a high degree of civilization.

Until Christ returns in glory we have an urgent mission to perform. We may not fail. We may not be faint-hearted. May we see our mission with clear heads and the steady eye of true faith. With all industry and intelligence we must press forward on our mission. Let it never be said of us that the process of decay was hastened because we failed to perform our urgent mission.

EDWARD HEEREMA

Address before the National Union of Christian Schools Convention, Grand Rapids, Michigan, August, 1950.

Key Thoughts:

1. Our task in education is to be accomplished in an era when the common man who recognizes no real standards has risen to power. It is an era of revolt of the masses that has broken with norms of life recognized in earlier days, though not always obeyed.

2. The intellectual climate is one of hopelessness and despair. All sense of truth is lost in the wilderness of relativism. The only truth is that there is no truth.

3. Psychology has discovered that not intellect, as the Greeks thought, but driving, pushing energy makes man go.

4. Our mission lies in the area of human personality. We must seek to develop "that kind of personality that will so express the energies within himself that they are freely directed toward the proper ends and subjected to the proper controls."

5. Our mission is true education for the common man, not for the privileged few, but for all children of the covenant of grace.

6. True education is education in truth as revealed by God.

7. It is education of the total man. Hence, we insist on two things:

   a. It must be religious to the very core.

   b. All of man's experience must be brought within the sweep of a God-centered life.

8. Correlate the final unity of experience, fellowship with God, with the unity of experience in the child's most impressionable years, parent-child relationship. This is covenant education of the total man.

Comment:

The Christian school, the Christian teacher to be more specific, has a mission and should be mission conscious. The Christian teacher is sent and has a Sender. He is sent with a message. The message is clear.

True education is for all covenant youth, not only for the gifted among them. It is, to be sure, for them too, and in special measure; but also for the less gifted. For them too the Lord has a place in life.

Far be it from the Christian school to cultivate an intellectually elite group. All covenant youth are stewards. The teacher works with all in the area of their total personality. All the energies of their personalities are to be directed to ends that are God-ordained, and they are to be disciplined by those ends.

The Christian school fulfills its mission to the life of youth in the unity of their experience. It is in the unity of experience that he develops the feeling of security for genuine fellowship. And it is in the fellowship of love that he reaches out confidently for enrichment and enlargement of experience.

7

End Time Education

This is end time, and our education must be geared to meet this end time challenge. Let us think about these two points: end time education evidences and end time education requirements.

End Time Evidences

Under evidences, I would posit two propositions. First, today's world struggle is a manifest sign of the times, a sign of the latter days. Our mind may still debate it but in our hearts we feel and believe it. We believe this notwithstanding our fear of too specific eschatological predictions. Our Reformed doctrine books usually present a number of things that still have to take place before the return of Christ. Nevertheless, we know the time of His coming is drawing nigh, and I firmly believe that it is a much healthier spiritual position to speak of latter days than to calm the people by saying, "the time is not yet." It is later now than we think.

It is not that ministers and spiritual leaders only are blowing the trumpet, but news commentators, world historians and secular leaders are all sounding that note. It is the fulfillment of Christ's word that "perilous times shall come and men's hearts shall fail them for fear." Professor Harold Urey, a Nobel prize winning scientist, says pessimistically, "I am a frightened man. All the scientists I know are frightened men." Governor Earle, former governor of Pennsylvania, upon return from a European tour stated, "There is less than an even chance that ten percent of us will be alive in five years." General Douglas Mac Arthur at the signing of the Japanese surrender, warned, "Humanity has had its last chance." When President Truman announced his momentous decision authorizing the construction of the H-Bomb, Dr. Albert Einstein declared that through "radioactive poisoning of the atmosphere," "the annihilation of any life on earth" is "within the range of technical possibility."

The following recent book titles and magazine headlines carry their own astounding message: "Shall We Hide?" "No Place to Hide."

"There is No Defense." "How Close Is the Danger?" "A Conspiracy to Commit Genocide." "The Soul Searchers Find No Answers."

A recent editorial in *Business Week* says, "These last few months there has been a special touch of horror in the deadly bickerings between the eastern and western worlds. Suddenly, and in the most coldly literal sense, the human race has turned a corner. It must learn to get along better with itself or expect to wipe itself out sometime in the second half of the twentieth century."

Our second proposition under end time evidences is that today's world struggle is in terms of education. A very great part of the blame of the world situation is laid at the feet of modern education. Who are these monsters that we fear today in our modern age? They are our own children, whom we have taught. Think of modern education based on natural science as it has molded our race. Think of the despair of men today as they worry about the morals of our age which has not kept up with the intellectual development. One educator has put it thus: "Tomorrow's school will stress human relationships and civic responsibilities, with the emphasis that in an age of atomic and hydrogen bombs and the possibilities of biological warfare that mankind must learn to live together and to get along with each other. The first fifty years of the twentieth century having already witnessed the death of more persons in warfare than in all of the other centuries of man's recorded experience and with society having perfected the tools and instruments for mass suicide there is the sobering influence that the next war may be the last." In the light of this dilemma, let us think of the picture in Revelation 13. That second beast rising up out of the earth gives us the educational picture. It is a philosophy. Note that beast came up out of the earth — naturalistic is it not? It represents a religion — it is a beast that is worshipped — and men today worship at the shrine of natural science. It also concentrates all its efforts so we learn, in terms of the Lord's return. Summing up this first point we note that the educational dilemma is a leading part of the world dilemma, and is a sign of the times.

End Time Requirements

What must we do about all this? We should avoid two extremes. We should not slip into an hysteria complex, and feel as though all we can do is save a remnant. Sometimes in the educational world one is almost filled with despair when one thinks of the American movie as doing more than one half of the educational job, when 80 million people attend the movies each week; and our hopes almost sink when we learn that the three main families who own most of the movie industry are all Russian born. Nor should we feel that our small constituency shall save the world in its present dilemma. We are to follow a determinate course in the light of facts and prophecy. Let us dedicate ourselves to an education which stresses these requirements:

A "back to basics" education

First things must be first. This is no time for non-essentials and for time-consuming experiments. Remember time is precious in what we face today. Yes, it is back to basics — master the subjects, but also teach the basics about *authority, virtue and ethics;* teach the fact of *sin* and *salvation.* They are basic in our Christian school.

An antithesis education

Christian education is always conscious of an antithesis — the antithesis between God and Satan, light and darkness, life and death. There are in the final analysis only two camps. In the world today these two sides are linking up against each other. As time is running out Satan is becoming very bold. The war we are fighting is not a territorial aggression but a war of ideologies. Our youth must be instructed to see these camps as they take shape in our day.

An accelerated program

Education certainly can be accelerated. If Dodd Harris School in Chicago can condense four years of high school into a twelve months solid schedule and give a certificate that satisfies the regents of the University of Illinois, then most of us too can press the schedule. Certainly this is no time, I would say, to spend more time on added athletics and extra curricular activities. We must adhere to our main business of essentials in education — in a time like this.

Redblooded-covenantal education

I mean here a covenantal parental education that sounds the redemptive note throughout. Do not be afraid to stress the personal salvation note in teaching. Sometimes I fear that we have allowed the pendulum to swing toward an altogether impersonal, objective, theistic extreme without a Christ. A few weeks ago I had the privilege to talk with a group of junior high students who remarked that their teacher (may God bless her) had taken time to have a personal talk with her students on personal saving faith in the Lord Jesus. She had distinguished between various types of faith and had pointed to true saving faith for her pupils. One of the students remarked that she had been too personally concerned about them; that was the field of the pastor in catechism but not the task of the teacher in school. Have our pupils disassociated anything evangelical with covenantal education? Too bad if so!

An all out Christian education

Are there still some who argue and question whether we need Christian schools? This end time consciousness should scream for the best, the only kind of education. There is no time to lose. The best is none too good. If the covenant doctrine does not convince a man to Christian education will he listen to the argument of end time urgency?

An eternity education

We call our education a teaching of a world and life view. We speak about training for life and Christian citizenship. But we must recognize that it extends way beyond this life. It reaches out into eternity.

I love to think of Moses' training — through the faith of Moses' parents (see Hebrews 11:23-27). There are several scenes in his life. First, we see him at his mother's knee, receiving instruction in the truths and values of the God of the Fathers. Then we see him at Pharoah's court being instructed and gaining the best in the secular knowledge of the day. We see him then at the threshold of an imperial life — but he forsook Egypt. Note the verbs in the choice of Moses — he *refused* to be called the son of Pharoah's daughter; he *chose* to share ill treatment with the people; he *accounted* the reproach of Christ greater riches; he *looked* unto the recompense of the reward; he *endured* as seeing the invisible. Where did he receive such a sense of values in life? From his education by his parents.

A sense of values, in the light of eternity, is what we need for ourselves and our children. Now we evaluate the tangible and the material, but the time is coming when these earthly things fall away. Recently I read an account of a missionary who related the changed sense of values in time of calamity, when soldiers were coming. The merchants closed their shops and dismissed their frightened clerks. He saw them fleeing for their lives. He saw the banks close their doors and bankers flee for their lives. He saw the post-office workers flee for their lives. He saw the doctors and nurses in the general hospital put their weak, sick patients out on the sidewalks, and then flee for their lives. Out at the zoo the keepers of the animals shot the lions and the tigers and then fled for their lives. At the leper and insane asylums the wardens opened the doors and let the loathsome and unfortunate people come into town, while they too ran for their lives. From the jail three thousand criminals were set at liberty, when keepers and policemen fled for their lives. He was in the church and played the organ for the last, last time — it was the last hymn that organ ever played, for the invading army broke it up and used it for firewood. He closed the Bible on the pulpit. He left the church and turned the key in the door. The account makes us think of the poem with which I wish to close.

What Then?

When the great plants of our cities
    Have turned out their last finished work;
When the merchant has sold his last yard of silk
    And dismissed his last tired clerk;
When the banks have rolled in their last dollar
    And paid out their last dividend;
And the Judge of the world says,
    "Close for the night," and calls for a balance —
        What then?

When the choir has sung its last anthem,
    And the preacher has said his last prayer;
When the organ has pealed its last echo,
    And the sound has died in the air;
When the Bible has closed on the altar,
    And the pews are all empty of men;
And each soul stands facing his record,
    And the Great Book is opened —
        What then?

When the actor has played his last drama,
    And the mimic has made his last fun;
When the movie has flashed its last picture,
    And the billboards displayed their last run;
When the crowds seeking pleasure have vanished,
    And gone out into darkness again;
And a world that rejected its Saviour,
    Is asked for a reason —
        What then?

When the bugle dies out in the silence,
   And the long marching columns are still;
When the millions of earth are gathered
   From ocean and valley and hill;
When the day that has no morrow
   Has come to the last, last end;
And the voice of God from the heaven
   Says, "It is done" —
                 What then?

D. H. WALTERS
Address before the National Union of
Christian Schools Convention, Grand
Rapids, Michigan, August 1950.

Key Thoughts:

1. The evidences for the return of our Savior and Lord are increasing. We should be diligent students of the time in which we live to be alerted to the signs of the times.
2. These evidences point to a needed emphasis in Christian education in our schools.
3. First things must be first, in Christian education too. Because the fact of sin and salvation is first in Christian experience to come to a fruitful Christian life, it should occupy a major emphasis in teaching in the Christian school.
4. The Christian school is needed more than ever to give the education of our covenant youth the perspective of eternity. Christian education involves more than a world and life view, it involves the view of eternity.

Comment:

Christian education seeks to mature children in the perspective of eternity.

Two things are often neglected in the Christian school, the subject of missions and the consciousness of the Lord's return. Children will learn the industries and products of Korea, but never learn of the great work Christ has done there through his church. Likewise we seek to give the children a life and world view, but develop little longing for the Lord's blessed return. I wonder what Jesus would regard more important?

Balanced we must be. But are we balanced in our education when it generates no longing for Christ's return? We too are not balanced when we have the longing but fail to see our task in this world. It is the longing Christian whose heart is on fire for the Lord. Christian education too has a task to perform in developing this balance.

SECTION THREE

ORGANIZATION AND IMPLEMENTATION OF THE PROGRAM OF CHRISTIAN EDUCATION

1. Principles Underlying Curriculum Making for the Christian School

2. The Christian View of the School Curriculum

3. Improvement of the Curriculum

4. Integration

5. Implications of the Principle of Integration

6. Implications of Making the Unity of Life Central

7. Teaching According to the Ways of Child Life

8. Humanism in the Life of the School

9. The New Obedience

10. Education for Self-Direction

11. The Problem of Giving a Child a Biblical Conception of his Fourfold Relationship in Life Through the Classroom

12. Learning Through Understanding

13. Intellectualism in Education

14. Knowledge and Wisdom

15. The Discipline of the Christian School

16. Discipline in the Christian School

17. The Great Office of the Teacher in Preparing the Child for the Complete Life

18. The Teacher and Vitalized Teaching

19. Choice of Technique in Teaching

20. The Social Trend in Education

21. Philosophy and Educational Trends

1

Principles Underlying Curriculum Making for the Christian School

This subject is mainly concerned with the choice and the organization of the subject-matter to be taught in the Christian schools. Its range is very definitely circumscribed by the qualification, *underlying* principles, so that any consideration with reference to practical curriculum building must be guarded against as a digression from the central theme. It may, perhaps, be thought hardly admissible to point out in a very general way in what manner the underlying principles determine the actual building of the curriculum.

I would not be at all surprised should some of our practical schoolmen feel inclined to object: "What's the use of all this theorizing, this discussion of principles; where does the value of all these considerations come in for the teacher who is wrestling day after day with the practical problems of classroom instruction and discipline? Is not our age the day of the *praxis,* the time of all times that stresses the application of scientific discoveries, and of religious and moral sentiments? And is not the educational book market flooded with literature that suggests all manner of new methods and untried devices, tending to revolutionize the art of teaching?"

There is the rub. The veritable deluge of professional literature suggesting now this, then that, scheme of operation to the classroom teacher makes it more than ever obligatory upon the teacher in the Christian school to select from the multitude of offerings with scrupulous care under the guidance of well-defined and thoroughly mastered principles, lest he introduce into the school (which is by reason of its very existence a protest against the spirit of the times that deprecate its most fundamental conceptions) practices which will ultimately nullify the original purposes of the patrons of these Christian schools. For though the teacher may be anxious to avail himself of the practical values that seem inherent in certain recommended devices, there may lie concealed in the warp and woof of the plans the weaving of patterns that would sadly mar the product of the teacher's efforts. For let not our practical man or woman overlook the fact that behind

217

all these devices lie motives of far-reaching formative significance. It is necessary that teachers be able to choose sagaciously and prudently, lest they dish up a diluted form of modern paganism under the flag of Calvinism. That is one danger inherent in an over-practical attitude toward school matters.

Another danger, scarcely less inimical than the first, is that for very fear of transplanting some exotic flowers into our pedogogical garden we should reject any and all of the rich flora that bloom in soil contingent to our tiny patch. Thereby we should deprive our institutions of the indispensable tools needed for the progressive development of our educational system in accord with modern times. This policy of stark conservatism would defeat with equal fatality the very purpose of our schools, even though it may appear to some that to err on this side is less deadly than the policy of indiscriminate imitation would be. For this course of action — or rather of inaction — would result in a petrified system out of tune with the historical development of life.

But the vital question in this connection is the one that confronts us when we consider the question of our own definite aims. We must build what we intend to raise. We must know what we desire to accomplish with our educational policies. What kind of men and women do we want to train? Sparta desired soldier-patriots and trained its youth accordingly; Athens entertained different ambitions for her future citizens and therefore offered an entirely different course in training for her democracy of leisure and intelligence; Rome likewise suited her training to her preconceived notions commensurate with the ideals of world dominion. The philosophers of all ages have advocated educational policies in accordance with their life and world views. Thus have at all times the dominant groups in any civilization prescribed for the schools of the nation whose policies they controlled a system of education agreeable with their fundamental concepts of life.

This fact has been clearly demonstrated. All education is in a large sense social as well as individual. Society attempts through education the shaping of the young life after the pattern of her own conception of what constitutes an ideal state of society. And it is plain that the state of society is determined by the quality of the individuals of which it is composed. Hence the vital interest society possesses in the education of those that are to be admitted within its circles for weal or woe.

Since the Christian and particularly the reformed Christian has a very pronouncedly distinct view of life, it is inevitable that he should desire to incorporate these ideas and ideals of his into the curriculum of the schools that are charged with the rearing of his children. And since John Calvin of Geneva was of all other leaders of the Reformation the keenest thinker, as well as the sanest mystic, it was he who succeeded better than any other genius to construct a system of thought which for comprehensiveness of scope and depth of insight stands without equal in the sphere of philosophy. For Calvinism sweeps all that is in the heavens above or on the earth beneath within its all-embracing grasp. It is both simple and complex. It has a single purpose, the glory of God most high; and therefore it lays all creation in heaven and upon earth under tribute to its Maker and Redeemer. Like David of old the Calvinist calls upon the angels in heaven, as well as upon the mountains and the seas, the wild beasts of the forests and creeping things on the earth, the cedars of the Lebanon and the mountains of Bashan to recognize the supreme power and majesty of the Lord of hosts that they may pay homage to Him. Like all other systems of thought Calvinism rests upon faith; but unlike any other philosophy its faith is not pinned to a hypothesis, hatched in the fertile but errant brain of man. It rests upon the immovable Rock of the Ages, the eternal Word, the Logos, concerning whose revelation we have the assurance that no tittle or iota shall ever fall to the ground.

No surer foundation can ever be laid. Storms may rage and rains may beat against this house of faith; the heathen may rave and the nations may threaten to overwhelm it; they can only bruise their heads without affecting this firm foundation. The life view of the Calvinist is a philosophy of revelation. Not man's wisdom but God's revelation is the loadstar of the Calvinist who believes with Paul that "the foolishness of God is wiser than men, and the weakness of God stronger than men" (I Cor. 1:25).

Philosophically speaking, Christ is the corner stone of the only rational and the only complete system of thought that rests in faith, the faith that conquers the worlds of science and art and religion. Christ is not only the Redeemer of fallen man, but the Restorer of all things to more than pristine beauty and perfection. The Calvinist sees creation suited to and destined for restoration in Christ, the entire cosmos finding its purposeful consummation in this process of redemption whereby Christ makes all things new to the glory of God the Father. And he understands by faith that men who are chosen and called are co-workers with God in this great business of the restoration of all things in Christ in spite of the fierce opposition of Satan and all his host. This partnership with God is possible to men because God is in immediate communion with His own who in turn, bowing before the sovereignty of High God, live their whole lives in His presence. There is no life, regenerate or unregenerate, possible without God, as Paul informed the Athenians from their own Areopagus when he uttered that memorable dictum: "For in him we live, and move, and have our being" (Acts 17:28). In this Pauline expression we deal however with the life that moves by the power and the favor of God's common grace, which life does not imply conscious fellowship with God; but those who live their whole lives in His presence possess the new life, "the earnest of the spirit" (II Cor. 1:22), the life "that is hid with Christ in God" (Col. 3:3). This new life, which is in Christ, is the prerequisite gift of God to the Calvinist, for Calvinism is the full-blown flower of the Spirit of adoption whereby we cry: "Abba Father." For that very reason Calvinism embraces not only all things above and below, but it also comprises, according to the measure of the gift of that self-same Spirit to man, both time and eternity. And this new life is also, thanks to the grace of our covenant God, the basis of Christian education as ideally conceived by the supporters of our Christian schools.

*   *   *

The curriculum of our Christian schools is accordingly based upon at least three distinctive, fundamental concepts. In the first place Calvinism views the child from the standpoint of creation, fall, and redemption. In the second place, Calvinism seeks to accomplish a distinctive purpose through the education of the Christian home, the Christian school, and the Church. It is a self-evident truth that the determination of the purpose of education as one of the basic principles for curriculum building pre-supposes a knowledge of the child as the object of the educational process. For the physical, moral and religious characteristics of the child determine the nature and the scope of the educational program through the activities of which the educator hopes to realize his aims in conjunction with the indispensable self-activity of the child.

What we have said thus far indicates only in a general way how the Christian school views the child. But we have seen that the child is to be taken as a child of God in Christ, as a citizen of the Kingdom of Restoration. From this premise we may safely deduce that this child is destined by his Creator and Redeemer to live his life in the presence of God and to His glory alone. Moreover, it appears from this that the child is to accomplish this purpose through the instrumentality of all things over which God has placed man in authority, and that he is to gain this end in cooperation with his fellow-men, both believers and unbelievers. For this reason the Christian believes in the fullest development of every side of human nature, the development of his relation to nature, to the animal world, to his fellow-men, and to his God. The Christian believes in the organic nature of all creation and must consistently stress this in his ideal of education. This involves the individual as well as the social ends of education, since the latter can only be attained through the former. The highest development of the individual insures *ipso facto* the highest organization of society. Here lies revealed the strongly individualistic idea of Calvinism. But it is an individualism not for its own sake, but for the sake of service: the service of God in and through and for his fellow men. Calvinism is never one-sided, but always comprehensive. It has room for all that is true and good and beautiful in the world of nature and in the thoughts of men; but it shuns all extremes in the development of one thing or feature of things at the expense of another. All true ideals are Calvinistic, for they are facades of the one genuine diamond of *truth* and *goodness* and *beauty,* the diadem that the devout Calvinist yearns to lay down at the feet of his Master in gratitude for His erstwhile wearing of the crown of thorns that pierced His brow.

Yet, even so, there is a certain vagueness in the definition of our educational purpose. What do we mean when we speak of true piety, thorough knowledge, and genuine culture, and what is their organic relation? We are in evident need of assistance from a philosophical anthropology in order that we may ascertain the central relation of man to the universe so that we may have a clear perception of man's exact position with reference to the totality of all things. Then we shall be able to discover the unity in the manifold purposes of education. A Calvinistic anthropology would aid us in placing proper emphasis upon the fact that the universality of our educational purpose must at the same time include the particular purposes for each individual life. For, though the purpose of education is general, education itself is always individual. This fact must be taken into consideration in the framing of our educational purpose. The individual must, to be sure, have a clear and distinct understanding of the general purpose of all life, of the whole cosmos; but this knowledge will not of and by itself enable him to locate his own particular place in the totality of things. And if he is going to add his mite toward the harmonious development of the universe to the glory of God, it becomes to him a very urgent and exceedingly practical question in which way, and at what place he should labor toward that one great universal end. The Christian school must keep in mind this very particular and personal problem that each child must be prepared to answer at some time in his life.

This individualistic nature of education clearly points, it seems to me, to an important underlying principle for curriculum making, *viz.,* that for each clearly defined district or territory the application of the general principles of education must be adjusted to the peculiar life situations and the characteristic social and industrial relations that obtain within its boundaries. Besides it would seem that each local school should adapt its course with a view to the conditions of its patron homes. Furthermore, this question is largely of a psychological nature, involving as it does the problem of the subjective experiencing of objective relationships. The universe in which we live is a rich field of objective facts and phenomena in which diverse individuals share in accordance with their psychological make-up. They do not all react upon the given phenomena of life in the same manner, or to the same extent. Some have, *e.g.,* an ear for music, others have not; some enjoy the harmonious blending of colors, others are blind to their effects; some are adept in linguistic expression, others are skilful in the handling of the brush; some are captivated by the sublimity of abstract truth, others revel in the doing of practical work; and so on. Here is a rich field for the empirical psychologist.

But, you may object, if this individualistic phase of education is to be given proper attention what remains of the many-sidedness, the comprehensiveness of Calvinism as a view of life that must be shared by each individual Calvinist? To this I would reply that it is possible for each individual to have an idea of the general fundamental principles, the central thought of Calvinism so that he may learn to adjust his personal life in harmony with the whole, even though he finds himself incapable to participate completely in all the richly variegated experiences of human life. It is indeed necessary that each budding Calvinist learn to live his own individual life subjectively under the inspiration of the general principle, and live it so intensely that he may learn to lose himself in order to gain the true life that is in Christ. Thus will the life of all the individuals blend into one glorious and harmonious composite, focussed upon the adoration of the Maker who is all and in all. Here we understand that the hand cannot say to the foot I have no need of you, nor the eye to the hand, and vice versa; for all are members of one body whose head is Christ. Each one must, therefore, know himself a debtor to employ his gifts for the welfare of his brethren, as no one is sufficient unto himself alone, but all complement each the other for the perfecting of the whole. Calvinism demands in truth the highest development of the social ideal in man. Only it is not *founded* in man; but is the fruit of the all-controlling ideal of Calvinism: love to God.

*   *   *

Having then briefly considered the object of education and the purpose both general and particular, let us next inquire into the choice of subject-matter and methods.

Which are the underlying principles that should govern the choice of subject-matter in the curriculum of the Christian school?

Since the fear of the Lord is the beginning of all wisdom, and since the purpose of Christian education is true piety organically related with thorough knowledge and genuine culture, it seems plain that the first consideration in this respect must concentrate upon man's relation to God as the controlling factor in the choice of subject-matter. Hence the study of the Word as the divine revelation of God to man comes in for first consideration. This Word must be and *is* to the child of the covenant *the* light upon life's pathway. According to the measure of his insight the child is able thereby to discern both good and evil, truth and falsehood, right and wrong. Bible study is then the dominant branch of study in the curriculum. It should be allowed a generous share of the precious school time. No frills and fads must be allowed to encroach upon the time allotment for Bible study. Besides, the curriculum as a whole, that is, the entire body of organically related subject-matter must be consolidated by the truth that springs from the Fountainhead of all wisdom.

A fundamental principle of curriculum building is undoubtedly the demand that education must prepare the child for that child's own time, *i.e.,* the school must maintain adequate relationship with the present. The character of the times conditions in no small measure the processes of education. This principle exerts its influence upon Bible study as well as upon any other branch of study. Not, of course, in the sense that changing times affect divine truth; but, to the contrary, in the sense that divine revelation contains a message for every time, because God's truth abideth forever. The times themselves shed light upon the meaning of the sacred pages to the believing heart so that with heart uplifted and with soul inspired he may serve his Master in *his* day.

To illustrate, our own period seems to be that which is described in Scripture as the period of apostasy, the churches forsaking the truth as it is in Christ to believe a lie (II Thess. 2:11), turning away their ears from the truth in order to embrace fables (II Tim. 4:4). Now Scripture foretells us that this period is to be followed by times of fierce persecution, "perilous times" as Paul calls them (II Tim. 3:1). Will it not be incumbent upon the Christian educator of our times then to emphasize in his instruction that part of revelation which is calculated to inspire the souls of the pupils with the courage to hold fast to the truth that abides forever, and to cling to the faith that overcomes the world? In this connection appears the importance of the study of history from the biblical standpoint, especially the history of the church of God as an influence in the history of the world. Closely bound up with this is the study of the world's literary productions, serving to aid the students in the mental construction of a vivid panorama of the world's course from creation to parousia. Thus conceived history will afford the student a means to arrive at a correct estimation of the significance of his own time in which he is destined to take an active part.

Of great value also is the study of nature in its broadest sense. The wisdom and goodness, the glory and majesty of the Creator is reflected in endless variations by mountain and rill, in daffodil and oak; His divine attributes shine forth in the tiniest insect and in the lumbering pachyderm, in the elusive minnow of the brook and in the giant whale of the ocean deep. Our curriculum builders may well consider whether we have, perhaps, in the past been guilty of over-emphasizing such branches as spelling and numbers at the expense of nature study. Geography as a study of the earth which the Lord has given to the children of men (Ps. 115:16), and which is full of His riches (Ps. 104:24), is intimately related to the afore-mentioned subjects, as the habitation of man and as his workshop wherein he is to labor for the glory of his Maker.

The induction of the pupils into the arts of reading, writing and language must, of course, be provided for in the curriculum in view of their instrumental value both for the affairs of practical life, and for the cultural side of human intercourse.

Another underlying principle of curriculum construction is found in the fact that a course of study is of necessity conditioned by the nature of the child that is to be taught. Since the praxis in education is as we have seen always individual, and since the interest of the child, according to his way, is of prime importance in education; it follows that the psychology of the child must enter largely into the consideration of the underlying principles of curriculum making. And here once more we find light upon our pathway from the Scriptures that teach us that God has laid the times into the heart of man so that we may expect to find interest in the hearts of the coming generation for the things that concern the problems of their own age. The aptitudes and sentiments of the child may thus be enlisted in the processes of an education such that it will fit the child for active participation in the affairs of his own environment. Lack of interest in the classroom may well result from the neglect of this principle on the part of curriculum makers. There is a creatively given and a historically provided harmony between the psychological equipment of the child and the actual environment to which that child reacts. A similar congruence obtains with reference to the ideal and the practical values, the material worth and formative virtues of various branches of study —

such qualities being frequently found united in one and the same study. It is the business of the teacher to bring this out, guided by the well-made curriculum.

The underlying principles of curriculum making in regard to methodology must in the nature of the case be largely derived from psychology, especially from the results obtained by the authorities in the field of child psychology. To obtain the active interest of the child's mind one must know and understand the workings of the child's mind. Says Van Der Kooy: "Scripture itself points in this direction when it says, 'Rear the child in the way he should go.' In order to be able to do that, the 'way' of the child must first be known" (*Distinctive Features of the Christian School,* p. 55).

In the discovering of the divine laws that govern the development of the human soul others than Calvinists may well render valuable assistance. The Christian school may well profit from the labors of unbelieving research workers in the field of empirical psychology. For the Lord teaches man how to labor in every sphere of human activity, for through the instrumentality of man it pleases God to unfold the greatness of His works throughout all the earth. The Calvinist then, may, guided by his own principles, make grateful use of the genuinely scientific work performed by unbelieving scholars, in this instance of the psychologists. True, care must be had to distinguish in this connection between actual scientific facts, and the interpretations put upon these facts by men whose minds boast not in the freedom of the children of God but in the anarchy and license of the infidel. All facts are common property of infidel and Christian; but the understanding of the wise pertains to God alone. Modern investigators are too often found buttressing their pet theories with facts which do not warrant the acceptance of such theories. So, *e.g.,* the idea that nothing which the child is unable to comprehend should be taught him — a notion unreasonable as any, since even the adult must perforce accept many things he cannot understand. Another source of confusion in educational practice rose from the extreme application of the postulate that the teacher must always descend to the mental level of the child — an excellent rule in itself. But sound pedagogy will only descend in order to raise the child to higher level instead of remaining on the level of the child.

On the other hand, the principle of self-activity, discovered outside of our circles, is a very valuable lever in the skilful hand of the teacher for the education of the young. Only — here too, it should never be forgotten that *mere* activity as such can never be an end in itself: a method may never become the purpose of educational activity. Artificial devices encouraging physical activities where only mental effort will accomplish the desired ends are harmful to the child. The finding of knowledge and truth is to the Calvinist of greater importance than the seeking after it. The curriculum maker must therefore bear in mind that all truth is God's truth, but he must at the same time remember that man can see the light only by His Light.

* * *

Following these underlying principles, briefly and imperfectly described, we may build for our schools a curriculum, distinct from similar instruments reared upon the principles of modern hypotheses. It will be founded upon the revealed truth of God, resting upon solid values that are not subject to intrinsic mutations of texture though capable of adaptive application in accordance with the dispensations of time. Amid the turmoil and confusion in the minds of men who have cut loose from the bearings in the Logos, there will be found in the Christian school a calm objectivity of purpose throughout the coming ages; not the calm, however, of a stagnant pool; but that of a mighty river flowing steadily onward toward the sea, gaining momentum as it proceeds from its accumulated volume, contributed to it by numerous sources whose accretions can only reach their ultimate destiny through the channel of this mighty stream. But the muddy, swirling eddies from the mountain rivulets are allowed to sink their sediment into the greater depth of the mother stream towards whose volume they only add the pure water that needs not the super-gravitational force of rapids and falls — that carried the silt along — in order to pursue its course. The central principle of Calvinism that all things consist together in the Logos (Col. 1:17) and that all things must contribute to His glory operates like a sieve that strains out all impurities, yet leaves an unobstructed pathway for the limpid liquid of unalloyed truth.

Thus there is secured for the Christian school a curriculum that represents on the one hand stability and certainty and on the other, constant progress and continual adjustment with reference to the times decreed by the Almighty over the lives of the children of men. This adjustment and development — for it is both — points to the necessity of unremitting toil in the service of perennial reformation. This means evolution in the true sense of that much abused word, historical development, predetermined by the counsel of God. Calvinism as applied to our topic means here as ever, construction; never destruction. Calvinism, I think, is greater than any one man. Who can fully comprehend all it means? Where is the man that can live subjectively a hundred per cent Calvinistic life?

And still it is the most practical system in the world. It has the long-range vision. It is not for this fleeting moment of time alone; it builds for eternity. If the wise of this world would but become fools listening to the wisdom of God, the nations of this sin-sick world would not now be trembling with the expectancy of impending destruction and blasted hopes. But it brings its fruit of peace and joy only to those who have lost their lives in active service in order that they may gain it.

A. S. De Jong

Address before the National Union of
Christian Schools Convention, Grand
Haven, Michigan, August 31, 1927.

Key Thoughts:

1. The curriculum as a whole is the entire body of organically related subject-matter.

2. We must be clear on the underlying principles that determine the actual building of the curriculum. Clear principles are necessary "that our teachers be able to choose sagaciously and prudently." Absence of clarity on this point may lead to a dishing up in our schools of "a diluted form of modern paganism under the flag of Calvinism." We need clarity to avoid a "petrified system out of tune with the historical development of life." We must build by profiting from ideas of others.

3. We must build what we intend to raise. We must know what we desire to accomplish with our educational policies. And the Christian, particularly the Christian of Reformed persuasion, holds a distinct view of life based on the Scripture. It is inevitable that he should desire to incorporate the ideas and ideals of his view into the curriculum of the schools that are charged with the rearing of his children.

4. The curriculum in the Christian school is, accordingly, based on three distinct concepts.

    a. Calvinism views the child from the standpoint of creation, fall, and redemption.

    b. Calvinism views the child as a child of God in Christ; hence Christian education has a distinctive purpose.

    c. Calvinism holds that the universality of our educational purpose for the Kingdom must at the same time include the particular purpose for each individual life.

5. Central to the entire curriculum is the study of the Word of God as His divine revelation to man.

6. Closely related is the study of history from a biblical standpoint, especially the history of the church of God as an influence in the history of the world. And closely bound up with history is the study of the world's literary productions. Together they afford the student a means for sound appraisal of his own time of which he is a part.

7. A study of nature in its broadest sense reflects the wisdom and goodness, the glory and majesty of the Creator. This includes geography as a study of the earth which the Lord has given to the children of men.

8. Then the child is to be introduced to the arts of reading, writing, and language in view of their instrumental value, both for their practical value, and for the cultural side of human intercourse.

9. The course of study is conditioned by the nature of the child that is to be taught. Lack of interest in the classroom may well result from the neglect of this principle on the part of curriculum makers.

Comment:

The curriculum is the medium which the school employs to realize the ends of Christian education. It is the given that makes the school a school. It represents the cumulative culture of the race as the work of God among and through men. It has its center in the living, inscripturated Word as directed to men. Neither the child nor the school determine the curriculum. It is determined for both the child and the school in the totality of life as viewed according to the Scripture.

But the curriculum needs design for effective learning if the desired ends are to be realized. It is in the course of study that the curriculum is given design. Basic facts and principles of child development set the stage for curriculum design. These basic facts and principles too are to be viewed in the light of what God's Word tells us about man and child life.

2

The Christian View of the School Curriculum

When we speak of the curriculum with reference to the schools, we are thinking of areas or fields of subject matter as learning areas, however they may be organized. Throughout the centuries we have taken the cultural product of the human race and organized and adapted it to learning areas appropriate for learners at various levels of maturity. So we have thought that the coming generation must have some systematic knowledge of the past in order to have a conscious link with historical continuity and to enter understandingly into the issues of the present. Hence, we have included history in some form among the learning areas in the schoolroom. In order to graduate the learning materials of history according to the learning readiness of the learner we have tried to ascertain whether a biographical approach, or a logical approach, or a problem approach, etc., was psychologically and sociologically most sound. Thus the various areas of learning have taken shape more or less scientifically and now constitute the curricula of our schools.

The question for our discussion now is whether there is a distinctively Christian view of the curriculum. Can we say amidst all the controversy in the field of education that Christianity lays down certain basic principles with reference to the nature and meaning of the curriculum?

What determines the Christian view of anything? What determines the Christian view of government, of the economic life, of war and peace, etc.? One might reply the Bible, for it is our only infallible rule of faith and life. In a general sense this is true. But the question of what is the Christian view of this or that is not so easily or naively answered. Genuine honesty, for example, is required of every Christian. The Bible is crystal-clear on this requirement for Christian living. But in our complicated culture it is not always clear what is the honest thing to do. And sometimes the choice is between two evils rather than the good and the evil.

I think with reference to education this may be said. The end which education is made to serve determines whether it is Christian, when we consider that this end is present at the very beginning and judges the process throughout.

Let me attempt to make my point clear. Our cultural activity we have in common with all men. We build bridges, sell products of our farms and factories, engage in laboratory research, etc. All of this activity, however, needs an end or destiny for its justification. From the Greek-Roman classical world we have received two ends or destinies. One is the natural, the end or destiny that finds the justification of all human activity in the fulfilment of man's natural propensities. It is a naturalism, to be distinguished from a materialism. The other is the ideal, the end or destiny that finds the justification of all human activity in the realization of an ideal life of reason. It is an idealism. The Hebrew-Christian tradition confronts us with the rule of God centered in the heart of man, the center of his very personality as a created being. It finds the justification of all human activity in the glory of the Creator. There is a third end or destiny for all cultural activity of man which recognizes no final purpose anywhere. It finds the justification of human activity in meeting human needs as human only. It is the Renaissance-modern interpretation of life and its meaning and purpose.

Bringing this over into the field of education, we have this qualification of it as Christian. Education is distinctively Christian when the authority of Christ and the realization of his authority in the lives of men is the justification of all educational activity. This is very definitely according to the Hebrew-Christian tradition.

It is our responsibility to indicate how this concept of Christian education can be implemented in the construction of curricula. To do this we should try to answer three questions. (1) What are the views of the nature of curricula? (2) How do we appraise these views in the light of the above concept of Christian education? (3) How can we make curricula distinctively Christian?

Views of the Nature of Curriculum

In the history of education we discern four major curriculum concepts. By this I mean that instructional materials or learning areas have been organized and adapted for learning purposes with one of four major purposes in mind. They are: the information or knowledge-getting concept, the disciplinary concept, the social concept, and the creative concept.

In the first or knowledge-getting concept the factual material of subject matter is organized for mastery. The gradation of subject matter is based on a quantitative increase of amount and complexity from level to level. Finally one's education is measured in terms of the amount of information he has stored up during the years. The human mind is viewed as a sort of container into which one pours content at will, with this exception that it has the capacity to organize and recall, also at will, any combination of previously acquired information. The emphasis is on memorization or recall.

The disciplinary concept looks upon subject matter as a means of forming the learner in his mental powers. It is generally based on some form of faculty psychology. The mind is in possession of certain powers or faculties which are exercised and molded in the process of mastering essentials of subject matter. What is learned is not as important as the sustained effort involved in its mastery. Then too, there is an external mold or pattern according to which the learner is to be formed. In the process of learning he begins to take on this form of things.

The two curriculum concepts referred to thus far have come down to us from ancient times. Early schools and those of the Middle Ages were entirely dominated by them. Only occasionally were they called in question. It was not till the modern period that other concepts began to prevail.

The social concept is more of a utilitarian nature. From a survey of the needs of the individual with reference to his successfully functioning in society it is determined what learning activities and materials must be included in the curriculum. Our modern industrial society in which the worker rightly makes his just claims and which operates in the framework of the democratic ideal provides the pattern for curriculum construction in our time. The question, which is paramount, is what does the learner need to know and to do in order to participate in this kind of society for the welfare of all concerned? What kind of mathematics will he be called upon to know and use? How much history must he know and how is it to be organized and interpreted that he may be able to enter intelligently into the issues of the day? Knowledge-getting in itself is meaningless apart from the social structure in which it must function. As a discipline education must take account of the relationship of the individual to the social whole.

The fourth concept we mentioned turns to the individual in his psychological make-up for its basis of the curriculum. It recognizes in man a creative capacity which, though varying in degree among individuals, is the primary goal in education. The development of man as a creator is the primary concern of a society that seeks not merely its self-preservation but that seeks social progress. Learning activities are organized to call forth the creative expression of learners.

Learning is a cooperative activity in which the learners launch on an exploratory tour. Self-expression, self-appraisal, motivation, self-activity, and the like are the key words in learning as a great enterprise. The curriculum consists of activities which vary according to pupil needs. In some quarters it is known as the experience-curriculum.

Here we have the four common views of the curriculum. They should not be thought of as chronologically following each other. The first two, as we said, are of ancient date. They survive today, however, in several ways. Tests and examinations frequently give evidence of the knowledge-getting emphasis when they are almost exclusively factual in character. When the classroom recitation is but a "giving back" what the teacher said or what was read in the textbook, the knowledge-getting or information concept is supreme. Arithmetic and higher mathematics textbooks still contain problems of mental gymnastics, and lecture notes are still reminiscent of memory exercises for their own sake. The social concept is used by some as the basis of a curriculum for social and political regimentation, and by others more democratically as the social orientation of the individual. It is obvious that the creative concept of education is compatible only with a social order which commits itself to the potential integrity of the individual.

What shall we say about each of these concepts when viewed in the light of the Scriptural teaching of man and his place in this world?

Appraisal of Curriculum Concepts from the Christian View

We must base our appraisal on certain essential teachings of the Scriptures with reference to man and his place in this world, for it is with these that education as a process is primarily concerned.

As to the nature of man and his needs, let us note first that education is concerned with man as a whole. He never functions mentally apart from his emotions. Never can we seek his mental development without affecting him spiritually. His social growth is involved in the mental and emotional. And his physical progress affects his emotional adjustment. It is comparatively recent that we learned that an infant needs emotional satisfaction as much as food. As a matter of fact the feeding problem of children is as much emotional as it is physical. Hospitals are adjusting maternity wards to this fact. Let it be remembered likewise that the whole child goes to school, and the whole child is involved in every learning activity.

Furthermore, it should be noted that the whole person in all his resources, physically, emotionally, socially, mentally, and spiritually was created to be patterned after the excellences of the Creator. This is what we understand by the Scriptural teaching that God created man in his image.   In all his resources he is responsive to his world about him that being activated by it he can be formed and form himself after the nature of it, above all after the nature of God himself.   This is man's supreme prerogative among God's creatures.   This means that education is a process of man-making, not merely a training of the intellect or stuffing the mind or adjusting the human organism, etc.

We must follow this observation immediately with the fact, however, that the perfection of which man was capable in all his resources by creation has been lost by the disastrous consequences of sin.   By voluntary act of disobedience man deprived himself of the one source according to which he was to pattern himself that in his response to the world about him he might cultivate the perfections of which he was capable.   This source is God himself.   Having thus deprived himself, he did not cease to be a responsive being, but continued to function thus and according to the natural inclinations of a heart inclined toward self and its indulgence rather than the fulfilment of his original nature according to creation.   The natural man of sin is involved in the tragedy of history, unable to extricate himself.   In all his resources he is perverted and unable to respond according to his created nature.   It is particularly in his mental and spiritual resources that distortions have been so damaging.   Because he is mental and spiritual he is a creative being, rational and moral.   He has created a culture made to serve himself according to his perverted heart.   The final culmination will be the full realization of his own perversion, unrestrained by influences in this world reminiscent of his origin.   What a tragedy!   Education which fails to recognize this awful reality is not true education, but mal-education.

Thanks be to God that we can follow this tragedy of tragedies by the glorious truth that God is in Christ reconciling men and the world unto himself.   There is hope!   There is salvation!   There is redemption!   Man can again be made responsive to God and thereby responsive to the truth of his world in all his resources.   He can again be formed, patterned after the excellences of his Creator.   This is the gospel of the risen Christ.   Education to be true must now be redemptive.   It must cultivate the individual in all his resources in keeping with the awful reality of sin and all its tragic consequences and the saving grace of God in Christ Jesus that delivers him from the human tragedy to be made responsive to the truth and to be formed or patterned after it.

Now, what are man's primary needs in view of these teachings of the Scriptures?   First, that before he is conscious of the truth about himself and about his world he be surrounded by influences which take into full account this truth.   Though the child is unresponsive to the truth by natural inclination of the heart, Christian parents have the promise of God himself, "Bring up a child in the way he should go and when he is old he will not depart from it." The Holy Spirit alone can transform hearts, but he promises to accompany the word of truth and make hearts responsive. Second, we must continue this influence according to the needs of our time by soliciting the growing consciousness of the learner in the understanding and mastery of the truth and the commitment to the truth to be disciplined by it. The latter is the special task of the school on its various levels. Surely, the home, the church, and the community play a large part in this task, but in our modern society it is the formal schooling of the youth which officially assumes this responsibility. Education which fails to meet this basic need is mal-education and will fail of its most cherished goals.

There is another criterion by which we must judge the curriculum concepts which we listed. We must ask the question, What is man's place in this world? In the language of Christ himself this is described as being *in* this world but *not of* it. The meaning of this should become clear later. But we should ask of each of these concepts whether it will give us a curriculum which will help us function *in* this world *as not of* it or whether it will cause us to function *as of* it. For Christianity this is of utmost importance. To live in this world as of it is to be worldly. To live in this world as not in it is world-flight. To live in this world as not of it is to fulfil one's Christian task or God-given calling. This is education's task in our world.

Now we must return to each of the curriculum concepts briefly to appraise each in the light of the criteria presented.

The information or knowledge-getting concept is right when it asserts that there is objective, preëxistent truth to be apprehended. There can be no true education without understanding it and mastering it for recognition and recall, at least to a degree. There is need for logical organization of the materials of knowledge that it may tend to form the learner's thinking.

But a curriculum organized on the basis of knowledge-getting fails to take account of the whole man. It leaves all resources other than the mental resource of man, and even some aspects of the mental, a sort of accidental in education. Little thought is given to them and no phase of the curriculum aims specifically at their activation and forming. Benefits may accrue to the cultivation of other resources, such as the emotional, but they will be quite incidental. On the other hand there is great danger that erudition may be achieved at the expense of the emotional or the social. And on the religious side we know that informational knowledge about God is not synonymous with knowing God unto salvation.

The discipline concept is right when it calls attention to the fact that the mental resources of the individual are strengthened by their exercise and that they must undergo a forming according to the pattern of real being. There are basic laws of logic which must mold our intellect. There are basic principles underlying effective memorization for retention and recall.

A curriculum organized essentially in terms of this concept, however, fills textbooks and learning activities with exercises in mental gymnastics with little regard for the value of subject matter in itself. Mental acuity may be achieved at the expense of desirable emotional and social growth. It can produce debaters and arguers, but will make only incidentally lovers of the truth, if at all. To make lovers of wisdom requires more than either a storehouse of information or a well-disciplined mind.

The social concept is right when it emphasizes the social resources of the individual. Man is a social being. Cooperative activity in the interest of a great cause is difficult for one who has not matured socially. Maturation socially is no more an automatic process than is intellectual maturation. Education must be directed at certain essential social qualities as well as at necessary basic knowledge and intellectual skills.

When the social concept of education makes social adjustment the end and criterion for all educative activity, we respond by saying that the fulfilment of man's deepest needs transcends the social milieu. Society needs an end or destiny beyond itself for justification. A curriculum organized on the basis of the social concept will fall short of developing basic knowledges and understandings, and will neglect the forming of the intellect according to patterns of truth. It will either regiment forcefully or propagandize the individual to the end that he conform to the social context of his time.

The creative concept is right when it calls attention to one of the greatest capacities of the human personality, namely, through insight to reorganize past experience that relatively new patterns of thought and action are produced. This originality is not limited to the few geniuses who write poetry, sculpture human forms, invent machines, etc. It is an integral part of the whole learning process. From the kindergarten through the university we encourage originality. To repress it is to squelch essential motivating drives toward growth.

A curriculum organized on this concept, however, will neglect the forming of the individual according to preëxistent patterns of thought and action. Emphasis will fall on expression with little to express. Norms for judging the quality of expression will be lacking. The individual becomes a law unto himself. All systematic learning ceases.

Education as a process is aimless, lawless, and capricious. The individual learner determines the curriculum.

Let us summarize our appraisal. All the curriculum concepts we discussed have elements or aspects of truth, according to the criteria we secure from the Scriptures. There is preëxistent truth to be understood and mastered. Our mental resources gain power through their exercise in knowledge-getting. Our social resources are responsive and must be cultivated. And finally, we are creative beings, and our capacity for originality must be given opportunity for expression.

We should add immediately that all four concepts are found wanting on essential counts in the light of the same criteria. Every one fails to take account of the individual in all his resources. Especially the social and creative concepts fail to recognize a preëxistent order of truth to be understood and take no account of the great tragedy of human history and its dire consequences. Likewise they find no need for a process of redemption outside and independent of man's own efforts.

A combination of these concepts in eclectic fashion will not do for a Christian view of the school curriculum. They are all essentially rooted in a view of man and his world contrary to the teachings of the Scriptures. And, let it be said that any view of anything to be Christian must take its departure from the basic tenets of the Scriptures. I say, its basic departure. By this I mean that the Scriptures as the revelation of God, in which God has spoken, are for us the corrective, the one true orientation of ourselves and to our world because it reorients us to God.

The Christian View

The basic criteria for appraisal discussed before send us in another direction for educational concepts. In keeping with these criteria we must ask three questions: (1) What materials are available to us for educational purposes? (2) What end or destiny must they serve? (3) How shall we select curriculum materials?

First, then, what materials have we available? Here we generally think of areas of subject matter such as history, geography, language, etc. And this is correct. But to appraise them as educational media, we must look a little deeper than to view them as organized bodies of knowledge.

What is subject matter? It embodies in organized form the cultural and spiritual products of man. These products are the fruit of cultural and spiritual activity through the ages. Let me try to make these statements clear by illustration. There is a given in the world of nature outside of man which constitutes his environment. There is the sunshine and the rain. According to the alternation of these in a given geographic area man develops an agricultural practice and technique which produces the necessary victuals for his consumption. A system of exchange is developed to profit from each other's enterprise. In a similar way communication, transportation, manufacture, construction, etc., are the products of man's use of the naturally given to create for himself the means for life and its enrichment. This activity we call man's cultural activity, using the word culture in its broadest sense.

It is this cultural activity and the cultural product which have constituted the media for the education of the growing generation throughout the ages. In the course of history the cultural product was organized into systematic bodies of knowledge or information. These bodies of knowledge variously organized became the curricula of the schools. They constitute our subject matter today.

But we cannot stop at this point to find the ground for subject matter. There is another given that is presented to man. It does not come to us in the form of nature, as nature is generally understood, that is the world of creation. This given is God himself as he comes to us in his word, in Jesus Christ the Word made flesh and in the inscripturated word, and in the Holy Spirit as he accompanies that word in our consciousness. Man's response to this given is man's spiritual activity, in distinction from his cultural activity.

Now it is peculiar to the Christian that he engages in both. He is in this world and as such is involved in the activities related to this world. But he is not of this world. And it is precisely his spiritual activity that gives direction to his cultural activity. His citizenship is in heaven.

Here we could at length enter into the discussion of the tension this creates in the Christian's life. How can the Christian cultivate his spiritual activity in a mixed culture? How can his heart be set aglow with love for Christ in a world so full of enmity to Christ? This tension is reflected in the Christian view of the curriculum as we shall see.

It should be said that man's spiritual and cultural activities find their justification in a common end, that the authority of Christ may be realized and manifest. This is our citizenship. Hence, the Christian says with Paul, "to be with Christ is far better." He cannot rest until the Christ within him has come to full expression. He longs to be delivered. But with Paul, too, he finds himself in a dilemma. He would fill his place in this world in keeping with God's will for him and abide God's time for his deliverence. In his cultural activity he will struggle to make the claim of Christ upon his life effective. In his spiritual activity he will cultivate a personal fellowship with God in Christ which gives direction to his cultural activity. The Christian's end or destiny is his heavenly citizenship. All his spiritual and cultural activity finds its justification in this end. And it is from the spiritual and cultural products that we have our curriculum or media for education.

What concept do we need to select curriculum materials from our spiritual and cultural products to the end that "the man of God may be perfect and thoroughly equipped to every good work," which is the same as saying that one may exercise his heavenly citizenship? We have found the four concepts that have prevailed in the history of education inadequate. I trust this is even clearer now after the discussion of the Christian's spiritual and cultural activities and their destiny. But can we find a comparable concept that will serve our purpose?

We are concerned with men as creatures of God who have fallen from their God-given state and, who, in the face of the tragedy of a perverted heart and world, are called to turn to Christ in whom God is reconciling man and the world unto himself. We are concerned with the whole man, the individual in all his resources. We recognize man's primary need to be his personal restoration of fellowship with God. He must be saved. We recognize too that the media at our disposal must be employed to realize the meaning of a saved life for this world and the world to come. The best concept I know is that of the Scriptures, citizenship of heaven. We may also call it citizenship of the kingdom of God when this kingdom is placed over against the kingdom of darkness or the devil. To be subjects of Christ in this world, this is our citizenship. Our curriculum materials must be selected to cultivate this citizenship.

What we want, then, are curriculum materials taken from the spiritual product and cultural product that will energize, direct, and form the learner on his level unto citizenship of heaven. This is Christian education's task. Without the destiny of citizenship, education cannot be Christian. Without the cultural product it cannot be education. Without consideration of level it cannot take into account the whole man. Such is our curriculum problem.

The Curriculum Itself

We can divide the areas of subject matter into seven major groups: religion, language arts, philosophy, historical sciences, social sciences, natural sciences, and creative arts. What can each of these areas contribute to the energizing, the directing, and the forming of the individual in all his resources as a citizen of heaven?

The primary task of Christian education in each of these areas is to cause the learner to face God. In every area he should encounter the demands of God upon his life in an attitude of submissiveness to that demand. Heart attitude is our primary objective. The very center of the human personality must be inclined to the divine order and the patterning of the individual in keeping with that order. This is the essence of a heavenly citizenship.

Our first criterion, therefore, in the selection of areas and of subject matter within these areas is, can the learner on his level be directed to face God and God's demands upon his life that he may come consciously to submit to this demand? Let me illustrate this criterion on two levels. First on the primary level, the first level of formal schooling; and then on the level of what we call secondary education, especially the senior level, which are grades ten to twelve.

On the primary level the child, of seven or eight say, hears and reads Bible stories, first largely centered in great Bible characters and later in the form of narration of events. He joins the teacher and the class in prayer, in the singing of sacred songs, and in devotional reading of the word of God. He comes face to face with God in his direct dealings with men in the history of the people of God. He faces God as he joins in group devotions in which he takes an active part. Throughout these activities the demands of God upon his life enter his consciousness.

In the language arts he learns to interpret the printed page and to express himself orally and in writing. His reading material deals with real life as he lives it in a Christian community, including its hazards, its joys, and its responsibilities. Speaking and writing is gauged by the standard of our companionship in which Christ is the unseen guest on every occasion.

The historical, social, and natural sciences at this level come in the form of readings, stories, and individual and group projects aiming at an initial understanding of our world through the world closest to our present interests. This may be our immediate community or it may be the children and their way of life in other lands. Let it be, for example, the Eskimo children. How are they living without the Christ? What is being done to bring the Christ? What is our obligation who know the Christ to them who know him not?

The creative arts take the form of construction, coloring, cutting, etc. Some pupils may begin to show talent in composing prose or poetry, or in color, or in mechanical arts, etc. What are we doing with the special talents God has given us? How well do we cooperate with others in the use of tools, etc.? Can we make or do something to make others happy?

Now an illustration of how this criterion applies to the secondary level. Through a study of the Bible and its doctrines and through the study of the history of the Christian church through the ages since the New Testament days, the learner enters more rationally and intelligently into the religious life. He is confronted with the claim of God upon his intellectual life as well as his moral and devotional life. Class devotions in which all participate take on a more mature character of intercessary prayer and personal consecration. Exchange of religious experiences can be productive of energizing and directing one another if wisely guided by a spiritually mature and tactful teacher.

In the language arts young people are stimulated to read and express themselves. A more mature study of language in its structure and function becomes necessary. Here too we remember that language is our means of communication. The fellowship we keep will determine largely the kind of language we use. When Jesus is our constant companion in all the company we keep, our language will be qualified accordingly. What language is appropriate to this company? What language is in keeping with the citizenship we cultivate?

Of the sciences I shall refer to the historical only. We meet with God in his inscrutable wisdom and purpose when we note that he permitted the devout Huguenots to perish when the Pilgrims were saved in their journey over Holland to America. We meet God when we see the Christian church going down in times of cultural productivity but standing firm when shorn of this opportunity and bitterly persecuted. The learner faces the claim of God upon his life when he begins to ascertain his position in this kind of world.

Thus without sermonizing, moralizing, or preaching, the claim of God upon each individual life enters the consciousness of the learner. It is the primary criterion for the selection of curriculum materials. Curriculum materials are selected and organized with this primary end in view.

I shall have to confine myself to the brief mention of two other criteria. A citizen of heaven in this world faces the tension, as we say, of keeping himself unspotted from the evils of the world while trying to make his citizenship of heaven effective in the mixed cultural activity of our time. Curriculum materials must be selected to make victory over the evil in our cultural activity the freely chosen pursuit of the learner. The areas of subject matter are to be explored that the learner on his level is cultivated in all his resources according to their respective functions in the life of the individual to discern among cultural products and in his cultural activity. As a member of a productive unit in industry he must understand his position as a citizen of heaven. As participant in governmental affairs he must discern in what he is involved.

I think a third criterion with reference to the selection of curriculum materials should be mentioned. As citizens of heaven in this world we are called upon to be workers. Curriculum materials are to be selected and organized in view of the various callings of life. In this rapidly changing and uncertain socio-economic order the call upon one's life for service presents a most perplexing problem to the Christian. The curriculum materials of the various areas of subject matter present opportunities for guidance with reference to this problem. Curriculum makers are to take this problem into account.

In selecting and organizing curriculum materials, therefore, for any level of Christian education, we ask three important questions. First, what is needed on this level to have the learner face God and God's claim upon his life? Second, what is needed to have the learner discern the cultural product and cultural activity of man with reference to his heavenly citizenship? Third, what is needed to have the learner face the call of service as a worker?

I have endeavored to place before you the basic principles involved in the Christian view of the school curriculum. I believe these principles are universally applicable in whatever community Christian education is taken seriously.

Permit me to recapitulate. The curriculum for Christian education is selected and organized from the areas of subject matter embodying the spiritual and cultural products available to us. These areas of subject matter constitute the media for energizing, directing, and forming the individual in all his resources unto his heavenly citizenship. Curriculum materials are selected and organized for the various levels according to the basic criteria as stated before.

It is obvious that only a Christian school wholly committed to the concept of Christian education included in this discussion can prepare the curriculum according to the principles set forth here. No half-way measure is possible. In no sense can a school be called Christian which fails to make the citizenship of heaven its destiny. In no way can a school be a school which fails to employ the cultural product meaningfully toward a destiny or purpose. The Christian school is the answer to the confusion of the educational scene.

CORNELIUS JAARSMA

Address before Schools Section of
Graduate Fellowship, London,
England, September, 1950.

Key Thoughts:

1. Education is distinctively Christian when the authority of Christ and the realization of His authority in the lives of men is the justification of all educational activity.

2. In the light of this criterion the curriculum concepts of the past are found wanting though all make a contribution to curriculum planning.

3. The curriculum concept for Christian education is best expressed in terms of citizenship. But it is the citizenship that bows before the authority of Christ from the heart. It is citizenship in the kingdom of God.

4. Curriculum design follows the pattern of this citizenship as it develops in the immature according to facts and principles observed in child life.

3

Improvement of the Curriculum

That the curriculum of our schools needs constant improvement is commonly accepted. The curriculum does not come to us authoritatively from some power above us, but is developed in the process of education. In spite of this constant desire for improvement, however, we recognize that the curriculum is not the product of caprice. There is something normative about curriculum construction. In the making of the curriculum we subject ourselves to norms. Hence no discussion of curriculum improvement can be carried on without the consciousness of norms.

Where do we get our norms for curriculum construction in Christian education? As Christians of Reformed persuasion we would regard Reformed dogmatics and ethics as normative. Philosophy as the total view of things from the scriptural point of view, logic, and aesthetics would be normative. These must all be in the back of our mind, so to speak, as we talk about curriculum construction. But this is not all. Not only normative fields of learning, but certain descriptive ones too make their contribution to curriculum construction. They are especially psychology, sociology, anthropology, and history of education. It is obviously impossible in this brief discussion to turn to all these sources for specific considerations that should guide us.

What can we do to lay a sound foundation for curriculum improvement? We are concerned with Christian education. This means we are concerned with education in the light of the Word of God. Nothing can be called Christian which does not find its first and foundational departure in the Scriptures. We can ask then, what is the scriptural basis for the curriculum? The normative and descriptive sciences we spoke of will implicitly be involved.

We address ourselves to the task of seeking curriculum improvement along scriptural lines. Before we undertake this difficult task, it seems necessary for clear understanding that we make some pertinent observations relative to our discussion though they are not immediately involved in our problem.

We should bear in mind that the modern school is still, historically speaking, in its infancy. It is not more than one hundred years "young." It is an invention of our modern society. Its inner structure and general organization originated in the philosophical and social movement of the eighteenth century known as the Enlightenment. The humanistic-rationalistic-empiricistic character of this great historical movement is well known to all who know modern history.

Christian schools had their beginning in the matrix of this movement. When Reformed people in the Netherlands became fully aware of the thrust of the Enlightenment school and its effect upon the Christian faith, they launched the Christian school movement. The inner structure of the school remained unaltered except for the reforming of the teaching of Bible history, Christian songs, prayer, and the personal influence of Christian teachers. Now, this was no small thing, this addition of Christian influence. It had all the potency of ultimately permeating the whole structure. But, you see, this is precisely what did not happen. The educative process as such remained unchanged, that is, educational theory and practice. As a matter of fact, Bible history itself was cast in the mold of the educational theory of the Enlightenment school.

We have the Enlightenment school still with us. Only where a classroom is blessed with a genuinely consecrated Christian teacher is the educational structure significantly affected in favor of Christian education. And this can happen in a little one-room rural Christian school as well as in one of our well-equipped Christian schools of urban areas.

In our country as well as in Europe, educational reform is under way. Here in America, educational reform is generally associated with John Dewey and the progressive movement that claims him as its leader. After a couple of decades of uncontrolled excess and recent reactions in certain areas, this reform movement is now beginning to crystallize into a well-defined educational program. Our Christian schools too have felt the influence of this reform in several ways. This reform has a contribution to make, but it will do this with great damage to the Christian school, unless we develop a sound scriptural basis for educational theory and practice.

As we continue with our problem, I am not at all sure that the word curriculum conjures up the same idea to all of us. It should be clear that the teacher's art has two raw materials, so to speak, at its disposal. The first is the child's personality, his personal resources. The second is the cultural milieu. The cultural milieu consists of man and his cultural products. Throughout the centuries man has used the given of God's creation as means to certain ends. Means and ends have accumulated as a cultural product which we all share to some degree. The cultural milieu has been the curriculum for education from the beginning. The modern school organized the cultural milieu for educational purposes to conform to its structure. Whether the school breaks up the cultural milieu into isolated areas of subject matter or whether the school maintains to a degree the wholeness of life in the cultural milieu matters not as far as the meaning of the word curriculum is concerned. The curriculum is the second of the raw materials of the teacher's art.

With these considerations in mind let us try to attack our problem fundamentally. Let us do so in the full consciousness and the desire to build together in the interest of the Kingdom of Christ.

Scriptural Basis for the Curriculum

When we take the scriptural view, we assume a vantage point outside of creation, and, therefore, outside of the cultural milieu. For what is the Scripture? It is the supernaturally inspired and recorded Word of God. In it God speaks to man from the only true vantage point, that of the Creator. It is the truly and completely transcendent point of view. It is the only position from which all things can be seen coherently. Every other view results in error because it fails to see things in their true relationship.

Why do we insist upon this point of view and tolerate no other? Because we are Christians. Our hearts have been transformed by the renewing power of the Holy Spirit and we are daily being renewed by the Spirit in the image of the crucified Christ. It is the transformation of heart that gives us the true life and world view. Do not confuse life and world view with philosophy. Our life and world view comes from the heart. Not philosophy, but only the Holy Spirit can give us the true view of things. It is in the scriptures that the renewed heart views things truly.

Important distinctions must be made here.

The unregenerate man too views things from the heart. But he cannot view them truly for he is confined to a viewpoint from within creation. The reading of the Scriptures as such does not give him the true point of view. Intellectual apprehension and consent to scriptural truth gives no one an understanding heart. The nominal Christian finds himself in this sad plight. Having consented to the Scripture, he has not accepted it in his heart. Only the Holy Spirit can change the heart of man.

One might be a Christian and have had a change of heart, but be a very disobedient Christian. He has the true life and world view but it is sadly obscured by barriers of personality. To be sure we all have but a small degree of this obedience. Christians vary in the clarity of their life and world view because they do not walk equally close with God. We as Christian teachers are called upon to live out of the Word of God if we would see our task clearly.

There are genuinely consecrated Christian people who cause one to marvel at their insight into truth. They school themselves in the Word as those hungering and thirsting for the righteousness of Christ. They view life and see it whole, in coherence, meaningfully. They have come to accept life lived out of the Word. They are found among the erudite, but as often, if not more often, among the unschooled in the academic sense.

For Christian teachers this distinction is important. Christian schools as well as all Kingdom work suffer more from lack of what is sometimes called spirituality than from other inadequacies. To give Christian education a sound scriptural basis we must consecrate ourselves to the Christ who has first loved us. Then the true vantage point we have received in transformed hearts will enable us to see our problem coherently according to the scriptures.

The Vantage Point

Before we try to discover what the Scriptures give us as a basis for curriculum study, we should inquire a little further into the nature of our point of view. We learn essentially three things from the Scriptures on this point.

First of all we are told of the absolute distinction between Creator and creation. God has set a boundary for, a limit upon creation. Man, the acme of God's creation, has a limit placed upon him. Though God made man in his own image, he did not make him god. There is a line of distinction between God and creation. In faith man reaches the border line of this distinction, but he cannot cross the line. God crosses the line from his side in his providence by which He upholds all things by his divine power, in his communion with man, and especially in the incarnation as the Son of God.

In the second place we learn that God makes himself known. He has spoken. He communicates with man and fellowships with him. He gives his people a life and world view in a transformed heart and speaks to them from the vantage point of his great works. He does not even leave himself without witness to the ungodly that they may have no excuse.

We learn too that man lives by faith. God so made him. Faith is the highest act of man that brings him to the very boundary line between God and creation. When man in faith lays hold upon God, he lives in the light. When, on the other hand, man's faith is turned from God, it turns upon man himself and through him upon the world. This is darkness for man. No one is without faith. Man surrenders to what he believes to be true. The unbeliever is not without faith. His faith is directed away from God.

In the transformed heart man's faith is turned to God. From his new vantage point he lives by faith in God and in his Word. It is by faith that Abraham, that Isaac, that Jacob, that Moses, etc. The Christian faith is not a leap in the dark where knowledge fails, but the act by which the transformed heart accepts life lived out of the Word of God.

More could be said concerning our vantage point, but these suffice to show that we have ground under our feet the world knows not of. We stand on solid ground and must not permit our thinking to become adulterated by views not in keeping with these basic truths. It is from this vantage point, then, that we follow the Scriptures to lead us into a better understanding of the problem before us and to show us the way in the solution.

God has spoken. And He has spoken to man with reference to the fullness of human life. Man has the capacity for faith. He lives by faith. By transforming the heart of God's chosen ones, the Holy Spirit has directed their faith to God that they say from the heart "Speak, Lord, for thy servant heareth." God gives us, his children, the true perspective of life in all its fullness; He gives us the true life and world view. We come to life's problems with a transformed heart which gives us eyes to see and ears to hear that in God's light we may see light.

The Primacy of Love

From among the teachings of the Scriptures basic to Christian education I select those having direct bearing on the problem before us. I believe that the first in order and most basic of these is love. The Scriptures are replete with the gospel of love. "For God so loved the world. . . ." The love of God in Christ Jesus is shed abroad in the heart of the believer that he may love God and man. Love is the fulfilment of the law.

What is love? Somehow we feel that we cannot confine it to the emotional life. It involves the whole man. Even of God we are told that God is love. Someone has spoken of it as a mode of man's being. This idea leads us, it seems, to the very essence of it. To love at all is to love from the heart, and this means with the whole man. You just cannot love with your head, nor with your feeling, nor with your emotions.

The best I can do, I believe, to clarify the meaning of love is to refer you to a psychologist at the Free University in Amsterdam, Dr. H. R. Wyngaarden. "Love is not a matter of the affection, a mood, is not merely a concern for, but is the acceptance of a binding together in being; in other words, it is that mode of being of man, in which he truly, without reserve, turns to another and opens himself to the other. It does not overpower the other, but draws the other to himself. In the surrender of love one abolishes voluntarily the rather arbitrary action of the I, the ego; while maintaining his independence, man places himself at the disposal for (not of) another, participates in his life, and thereby enlarges and deepens his own life. He is thus, without reserve, involved in the other, 'with heart and soul,' with all his functions and faculties. Love that is not total, i.e., does not involve the whole man, is not true love." (*Hoofd problemen der Volwassenheid,* p. 140).

Love as here described involves the whole person freely. It characterized man basically before the fall. But sin has turned man inward upon himself and in himself upon the world. This is the very opposite of love. Man is no longer capable of love. However, when by the grace of God in Christ Jesus, the love of Christ is shed abroad in our hearts, his love will constrain us, and we are once again enabled to love. Hence, only the true Christian can love. The non-Christian can only make adaptations and adjustments which resemble love.

When this love by the grace of God becomes ours in the new life, all things become new. Our rationality, our morality, our fellowship, our feeling, our willing, and every other capacity and function take on a new direction. If any capacity or function of man is made primary, as the unbeliever of necessity does, rather than the mode of being called love, one faculty or function dominates. However, when love, which involves the whole man in his basic motivation, is considered primary, all human capacities form a coherent whole directed to God.

Now, why do I begin with this treatise on love in laying the foundation for the study of our problem? Because it is the first principle, the foundational principle, of all educational theory and practice that would claim the name Christian. Our whole methodology rests on it, as well as the curriculum as such. Only he is a Christian teacher who, constrained by the love of Christ, loves as here described by Dr. Wyngaarden. We simply have no Christian education without it. Education without it is mere adjustment.

Because love is so basic to the whole of the Christian life, it is basic to Christian education and therefore to the curriculum. We often speak of educating the whole child. Many educators today are coming to see the futility of directing education at any one time to any one specific function or capacity of the child. It is especially the school of analysis in psychology, known as the depth or dynamics in psychology, that is convincing many educators of the wholeness, the unity of human life at *all* times under *all* circumstances. To deal with any aspect of it in isolation at any given time is not only futile, but fraught with danger to the subject. However, it is only the mode of being we call love which involves the whole man.

If we are going to find a basic unity for the educative process, we shall have to look to the principle of love. The principle of integration is not first of all a matter of intelligence or analysis, nor of feeling, nor of volition and choice, but an action of the heart. This truth becomes very important to us in curriculum construction.

The Christian Educational Structure

It is especially when we come to consider the structure of Christian education that we come to recognize the basic character of love as a mode of being of man.

What do I mean by the structure of education? Let me give a rather prosaic sort of illustration. It may help to get clearly in mind what I mean. You go to view a house. As you view it from the outside, you notice a bit of careless, rough carpentry here and there. You inspect the inside, first and second floors, and you observe that the paint job is not first-class either. When you get to the basement you note the foundation, steel support, and inner construction of the house. You conclude that the structure of this house is sound and durable. What you mean is that what really counts in building, that which holds the house together in all its parts, is essentially sound.

When we study the history of education we note that education in every age can be gauged by an inner structure, or that which constitutes it in a coherent way. So we find the structure in Greek education to be loyalty and eloquence; among the Israelites knowledge of the law and obedience; in the middle ages knowledge and discipline, etc. By structure we mean that which holds education together coherently.

What is the Christian educational structure? Consider the words of Dr. J. Waterink, veteran student and teacher of psychology and educational at the Free University in Amsterdam. Says he: "The depth which the wisdom of Greece could not fathom, which the organizational power of Rome could not attain, Christianity contributed to education. For in reference to education it is not the head which is primary, not the hand which has priority, but it is the heart which gives both wisdom and power. It is therefore not in the emphasis upon love that Christianity has failed education. Throughout history Christianity has failed to find the unity of heart and head; it has failed to circumscribe knowledge in fellowship with love. Christianity has not always succeeded to keep clearly in view what is primary in love; the love of God for his people which is so singularly expressed in the covenant relationship." (*De Geschiedenis der Paedagogiek,* Vol. IIa, p. 212).

We might consider love, as does Waterink, as the structure of Christian education. In vain do we look for it among the Greeks and the Romans. As pagans they simply did not know what love is. No less do we find it among non-Christians today. Though we find love in the lives of Christians through the ages, it was conceived largely in religious and ethical terms. And education was concerned with mental or intellectual discipline. This accounts largely for the inhumanity to man in schoolrooms of earlier years. There have always been genuinely Christian teachers who implicitly made love the structure of education in spite of the educational theory and practice commonly accepted.

I think, however, that two additional structures, or better said, two other integral parts of the Christian educational structure, should be considered. One might consider them as the two other sides of an equilateral triangle. They are faith and obedience.

When the love of God in Christ Jesus is shed abroad in the heart and the heart is thereby transformed to the disposition to love truly, the capacity of faith is turned God-ward. The whole man in his new disposition to love lays hold by faith upon God and his Word. That Word, which remained a closed book to him before no matter how he read it or studied it, now opens up life in all its fullness to the view of the redeemed. Faith now opens the way to true knowledge and understanding. Love and faith belong together.

Obedience too is an integral part of the educational structure. Dr. Wyngaarden's description of love, which I quoted before, makes this clear. I quote again: "In the surrender of love," says Wyngaarden, "one abolishes voluntarily the rather arbitrary action of the ego or I." There is surrender in love. In faith the whole man is directed God-ward. No longer does the ego turn upon the self and in self upon the world, but the ego is God-directed. Not only does the outlook change, but the whole course of life changes.

The non-Christian too surrenders in faith. But the non-Christian surrenders to life as viewed from his immanent position. All men live by faith and surrender to what they believe to be true. So man was created. It is involved in his being man. But his surrender is not in love, but a necessary acceptance to make adjustment. His adjustment gives him a measure of integration, but in it he moves away from God. He is hell-ward bound.

Now all of this is of tremendous importance for our discussion, as I see it. The importance is especially emphasized in our minds when we see in the study of the history of education how little attention was given in education to the Christian educational structure. It did not dominate the Enlightenment and the nineteenth century school which was its product. And we cannot say that it dominates Christian education today. If love, faith, and obedience are the structure of Christian education, then we must all admit that in educational theory and practice we are still far removed from where we should be in our Christian schools.

Yes, there are consecrated Christian teachers who, because they walk with God, intuitively, spontaneously teach in the framework of this structure to a large degree. They are restricted, however, by a curriculum and methodology better suited to the Enlightenment school than the Christian educational structure. We need a psychology, a sociology, an anthropology, and a history of education which can contribute vitally to a curriculum and methodology appropriate to this structure. But where are they? Because we lack a scriptural approach and development of these fields of study, our teachers must rely upon these contributing fields as viewed from a non-Christian, immanentistic point of view. In this regard we have failed in a crucial task so essential for the task of Christian education.

But we must hasten on. None of these basic considerations can be treated exhaustively. Two more demand our attention to guide us in curriculum study.

The Christian View of Culture

Earlier I said that the cultural milieu is our curriculum. It is the only medium available to us for teaching. It is well that we understand the meaning of culture as viewed in the light of the Scriptures.

Man was placed in this world by God charged with a definite responsibility. He was given a cultural mandate. Said God, "Be fruitful, and multiply and replenish the earth, and subdue it; and have dominion over the fish of the sea, and over the birds of the heavens, and over every living thing that moveth upon the earth." What does this mandate mean? Man was charged with the task to develop and master the given of God's creation under God and in his service. In this great work man would find the fulfilment of himself as man.

But we know the tragedy that came to pass. Man turned from God. In his heart he accepted the world without God. Man's capacity for his great task was seriously affected at its very source. And upon the given world itself he brought the curse of God. In his blind immanentism he continues his cultural activity. From the world on which rests the curse of God he wrests a meager product compared with what could have been.

God acts in the midst of this awful tragedy and sets in motion the great process by which his creation will ultimately be saved for greater glory. By regenerating lives God gathers unto himself in Christ a people who will carry out his mandate. But the mandate is quite different now. The cultural mandate has not been revoked. But the witness to the gospel must now take priority. The people of God are to exercise their cultural mandate against the background of, or better said, rooted in the gospel.

To make the great work of redemption possible throughout the ages, God restrains the power of sin and overrules it. The natural man of sin continues with his cultural activity in the blindness of his immanentism under the restraining power of God. The cultural product is not all wrong; it has much that is good. But in the cultural activity man moves away from God.

The man of God prompted by the gospel shares much of the cultural product and carries a cultural mandate based on the gospel. A mixed cultural product is in evidence which two classes of people appropriate for two conflicting ends.

Man and his cultural product constitute the cultural milieu. It constitutes the curriculum or educational medium. Human life in its fullness embodies the cultural milieu in the mixed form of good and evil, righteous and unrighteous. The individual is being constantly patterned by it and according to it. The best the natural man can do is to accept life as patterned by the cultural milieu and direct his way accordingly for human ends. His school needs a curriculum which will help him to accept life intelligently, meaningfully, according to his immanentism.

The Christian, however, occupies another position. His new life and world view gives him another approach to the cultural milieu and another end for his cultural activity. He too comes to accept life, but he sees life as a coherent whole in relation to the God of life and as centered in the gospel. Rather than being patterned by the cultural milieu, he appraises it for the new life that lives out of the

Scriptures. His school needs a curriculum which will help him live this new life to the praise of the God of his life.

When we set up a curriculum for Christian education, not the cultural milieu as given becomes the pattern, but the new life lived out of the Word of God. To be sure the cultural product is our medium for education, but it is in the appraisal of it for the new life that we find our curriculum.

The Christian View of Learning

We turn our attention to another basic consideration, the theory of learning. Psychologies today confront us with varying theories of learning. The conditioned response and trial and error theories once occupying a prominent place are now recognized as inadequate for the higher processes in human learning. Man learns by sudden insight too, it has been found. And the depth psychology has caused some psychologists to extend insight as a principle of learning to include the whole man in the process. W. H. Kilpatrick in his recent book on the philosophy of education makes the bold assertion that one has not learned anything until he has accepted it in his heart. Prof. Kilpatrick, the popularizer of Dewey, has come a long ways in his view of learning since the day of his *Foundations of Method,* first published in 1925. Of course, he does not accept the scriptural denotation of heart, though he borrows the Christian expression.

The Scriptures very clearly tell us that the understanding heart is to be desired. Nothing is really learned until one accepts it in his heart. "Thy word have I hid in my heart, that I might not sin against thee." The word may be in the head, but sin will still run uncontrolled in life. But in the heart it accomplishes its purpose. Nothing is really learned in school until a child comes to accept it in his heart. This is the scriptural view of learning. It does not deny that certain psychosomatic behavior is acquired by conditioning and trial and error. Neither does it deny that insight gives intellectual comprehension. But learning is more than a modification of behavior and assimilation of knowledge. Learning is heart acceptance.

How can we get the child to accept in his heart what he ought? This is a staggering problem. It is in part a question of methodology. We enter here into the sphere of regeneration. The capacity for heart acceptance of the truth is not ours to give. By nature no man has it, for sin turned man from God. But in the covenant of grace we have the promise. Our view of the curriculum must take note of the promise.

What Curriculum Views Do We Reject?

Having taken the scriptural position on the nature of the educational structure, on the meaning of culture, and on the view of learning, current curriculum views come in for critical appraisal.

Earlier we have said that the natural man seeks to view the whole, the totality of life from some position or point of view within life. This is all he can do. His is not the transcendent point of view of the heart renewed by the Holy Spirit. Because he believes his point of view to be true, he accepts life as he views it from his immanent position. Some phase of life he glorifies above the other phases.

This is also true in education. When we come to examine educational philosophies not founded on the Scriptures, we find that some aspect is glorified above the other phases of education. So it is that either knowledge or personality has been glorified.

The curriculum which glorifies knowledge makes mental discipline, intellectual comprehension, logical demonstration, etc., the *conditio sine qua non* for the educated man. It is the man who can think logically, who is erudite, who has much book knowledge who is really educated. It often passes under the name of liberal education. It worships knowledge as virtue or as power. It says we learn what we come to know.

The curriculum which glorifies personality claims to have a monopoly on integration and unification of human life. Adjustment is what counts. Every quality of human personality must be developed harmoniously in relation to every other quality to effect the adjustment of the whole person to the flux of life. It says we learn what we come to live.

Both views are very critical of each other. The former accuses the latter of superficiality and sentimentality. The latter charges the former with intellectual aristocracy and traditionalism. But on scriptural grounds both are weighed in the balances and are found wanting.

What are our objections to curriculum views glorifying either knowledge or personality? First of all, both belong to the immanence perspective of life. Some have made the intellect primary among man's capacities or faculties. Others the feeling function. Still others the will. The faculty psychology has done much damage to Christian education. It is Greek and pagan in its origin, not scriptural.

The second objection follows from the first. Both view life empirically-rationally or ideally-rationally. The former is the modern scientific approach; the latter the deductive-logical approach. The former claims to reason from observed fact only; the latter reasons from logical propositions rationally or propositionally deduced. Revelational thinking puts both in their proper place without denying either. Both propositional thinking and induction from observed fact are necessary for the extension of knowledge, but both need the orientation and direction of the Christian faith to escape the limitation of their immanence.

There is a third objection. The glorification of knowledge as the all-in-all in education ignores what has been called the whole-person-in-action. By this is meant that this view fails to see that the knowing function of man is involved in his total action. Learning is more than an accretion of knowledge or a discipline of the power to think. The whole man in all his psycho-somatic processes as issuing from the heart is involved in learning. One may acquire right knowledge and develop the power to think clearly, but fail to develop an understanding heart.

On the other hand, the glorification of personality which speaks so much of the whole person in the learning process *limits* its view to the whole-man-in-*action*. Personality and selfhood do not exhaust man anthropologically. Man is spirit, ego, I. The heart, as the Scriptures speak of man, is ego, is the very center, the directing essence of man. The heart is at the very center of the psycho-somatic. The whole-man-in-action is the heart issuing forth in the psycho-somatic. This is called an anthropological psychology according to the scriptural view of man. The glorification of personality in education ignores man in his deepest nature. The depth psychology thinks to have found human nature in the *id*, but fails to recognize the spirit of man, and consequently goes wrong in both the ego and in its motivations.

It should be clear that we cannot compromise with current views of the curriculum. A truly transcendent view of man and his culture challenges us to a diligent study of the curriculum as a medium for a distinctive Christian education.

A Christian View of the Curriculum

I now turn to the curriculum proper. Against the background of and on the basis of what I have been saying, I shall try to state certain principles basic to curriculum construction in our Christian schools. Far be it from me to claim that they are exhaustive. Let us keep working at their modification, clarification, and extension. The order in which I state them has no necessary significance of logical priority. The order is more psychological than logical.

Principle I

The curriculum is the medium the teacher-artist has at hand to guide the learning of the child according to the Christian educational structure.

I think every term used in this principle has been explained in the previous discussion, except the words guide and medium. The latter has been used on occasion but not explained. Hence, I shall enlarge on these only.

Some may feel that the word guide is too weak. What then happens to indoctrination, discipline, and forming, all of which surely have a place in Christian education? Remember that the Scriptures teach us that nothing is really learned until it is accepted in the heart. It is obvious then from the Scriptures as well as from psychological study of the learning process that you cannot make anyone learn anything. When the Christian educational structure functions in teaching and learning, guidance will be purposeful, firm, enlightening, challenging, and understanding. Guidance involves instruction, admonition, discipline, and direction, but always in the full consciousness that the subject must act by acceptance in his heart.

I should make some explanation of medium too. This should not be interpreted to mean that the curriculum is a means to an end. No more than life is a means to an end. The true end of man is to glorify God. But we can glorify God only in the life He gives us. We cannot glorify God apart from life. But my life is not I. Life is a medium with respect to the I. As a medium it is involved in the end, but it is not the end. But life is more than means, too. Likewise the curriculum is not the end of the learning process, but it is very much involved in the end. It embodies values the learner must come to accept. It is the medium in which the learner realizes his end.

Principle II

The curriculum in the Christian educational structure affords a continuity for learning.

Education aims at bringing the individual to maturity. The chief mark of maturity is that one accepts life. He does not come to acceptance of it piecemeal. He comes to accept it in coherent relationship. He accepts it from a point of view, consciously or unconsciously, he assumes or believes. The Christian comes to accept life from a transformed heart. He has the truly unified, coherent point of view. The Christian educational structure gives true coherence to education. It demands an interrelatedness of curriculum of such a nature that it facilitates the learner's acceptance of life coherently. A chopped-up curriculum of isolated facts glorifies knowledge. An experience curriculum seeks unification in terms of the whole-man-in-*action*. Only Christian education is capable of genuine unification of curriculum for continuity of learning.

Principle III

The continuity of learning in a unified curriculum has its center in the Scriptures.

The transcendent view of life and the world is the possession of every Christian. In the Scriptures the Lord gives the light in which the children of light see the light. The Scriptures are norm for faith and life in all fullness. The Christian developing into maturity comes to accept life lived out of the Scriptures. Like life, the curriculum in its coherent relationships lives out of the Scriptures.

How does one live out of the Scriptures? The Christian's devotions are a response to the hunger and thirst for personal fellowship with God. In prayer and searching of the Scriptures the understanding heart matures. The Christian lives out of the taproot, if you will, of his life, which is Christ. He subjects himself to the norms of the Scriptures and accepts life in the light of these norms.

Principle IV

Continuity and coherence of learning is primary in curriculum organization.

This principle, it seems to me, follows from the previous. If the curriculum as a medium affords a continuity for learning in the Christian educational structure having its center in the Scriptures, continuity and coherence must be a basic consideration in curriculum organization. Arbitrarily to chop up a curriculum for mastery of isolated skills and knowledges, even if based on experimental studies, violates this very principle. Organization will vary with levels according to the maturity of the learner. A twelve-year-old, for example, can study arithmetical facts and skills for a prolonged period of time and later relate these on the level of insight and understanding coherently to life, but a seven-year-old lacks this capacity. The eighteen-year-old can normally deal with not too involved a problem of government for a time in somewhat isolated fashion and meaningfully come to relate it to life under guidance. The twelve-year-old lacks this capacity for concentration and insight.

No learner comes to accept in his heart what appears to him unrelated to life. Intellectual comprehension is not a prerequisite to heart acceptance. Faith is of a higher order in life than analysis. Meaningful relationship in the unity of life is more important for acceptance than intellectual comprehension. How many unschooled Christians accept life truly and coherently when often erudite scholars find less coherence and unity in life because they have not surrendered in love to the God-related life.

A curriculum consisting of isolated skills and knowledges highly compartmentalized constitutes actually a barrier to life acceptance. Only in so far as it is supplemented outside of school from life does it acquire genuine educational significance. The genuine Christian teacher who in his teaching art makes the classroom live out of the Scriptures for the learners in spite of a compartmentalized series of exercises is not common, but not rare either. We need more of such teachers.

Suggested Implementation

We have now come to what some would call the practical phase of our discussion. For want of a better word, I shall call this part the implementation of what has gone before. It seemed a long time in coming. But I could not have said less, as I see it, to try to make clear the basis on which the curriculum rests.

As I said at the outset, in a sense a curriculum is never complete. We must keep improving it constantly. As our insight into the problem deepens and extends, new vistas for revision loom up. Needed reform will ever be with us.

The foregoing represents a humble attempt to lay a scriptural foundation for continued curriculum improvement. I do not mean to infer either that the scriptural foundation as I have tried to outline it needs no revision. Only the Word of the Lord abides. Though born again of the Holy Spirit and viewing things as we do in the newness of life according to the Scriptures, we still see "things" as in a mirror, obscurely (I Cor. 13:12) for we have not attained to the fullness of our life in Christ. I venture, then, to concretize for our schools some of the things I have said and present them for your deliberation.

First, the Christian view of learning makes the teacher-pupil relationship basic to the pupil-curriculum relationship.

The Christian view of learning which says that learning is heart acceptance, grounds the learning process in the anthropological view of man as taught in the Scriptures. As I said before, the teacher-artist has two raw materials at his disposal, the pupil and the cultural milieu. The pupil is a subject, not an object. The cultural milieu is the object. The Mark Hopkins analogy is a scriptural idea. The curriculum can be effective only in the hands of a teacher-artist, that is a teacher who has learned how to use the cultural milieu for educational purposes in the Christian educational structure.

A genuine Christian teacher-artist makes his curriculum. He knows and understands the cultural milieu. He is able to plan and execute his plan in the Christian educational structure. He knows the learner and is able to stimulate him into action from the heart. He looks prayerfully to the grace of God to move the learner to heart acceptance of the truth.

This does not obviate the necessity of a recorded, ready-made curriculum for the schools. First of all there must be organization and articulation among the various levels of schooling, and a ready-made curriculum accomplishes this organization. To a competent teacher this curriculum will be no more than a tool by means of which he regulates his planning. In the second place, not all teachers are competent. We shall always have the latter kind with us. And there are the neophytes. They need much help. A planned curriculum for our schools is necessary.

We shall make a mistake, however, if we think a well-organized course of study can accomplish for Christian education what the genuine Christian teacher-artist accomplishes. The same is true of textbooks. We must concentrate on the teacher, his recruiting, pre-service, and in-service education. Here is the heart of Christian education.

Second, curriculum coherence demands unified areas of learning in keeping with the fulness of life if acceptance of life in the heart is to be achieved.

This statement is in keeping with what I said earlier about accepting life in its fulness. Life must be divided for purpose of analysis. One cannot learn or grasp it as a whole in one look, so to speak. Acceptance in the heart, however, can come only when life is seen coherently. Facts can be memorized in isolation, skills and ideas can be acquired in compartments, and logical thinking can be developed in academic areas of study, but to surrender to and take possession of (for this is what acceptance really means) requires a grasp of coherent relationships of life in its wholeness.

Permit me to illustrate this point from Christian worship. I think the point I am trying to make is evident to all who worship the Lord in truth. One may acquire knowledge of the great doctrine of providence. One learns what it means from compendium and catechism. One hears it expounded in sermons. One even argues the point doctrinally with others who allow for a degree of chance or fate in life. But when has one come to accept this great doctrine? When in the fulness of life this doctrine is seen coherently. The time comes when grief and distress crowd in upon one. To say then from the heart, "All things work together for good to those who love God . . ." and "The Lord has given, the Lord has taken, blessed be the name of the Lord" constitutes acceptance. The great truths of the Christian faith are learned in the coherent relationships of life. We have not learned these truths until they have been accepted in our hearts.

But we cannot reproduce the fulness of life in the school, you say. No. But we can give the curriculum the unity and coherence which resembles life. And this can be accomplished by unified areas of learning.

Third, the Scriptures must permeate unified areas of learning with their perspective and mandates.

We talk much of permeating all of education with our life and world view. This is genuine Calvinism we say. We are no more finished making the statement and we wonder how this can be done in arithmetic, or spelling, or mathematics, etc.

Now it must be granted that this is no easy task. We as Christians have a life and world view from the heart, as we saw earlier, which is transcendent in character, revelational, and, therefore, the only true point of view. We have the Word of God to unfold to us from this transcendent point of view the truth about our world. Only to the degree that this light permeates life can we see life truly, coherently.

But one reason why we have such great difficulty with permeating the curriculum with scriptural truth is that the nineteenth century school, which still predominates among us too, is so far removed from life in its educative process. Learning is not taken as acceptance in the heart, but as assimilation by the mind or intellect. There is very little scriptural application to the abstractions of our curriculum when these are set up in compartmentalized facts, skills, and ideas.

To be sure we cannot join with the current educational theory and practice that would seek unity and coherence from life. It views life from a point within life and applies human criteria. It seeks unity of life without God.

If we mean business with a distinctive approach to the curriculum on scriptural ground, I firmly believe we shall find new possibilities for what we have been talking about for so long a time, namely permeate the whole educational program with revealed truth.

Suggested Areas of Coherence

I have tried to suggest the broad lines along which, I believe, improvement of the curriculum in Christian education should take place. I make bold to say more by way of implementation. I shall suggest areas of coherence within the framework of the school set-up.

We must work in the framework of the graded structure of our modern school. In many ways this nineteenth century school constitutes a barrier to genuine Christian education. This school is not the fruit of Christian thinking and the planning of education within the Christian educational structure. This school is a product of the Enlightenment, the very enemy of scriptural truth. We have taken this school over for Christian ends. But at best it remains a setup which works more into the hands of the non-Christian world than for the kingdom of God. But I am not minded to suggest a reformation on this score, nor am I prepared to recommend a substitute. Even if we should try to reform the school in its framework, the community would find it difficult to follow. You know what community resistance is experienced in the change of a marking system. What would happen if we abolished grades, report cards as we know them, and substitute home visits by teachers, and the like? So, work in our present framework we must.

On the basis of our present school organization let us think of three divisions prior to the senior high school. They are the kindergarten-primary division comprising the kindergarten and first two grades; the intermediate division comprising grades three to six inclusive; and the junior high school grades seven to nine inclusive.

For the first division I would suggest the language arts as the coherent area of learning. Everything done in these grades seeks oral and written expression, including reading. All knowledges and skills are subordinated to and developed for the purpose of the ability to use language as our mode of communication. All activities have this one major purpose. The child is learning to accept life in the medium of the language arts. This is not the same as saying that he is learning language. That makes language an end in itself. He is learning to accept life coherently as he lives it in the language arts.

On the next level the medium by which life is accepted in ever enriching fulness is extended. We continue with the language arts, but it is no longer an adequate medium for a fuller life. I would add the natural sciences. Knowledges and skills formerly subsumed under language arts and developed for extended and enriched communication outgrow this limited area. Arithmetic, for example, becomes a knowledge and skill that opens up life in the natural world about us. The learner comes to accept a larger world than the world of communication. The same is true of hygiene, geography, and even of history. The learner is not yet ready for the historical grasp.

On the junior high school level the two previous areas are continued. A third becomes necessary to enrich the life the learner must come to accept. It is the area of the historical and social sciences. The language arts, the natural sciences, and the social sciences now constitute the areas of learning, the media of coherent learning by which life in greater fulness comes to be accepted in the heart of the pupil.

What am I really advocating? Not a lumping together of discrete subject matter over-arched by some inclusive concept for logical classification. External organization never makes for coherence. Nor do I advocate what some educators speak of as fusion. So often the values of the medium are lost by fusion in a colorless mass. Fusion becomes confusion. This is hardly coherence, for the integral parts lose their identity in the whole.

Not these, but I am advocating a continuity representative of life. If maturity is characterized by the acceptance of life from the heart, if the school aims at maturity, then the school must deal with life. Christian education is concerned with the acceptance of life as viewed from the Scriptures. It too must lead the learner to understand life coherently. Life cannot be understood any other way. It is not accepted, as we saw, in the heart in compartmentalized form.

For learning purposes we must deal with aspects of life according to the level of comprehension of the learner. The graduate school student can deal with isolated areas for concentrated study for long periods and come to relate these to life (some do not on this level) but in childhood we are dealing with another level. And these levels are different, not merely quantitatively. There is a qualitative difference, difference in kind, of comprehension. Hence, I am suggesting these areas.

Let me use an illustration for the intermediate level. We teach fractions. This is necessary. The fulness of life demands it. They have real significance, not only in arithmetic, but in the area of life represented by the natural sciences. In learning to understand fractions and how to manipulate them, this whole area is involved. Life as represented in the natural sciences includes fractions. They come to be accepted in their coherent relationship when organically related to life in this area.

Having traversed the curriculum as one of the raw materials the teacher-artist has at hand in a unified and coherent way, the learner comes to accept life and not merely retain compartmentalized knowledges. I suggest when the pupil leaves the junior high school, having followed such a curriculum, he has viewed life coherently as represented in the language arts, in the natural sciences and in the historical and social sciences. He has viewed life coherently for he viewed it from the transcendent vantage point of revealed truth. If it pleases the Lord to transform his heart, the pupil has made a significant beginning with the Christian life. If not, Christian education has pointed the way to heart acceptance of life embodying truth but viewed immanently. The direction of human faith is not ours to give.

You may conclude I neglected Bible as a part of the Christian school curriculum because I did not mention it as a subject of study. The central place I have given the Scriptures as revealed truth throughout hardly makes it necessary for me, it seems, to enlarge upon Bible in its significance for Christian education. I am not in agreement with those who think we would still have Christian education though Bible and worship were excluded as long as the curriculum is interpreted from a Christian point of view. This reasoning betrays a Thomistic dualism of faith and knowledge. If Christian education is what I have tried to say it is, Bible and worship will be an integral, dynamic part of the school. As there is no Christian life except the life lived out of the Scriptures, so there is no Christian education without a living contact with God in his Word. This requires worship as well as Bible study.

If the Christian school is to survive among us it must become more distinctively Christian. So positively Christian must it be that the non-Christian does not feel at home unless he too begins to accept from the heart the life lived with God. The Christian religion embraces the whole life. Our boys and girls of Christian homes, members of the church of Christ, will mature in the Christian life when they come to accept in their hearts life in its fulness. The Christian school is Christian when it is staffed with teachers who have accepted life from the vantage point of the new life in Christ and are the artists who know how to use the medium of the cultural milieu to guide the immature to the acceptance of life.

Cornelius Jaarsma

Address before Christian School
Principals Conference, Grand Rapids,
Michigan, August, 1951.

Key Thoughts:

1. School reform is here, both in Christian education and in secular education. There is no return to the Enlightenment school of the nineteenth century. It never was Christian. It merely added some Christian features to a learning process essentially non-Christian.

2. There is a scriptural basis for the curriculum. It is found in the primacy of love. The entire Christian educational structure, love,

faith and obedience, lays the foundation for the curriculum in Christian education.

3. The cultural milieu is appraised for its contribution to the development of the new life in Christ in planning the Christian school curriculum.

4. Learning is essentially heart acceptance. Curriculum design in the Christian school is based on this principle.

5. The curriculum in the Christian school avoids the extremes of knowledge-getting and personality as bases for design.

6. Basic principles of curriculum construction and their implementation for our Christian schools are necessary if they are to become better schools and more distinctly Christian.

4

Integration

A well-known and famous thought that we would make central and point of departure is this: that the school must take its place in the fullness of life, that all school activity must be as closely related to the fullness of life as possible. Life must not be viewed too "practically," must not be exclusively oriented in the here and now, not exhausted in the material and mundane, but it must constantly be viewed in the light of eternity, in the light shed on it by Jesus Christ. Hence, there should be no optimistic camouflage of the vulgar and sinful, but through it, God be praised, an eye for the restoration of all things in Christ Jesus, for the kingship of Christ, his purpose with it all.

This orientation in the beyond gives us insight in the fundamental unity of life. For life is one and at the same time a manifold of individual variations. A unity, not in its uniformity, but in its pluriformity. A unity with qualitative variation; with main and subheadings (authority); not only with counsel, but also with final relations. A unity that does not find its analogy in a stream, but in an organism — an analogy two thousand years old. Essential to it is balance and harmony, mutual aid, promotion and restraint.

This unity of life that proceeds from God and returns to God gives us the correct view of the tension which we meet constantly in life and in educational theory, the polarity of the individual and the group. This is a tension that calls for a balanced solution by choosing one or the other, but over against this we maintain the Christian demand of harmony and reconciliation of the opposites. Not either-or, but and-and must be the departure. Not a fearful abstaining from certain educational techniques out of "respect" for the individual, anxious lest he manifest unbridled expression — nor a social education that one-sidedly finds all norms in the (supposed) welfare of society. We should reverence life, both in its individual and in its collective manifestations. No one places higher value on the individual than does Christ (what profit is it to a man, though he gain the whole world and lose his soul) — but no one is clearer than He in setting boundaries to individualism (he that would save his life shall lose it), and that the one must view his calling in life in the service of others (love your neighbor as yourself). Hence, as Gunning says somewhere, for the Christian the welfare of society is not the norm for education, but the natural fruit of it.

L. VANDER ZWEEP, G. WIELENGA AND J. W. VAN HULST
*Guide for a Course of Study
for the Christian Schools*, pp. 6-7.

Comment:

The school takes its place in the fullness of life. Its integration is had from the organic unity of life. This unity must be maintained in the learning process if integration of the personality is to take place. The unity of life is of God. Man's systems are of his own making. He needs them to help him think about life. But only when they return one to life with greater clarity of insight are they educational.

5

Implications of the Principle of Integration

If we proceed from the *unity of life in the collective whole,* we come to the following thoughts:

A. The school must form the child into a living member of society by cultivating a group consciousness. This cannot be accomplished by talking about it, but only by creating an atmosphere in which the child lives the true community life. The contrast between the "listening school" and the "doing school" is not in the first place between the school where a child listens and the school where he works with his hands, but between the school where he hears life's task and life's calling talked about only, and the school where in real living he experiences daily what is spoken of in theory.

1. In every class, the community idea must prevail, every class must be a community. A community is a unity with a purpose, or otherwise said, nothing cultivates a community consciousness as does the possessing of a community purpose, the working together at a common task. It will be of great importance, therefore, that we cultivate in class a group consciousness, for example, to challenge children constantly by an attainable goal. The group must not be too large that the individual be not lost in it. Hence, let children work in groups. Will this not cause some disorder in class? There is no ground for concern here! And do not forget that this is excellent practice in group consciousness, for is not the secret of this the taking account of others, feeling responsible to others? By thus working at a common task, competition makes place for cooperation, and destructive criticism for mutual appreciation. This helpful and appreciative attitude we ourselves must demonstrate, and must stimulate in our pupils. For example, we do not merely call attention to errors made on the blackboard, but ask, "What is particularly well done?" But especially is the community spirit advanced by living and sharing together common joys, sorrows and admiration, but also zest for work that becomes contagious and is even caught by slow learners. This is an experience in which the teacher too must share, in which he even takes the lead that it may be transmitted to the class. For he must not only be the leader of this community called the class, but he is an integrating, cooperating, inspiring part of it.

2.   This class community must not stand by itself. The circle must be enlarged, it must itself be a part of the larger community, the school, with a sense of responsibility of the older for the younger. Such an atmosphere cannot exist, however, without the spirit of confidence generated by the relationship among the teaching personnel. This can be if schoolwork is viewed as a community task and each one stimulates and helps the other, for example, by exchanging ideas and discussing attempts at improvement (successful as well as unsuccessful). The school community should include parents and members of the board. Parents can have a part in providing materials for the school, pupils can organize exhibitions for parent evenings, etc.

3.   The circle must be enlarged still further. The child must acquire a vision of the larger community, in which he still occupies a passive position but in which he will some time play an active part. There must be a strengthening of national consciousness (by commemorating national events in relation to school life) and we must direct education purposefully in channels of Christian-democratic principles, wherein the emphasis falls on responsibility to our neighbors in word and in deed, also in our school work (good workmanship).

B.   The school must form the child into *an active member of the community* by developing a *dynamic cultural interest,* an openness along various channels.   The community needs *active people* who throw themselves into the fullness of life and take a vital part in it, who have a real interest in and an eye for problems pertaining to church, state and society. People who love to read a book (and not the devotional kind only) ; people who love to sing and enjoy music (and not only via the radio) ; people who have a vital interest in educational issues (and not only to criticize the teacher). The last example clarifies what we have in mind. In school, it stands to reason, such problems cannot be introduced. But our purpose is to cultivate such a mental attitude that one senses the problem (when met in life) and seeks the information and enlightenment necessary to arrive at an independent judgment. This does not require first of all the accumulation of much knowledge, but rather a harmonious development of intellect, heart and will. Not too much "knowledge," for this only makes know-alls, and parading knowledge is worse than ignorance.

We seek, therefore, a mental attitude which is characterized by vital interest, critical appraisal, and unpretending; hence:

1.   Do not equip a child with all kinds of erudition prematurely. Self-restraint is called for here, for we easily permit ourselves to be guided by what we find attractive and interesting. For unassimilated and indigestible knowledge does not arouse interest (nor later in life), but indifference and aversion. Not what we find of interest first of all,

but what has or can stimulate the inward appeal of the child, constitutes the criterion. Connection must be sought with this inward appeal; it must be developed, and directed into wider channels.

2. Cultivate *people who can help themselves.* Not a complete systematization of all kinds of knowledge is the ideal, but a well-chosen selection of key-concepts. Equipped herewith, the child can learn to use the means or aids for self-development. A small library of reference works is a great help (Why should not the school try to collect such a library through pupil's savings?).

Our attention must reach beyond this. Also the aids for self-development that play a major part in later life, as the press, film, and radio, must be incorporated in our instruction, their proper use must be learned; especially ability for critical appraisal must be developed.

A constructive, critical attitude is of great importance. This is difficult too, even for adults, but especially for children, for it seems to run counter to their suggestible nature, their dependence, which is frequently intensified by the school.

Attempt by your questions to get the young people to *think,* not to *guess;* try, if at all possible, to have them undertake something independently, and teach them to read and listen critically. This may not degenerate, understandably, into a hunting for all kinds of error (there is room for critical appreciation), but they must accustom themselves to an objective search for error, and not uncritically accept everything.

Of importance is the analysis and valuing of error, for we are especially concerned with the reason for making such an error. This constantly asking for the why of an error takes the attention off the one making the error and turns it upon the object itself. The teacher should put this constantly into practice that youth may become accustomed to a matter-of-factness. Especially must criticism be turned upon one's own work. This is even more difficult for a child, but of great value. The pupil's work must be appraised by the teacher, constructively, and by himself. Modesty is a beautiful virtue.

However, the teacher must act with caution and great tact. Especially at this point can and may children not be treated alike, for not all children need to learn modesty. The timid children must have their eyes opened for their achievements. In general, encouragement is a greater stimulus to independent activity than criticism, but this does not minimize the significance of objective self-criticism for later life.

3. No matter how much we command the development of an active interest, the acquisition of basic knowledge is essential. The necessary amount must be thoroughly mastered and in readiness for use. But here we must caution too: not too early! Seed sown in infertile soil will not take root. Knowledge for which the child is not ready, in

which a child has no insight, and with which he has no contact, the child's psyche will throw off in sort of self-defense, and will therefore soon be forgotten. It is much more economical to wait with sowing and planting till the child is ready.

C. The school must take full account of *the child's interrelation with his environment*. When we speak of the unity of life, we mean first of all the life of the child. Much more than the adult, the child is in his feeling and willing, but also in his ideas and his thinking, bound by and dependent upon concrete experiences. As we have great difficulty to conceive of and think about things with which we have had no contact, likewise the child, and even more so. Hence, we must proceed in our instruction from the immediate environment of the child, from his daily experience. This does not mean, of course, that we confine ourselves to this narrow circle and passively wait till it enlarges itself. We shall very actively try to widen the horizon and extend the circle constantly with the child as center. But point of departure and point of contact will always be found in the child's concrete experience.

D. The school must take full account of the unity of life *in the organic relationship of subjects*. The organic concept of the relationships of life demands that all the various divisions of subject matter be organized into one whole. The much-criticized separated areas of subject matter, though sometimes commendable from a point of view of method, do indeed threaten to disrupt all the interrelations of life. Without forcing everything into an "organic" straitjacket, we should at least take account of the following.

1. There is a close relation between *place* and *historic event* (and "historic" does not have to mean "in the dim past"). Nothing happens or it happens somewhere, and a place is of significance only when something happens there! That "something" is of historical and social significance. Therefore, geography and history must be brought into close relationship; yes, history (even Bible history) cannot be taught without constantly using a map. From the very beginning, when geographic concepts are used and when the map as a symbol is introduced, we take account of this. When the surroundings of the school are drawn in the form of a map, this must be interwoven with school life as a whole, our going to school and school events — this happened here and that happened there. By including the experiences of the children, purpose and relationship are experienced and firmly established.

Also at the outset of the learning of history, we must take care that the place where something happened is emphasized. What really counts is that at the outset the geography of the immediate environment be interwoven with its history into one complex whole. This complex is then again related to the complex of "the knowledge of nature," for also this subject must begin with the immediate locality and be combined with the other subjects.

But this relationship must *continue*. It will be necessary first of all to learn the basic geographic tools, reading of a map and the chief concepts (means of transportation, centers of transportation). But this is soon followed by the extent and position of our country. History is then learned from the very beginning and likewise the geography of Europe and the world is extended in connection with the study of history (discovery and exploration, trade and the wars brought about thereby). In the higher grades, these subjects are interwoven still further and proceeding from the contemporary geographic and economic situation, linear developments in history are traced.

2. Organic unity is also attained by a unitary view of all events; that is, to view all things in the light of eternity. If we help the child in all things to see God as Creator and Provider, God's greatness in his works, God's guidance in his deeds, these will provide a concentration of and a golden thread through all school activity; that is, they provide the opportunity for continued development. But it must be a concrete manifestation, a helping him live it (for we ourselves live it), and especially not a series of cerebral expositions in a multiplicity of words. This view of the unity of life, of God and to God, translated into a living reality is the ideal. To mention one concrete example: let not the church — and especially not the history of missions — be buried in a special hour in the higher grades, but let missions be a much-discussed subject in connection with geography. The economic and sociological aspects are not the most important.

* * *

If we proceed from the *unity of life in the individual,* we come to the following thoughts:

A. Of fundamental importance for the right view of our school activity is the relationship of instruction to the bringing up of the child in the school.

This is not the place to consider all the arguments that are raised in connection with this problem. In discussions of this nature, we must be constantly on our guard lest we permit distinctions made among concepts (by which the concept "instruction" refers to the accumulation of knowledge and skills and the concept "bringing up" points to character and conscience) to be applied without further qualification to real life. The contact of the pupil and the teacher is never enacted only on the level of the intellectual. To deny this is to cut life into fragments, is to deny the unity of life. Even though at times we are almost exclusively occupied with knowledge content, and justifiably, of necessity, so we are still engaged in deepening pedagogical influences. For we are occupied with teaching a lesson, and a lesson in which we all work with animation forms character, but a dull lesson in which we are bored misforms character.

To cite Waterink here, "For that matter, what else can we expect than that the school, while primarily an instructional institution, at the same time must be an institution that brings up youth. For a child is occupied with becoming an adult, is he not? The entire inner structure of the child asks for guidance, and also when this guidance is not intentional, the child is still being formed according to it and by it."

Instruction in school can therefore not be separated from the bringing up of the child. Through instruction, we bring him up and labor toward the forming of the total personality. If this is so, then in formulating the objectives of our instruction we shall have to give a central place to that which occupies the central place in our life, our relationship to Christ, the Lord. Hence, the religious element, especially the development of conscience, must undergird and permeate all school activity.

A pure conscience is of fundamental importance for the individual and (thereby) for the community. For on the one hand an undeveloped conscience brings unrest and uncertainty in the total attitude of man, while on the other hand in all reformation activity the "for conscience sake" motive is a compelling force. This is a most difficult subject. To mention but one example: the complacency with which cribbing is accepted and even justified can only create moral confusion. Intentional measures are generally of little effect. Especially admonitions that are not underscored by an exemplary life are of no value — what is worse, they defeat their own purpose. Here is applicable in even greater degree what we posited in connection with the cultivation of group or community consciousness; namely, if we would accomplish well our educational task, the child must see in our life and in our leadership of group relations of the class experience first hand what it means to serve God willingly.

It should be clear that a free and pure conscience represents a free, strong and well-directed will. The best means for the forming of conscience is found in the strengthening of the will to obedience. And this, too, is not something to be talked about, but to be demonstrated. It is not subject to punishment either. Rather must we try to cultivate positive strength latent in the child by demanding constructive achievement in service of the community and appropriate to his capacity. Let the child learn to work hard for an attainable goal, for herein lies an important character-forming function for intellectual instruction too. Especially should an atmosphere of systematic work, good control and discipline prevail in the class community, sustained by a cheerful spirit, with an absence of too many coercive techniques.

B. The school should take full account of the meaning of inner experience and the will for learning to know. If there is one thing established by modern psychology it is the inseparable relationship of the act of coming to know with volitional experience and the feeling experience, especially in the life of the child. This is one of the chief grounds for the contention that all instructional activity is pedagogical (bring up) in character.

True, vital, functional knowledge is not cerebral, but total; it is knowing with the heart. Not only will we fail to do justice to the pedagogical aspect of our school task without inner experiencing, but for all instruction in the narrower sense it is the necessary condition, for without getting inside of, without inner contact with the object we shall lack insight and grasp; no knowledge is possible. The accent falls upon the "inner," for only inward experiencing, which touches the personality more deeply than being affected by or experiencing with, as in the case of accompanying events, grips the heart of the child, leaves permanent traces and abiding knowledge. By gripping the child in his heart, true inner attentiveness is aroused, which leads to genuine natural activity. These three, experience, attention and activity, when not viewed externally, but in their inner functioning, are very closely related, and constantly interacting. We may not ignore them, but must use them as point of departure of our purposeful educational activity.

Every one who has observed children knows that the child manifests the impulse for physical and mental growth and development. The vital desires of the child correspond largely with this need for the unfolding of his own nature. It is an impulse placed in the child by God which manifests itself in all his play activities and in his questions. It directs the interest, stimulates to activity, and is involved in every experience.

But to proceed from these impulses is easier said than done, for the desires and needs of the child are so diffused, divergent and chaotic, that it seems almost impossible to select among them for a given purpose. And we must look beyond the momentary interest, and certainly not permit the child to do as he pleases.

The child must learn to obey, must learn to master the evil impulses, and learn to exert himself. But this need not be accompanied by strong distaste. The task itself, the way to the realization of a set purpose, must not be easy, but the task must be worth doing also for the child; it must be accommodated to the natural needs and interests of the child. A worthwhile objective for later life generally does not originate spontaneously in the child, for he does not project his view that far ahead; but the purpose must find response in his inner life, must be acceptable to the child. We must not permit the child to do as he pleases, but let him please to do what he must. Only then will he mobilize all mental power and we shall find in him an ally instead of an antagonist, and the knowledge that he readily attacks is assimilated more adequately and retained longer than much learning that he acquires with dislike and hence soon forgets.

When so considered, the task of the teacher will be to stimulate, inspire, suggest attention; his greatest asset will be enthusiasm, psychological understanding, keen observation (not erudition). He must not pour in knowledge that the child may need at some future time, but let the child feel and experience the value of a task and of the knowledge needed; that is, teach the child to love his task and to give himself to its performance.

This requires that the child have adequate background in real experience for that which is to be learned. There must be a readiness, for seed needs a fertile soil for germination and growth. Hence, take account of, accommodate to the child's interaction with his environment, draw the material as much as possible from his immediate community activity and from his play and recreational life, but also from his religious and esthetic life as a child. We mean to say, for young children begin with play needs, use as experience background their immediate environment; and for older children begin with intellectual needs, using social life as experience background.

Not only in the case of interesting material must we follow this course. But this also holds for drill, for mastery of the necessary minimum of basic knowledges and the practice in skills. Also in these the child must get insight into the need and come to accept them. And this can be accomplished if we accommodate these to child life and have him experience the practical value of it.

Also, by and by in social life the knowledge attained in school will prove inadequate. We know the complaints: uncertain, inadequate mastery, inadequate organization. We shall continue to hear these to greater or lesser degree. But what was said above is the only possibility, at least in part, to meet these criticisms. This seems the only way to achieve a vital, functional knowledge, assimilated in the total personality.

Something should be added to this. Knowledge will be assimilated more easily and effectively, but work with animation at a task in school has the greatest significance for character education. For the methodology in keeping herewith (*e.g.*: projects and beginning with centers of interest) frequently requires that children work in small groups, which leads to team work. The value of this should be much emphasized. When a child is active at a task he has accepted, his power of concentration is so much the greater that he can work more independently in keeping with his age and exploit his own initiative. Even more than these, he will be inspired to greater sense of responsibility for his own task and to an attitude of self-criticism.

C. The school, however, must take full account of the meaning of knowledge for *the life of feeling and willing*. By placing in the foreground the feeling and willing of man, we may run the danger of minimizing the acquisition of knowledge and lose sight of the fact that the school is primarily an institution for instruction. We should warn of the possible excess of emotion and be on our guard against the sentimental.

For the forming of the harmonious personality, the right balance of the intellectual, volitional, and emotional aspects of soul-life is very necessary, while for the social life knowledge, insight and understanding are indispensable. Otherwise expressed, for the life of the individual and for the life of the community, an objective, matter-of-fact attitude toward oneself and the environment is of the utmost importance. Contact with cultural values will be enriched structurally by insight and understanding, and furthermore, for the pure functioning of conscience, a clear insight into our motives is essential.

Therefore, we shall have to be on our guard against an overvaluing of knowledge, but also to an undervaluing of it. Especially in the teaching of Bible history we may not yield to the inclination to regard knowledge of little value, because leading the child to Jesus is, naturally, the most important. We must love God, too, with the understanding, and abiding, retained knowledge is also for instruction in the worship of God our objective.

D. *Knowledge and cultural interest* must be *grounded emotionally*. In the unity of life, knowledge plays an important roll. With this restriction, however, that it is not a cerebral, intellectualistic knowledge, but one grounded inwardly in the experiential. For this reason, stimulation and suggestion of class interest and striving to cultivate a vital cultural interest must not be confined to the intellectual sphere. In both respects, interest must be grounded emotionally; immediate and remote aims must be experienced as worthwhile! In this attempt the following factors, among others, play an important role:

1. The joy of discovery. Something that one discovers for himself is valued, subjectively, more highly than knowledge which is merely imparted to one. Discounting the fact that the latter may remain

quite superficial, insight and discernment are necessary for the latter. We should allow our pupils the privilege of discovery, rather than prematurely impart things to them for mastery that they can later discover for themselves.

2. The admiration for imparted knowledge, which in reality should be an admiration and reverence for God and his great work. God manifests his omnipotence, wisdom and grace in his dealing with the human race as he does in the entire creation, and we must help the children see God therein and have them experience His greatness. The necessary condition is that we ourselves are filled with admiration and love for Him. No one can lay hold upon the child's heart who has not been laid hold upon himself.

3. The joy the teacher experiences in his task. If the atmosphere of a work-fellowship constitutes the spirit of the class and of the entire school, the soil of the child's innermost life is prepared to receive the seed. This atmosphere is rooted in and springs forth out of a common experience, the experience of unitedly accepting an aim, of feeling together a responsibility in our task before God and man.

The community life of the class must be directed, undergirded, and inspired by the man or woman in charge of the class. He must be able to create a class spirit which chokes off all evil and causes the good to prosper. He must be able to suggest ends and means that make the child work in love. All this must be realized in an atmosphere of order and discipline, but above all of cheerful disposition, humor, and buoyancy, animated by that joyful spirit which is the chief asset of the teacher. The joy the teacher manifests in his task is the best sounding board for his own experience and thus the first condition for responsiveness of the learner in his youthful inner life. The joy of reflecting a bit of our own life, of the love of God, of the beauty of nature, of the rhythm of numbers is the surest approach to the heart and the head of youth. To quote Augustine, "It is obviously a fact that others listen to us in a measure to which we enjoy our teaching; our words then give evidence of our joy, come to us more easily and with greater pleasure."

So, the deciding factor in all revitalized instruction is the enthusiasm of the teacher. First of all, because his own enthusiasm carries away the learner, but also because he will need a large measure of enthusiasm to counter all the disappointments that arise. This should not be thought of as a recipe. We must not proceed from the idea that if we apply all this wisdom faithfully success will be assured and our further pathway will be strewn with roses. Everyone who knows from practical school-life the (mis) behavior of himself and of youth sees the foolishness of this idea, and he who does not see it will experience it early.

Teaching is an art. There are some pedagogical and psychological pointers to which the teacher should give heed. But the most important for him is whether he can, as a re-creating artist, give body to these basic ideas in his work with the class.

L. VANDER ZWEEP, G. WIELENGA AND J. W. VAN HULST
Guide for a Course of Study
for the Christian Schools, pp. 6-19.

Key Thoughts:

1. The unity of life precedes all analysis. Genuine understanding comes from this unity only. Momentary analysis must return to the unity of life to give the former meaning. We proceed from the unity of life as we try to understand education.

2. When we proceed from the unity of life in the collective whole, we learn that the school is a community of children where group consciousness is cultivated. As the child becomes an active member of this community he develops a dynamic cultural interest. Subject matter acquires its organic relationship in this unity.

3. When we proceed from the unity of life in the individual, we learn the right relationship of instruction to the bringing up of the child. There is an inseparable relationship between coming to know and the feeling and willing of the child. All true, vital knowledge is knowledge of the heart. Only as a child is gripped in his heart will true learning take place. The child's true needs must be activated and vitally brought to his consciousness. Knowing will then be integrated in feeling and willing. The whole child will reach out to the new. Knowledge can be grounded emotionally in the joy of discovery, in the child's admiration for new knowledge to be attained, in catching the joy the teacher manifests in his task.

4. Vitalized instruction depends most of all on the enthusiasm of the teacher.

Comment:

Among the first principles to guide us in designing a curriculum for the elementary and secondary schools is the fact of the unity of life in the individual and in the collective whole. God has so created life in the individual and in the organic unity of the race. Subjects are man-made systems. They will fail to enlist the learnings in the whole person unless they receive their organic unity from life in the learning process. This is a basic principle in Christian education.

6

Implications of Making the Unity of Life Central

What implications for the organization of the school and the construction of the curriculum and the daily program follow from the principle that the unity of life is to be central? Some have supposed that the school should be organized as the family life. Others have declared that Christian principles demand a school organization similar to the Dalton plan. Still others have advocated an organic curriculum that crosses the boundary lines of separate subjects. It has become an obsession in The Netherlands, too, to name a school according to a system as Montessori, Decroly, or Dalton. Further examination of the practice of these progressive schools often leads to disappointment. One is frequently reminded of the subtitle of James' *Pragmatism*, "A new name for old ways of thinking."

We think the time has not arrived for attempts at extreme reform. Such reform, it seems to us, would have to be preceded by a revised pre-service education and wide-spread justifiable experimentation. Experimentation can be justified only when the experimenter knows where he is going. This is attained only after thorough study and careful observation at experimental schools.

This guide is for the normal, common school. We shall maintain the graded system, be it in mitigated form, and the traditional school program, be it in a more flexible form.

The tempering of the disadvantages of our graded system can be accomplished especially by removing the curse of failure.

(The authors continue from here on to make applications to local curricula as found in the Netherlands. It represents an attempt at gradual transition to practices more in keeping with the principles they discussed, and here quoted. J.)

L. Vander Zweep, G. Wielenga and J. W. Van Hulst
*Guide for a Course of Study
for the Christian Schools*, pp. 19-20.

Comment:

That the unity of life of the individual and of the collective whole must be central in designing the curriculum in our Christian schools and in the organization and administration of these schools seems to be beyond all controversy in the light of the Scripture. But this unity is God-centered in Christ. Hence, it deviates fundamentally from the unity secular education seeks.

How can we make this unity effective in our schools? Radical reform movements are always reactionary rather than constructive in their effect.

We must begin with our teaching personnel, both with in-service and pre-service education. Our efforts must extend to the constituency, the Christian community. When together we shall see the function of the school of today in the light of the Word of God, we shall develop schools which are genuinely Christian.

The redeeming feature today as well as of the past is that we have individual teachers who implicitly feel this very principle. They make school live by their consecrated lives and personal enthusiasm. But with them too this insight must become explicit that they may rightly appraise their work and understandingly contribute to the whole of the Christian school.

7

Teaching According to the Ways of Child Life

We need to explore the nature and needs of child life with reference to the learning process. In our search for a philosophy of Christian education, a scripturally oriented understanding of childhood is essential. The child in his developing personality is the focal point in the learning process. Right understanding of the child, or rather of children, is basic to effective teaching. How to teach is determined largely by how the child learns. The teacher does not prescribe the learning process. Rather should we say that the learning process is determined by the ways of child life and these ways are God-ordained ways. They are God-ordained ways as much as the laws of thought and the law of gravity. We shall view the ways of child life in their religious root, in their racial continuity, in their unity in the person of the child, in their educability, in their relationship to the learning process, and in their involvement in the totality of life.

I. Common Religious Root

The ways of child life have a common religious root. By this we mean that they go back to a common origin. They are essentially religious in character. Why? Because the child is a religious being.

When we say man is a religious being, we are not saying that among other tendencies and capacities man has that of religious experience. Not at all. The Scriptures tell us that man as man in his totality must be explained out of a religious root. All he is and does has its origin in this great fact. To understand the child aright this fact and its meaning should be clear. Current child psychology either ignores this truth or openly denies it. We begin with it in our study of the child. His nature and needs are defined by it.

The common religious root of man is very clearly explained to us in the first three chapters of the Bible. In these chapters we read of the four developments in man's beginning that characterize his common religious root. They are his creation, his mandate, his fall into sin, and the antithesis. These four developments have determinative significance in our thinking about life. To ignore them is to let other considerations take their place. We want to explore them briefly with reference to education.

Man's Creation

What does the Bible say about man's origin? For the Christian who accepts the Bible as the infallible, divinely inspired Word of God, in which God the Holy Spirit has recorded for us through the agency of men, divinely chosen, what God deems necessary for us to know to accept Him by faith, this question is answered clearly and conclusively. Genesis 1:26-27 tells us, "And God said, Let us make man in our image, after our likeness. . . . And God created man in his own image, in the image of God created he him; male and female created he them." Genesis 2:7 continues, "And Jehovah God formed man of the dust of the ground, and breathed into his nostrils the breath of life; and man became a living soul."

Two things especially should we note in these passages which have bearing upon our discussion. Man was made in God's likeness, and man became a living soul. Here we have the beginning of our common religious root, man in the likeness of God and man a living soul. This is man's humanity; it describes man as man.

Another point should be noted for our purpose. These two qualities, man made in the likeness of God and man becoming a living soul, place man in personal fellowship with God. It is, however, a fellowship of dependence. There is a fellowship within the Godhead too, the fellowship of Father, Son, and Holy Spirit. This is a fellowship of equality among the members. Man's fellowship with God, however, is a fellowship of inequality. God takes the initiative in this fellowship, and man as a creature shares the fellowship of God. Man's fellowship with God is the prerequisite for the fulfilment of himself as man. Outside of God's fellowship man lives in total darkness and must suffer the consequences of this darkness.

Here we have the beginning of man's common religious root. Man was made in the likeness of God and became a living soul that he might fellowship with God. God provides for all creatures, but among all earthly creatures He can fellowship only with man, for only man possesses the qualities which make fellowship possible. He is a person, an ego, an I, a spirit. He is made for fellowship.

We should note here what this fellowship involves. The gregarious and social tendencies in man as described for us in psychology and sociology are to be explained in the light of what the Scriptures teach about fellowship, but come nowhere near exhausting its meaning. Neither does man's need for the sense or feeling of security explain this fellowship. Security is involved in this fellowship. But if we would understand the meaning of Christian education, we must understand man's need for fellowship with God.

It is a fellowship of rational communication. Yes, God makes himself known to man. Man is a rational being because he is made in God's likeness. He comes to know God as God makes himself known on the human level. It is a fellowship of feeling. Man feels in the very depths of his being his dependence upon God and finds his security in having his feeling satisfied in God's very presence, with Him. He comes to know the will of God and wills to bring his will in line with God's will.

All of these are involved in man's fellowship with God. But they are not all and do not go to the root of this fellowship. Our thinking, our knowing function, and our feeling are involved in genuine fellowship. Our willing as the determinative expression of the whole person is involved too. But genuine fellowship, according to the Scriptures, is the fellowship in love. Love involves the totality of man. It is the prime motivator of all our action. God is love and He loves man as the acme of His creation, made in His likeness. In His love for man He draws man to himself. Man responds in love and is in turn constrained, overmastered, by the love of God. It is in the primacy of love that we find the meaning of genuine fellowship. Without it fellowship degenerates into adaptation and adjustment. There is no giving of ourself and drawing to oneself and being overmastered by another in adjustment. Only in love are these qualities manifested.

This is the common root of all men and, therefore, the first principle for the explanation of human life. And, as we shall see, education can be understood only in terms of life. Therefore, it is the first principle of education.

The Divine Mandate

We learn further from the Bible that God gave man a mandate, a commission, a charge. We read in Gen. 1:28, "And God blessed them; and God said unto them, Be fruitful, and multiply, and replenish the earth, and subdue it; and have dominion over the fish of the sea, and over the birds of the heavens, and over every living thing that moveth upon the earth." The Bible continues in Gen. 2:8-9, "And Jehovah God planted a garden eastward, in Eden, and there he put the man whom he had formed. And out of the ground made Jehovah God to grow every tree that is pleasant to the sight, and good for food; the tree of life also in the midst of the garden, and the tree of knowledge of good and evil." Genesis 2 continues in vs. 15-17, "And Jehovah

God took the man, and put him into the garden of Eden to dress it and keep it. And Jehovah God commanded the man, saying, Of every tree of the garden thou mayest freely eat; but of the tree of the knowledge of good and evil, thou shalt not eat of it; for in the day thou eatest thereof, thou shalt surely die."

Man's mandate or commission is clear. He is to build a race of men competent, under God, to cultivate and manage the great potentialities Jehovah God, the Creator, pleased to contain in the animate and inanimate world about him. It is a tremendous task. It demands a supreme test at the outset. It must be a test of the whole man in interpreting his fellowship aright. Will it be a fellowship in which the drawing power of God's love so constrains him that he voluntarily commits himself, surrenders in faith to God's command? Or will man seek a fellowship in which love goes out first of all to himself in his own ego? His choice will determine his ability to assume the great mandate given him.

Here we have another phase of the common root of man. It is a religious root. Man's ability to carry out his divine mandate depended not upon the inherent quality of man as a creature, but on his continued fellowship with God. As a living soul, made in God's likeness, man cannot escape commitment or surrender to a power beyond him. He, as man, commits himself to the fellowship of God, or he commits himself to another fellowship. His commitment is an act, not merely of the intellect or of his feeling, but of his whole being. It is always, therefore, a religious act. Man cannot escape religion. His every thought and deed is basically religious; each comes up out of a commitment. His mandate is religious in character in that it is based upon man's continued voluntary fellowship with God, or a commitment to another fellowship.

Man, the Sinner

We cannot stop here in our analysis of the common root of man. Subsequent developments further qualify this root. To understand life aright the two major developments that follow are indispensable. Yet they must be understood against the background of what was said before.

What does the Bible tell us? We all know this well. It is the tragic story of the fall. Read Genesis 3 again before you continue reading this. Read it with what we have said in mind — and subsequent history too.

What happened? Man failed his supreme test. The human race failed and was doomed to tragic failure in subsequent history. Man proposed to put his vaunted self-sufficiency ahead of fellowship with

God. He proposed to build a race sufficient in its inherent competency to master the created world about him. In doing so he brought the curse of the holy God upon him and in him upon creation as a whole.

Man surrenders — for surrender he must, he was made that way — but not to God who loves him, but to the devil who would exploit him for his own wicked purpose. He seeks a fellowship, but not a fellowship prompted by love. His fellowship degenerates into mere adjustment seeking to satisfy basic needs not fully comprehended by himself. He fixes his heart, the very center of his life, upon the object of his choice, not God, but himself. He sets his face away from God, to travel hellward. And, tragedy of all tragedies, from his choice there is no return for him and his posterity. God once initiated a genuine fellowship with man. Man cannot restore this fellowship, now that he has broken it.

I say we have another phase here of our common root. It is a religious root. Man's choice is a religious choice. It is a choice involving the whole man in a commitment which turns man from God. Man as man has surrendered to a power other than himself contrary to God. Life, and therefore education, must be understood out of this phase of our common root too. Failure to do so has led to many an error in educational theory and practice.

The Antithesis

In the midst of chapter three of Genesis we read, vs. 15, "And I will put enmity between thee and the woman, and between thy seed and her seed; he shall bruise thy head, and thou shalt bruise his heel." It is a word spoken to the devil, but prophetic of a great intervention by God himself. Only in the light of subsequent revelation do we learn to understand the fuller significance of this prophetic utterance by God himself.

God marks out a thesis and an anti-thesis. There is no synthesis of these two. The two lines Jehovah God marks out shall never meet. They constitute the conflict in the light of which all subsequent history must be understood; education too.

In the antithesis we too have a common religious root. The distinction between the two classes of men, Christian and non- (anti-) Christian, in this world is basically a religious distinction. One consciously or unconsciously surrenders to a power not himself. He lives for a chosen end.

In His sovereign grace God creates a restored fellowship out of the root which is Christ. Out of a dying human race God redeems a new race unto himself. For this race all things have become new. There is a new fellowship in Christ and a new mandate (Matt. 28:18-20). The mandate of creation has a new setting: no longer man the sinner, but man the saint.

II. Significance of Our Common Religious Root

Modern View of Child Development

Commonly the study of the child is begun quite differently, as those who have studied psychology well know. The child is studied in his hereditary background, for in part he is what his ancestry is and was. His environmental opportunities are appraised with reference to what the child can become. He is further studied in his physiological (also known as somatic), emotional, intellectual, and social development. His development is then viewed in three dimensions; physiological, intellectual, and social-emotional.

Immediately the question occurs to the Christian student, Where does the moral-spiritual come in on the basis of this three-dimensional development? The moral and spiritual are included, we are told. For what is the moral but the mores of the race and civilization of which one is a part? And conscience is the internalization of the mores, the mores having become part of one. The mores become part of the life style of the individual. And the spiritual? If one means thereby the religious, it too is included in the social-emotional dimension. For what else is religion but a feeling of dependence upon some power beyond us? Hence, we do not all need the same religion to satisfy this feeling.

Scriptural View of Child Development

But as we of the household of faith turn to the Word of God, we come to view the nature and needs of the child quite differently. It is not merely that we add a fourth dimension, the moral-spiritual. This we do, of course. We view the child, however, in his religious root from the very beginning.

Originally the human race was made pregnant with the self-expression of God and every member of the race to be born in the future was to share in this image of God. But the tragedy of sin ruined all prospects of realizing a glorious harmony of the qualities God placed in the human race. The fulfillment of the self-expression of God with which the human race was potentially equipped is no longer possible of realization, for the ego, I, spirit of man, once focused on God and embraced in the fellowship of His love, is directed away from God and has become diffused in its direction.

But, thanks be to God's unfailing love in Christ this fellowship is restored to the human race in those members of the race individually who, in God's electing grace, are ingrafted into Christ. In regeneration the I, ego, or spirit is again focused on God. It is not a process of adding the fourth dimension. No, something much more fundamental takes place. In Christ God gets to the very core or heart of the race. Christ's incarnation is the basis of this change in man's heart. In his becoming one of us, really man, as well as being really God, he restores man to the fellowship of God's love. But as man was given the freedom originally to realize the self-expression of God, so he is free to accept or reject this restored fellowship. This is man's common religious root as it existed prior to the fall of man and as it is subsequent to this awful tragedy.

Christian Teachers and Modern Psychologies

We hold to this common religious root in distinction from those who view man as a biological organism that develops human characteristics collectively referred to as personality. We hold it too in distinction from those who consider man a rational animal, that is, an animal which possesses the unique capacity for reflection, reasoning, purposing, etc. Likewise we take this position with equal emphasis over against those who speak of man as a rational-moral being and give him supreme cosmic significance in that in him the rational and moral qualities of the universe came to self-consciousness.

Teachers should be fully aware of the fact that nearly all psychologies are written from the point of view of one of these unscriptural positions. Very little of note has been written for teachers from the viewpoint of man's religious root. It is my firm conviction that we shall not get into the clear on the subject of Christian education until we explore this root further. It is for this reason that I have begun with the child. Not because the child is central in our philosophy of education, but because the child as subject must be understand in the light of God's truth, would we educate aright.

We understand the child, then, in the common religious root of the human race. What benefits accrue to us for our educational thinking as a result of this great truth?

Basic Principles of Christian Education

First, our common origin is to be understood primarily in terms of the spirit, the ego, the I. We have been created of one blood. In Acts 17:26 we read, "He caused to spring from one forefather people of every race" (Weymouth translation). This is important particularly with reference to the continuity and organic character of the race. But this is not of first consideration. Man has a cosmic origin too. He was made of the "dust of the ground" (Gen. 2:7). He is likewise biological in origin. We know of man's animal life especially from physiology. How his animal life is related to his becoming a living soul we do not know. Scripture does ascribe soul-life to the animal, but not in the sense of spirit. We shall have something to say about this in connection with discussion of the personal unity of the child. But neither man's cosmic origin nor his animal origin are primary.

It is in his ego, spirit, I, in fellowship with God that we find man's distinctive origin. In the spirit man is rational, moral, social, free, and responsible. In his spirit he was originally focused upon God. In his love God embraced man in his spirit and drew him into fellowship. In the spirit he was free to respond to God's love by complete surrender in love.

Second, man is therefore basically religious in nature. God linked man to himself, the Creator, in a personal manner, as person to person. Among all God's creatures on this earth, God can fellowship with man only, for only he is spirit. No one can worship God except in spirit and in truth, as Jesus told the Samaritan woman. This link then is God's personal fellowship with man in love.

God communicated with man, and man walked with God. All that follows in the constitution of himself as a personality and in the exercise of his mandate flows from this personal link. When we say man is a religious being, we mean, according to the Scriptures, that God created man to fellowship with him in love, and in that fellowship to bring to fruition the self-expression of God with which he was endowed. We fail to understand man in his deepest nature and in his greatest need, and therefore the child likewise as a member of the human race, if this great scriptural truth is not foremost in our thinking.

Third, man's mandate is religious in scope. We saw earlier that man's mandate, commission, or charge, given him by God, was in keeping with the position God gave him among God's creatures. This commission was nothing less than to build a race of men competent, under God, to cultivate and manage the great potentialities Jehovah God pleased to contain in the animate and inanimate world about man. This great task was to be exercised in the service of God, that He receive all the praise and glory as His mighty deeds are unfolded in man and in man's work. Man's charge was therefore a religious one. It was the task of rendering all things to the service of God. To do so would be natural for man. Not to do so would be unnatural. But the natural became unnatural and the unnatural natural.

Fourth, man's deepest need is religious in character. What we have said about man in his basically religious nature and about the religious scope of his mandate is not abrogated, annulled, by the awful tragedy of sin, great as this is. Man out of fellowship with God did not lose the need for that fellowship. The need remains in him as a drive or motivation. He lost awareness of this need and the desire for it. But at the root of all this striving lies the need for the presence of God in his life and the need for rendering all things unto God. This is the religious motivation, the most basic of motivations in man. All that man thinks and does must be explained out of this motivation to understand his ways. Man out of fellowship with God lives in darkness. He has his back turned to the light and stares into the darkness. Whatever light breaks through into his darkness is lost in the darkness of his perspective, for he peers into the darkness. He gropes, as it were, in response to a need he fails to understand. In his blindness he grasps the ear of the blind man's elephant and calls him a fan. From his limited perspective he views the whole and surrenders to the errors of his judgment. In his commitment he tries to find satisfaction. But his soul will not rest until he rests in God. Man's nature and need are religious in character. Of every child born this is true. All we do for and to the child, and all that the child is led to do for himself, must be done in keeping with this greatest of all needs. Failure to do so spells ultimate defeat at our task.

Fifth, the religious need of the child is the focal point in his education. Education in the scriptural sense means the nurture, rearing, bringing up of the child to maturity. Both in terminology and in context this is abundantly clear from the Bible, especially the New Testament. We have permitted our secularized culture to adulterate the scriptural use of the word education. Bringing up a child to maturity cannot be accomplished in harmony with his need as a member of the human race unless his deepest need is met. He cannot become the full-grown man in Christ (Eph. 4:13) unless the redirected ego, once again focused on God and reestablished in his fellowship in Christ, is led to unify the whole child into harmonious expression of the self-expression of God of which he is made capable in regeneration. Here God's part and our part in the process meet.

Sixth, it is in meeting the child's religious need that we find unity or integration in learning and in teaching. We said that in meeting the religious need of the child we have the focal point in his education. Every activity revolves about it and is measured or valued by it. In bringing up a child to maturity we must relate every part meaningfully to the whole. We have the whole circumscribed for us in the fellow-ship of love. With the love of Christ established in his heart, the Christian is enabled to relate all things together in love. It is that love we seek to cultivate by the grace of God in the heart and from there in the life of the child. It is in the primacy of love as exercised by the ego that the parts are meaningfully integrated in the whole. The restoration of this fellowship in love meets the child's deepest need.

Seventh, it is the primacy of love that is of most worth in rearing the child to maturity. "What knowledge is of most worth?" asked Herbert Spencer in the previous century. His question was in keeping with the philosophy of the Enlightenment in education. He judged the natural sciences to give this knowledge. Today some would say the social sciences, or "the liberal arts." Our modern pragmatist would ask, not what knowledge is of most worth, but what kind of living is of most worth. And the American answers, democracy. Christian education must be conscious of the fact that neither knowledge nor life will have their meaningful place in bringing up the child to maturity unless love in Christ Jesus is primary. On that basis both knowledge and life will be given their right direction.

Finally, love is the basis for the Christian educational structure. What is the Christian educational structure? I have already tried to show you why love is its basis. On it as a base I suggest the following equilateral triangle:

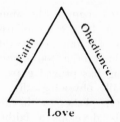

I believe this structure is entirely scriptural. The whole of the super-structure in bringing up the child to maturity must be built into this structure. It alone can hold all parts coherently together to develop the fullgrown man in Christ. On this foundation we are to build, not "timber, or hay, or straw" (I Cor. 3:13), but "gold, or silver, or costly stones." And the character of our work will appear.

III. Racial Continuity

We now turn to another phase of our subject. We have viewed the child in his religious root. We have seen that as subject, I, he is religious in nature. Security in the fellowship of God's love is his greatest need. Everything we can say about the child in his nature and in his needs is to be viewed in this light. He cannot be understood rightly in any phase of his life unless his original religious motivation is taken into account. Education is not Christian unless it recognizes this basic need of the child and meets this need in the God-appointed way. Though the religious nature of the child is the most basic and therefore the most important, it is not all-inclusive when we speak of the child's nature and needs. We must view him, too, in the life stream of the human race. We all have one ancestry (Acts 17:26). God so made us.

The question we ask ourselves now is, What does the child's racial history signify to us, in the light of the Word of God, with reference to his nature and his needs? This is not an easy question. We must run counter to the social anthropology, psychology, and sociology of our time when we try to answer it. We shall try to view the child in his racial continuity psycho-somatically and in his I or spirit. "Psycho-somatically" is used to express the interrelation of what is generally known as mind and body. For example, in fear certain body changes take place while we experience the emotion. I, spirit, is the subject who experiences fear.

Unity of the Race — Psycho-Somatically

In creation God related man to the animate and inanimate world (Gen. 2:7a). Because of the great similarity among God's creatures, we can study comparative anatomy, comparative physiology, biochemistry, and within greater limitations comparative psychology. The study of these areas of learning has proved extremely fruitful in the understanding of man, especially physiologically. Even in psychology there is a degree of similarity. Take, for instance, the dog. He can be stirred emotionally. He develops a faithfulness and loyalty which borders on the human. He crouches in fear with his eyes fixed with anticipation upon his master's every expression. Let his master but change the frown on his face slightly and the dog's tail begins to wag. He can respond warmly to tenderness of feeling and likewise turn coolly away. He understands, in a sense. Has he soul-life? When we get into the total psycho-somatic or psycho-physiological nature of man, all similarity ceases. Here animal psychology breaks down in its implications for human psychology. Learning as conditioning and as trial and error have for this reason been so misleading. We read that God made man a living soul. When he did so, he adapted the psycho-somatic to the structure of the spirit. The spirit is of God, and is not to be identified with the animal structure in kind. The animal structure is subject to the laws of the natural world, not the spirit. Animal life in man becomes distinctively human in its adaption to the spirit. So the difference between animal life and human life is not limited to the "higher" soul or spirit, but involves his entire psycho-somatic structure in its organic relationship to the spirit, I.

It is in the psycho-somatic that sin has had such telling effects. The processes of the psycho-somatic were harmoniously organized into organic relationship with the spirit, the subject, before the fall. The human person was an unbroken unity functioning in perfect harmony in every part and among the parts. Physical appetites, emotional drives, knowledge of the world around him, were subordinate to the rational purposes of the spirit, the I, the subject. But the turning of the I from the light of God's fellowship has cast the whole person in darkness and has set up tensions originating from within and from without. The mounting tensions through the centuries of man's history have left their record in the race. How could it be otherwise? We are so constituted that the past is recorded in our structure over a period of generations. Genetics has debated long and hard the inheritance of acquired characteristics, but must acknowledge the transmission of racially acquired traits. The pollution of sin is clearly taught in the Scripture and is confirmed genetically when the facts are viewed in the light of the Scripture.

The child is heir to the disharmony of the psycho-somatic structure of the race. He cannot escape the disorder of racial structure wrought over the centuries. His heredity is more deeply rooted than that from recent ancestors. In his nature and his needs, the child must be viewed as deeply embedded in his ancestry over the centuries. This relationship is not as simple as "a chip off the old block." It is more involved than patterns of genes and chromosomes express. Every child comes into the world as a person-with-a-history.

The Unity of the Race — in the I

Man became a living soul when God breathed in him the breath of life. He became spirit, I, ego. It is as subject, I, that he identifies himself in the flux of the psycho-somatic as a person. He knows himself to be the same person today as yesterday. Only the Bible gives an explanation for this certain self-knowledge, based not on our own observations, but on authentic truth make known to us. How philosophies, and more recently psychologies have struggled for some reasonable explanation for the immediate knowledge of selfawareness! But it lies beyond human understanding. The Christian knows this by faith in the Word of God. God in His self-revelation discloses to us the nature of our being as made in His image.

The Scripture tells us *who* we are. It does not tell us how we came to be. The human personality is a unity. This much is clear. Here, too, we should take note of the racial unity as it is expressed in the spirit. God deals with man in this unity at the very outset in the covenant of works. The probationary command is not only a test of obedience for our first parents, but it is that for the race. We are included in Adam in the spirit. In the spirit man is free and responsible. Created in the fellowship of God's love, the spirit of man can choose to continue and confirm this fellowship or follow his own autonomous way. The choice is a religious choice, for it involves the I, and the I, as we saw, is religious in character. God likewise deals with the human race as a unity in the covenant of grace. "Just as in Adam all die, so also in Christ all will be made alive again" (I Cor. 15:22). The race which died in Adam is made alive in Christ Jesus. But this living unity has reference to the spirit restored to the fellowship of God's love. The unity of the race in Adam is dissolved under the law of sin. True, the psycho-somatic unity continues. But in the spirit the original unity has disintegrated. There is only one racial unity in the spirit, the Church as the body of the Lord Jesus Christ, the invisible church, the redeemed.

So we recognize an original unity of the human race, now dead — spiritually as we usually say — and therefore not a unity anymore. Man was told by God, "Thou shalt dying die" (Gen. 2:17, also translated "thy life shall be a dying life"). In Christ the unity is restored for all those who by faith are ingrafted in Him as the vine. Man is by faith restored in his religious root. His greatest need, security of the spirit, is satisfied by a divine act of God's grace. The spirit is not in full control of the psycho-somatic in its broken state, but he is gaining through the discipline of the "new obedience." There is no racial unity in the spirit for the child outside of Christ. Born into this world he is one with the race psycho-somatically and subject to all the disharmony of it. The spirit dwelling in darkness is capable of only a measure of discipline but is headed for eternal doom. The unity of the race in Adam is dead. Thank God for His covenant faithfulness. "The promise is unto you and unto your children. . . ." Blessed the youth upon whom God lays His hand early in life!

The Fact of the Covenant

The covenant is a blessed fact. The Scripture begins with it, is replete with it throughout, and ends with it. What a blessed promise for Christian parents! But what a great responsibility, for their children are the Lord's!

I hasten to add, however, that this glorious truth may be abused and lull us into a false security. Covenant youth too must be converted. The "repent ye" comes to them too. To lead them to a decision for Christ is the goal of Christian education (Christian nurture), in the school as well as in the home and in the church, To underestimate the magnitude of this great task by excluding it from the school as a major objective is to undermine the very foundation of Christian education. Not the *truth* of the covenant encourages complacency of spirit, but wicked men who distort the truth, or God's children who fail to understand God's Word rightly.

In the divine order of things the human race restored in Christ is realized through the Christian home and the responsible task of the Christian parent, and in such as the Lord may call through the preaching of His Word. The family is the divine institution to provide the fellowship of love for all its members. It is that thing on earth which most nearly resembles the love of Christ for His church. God intended it to be the great school for the nurture of His children to maturity.

What a mess our modern society has made of the home! Modern man views it as an agent of society. It is a social institution, so it is said, called into existence to regulate the sex function of man and to provide the first social experience for society's children.

Christian parents may not permit such distortion of the divinely ordained order to affect their home and the Christian nurture of their children. The Lord has promised, "I will be a God unto thee and thy seed after thee," and "The promise is unto you and unto your children." But every covenant has two parts. We are obliged to do our part. That the covenant line seems so obscure at times can not be laid to God's charge. We as Christian parents are so unfaithful in fulfilling our part in the covenant that it is God's mercy that we still see the line to a degree in our own families. Our firm belief in the irresistible grace of God, so clearly taught in the Scripture, may not minimize our effort.

Does the church have a vital part in the covenant obligation? To raise the question is to answer it, it would seem. The parents are members of the visible church. They present their child for baptism before the congregation of God's people, and they vow before God and His church that they will be faithful in their covenant obligation. The child is a member of Christ's church according to the promise. The church, in its own right, has a vital part in the nurture of the child to maturity. Though the parental responsibility is all-inclusive, the church shares with the parents the spiritual nurture of the child.

And now the school! The great fact of the covenant and its promise to the parents is the basis for it. The Christian school is a parental school. It has no other basis. We may not permit the covenant basis of Christian schools to become adulterated with non-covenantal views. The fact of the covenant is so fundamental that the evangelical faith becomes irrelevant to what the school as school is called to do if that faith neglects the covenant of grace in Christ.

The Christian School for Covenant Youth

That the Christian school is the only place for covenant children needs no further substantiation. One might raise the question, is the Christian school for covenant youth only? Shall our schools admit children from families concerning which we have reasonable assurance that they are not Christian?

That the Christian school can prove a great blessing to homes where Christ, the King, is not worshipped goes without saying. The mission potential of Christian education has great appeal for all who love the Lord. In fact, I see no connection between our firm belief in the covenant and the blanket rejection of all children from non-Christian homes. It would seem that it is more in keeping with our personal witness to consider every case in relation to other, sometimes, more basic matters. We may not permit the chief task of the Christian school, namely, to lead covenant youth to Christ in personal commitment, to become obscured, however. The very structure of Christian education based on the covenant is involved. The task of the Christian school is not evangelism, in the sense that this is generally understood. As a school for covenant youth, the Christian school builds on the foundation laid in the Christian home. This is not evangelism but Christian education. They are not synonymous. Let Christian schools be cautious in admitting children from non-Christian homes.

We are called to be saints (Rom. 1:7), a holy people unto the Lord (I Peter 2:9) ; this is very clear from God's Word. Lives consecrated to a holy priesthood in this world can be cultivated only in the Christian educational structure. Education not in keeping with God's Word creates great hurdles to effective service of the consecrated life. We are to remember too that the Christian life in this world is always beset by the dangers of hypocrisy and phariseeism. It is relatively easy to go through the motions of Christian service for group approval among one's peers.

Earlier I emphasized the primacy of love in Christian nurture. If love is not primary in the Christian school, it is in great danger of snobbishness. Where the love of Christ (*your* Christ and *my* Christ — personal, you see) is really present, and where the teacher responds to the love of Christ in his life by embracing his pupils in love, we have the basis for Christian nurture. A school is not Christian without it. The scene of the feet washing at the last supper is then re-enacted in mutual service, when love is present. Such an atmosphere banishes all snobbishness, and kindles love in children's hearts.

IV. The Child in His Personal Unity

We now come to a very important phase of our discussion, a phase which not only has almost obvious implications for the curriculum and methodology of our schools but is also basic to Christian nurture in general. Very much of a parent's, teacher's, or pastor's work with children depends upon the right view of the whole child. We should always remember that we are working with *a* child in the concrete, never with *the* child in the abstract, nor with a class as a mass or aggregation. And this living child is a unity, an organic whole, who can say I, and meaningfully so. When he says I, he is not referring to an integration of processes, as modern psychology views the child, but he refers to his whole personality centered in the subject or person. The identification of himself in his self-conciousness discloses a unity, the human person.

To try to get a little understanding of this unity of the human person is not easy. We are not accustomed to thinking of the human person as one. But difficult as this may be, the right view of Christian education depends in part upon our understanding the child as a person, not merely in his personality. I trust the distinction I make here between person and personality will become clear as we proceed.

Earlier Misconceptions

The Christian who knows his Bible will soon point us to the Biblical distinction of soul and body, of mind and heart, of spirit and flesh, etc. True, but the Bible speaks likewise of bowels of mercy, of sinful flesh, of sinning in the body, etc. Is the Scripture confusing the parts which constitute the whole of man? Attempts have been made to write a Biblical psychology, that is, a psychology which sets forth Bible teaching concerning man in his personal make-up. I shall not try to enter into a discussion of the psychologies past and present to point out what they have done with the *I*. This constitutes an interesting story all by itself. After cutting up the human personality into faculties, or powers, into ideas, and into structures, psychology is emphasizing the unity of the self today. Organismic psychologies and psychoanalysis are equally alive to the unity of the human personality.

Shall we rejoice in this development in current psychology? Has it something to say to us as Christians as we try to understand a child? Our first reaction may be to put us on our guard. And we should be cautious. Too frequently we have permitted non-Christian theory and practice to slip into our schools because we have had no answer from a biblical point of view to the problems we faced. We should remember here that a sound psychology is based on a sound anthropology. Our first concern is who is man. This is the object of anthropological investigation, discussed above. It is on this basis that we build as we continue.

Unity — A Given Fact

The unitary character of a person is a given fact of experience. It is common knowledge to all of us. When I meet you, I view you as a person, not soul and body, not intellect, feeling, and will, not spirit and flesh. We meet as persons whose every part is related to every other part in an organic way such that we recognize one another conscious of ourselves as persons. No philosophy, psychology, sociology, anthropology, or any other study concerned with understanding man can violate this unity as a fact of experience and make sense. Human investigation and analysis does not destroy what is known as *naive* experience (given facts of every day observation) but seeks to understand it.

Non-Christian thinking constantly makes this mistake. It seeks to know the whole from a study of the parts. Invariably a part is lifted to the position from which to view the whole. The proverbial blindman policy, you see. How damaging this is for psychology is evident today. One finds the unity in the process of integration of human resources or capacities. Another finds it in the equilibrium of tensions within and without. Still another in organized wholes in our response to the environment. And so we might continue. But where is the person?

Not so in Christian thinking. God has spoken. He gives us in His Word a reference for experience which enables us to view things in their true relationship. In His self-revelation God has made known the meaning of His works. When we listen to Him and explore His works in that light we shall understand as it is given finite man in a world under the curse of sin to understand. God deals with man as a whole person. We are responsible for the lusts of the eye. The tongue is appraised as a member capable of great evil. The body is said to be the sanctuary of the Holy Spirit. These and similar expressions in the Scripture suggest unity of the person. The Bible makes no attempt to prove it. It does not even tell us how God made man a unity when he became a living soul. The unity of the person is an accepted fact in the Scripture. But the Bible does make distinctions. It speaks of soul, body, mind, spirit, heart, etc., with reference to man as a person. Analysis is necessary, but it is not in analysis that we understand the whole. Anatomy is not physiology, and neurology and endocrinology are not psychology. It is the influence of non-Christian philosophies, beginning with Greek thought, that have led Christians to speak of soul and body as distinct entities somehow interacting or paralleling one another. We went even further. We began to speak of faculties or compartments of the soul. We began to speak of training the mind or educating the intellect. We dreamed of liberating the mind by means of schooling the intellect in the liberating arts. Do not misunderstand me. There is an element of truth in these statements. But in general intent they represent attempts to do what non-Christian thinking does with the human person.

Let us do what God's word so clearly sets before us. Accept the human person in his organic unity and try to understand him as such. What is more, when we seek to educate a child, let us adhere to this God-ordained organic unity. The child in class has come to school in his whole person. To deal with him in parts is to violate the God-ordained fact of his unity. Academically to lift the intellect out of the unity of his personality is an abstraction which has disappointing results because it violates life.

How Understand This Unity?

But, you say, is it not true that in spite of our apparent unity we are broken finite beings in a broken world? Where is the unity in ourselves and in the world about us? Is it not true that in our inner disharmony we encounter a disharmonious world? The answer to each one of these questions is, yes, indeed, but you are confusing unity and coherence, or harmony. Our unity is an organic wholeness in which every part is involved in every other. Hence the Bible speaks of bowels of mercy and an understanding heart. But disharmony reigns in this unity. The Bible speaks of the flesh warring against the spirit though the body is the sanctuary of the Holy Spirit.

We can understand the wholeness of the child in the light of God's Word only. More than Scriptural intellectual presuppositions are necessary to understand the God-revealed unity. Only the regenerated heart seeking God in His holiness in the living Word can avail himself of the light of the Scriptural presuppositions.

When we thus understand the unity of the child as experienced daily, we may proceed to make the distinctions the Scripture makes. We can then observe the child in these distinctions of his make-up in the light of the Scripture. We shall not fall into the error of non-Christion thinking, namely, trying to understand the child in his parts.

I have used the words spirit and psycho-somatic in describing the human personality. The Bible uses *pneuma* and *psyche* with reference to the soul-life of man and *soma* for the physiological life. Rather than think of soul and body as discrete entities, we are closer to the intent of the Scripture, it seems, when we think of human life as one in the spirit or pneuma. Dr. J. Waterink calls our attention to the fact that the Greek *pneuma* and the Hebrew *rouach* are both to be translated *breath* or *spirit*. These words seem to refer to the condition for life in man. It is the life substance in distinction from the body. They seem to refer to a definite "moment" (meaning essential element or factor) in the human being. Man's true personal life seems to be designated thereby. In distinction from the word *pneuma*, Waterink continues, the Greek *psyche* and the Hebrew *nephesh* seem to refer to "moments" in the human being. They seem to give the idea of essential elements or factors associated with the individual life in particular.

Dr. H. Bavinck interprets the Bible as speaking of man being soul but having spirit. Though Bavinck made a laudable attempt to give psychology a scriptural reference, he was not close enough to the field of psychological investigation. Dr. Waterink's observations in the Child Study Institute under his supervision have sent him back to the Bible for closer study of scriptural thinking. He and his associates have been alerted to new developments in their clinical studies. Being genuine Christian men of Reformed outlook, they concluded a unity of the human person, scripturally oriented and based on observed facts in child life. There is the urge in Bavinck's discussion too for greater unity of the human person, but his observations were limited to theology, philosophy, and the psychology of the nineteenth century with no clinical contacts. As I see it the Lord is opening the way for greater clarity in understanding the soul-life of man. But then we must be willing to study man in life. A study of the soul in academic fashion will not help us. We must seek our understanding of the soul from the organic unity of life. The child must be viewed in life.

Unity of Human Personality

How must we view the unity of man in action? The diagram below may help. It is an adaptation from Waterink's *Our Soul-life* (*Ons Zieleleven*).

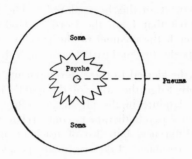

The spirit (pneuma) is the life-giving substance, the ego, I, subject, person. God places the spirit of man in organic relationship with the psycho-somatic. The unity of the personality is a given fact; the spirit is its explanation. It is in the pneuma, I, that man is rational, moral, free, and responsible. The psyche represents human life in its feeling, desiring, urges, drives, reasoning, willing, etc., in short the soul-life of man in relation to the body. The irregular line of the psyche means to indicate how the psyche and the soma (body) are involved in one another. Where the psyche leaves off and the body begins is difficult to determine. Endocrine gland secretions are involved in our emotions, but fear as an emotional experience is very much a psychical reality. Sensations, perceptions, ideas, thinking, etc., flow over into one another as in one organism. Waterink speaks of the psyche as the lower soul, while the I is the higher soul. This distinction is in order when we stop to consider the difference between attacking a problem in our reason and feeling the urge to pet a dog, between reflecting on a basic moral issue and trying to keep four balls in the air.

Psychotherapy has opened the field of the psycho-somatic as never before known. Every physician alert to developments in his field knows that a large percentage of his patients belong in a psychiatrist's office rather than in his. But to get them there!

The I is the person, the self-conscious center of our very being. The I is the explanation of the unity of the whole person or personality. The self is the psycho-somatic adapted to the life principle of the I. God so made us in His image. Our personality is the I as it operates through the psycho-somatic. The only contact we have with one another and with the world is in the self or psycho-somatic. The only approach the parent and the teacher have to the I of the child is by way of the psycho-somatic. This is life. Only God has direct approach to the I. What communication there is from spirit to spirit among men is not known. Can this be explored? The Holy Spirit can witness with my spirit that I am the Lord's. God speaks to us in His Holy Word through the channel of the psycho-somatic as we read or listen, but He speaks to our hearts accordingly by His Spirit.

Teachers must be alerted to these developments in psychology. When they fail to acknowledge the unity of the child's personality, they may add to the cases landing in the physician's office who should go to a psychiatrist. Many psychotherapists could relate sad cases of parental ignorance or indifference, but also of teachers' mistakes, at the basis of their patients' troubles. Likewise many people experience conflicts that they learn to live with more or less successfully, unless a major shock comes along.

Modern mental hygiene sends us up a blind alley. The bias of modern psychology distorts the view of man in the process of living. Invariably the I as subject is ignored or denied. The self and the I are identified. Man is what he is in the processes of thinking, feeling, purposing, desiring, etc. The rationalist reduces the subject to rationality; the moralist to morality; the voluntarist to purpose and drive; the organismic psychologist sees in the life-process the explanation of unity; and we might say the psycho-analyst views the ego as being formed out of unconscious bio-chemical mass, the tension of the unconscious and the culture that seeks to form him.

We thank God for a scriptural anthropology that gives us a basis in faith that, whatever knowledge we do lack about man, we have presented to us a unitary view. The human personality is a unity, coherently held together in a most harmonious way, with every part organically integrated with every other part, and the I focused on God and His will that the fellowship of God's love may motivate his every endeavor. This is how we might describe the original state of man according to the Scripture. God made man a religious being in that he was made capable of the self-expression of God harmoniously. In the creative expression of divine qualities with which man is endowed we see the pride and glory of man.

The Broken-I

But what an awful disharmony resulted when man in his I turned from God to give his allegiance to another. He forsook the fountain of living water for cisterns that hold no water. He forsook the security afforded by the fellowship of God's love for a vaunted security in the creature. His life became a dying life. All the disruption to which a dying life is subject became his.

Dr. H. R. Wyngaarden, associate of Waterink at the Free University, has graphically indicated the disruption of the human personality as a result of sin. The I here refers to the whole personality, as we understand it in our daily conversation. In a broad sense the I does refer to the entire personality. The diagrams below are adaptations from Wyngaarden's *Major Problems of Maturity* (*Hoofdproblemen der Volwassenheid*).

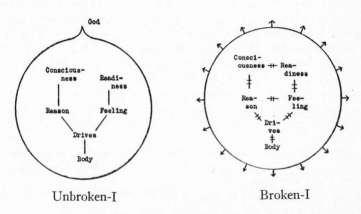

Unbroken-I   Broken-I

One need not grasp all the psychological implications of these two diagrams to recognize that the unbroken-I represents the total personality directed upon God in all his parts. The first represents the completely integrated person. In the second we see the personality still intact but sadly disrupted among the parts and headed in many directions at one time. God is gone as the focal point, as the determining object of man's fulfilment. Tensions, unresolved, remain his portion. There is no rest for the wicked. The soul does not rest until he rests in God.

As a member of the human race in Adam the child enters this world a broken-I. The spirit, the I in the restricted sense, is by act of God organically related to the psycho-somatic derived from the parents. The latter brings with it the disruptions inherent in a broken racial unity of which the pollution of sin is a major factor. The I, bringing with it the guilt of sin upon the human race, is steeped in spiritual darkness from the start, unless God in His saving grace determines otherwise. When regeneration takes place we know not. But if and when it takes place it means the re-birth of the I, a refocusing of the I upon God in Christ who has paid the debt of sin. The I is made alive in Christ in that the subject is re-established in racial unity in Christ, as a member of His body.

The broken-I is subject to the tensions of internal disruption. He enters a culture or life in tension by virtue of its being a human product. The natural world about him groans under a tension all its own by virtue of the curse of God's judgment upon sin. In the interaction of these factors, tension mounts. The natural man of sin dwells in darkness, so that he lacks power and perspective to clear up his tensions. Indeed, what we call normal on a general human basis is awfully abnormal viewed from the position of the unbroken-I. How the restraining power of God is in evidence when we see what the tragically abnormal man can accomplish in the midst of all his tensions! We see, too, the rare gifts with which God still pleases to endow men living in spiritual darkness, that even the darkness of sin may praise the Lord. But we see above all the saving grace of God in Christ as He redeems the broken-I and in the fellowship of redeemed sinners builds His church. God takes subjects, places them in the fellowship of His love by the regenerating power of His Spirit, directs them to His Word, and by Word and Spirit enables them to work out their own salvation by faith in Christ. Broken personalities are being restored to the harmonious self-expression of the Christ who is their very life, as branches ingrafted into the vine.

Do we now have our terminology clear? The I or subject (pneuma) is the person who is the explanation of the very life of the child. The I is placed in organic unity with the psycho-somatic (the soul-life of man involved in body processes, neural, chemical, etc.) by God. The psycho-somatic is adapted to the I such that our very humanity embodies spirit. The psycho-somatic is the self through which the I or spirit finds expression and receives impressions from the external world. Our personality is the I in its varied operation through the psycho-somatic. The personality is the I in the broad sense, as we employ I in conversation. In a restricted sense the I refers to the spirit, the subject, the person operating in the psycho-somatic. We speak of the unity of the person when we view this unity from the I; of the unity of the personality when we view the unity as a given fact of experience or in dealing with one another. This represents our working vocabulary for the present. We cannot employ the vocabulary of the modern psychologist without becoming involved in his thinking. There is overlapping, as we see.

In educating a child we deal with him in the unity of his person. This unity extends to every aspect of his developing personality. In order to understand him we must take a look at the essential parts that constitute his unity, but we can understand him only in his organic unity as every part is involved in every other in life. God thus deals with man. Our psychology as a science is man-made, but God makes a child. We as parents and teachers are privileged to be co-laborers with God in the integration of personalities in their basic unity. This may be called man-making. It is the bringing up, the nurture of the child to maturity. The Bible gives us the light we need to carry on our responsible task. It points us to the I and the self in which the I is involved organically to constitute the human personality. The broken character of the I, in the broad inclusive sense, does not destroy the unity of the child as a developing personality but points to absence of harmony or coherence to make the unity serve its original purpose, God's self-expression in man. In the regenerated child the original harmony is being restored by Christian nurture.

The I and the Unity of Personality

We have seen that the unity of personality is a given fact, assumed, not specifically demonstrated, in the Scriptures. According to the Bible, the explanation for this unity is found in the I, or the spirit. It is in the I that man is focused upon the Creator, or, one might say, incorporated in the fellowship of God. Man is spirit of Spirit in a created sense. God breathed in him the breath of life and he became a living soul. Man is, therefore, religious in the whole of his being. He is of the "breath" of God. Because he is of God, he can fellowship with God. "Religious" describes man in his whole being, in all dimensions of his personality. He is the image of God as the self-expression of God. Because man is religious, he is rational, he is moral, he is social, he is free, and he is responsible. These qualities are inherent in man as the self-expression of God.

Man is rational. This means that he can know the truth. Man can judge that which presents itself to him as object of knowledge as true or false. Rationality is the activity of the I in the organization of experience with reference to what he judges true or false. Because man is rational, he can abstract from experience, from life, what he selects for reflection. He can form ideas and generalize his findings on the level of imagination. He can state and solve problems "in mind." In short man can think; he can reason. In psychological terminology one might say, he can conceptualize the perceptual.

Man is moral. By this we mean that he can know the good. Man can judge life as being good or evil. Morality is the activity of the I in the organization of experience with reference to the good or the evil. Because man is moral, he has a conscience.

Man is social. By this we mean that he can fellowship. Man can enter into the life of others. Sociality is the activity of the I in organizing the person communally. Men do not herd together, but they form communities.

Man is free. By this we mean that he can choose. In his rationality-morality-sociality he has fundamentally two alternatives in the direction of which his choices lie. He can choose the fellowship of God's love and there find the fulfilment of his being which constitutes his abiding freedom. Or he can choose to go his way without the fellowship of God's love. This way is unnatural to his religious nature and therefore causes him in his rationality-morality-sociality to dwell in darkness. Instead of moving freely in the natural, he is bound by the unnatural.

Man is responsible. By this we mean that he is accountable for his judgments of truth and falsehood, of good and evil, for his choices and the exercise of these choices in life. Man can respond to the love of God by loving God, or he can spurn that love and subject himself in his rationality-morality-sociality to the divisiveness of the broken-I. God passes judgment upon man as an accountable person who responded to or spurned God's love.

Man is rational-moral-social and exercises these qualities freely and responsibly because he is religious. His basic motivation, therefore, is religious. All man's striving is basically religious in character, for it involves the I in all his qualities as the self-expression of God. Man in the totality of life can be explained truly and understandingly in his religious motivation.

The Psycho-Somatic and the Unity of Personality

The I, as we saw earlier, is the life principle of the psycho-somatic. The I is "moment" involved in all the moments of the psyche. The organic relationship of the I with the soma (body, physiological) through the psyche (soul-life in relationship to and involved in the soma) gives the psycho-somatic its humanity. It is because of this organic relationship that the Bible speaks of bowels of mercy (visceral action of the psyche), of the body as the temple of the Holy Spirit, of the understanding heart, and the like.

In the psycho-somatic we view the person-in-life. But we see him as the whole-person-in-life. Momentarily we must abstract certain aspects or phases of the unity of the person for analysis. But in order that the person be understood we must think of every phase as an integral part of an interrelated unity, organically one.

When we thus view the whole-person-in-life, we see him in three dimensions, or, one might say, a three-fold magnitude. We see him in his physiological-life, in his social-emotional-life, and in his knowing-life. Note that I use life as the common factor. What I mean to say is that we see the whole-person in his physiological-life dimension, in his social-emotional-life dimension, and in his knowing-life dimension. In every dimension we view the whole-person-in-life. I make this very emphatic, for the *person* is never viewed in parts. His anatomy may be. In a certain sense his physiology may be viewed in parts. Not his physiological-life, however. Here you view the whole-person, for the social-emotional-life and the knowing-life are involved in the physiological-life. Every dimension is involved in the other in the I and must be so understood.

We view the whole-person-in-life in his physiological-life. We study digestion, not merely as a physical or chemical process, but in its inter-relationship with accompanying and resulting effects upon the social-emotional security of the person, or with relation to concentration in the knowing-life. We study neural processes, not as neurology, but in their relationship to reaction time, sensory acuity, and the like, to understand the mechanism involved in being alerted to danger, or in resting comfortably in a chair.

We view the whole-person-in-life in his social-emotional dimension. Our emotional-life tells us "how we are doing." It is the "color" of personality. It expresses the feeling-tone of the person. What we call an emotion — grief for example — is never a simple something. There are no simple emotions. When you feel kindly disposed *you* are involved as the whole-person-in-life, never something *in you* merely. And then we hyphenate the social and the emotional. We never experience the one without the other. This is true of all dimensions, but more intensively so in the social-emotional. Every bit of our emotional life is social and all social life is wrapped up in emotional relations. The first evidences of emotional life of the infant, his response to the warmth of the nursery, has a social setting. The first social awareness calls forth an emotional response revealing a feeling-tone of the whole-person of the infant.

We view the whole-person-in-life in his knowing-life. The knowing-life has its beginning in the perceptual field. Objects are perceived in meaningful wholes so that the person can deal with them as wholes conceptually. I can plan my garden conceptually, as ideas, because I experienced a garden or gardens perceptually. I can so order the perceptual conceptually because I am subject, not object of my perceptual fields. The I in the qualities of rationality-morality-sociality is creative, he orders the ideas in the conceptual. Thus in the knowing-life the whole-person-in-life is creative. He orders ideas creatively into new patterns for expression. So the boy's bird cage comes into being, slightly different from the ones he has observed, because he planned it thus. In the knowing-life the whole-person-in-life remembers, imagines, thinks, purposes, judges, plans, etc.

The knowing-life involves what we have come to call intelligence. By it we mean the capacity of the whole-person-in-life to apprehend almost immediately the coherence of the objects of knowledge presented to him. Intelligence is not an entity or something in us. It is an activity in the knowing-life of the whole-person. We speak of a person as being of high, average, or low intelligence. What we really mean to say is that the whole-person-in-life can deal with situations he confronts with a degree of effectiveness. Some would make a distinction among abstract, social, and mechanical intelligence according to the character of the situation one faces. Some persons seem to have more of the one than of the other. The knowing-life must not be narrowly limited to what has been called intellectual apprehension. I have come to know that Chicago is located on the southwest shore of Lake Michigan. This knowledge consists of a perceptual field of geographic location which has been conceptualized. I can deal with it as idea. I also know this fact in relationship to historical development of Chicago as a loading center, transportation, communication, and the like. I know it in what it has become as a metropolis. Conceptually I have developed many generalizations in association with Chicago as a city, as an urban population, etc. Conceptually Chicago has a wealth of meaning for me in relation to other knowledge.

When I look into my knowing-life further I note that I have come to accept certain generalizations as truths which guide the I in ordering all dimensions of my personality. I should not want to live in Chicago, for example. I would much prefer a suburb. I have committed myself to certain basic principles which determine the totality of my life. It should be evident that in my acceptance of truth or principle I am dealing with a deeper phase of my knowing-life. In his rationality-morality-sociality the I freely and responsibly commits himself in the knowing-life. The other dimensions are involved, but, if all things are to be well with me in life, the other dimensions will follow the knowing-life. It is in this deeper sense that knowledge of the mind becomes knowledge of the heart. According to the Scriptures we come to accept in our hearts what we come to love in the understanding. The knowing-life, then, finds its highest realization in heart knowledge or personal commitment. The religious nature of the whole-person accounts for the deeper meaning of the knowing-life. The I focuses all dimensions of the whole-person-in-life upon the object of his love, and embraces it, and surrenders to it in commitment. "Know the truth, and the truth shall make you free." It is in commitment that the broken-I experiences his integration — when the object of commitment provides the fulfilment of his person. This is the person's security. Man finds peace only in surrender to the truth, not by merely acknowledging it conceptually. And this is the person's freedom.

What I have been trying to say is that the unity of the person can be seen only in relation to life. Therefore we speak of the whole-person-in-life. We see him in three dimensions, or in a three-fold magnitude. A simple illustration, all too inadequate, may help clarify the point. Driving down the road in my car, *I* come to a residential area. *I* see a sign (physiological-life) that reminds (knowing-life) me to slow down to twenty-five miles an hour. Because *I* have come to accept (knowing-life) responsibility for the safety of others (social-emotional life), *I* slow down promptly. Suddenly *I* see (physiological-life) children at play near the highway. My sense of responsibility (knowing-life closely interwoven with social-emotional-life) leads me to step on the brake (physiological-life) to slow down still more and to keep my eye (physiological-life) on the movements of the children. It is in the I that the three dimensions of my personality are integrated to effective unified action. This is the unity of the psycho-somatic in the total personality integrated in the spirit.

But what of the will? No more than emotion or intelligence is the will something *in* the person. The will describes the I as rationality-morality-sociality bent on action freely and responsibly. In the disharmony of the broken-I the I bent on action, which is the will, often runs into conflict with dimensions of the personality as expressed in the psycho-somatic. In the redeemed the I has been refocused upon God and reincorporated into the fellowship of his love. He is bent on action in keeping with the law of love, the will of God. But he runs into an undisciplined, recalcitrant psycho-somatic. This psychology harmonizes with Paul's account of his experience as recorded by inspiration of the Holy Spirit in Romans 7:14-23. Read this again, either in the revised or Weymouth version.

Can we bend the will of the child? No. Can we give the child a new will by teaching? No. Can we do anything about the child's will? Let us see.

Development of the Whole-Person-in-Life

How does the child become integrated in the three-fold magnitude of his personality? Is he a unity at birth, or does he become a unity in experience? The life of the infant has its origin psycho-somatically in the germ cell generated through the parents and in his person in the I or spirit placed there by an act of God. That germ cell, therefore, is more than a mass of protoplasm capable of differentiation. It is a unity in the I that in the process of cell division and differentiation develops a psycho-somatic adapted to the activity of the spirit. Thus this cell develops its humanity. There is present a development-urge characteristically human.

It is in the development-urge of the infant that he must be understood as image of God. When we study the development of the human being before and after birth we observe the following order: from unity without differentiation to unity within differentiation. The unity within differentiation begins to take the form of integration of the dimensions of personality.

In pre-natal development differentiation is largely physiological. The physiological satisfactions involved in nursing and suckling, in elimination, and in cuddling in the early infant stage manifest the first signs of differentiation in the psyche, the soul-life involved in the physiological life. Gradually the recognition of the nurse, mother, if she does the nursing, enters the field of early satisfactions. Social differentiations set in. In the babe reaching for the ball, later creeping to it, and deliberately throwing it, we see differentiations in the knowing-life.

To bring about integration among these differentiations in an underlying unity requires further development. As individual the child comes to identify himself in his unity as I. This we may call his individuality. But he comes to this discovery in relationship to a community. Integration of the dimensions of his personality as they continue differentiation takes place in this relationship. Integration will take place as he successfully maintains his individuality while accepting his widening community.

Space does not permit further detail on this development. Let us note one point very pertinent to schooling. Suppose the child has with reasonable success maintained the integrity of his individuality while he accepted the widening community of his pre-school life. Now time for schooling comes. This is a major transition in the acceptance of his community. All will go reasonably well if the continuity of life is not too greatly disturbed. The degree of continuity depends upon the degree to which the whole-child-in-life has matured in his differentiation, and upon the degree of differentiation demanded of him when he enters school. For this reason we make the kindergarten resemble family life as closely as possible.

The development-urge inherent in the immature is the basis for all successful differentiation and integration. It represents the God-ordained way of child development. There is inherent worth in the stages through which a child develops into maturity. To interpret them in adult terms or to value them according to adult patterns is to do grave injustice to divine ordinances for child-life. All this, and much more, is involved in a child becoming a man or a woman. Oh, Lord, how wonderful are Thy works! Blessed is he who can view these wonders in the light of God's Word. To him the works of creation, providence, and divine government are a revelation of God Himself.

Personal Unity of the Child and Education

What significance has all this for learning and teaching in Christian schools? When we stop to consider that we are not accustomed to thinking of the child in his unity, but as a dichotomy or trichotomy, the implications of a psychology which takes the unity of the child seriously are extensive. Are we aware of the degree to which our thinking in educational theory and practice has been influenced by other views of the child than the one presented here? If this unitary view is in keeping with scriptural anthropology, we shall be challenged to re-think both curriculum and methodology in the Christian school. Inasmuch as the next two topics deal with phases of educational psychology, I shall merely mention a few implications of the unitary view of the child here.

First, learning and teaching involve the whole child in all dimensions of his personality as subject. The child does not learn with one dimension of his personality without involving the others. Nor can we in teaching address ourselves to one dimension without affecting the other. This is true because he is a subject, not object, in the learning process. He is active in the whole of his person. We address him in teaching as a subject, as the whole-person-in-life. The more immature, the more extensive his total action. When the teacher tells a Bible story in the first grade, the whole person lives that story, though he may appear passive in his listening. His nervous system becomes very active. Endocrine glands respond. Visceral organs become more active than normally. More nervous energy is expended. No, perhaps the child has not moved. He listened with rapt attention. But he just burned up physical energy and was intensely active in his social-emotional-life. He shifted from insecurity to security, back again, began compensating, and what not. He is as busy as the variations in his unity permit at the level of his maturity. As subject he begins to integrate the increasing differentiations of his activity. He develops ability to focus the dimensions of his personality. He learns to concentrate. He is gaining control over the expression of the dimensions of his personality. Teachers must not forget that this control is long in coming in child life. Along the way interfering hurdles turn up in unexpected places and at moments when not anticipated.

Second, the psycho-somatic develops drives peculiar to it as soul-life involved in somatic activity. It has its own needs which develop into drives. The tensions created in the need for food give rise to a drive which we call hunger. The infant in his undifferentiated unity throws his whole-person into activity. The whole body is in action and emits sound which we call crying. This crying is not the social-emotional dimension of personality of later development. A more mature child asks for a cookie. The same urge becomes involved in the purpose of the subject to make a living by working. Psycho-somatic drives become involved in purposes of the I. How to inspire, instruct, and discipline the whole-person-in-life to incorporate his pyshco-somatic drives in productive purpose is one of the problems of teaching. As we shall see later, all learning is purposeful. At the basis of this principle lies the unity of child life. The teacher must understand the child in his needs and drives if learning is to proceed purposefully.

Third, because the basic motivation of the whole-person-in-life is religious, the direction of the learning process is determined religiously. The I in his religious nature is rational-moral-social and as such the active principle of integration in the whole-person-in-life. As he comes to love the truth in his knowing-life, he accepts it in his person and orders all dimensions of his personality accordingly. Curriculum and methodology in school which focus the knowing-life upon the truth in accordance with the development of the whole-person-in-life recognize the religious nature of the child. The skills the child masters, the information he acquires, the insights and understandings he achieves find their final significance in meeting the religious need of the child.

Fourth, as the child can be understood only as the whole-person-in-life, so he can be taught effectively only as he comes to know the truth in the context of life. The more immature the child, the less is he capable of abstracting truth from life for understanding. As in his unity he becomes more differentiated along the dimensions of his personality, he acquires increased ability to abstract in his knowing-life a body of truth momentarily for analysis, understanding, and mastery.

The Lord deals with us as whole-persons-in-life. He does not set before us a body of "structurated reality" or a "system of disciplines." Some of our systematic theologies have become just this, also, some systems in philosophy and the like. Now, there is merit in all of these systems. We need them. But they are man-made, let us not forget. They are not without merit and not without truth. But the Lord gave His living Word, inscripturated for us, to bring us up in the way we need to go to be saved and to serve Him. Hence, the Bible addresses itself to the whole-person-in-life.

God recognizes our immaturity when he speaks to us in His Word in terms of life. He did not prepare for babes in Christ a body of truth that represents a system or structurated reality. We are called upon to do the same with reference to the God-ordained way of child life. The development-urge native to child life requires an approach in learning and teaching which begins with life. The primary level of schooling permits less abstraction in subject matter organization than the junior high level. Subject matter divisions are to be defined according to stages of differentiation in child life.

You see what implications the God-ordained way of child life has for curriculum organization and methodology! Some people still seem to think that we must take adult subject matter in logical form, abstracted from life, reduce it in quantity and simplify it, and call it a curriculum for the child. In this form it is not too palatable, to be sure. So let's make it "lots of fun," or tell them they had better get it — or else. Let's devise ways of "making it interesting." This they call method. That many thinking people come to scorn this methodology is no surprise. Let a teacher master his logical subject matter and method will come, it is said. Perhaps a period of internship will do it, they claim.

I recognize that there is a body of truth according to which the person must come to form himself. This forming takes place as the I orders the dimensions of his personality according to the truth. It is an active, creative process from the beginning. Do not try to make the child docile. You will drive him into reverse gear in his I or side-track him, at least momentarily. If he gets going it will be in spite of you! The process can take place effectively only in keeping with the development-urge of the child. Only as he comes to accept the truth in his heart will he be educated.

In his *Psychology of the Elementary School Child,* Waterink says so aptly, "Before the class stands a *living* person. In the seat is a *living* child. This *living* person is bringing up a *living* child for *life* by presenting *living* subject matter in a way that it *lives* for the child. All this is done that the child may *live* for the God of *life*."

V. The Child in His Educability

So far we have considered the child in his religious root and motivation, in his racial continuity, and in his personal unity. Because in his person he is religious, he is rational-moral-social, and he can choose responsibly to direct his whole personality to God or away from God. In either case he will worship and serve as only a person can. Man cannot choose to be irreligious or non-religious. He is religious by creation. He will in obedience subject himself to the will of God, his Creator, or he will commit himself to the creature. Paul found the "men at Athens . . . in every respect remarkably religious" (Acts 17:23). And Athens, the cultural world of our time, is as religious as is Jerusalem, the Church of Christ in this world. Man can be understood only in his religious motivation. The child in his nature and in his needs must too be understood in his religious motivation.

The I enters the racial continuity in the psycho-somatic to constitute his humanity. In his organic unity with the psycho-somatic he is human. In this organic relationship he becomes subject to all the destructive divisiveness inherent in the race because of the guilt and pollution brought upon the race by sin. In Christ the redeemed are restored to a new racial unity in which the power of sin has been broken. By faith one is ingrafted in Christ. And this faith is the new life implanted by God. The I is reconstituted in the embrace of the fellowship of God's love in Christ. As a religious person he is directed toward God and lays hold upon him. To the child of Christian parents comes the promise of a covenant-keeping God. This child needs the bringing-up that will direct his life upon God. He needs covenant-keeping parents and covenant-conscious teachers.

In his personal unity the child comes to differentiate himself in response to his community. In doing so the organic unity in the I finds a fuller expression in the dimensions of his personality, in his physiological-life, in his social-emotional-life, and in his knowing-life. No dimension of his personality can be abstracted from the organic unity of his person except for momentary analysis. He can be understood and guided only in his unity. We must view the child in-life.

Education, then, is the process by which we bring up a child to maturity as a whole-person-in-life. There are two phases to this process. On the one hand we have the bringing-up process; on the other we have the developmental process. The former is the responsibility of the educator; the latter is the responsibility of the child. God has ordained a development-urge in the personal unity of the child that is the basis for maturing of the child into manhood and womanhood. God has also ordained ways in which the child is to be brought up that the God-ordained development-urge can realize in the child the mature man and woman. Both are involved in "the way of *his going*" (Prov. 22:6, the original of which, Bible scholars tell us, includes both the goal and course to this goal. It is the nature of the child which determines the course, when we take nature to mean God-ordained way of child life). We can know "his going," the God-ordained ways for child life, when we observe a child, children, in the light of God's Word. It is in the "nature of things" that God reveals Himself when we see "things" through the eyes of the living Word. And it is only *then* that we understand "things" truly.

Now, what about the educability of the child? That he is educable is too obvious to require verification. Other living creatures on this earth can learn, but only man can be educated. Other creatures can act intelligently, but only man can be wise and understanding. A child can be brought up to mature manhood or womanhood. It has always been done. It will continue to be done as long as human history continues prior to our Lord's return. The question, therefore, is not whether a child is educable. Rather are we asking ourselves, what is the nature of a child's educability?

Some Interpretations of Educability

To the question, what do you mean by a child's educability, some would answer that he can acquire knowledge. We are not interested just now in the deeper philosophical issues pertaining to knowing. These are involved, but their discussion here would carry us too far into philosophy. When we say acquire knowledge or speak of knowing we are quite agreed on the meaning in general. The common-sense meaning will do here. For example: The high school student has come to know that banks are depositories for money. In his social studies in high school he makes further study of banks and banking. He learns that banks are an integral part of a larger financial structure of our day. He comes to know some of the history of banking, of various kinds of banks, and even explores some career opportunities open to young people in banking. In his knowing-life he has come to master certain facts about banking and to understand some of the processes of banking. He has also come to make judgments about banking in relation to life. He should learn to value in this area too.

Now it is said that here you have the key to man's educability. It is in that he comes to know, that the child's education is really accomplished. It is readily admitted, of course, that intellectual apprehension or erudition is not sufficient. But when all is said and done it is knowledge that measures one's education. The *more than erudition or intellectual apprehension* is not clear. Knowledge is power. Knowledge is virtue. Knowledge is the source of power and virtue, it is thought. But knowledge-getting cannot qualify our educability. It is only a phase of the knowing-life, and the knowing-life is only one dimension of our personality.

There are others who hold that man is educable because he is adjustable; or better said, man's ability to adjust himself qualifies his educability. We live in a changing world, so it is said, especially today in a rapidly changing world. The world of tomorrow will be very different from the child's world of today. The child will make many readjustments in the course of his life, if he is allotted the normal life-span. A state superintendent of public instruction one time said, "One of the greatest things modern education is doing for our youth is to make them more adjustable." That youth is more adjustable cannot be denied. The evidence is at hand. That it is a great achievement, many doubt, yes, even deny vehemently. To live happily and successfully one must be able to establish equilibrium among tensions within and without, it is claimed. It is only amidst tensions that growth and development takes place. The child's educability consists in his ability to make changes within and to meet changes without. It is his ability to make adjustments to and adjustments of. But, we ask, is educability to be stated in terms of change only? Our pre-scientific commitment to the personal unity in the spirit, the I, makes this view impossible. Not change, but the identity of the I is basic in educability.

Closely related to the former, the so-called social educator of our time claims that the capacity of the individual for socialization constitutes his educability. The child comes into this world as a non-social being. He is neither anti-social nor social. He is born into a community, of which the family is the first step. The community must come to accept him and he must accept the community if all is to be well. He can learn to accept himself in relation to the community. This, says the social educator, is the child's educability. But, again, is the nature and meaning of man exhausted in the socializing process, be it democratic or collectivistic? What the Scripture teaches us about the image of God in humanity refutes a concept of life exhausted in the social. Not man's horizontal social relationship explains him, but his religious nature.

Space does not permit a more detailed appraisal of the above three interpretations of the child's educability. Knowledge getting, adjustment, and socialization are all involved in the child's education and in a degree define his educability. But they neither individually nor collectively or compositely tell us the nature of educability.

Meaning of the Child's Educability

What does educability mean? What do we mean when we say that a child can be educated? Perhaps it is more effective to ask first, what does educability not mean? It does not mean that in the process of education we can bring about any changes in the organic constitutional relationship of the human person, nor can he himself do so. He is spirit in organic relationship with the psycho-somatic and expresses himself in his personal unity through the three dimensions of his personality. The identity of the human person in his unity is clear from the Scripture and is a given in experience as viewed in the light of the Scripture. Nor does it mean that we can by education change the direction of the I as religious. Neither can we change the state of the I in his subjection to sin. *Sola fide; sola gratia* — it is by faith alone; it is by grace alone. And therefore, *soli deo gloria,* the glory to God only. But educability does not mean either that there is a stage of passivity, relatively at least, in the child's development when we can mold him in his person. No, the child is an active I from the very beginning, though in infancy and in early childhood largely unconsciously in the psycho-somatic. The child is never passive or docile. What some call docility and passivity is actually the activity of an undifferentiated or little differentiated unity of his person. To the Lord we can say, "Mold me and make me," for in His hands we are but as clay. But no creature can so make us. We make ourselves.

What then can educability mean? Before we try to answer this question we must remind ourselves again that we can view the child only as whole-person-in-life. To try to understand him otherwise is to abstract a part and try to view the whole in the part. God made a child, not parts that constitute a child. The child can only come to know himself in-life. We, as the child's parents and teachers, can deal with him only in-life.

Let me answer the question this way: educability means that we can build structure in the life of the child. This is only an assertion as it stands here, I realize. But the wording of the assertion is chosen in light of what we have said about the nature and need of the child thus far.

Note carefully what I am *not* saying. I am not saying we can structurate the child. Again let me emphasize that the child is not a docile object pliable to any mold to which we desire him to conform. He is active in the I from infancy, though not consciously and purposefully.

Neither am I saying we can build structure *in the child*. We can accomplish nothing *in the child*. It is his domain, subject only to

God, his Creator. We can say that we work with the child in-life that he may build structure in himself. We can build structure *in the life of the child*. But this is quite another thing than to say we structurate the child or we build structure in the child. No, this is not a play on words. The difference arises from an attempt to be true to the nature of things as we view them in the light of the scriptural view of man.

Educational Structure

What do we mean, then, by building structure in the life of the child? We want to build in the child's life that which will coherently hold together the bringing-up and developmental process by which he reaches maturity. It is in the structure that this process has its inception, its sustaining strength, and its direction. All that takes place in the bringing up and in the development of the child is given interrelationship in the structure such that the whole-child-in-life receives effective guidance in the integration of his differentiations. In his development-urge he comes to develop himself in this structure. As he matures he creatively comes into contact with varied structures. He comes to accept a structure and commits himself to it. This may or may not be the structure parents and teachers sought to build in his life, though they hope and pray it will be. The structure they build in the child's life becomes more or less the structure in which his personality is expressed.

Is this difficult? Let me illustrate. Every society has some conception of what its immature members should be like when they grow up. The members of adult society also develop some notion of how this is brought about. Adults take an active part in trying to bring up the immature to maturity according to their ideas. In trying to do so they give some concreteness to their ideas. In a primitive society they might say that for a boy to become mature he should know where to locate schools of fish in brook and lake. They proceed to build into *the life* of the boy the abilities needed to hold coherently together every differentiation of the boy in this direction. Every effort of the boy finds expression in this structure. One's view of what constitutes the educational structure is an important phase of his philosophy of education. The philosophy of education of the primitive society is that of survival on a primitive, nature-in-the-rough basis. Alertness, courage, and perseverance might be considered its structure. But let us go back to the three explanations of a child's educability which we discussed before.

Take the knowledge-getting theory. Those who advocate this theory would say that the educational structure is the disciplines as we have them in present-day subject matter. The logic of grammar is such a discipline, for example. So is the number system. The educational structure is an external, pre-existent form according to which the pupil is to be molded, or formed, or to which he is to be conformed, or informed. The forming referred to violates what we know about the child as a person viewed according to the Scripture.

The adjustment theory would find the structure in the individual's experience as he tries to equalize the tension created from within and from without. There is no educational structure prior to experience, they say. It is produced in the individual on the spot. Learning becomes indeed child-centered.

The social theory of education of the democratic variety finds the educational structure in the group relationship of the individual. The changing society determines the variation of structure, not the individual. There is educational structure prior to the individual's experience, but it has no pre-existent form except that of social change. Both the adjustment theory and the social theory recognize the creative nature of the human organism. They deny the passivity and docility of man.

Christian Educational Structure

We believe that God has made man as spirit in the psycho-physiological, responsive to His revelation of Himself. We know too that the child is born into this world as a person who in his development-urge is creative in his response to his community, or total environment. Furthermore, we know that the interrelationship of man and his community has been thrown into disharmony, which throughout the history of human culture has produced awful distortions of the truth. And what is more, the I is by nature focused upon the creature instead of upon the Creator. But we have the promise of the covenant, and our God is a covenant-keeping God. The second part of the covenant, however, is our responsibility. By faith we appropriate God's promises and work out our own salvation. In view of these great truths from the living Word, what is the Christian educational structure?

That we cannot build *vom Kinde aus* (from within the child), as the German has it, should be obvious from our previous discussion. There is pre-existent truth which makes absolute demands upon us. As a religious being the child does not find his fulfilment in himself, but in the God of truth. When we search the Scriptures diligently, we find the structure we need. We want to build into the life of the child that which will hold together coherently the process by which he becomes a mature person in Christ. This structure is love, faith, and obedience, put in the form of a triangle, indicating their integral significance one to the other (see p. 289).

What do we mean by love, faith, and obedience as the Christian educational structure? Can we give the child faith? No, especially not if by faith we mean the gift of God by grace, namely the new life and the way of the new life in Christ. This is not of ourselves. It is of God alone in His sovereign grace. What can we do? We as teachers can work with the child out of love as our motive, according to faith, and in the way of obedience. We inspire, instruct, and discipline him in this framework of relationship. It is faith working through love (Gal. 5:6) to obedience. We cannot make the child love, nor can we force him to accept faith as his guide, nor can we coerce him to obey. But we can build into the child's life the structure that will direct him in his expression.

The School and the Christian Educational Structure

How can the school proceed to build the Christian educational structure in the life of the child? The school stands in the middle of life as a cultural institution. By this we mean that it has been called into being in the complexity of modern life to accomplish a task which needs doing today. The parent is the responsible educator according to the Scripture. The school has been called into being as the extension of the home to aid the parents in their complicated task as demanded of them in the modern world.

The very place the school occupies in modern life gives it a special educational medium. It takes the cultural product of the race and adapts it to child life in its stages of development so that the child can learn. The stages of development in child life require organization of subject matter with a view to the development of the whole-child-in-life in all dimensions of his personality. A highly skilled task this is today both in view of what we have come to know about the development of personality and in view of the complexity of modern life.

Educability means, as we saw, that we can build structure in the life of the child so that the child begins to express himself in this structure. As he comes to express himself in this structure he develops his personality according to it in his commitment to the truth. The medium of the school, known as the curriculum, presents the truths to which he comes to commit his life. The medium is, therefore, to be truth-centered. The curriculum is planned and presented in such a way that the child is confronted with the truth to which he is called upon to surrender himself in all dimensions of his personality. It is in the hands of the teacher that this great task is accomplished. He is, therefore, not a peddler of ideas, nor one who pours knowledge into empty vessels, nor is he one who provides the exercises for some entity of the human mind (formal discipline). No, he is a guide to and in the truth.

We should understand the word guide correctly with reference to the immaturity of the child in his personal unity. The teacher as a guide *inspires* a child. He energizes him in the unity of his personality to call upon his resources for purposeful action. As the child in his whole person becomes active in a purposeful way, the teacher *instructs* him. He may do this directly by presenting in personal communication the informing material. Or he may do this indirectly by providing sources from which the child gathers the informing material by his own effort. In the former case the teacher tells, and the child listens. In the latter the child looks for the information. The teacher *disciplines* the learner by firmly directing him through inspiration and instruction. Guidance, then, is inspiring, instructing, and disciplining the child. Only the Lord can do more. He can directly lay hold upon the person. Not you and I.

The school which, as a cultural institution, understands its task in this way can operate in the Christian educational structure. When doing so, the Christian educational structure is built in the life of the learner. In the structure of love, faith, and obedience, we hope and pray the child will come to commit himself to the truth and express himself accordingly. In the I as rational-moral-social he will then freely be motivated by love, make faith the chart for his life, and obedience the course for his whole personality.

Degrees of Educability Vary

I trust that the discussion of the child's educability has shown that we are not merely speaking of intellectual capacity. Nor is educability described adequately in terms of one dimension of personality, as the knowing-life. When we speak of degrees of educability, we refer to a child's ability to avail himself in his ego or spirit of the medium presented in the structure which we build in life. That children vary greatly in this ability we all realize. But this difference is even more involved than we think it to be.

At a given time one child learns numbers more rapidly than another. The other may learn to read more readily. A third pupil seems to have above others a keen insight into mechanical things that call for manipulation. A fourth displays greater group consciousness. And a fifth seems consistently superior in all these things. Parents and teachers observe these differences constantly. They are never differences isolated or abstracted from the whole-person-in-life, but differentiations in a personal unity. And it is precisely the differentiations in the child's personal unity that give his variations their importance.

Scientific experimentation has given us valuable insights in education as it has done in many areas of study and observation. But it has done immeasurable damage through faulty interpretation, too. Among the most damaging results has been the practice of dealing with children in their differences in the abstract. I refer to intelligence testing and achievement measurement, for example. Homogeneous grouping has been one of the most vicious of practices to come from such abstraction. We have gotten away from this grouping to a large extent, though some schools still look to it as a solution to individual differences. Educational determinism based on test scores has been another practice that violated the unity of the child's person-in-life.

In our Christian schools too we must face the problem of varied educability. God has not made us all alike. And there is no aristocracy in God's kingdom, intellectual, nor otherwise. There are varied callings according to divine endowment of the person. Our study then, of varied educability should proceed on this basis. In the elementary and secondary schools, where the entire pupil population of the community is in attendance, this problem requires serious study.

How Determine Educability?

Immediately we think of verbal tests, when we raise the question of how to determine educability. And tests have their place, standardized as well as non-standardized, general intelligence as well as achievement tests. But when we learn to view the child as I believe he should be viewed according to the Scripture, we shall be extremely cautious in the use of test results, and even before that in the selection of tests.

To determine educability, as I believe we should view educability, is extremely difficult. We may abstract a dimension of a child's personality for momentary measurement and succeed in securing some qualitative, descriptive statement of value. But if what we have said about child life thus far is correct, that is if we are following lines marked out for us in a scriptural anthropology, we shall be on our guard against inroads of modern phychology, sociology, and educational theory. We have imbibed uncritically altogether too much already.

We face two serious limitations. First, in appraising a child in his educability we can deal with only a limited aspect of his personality at one time. We may come to describe him in a certain phase of his expression. We may observe whether he writes and speaks acceptable

English, for example. We may go a little further. We may observe whether a child's ability in a given area corresponds to his abilities in other areas of subject matter. But in so doing we are still in the knowing-life of the child, and in only a limited phase of this dimension of his personality.

We are further limited by our inability to view our measurement in relation to the unity of the person. In the knowing-life we make some fragmentary observations; in the social-emotional-life, and in the physiological-life too. But to relate them in the unity of the ego extreme caution is advised. Our appraisal is at best very inadequate.

Can we appraise at all with some assurance that we may have a measure of confidence in our guidance of a child? We can use tests in their best form, that is when they are reliable and valid. To be reliable they must measure what we seek to measure; to be valid they must show internal consistency among their parts in trying to measure what we set out to measure. Tests are a part of the cultural medium of the school. But we cannot abstract the knowing-life from the other dimensions for measurement or appraisal. If teaching is to be guidance in the Christian educational structure, more must be done than merely testing. The whole-person-in-life must be understood that we may not go wrong in directing ourselves to the knowing-life of the child. Every child should become a living personality to the teacher. When directing himself to the knowing-life of the child, he should do this as he knows Mary, Jane, Harry, and John in their individual life style and in all dimensions of their personality.

I know what teachers are ready to reply at this point. "Impossible. You ignore entirely the size of our classes, and in our high schools the total pupil load per teacher." They are right. It seems absurd even to suggest knowing the child in his own life style. In school language we would say, the ceiling is low; that is, the opportunity to engage in this task is beset by limitations beyond our control. If only school boards would recognize that large classes and large pupil load in our high schools defeat the very purpose of Christian education! In spite of the limitations, I venture to suggest that unless teachers catch the vision and develop the practice of understanding children the distinctive character of Christian schools will remain formal and on paper.

In anecdotal recording of child life and in sound interpretation of our findings we secure more valuable information for child guidance than in any amount of testing. Principal and teachers will spend hours and money in a "testing program." But very little time is devoted to first-hand study of life styles of children in many cases. Anecdotal recording will require home visits and many informal contacts of teachers and children. It demands on the part of the teacher an understanding of himself in the relationships of life. The time, energy, and money spent in ascertaining whether our boys and girls are up to "standard" are not always wisely used, but the effort that goes into the study of children in their life styles is always of value.

VI.   The Learning Process

Learning is a Fact

That a child learns is a common observation. The infant learns to walk. This is not as simple a process as it appears to the adult. The child learns to read and figure. The adolescent learns to know how the voting at the polls is related to government. All of these represent progress in the person over the infant stage in dealing with life. This is precisely what learning really is in its most general nature. It is the progress made in the person over earlier stages in life.

In this general sense animals learn too, that is, they make progress in the organism over earlier stages. The observations made of animal learning have frequently been used as a basis for interpreting human learning. It was realized of course, that human learning is more complex. Initial bias led psychologists to the wrong conclusions. They did not view man in his person as spirit. One's pre-scientific commitment is bound to make a fundamental difference in his interpretation of the learning process.

When we observe the facts and processes of learning, we do so as Christians, as committed to *the truth*. We make our observations not as the modern scientist who claims objectivity. He collects data without critically examining his pre-scientific commitments. As a religious person he makes his observations committed to a way of life. But he avoids careful scrutiny of his total position. As Christians we stand committed to the faith in which the Sovereign God has laid hold upon our lives, and we search for truth in the light that the Holy Spirit affords us in the written Word. Only one ingrafted in Christ and schooled in the Scriptures knows what this means.

Learning is a fact. We want to interpret it as a process in the development of the whole-child-in-life as we come to see it in the light of the Scriptures. It will help us to examine five commonly known interpretations of learning and to appraise them. Current discussions of educational theory and practice are bound to include one or more of these interpretations. Teachers in Christian schools should be alerted to these interpretations, lest theory and practice inconsistent with the Christian faith be brought into the classrooms.

Assimilation and Discipline

We begin with one of the oldest interpretations of learning. Though they might be considered independently, assimilation and discipline can be discussed and appraised as one. Historically they parallel one another. In their view of mind they agree.

This interpretation is predicated on the view that mind functions as an entity distinct from the rest of the human organism. As the stomach operates with food, and as the heart regulates the blood flow, so the mind operates with ideas. Some have held that the mind as generated out of the ancestry brings ideas with it. At least as an organ, the mind can be exercised in manipulating ideas. The mind can assimilate ideas and be disciplined in the use of them.

The mind was thought, too, to consist of various compartments and faculties. Those who did not like the idea of compartmentalizing the mind spoke of distinct functions of the mind. Some recognized two functions, knowing and feeling; others three, knowing, feeling, and willing. When the mental life of man became the object of closer observation, faculties or functions increased in number, some speaking of reasoning, imagination, memory, judgment, purpose, motivation, etc., as functions.

According to the faculty psychology, for so this view was labeled, learning is a process of taking in and assimilating ideas and of exercising and forming the mind according to these ideas. Some placed greater emphasis upon assimilation, others upon discipline, but all agreed that assimilation and discipline were both involved in learning. The teacher is a peddler of ideas and a coercive manager of the learner's mind in the use of these ideas. The teacher has the ideas; the learner does not. The teacher transmits ideas and compels action by the learner's mind in manipulating the ideas he transmits. All the faculties or functions of the mind need exercise to strengthen them; so ideas, ready-made, are selected and presented accordingly.

It was not until about the eighteenth or nineteenth century that this view was challenged. Until then it was the accepted thing. All teaching was based on it. Teaching was largely logical and deductive in character and, therefore, verbal memorization. Some teaching still is.

Association Psychology

But the challenge came. And when it did come, it came from sources that began to tamper with the nature of man as taught in the

Scriptures. The substance character of the distinctively human principle of life was questioned. What is mind, it was asked. Mind is the association of ideas. It is not an organ that assimilates ideas and exercises itself in the use of ideas. No, it is its ideas. For what are ideas but perceptions organized and retained as generalizations in the organism. Mind, then, is the cumulative effect of internalizing sensations and perceptions.

Philosophically some began to challenge the thought that mind is its ideas. It was thought that mind makes a contribution of itself in forms or categories. But this remained a theoretical discussion as far as psychology was concerned. Even the challengers of the empirical view of mind had no intention of going back to the faculty psychology.

On the basis of the association theory of mind, learning becomes a connection of ideas. Ideas are still treated as entities. In the individual they are associated according to certain laws and retained in organized form. Teaching is the presentation of ideas such that association with previously acquired ideas is facilitated. Ideas have the power to make the man. Such is the Herbartianism of the nineteenth century.

Association psychology became the basis for educational theory and practice when the faculty psychology began to lose its grip on pedagogics. In Europe and in America the development of Herbartianism and universal educational opportunity were contemporaneous. The nineteenth century intellectualism, as Herbartianism came to be known, became the methodology of the nineteenth century school.

Connectionism

At the turn of the century psychology and sociology became enamored with the success of the quantitative methodology of the modern natural sciences. With the substance character of mind disposed of, psychology turned to observation and experimentation for its data. Not ideas but the nervous system of the organism became the focal point. The mind was interpreted as neural connections particularly in the brain. If mind is to be localized anywhere it must be in the cortex of the human brain with its countless connections. Hence this psychology became known as connectionism.

Learning, in the mechanistic school of psychology known as connectionism, is a process of connecting stimuli and responses. What stimuli will bring forth desirable responses? How can desirable responses be stamped in for desirable behavior? From investigations seeking answers to these and similar questions we got certain laws of learning. Educational psychology based on connectionism introduced the scientific study of educational theory. A revised methodology was in the making.

Insight

But while connectionist psychology was getting hold of theory and practice in the schools, two new movements arose to challenge it in its atomistic character, not in its view of mind as such. No return to the substance view of mind was desired. But to view mind merely as a quantitative accumulation of connections, and to view learning as a stamping in of these connections by successful or satisfying practice, seems to violate the given wholeness or unity of the person and of life, it was thought.

It was demonstrated that animals react not to stimuli in isolation, but to situations in which parts are experienced in relationship. Man, even more than animals reacts to organized wholes. Learning does not merely consist of connecting stimuli and responses, of responses and responses, and a stamping in of responses, but is rather the organization of responses in relationship. Learning may seem to come as a flash when the whole is perceived. This sudden awareness was called insight. Teaching was regarded as the presentation of organized wholes perceptible to the learner.

Experiencing

With the turn of the century there arose a school of thought in educational theory and practice that challenged the individualistic emphasis in learning as present in association psychology and in the connectionist views. The insight people did not correct this, it was said. Human behavior is not individual, but social in character. Mind and personality must be thought of as experience. Experience is the interaction of the human organism with the environment. And the environment is largely social. Learning is, therefore, experiencing. Teaching is the guidance of the learner's experiences to achieve fore-seen ends felt as valuable. Connectionism is an oversimplification of what really takes place.

Creative Expression

Not to carry the survey of theories of learning too far, I shall mention one more. It is the effect of several recent developments in psycology and sociology. It is eclectic in character and presents a complicated picture. But I shall confine this discussion to mere mention of some of its features. It is gaining ground in educational theory and practice by way of the psychological clinic and psycho-therapy.

First, there is the angle that says learning is really expression. Not unrestrained and unlimited expression, of course. But in the interaction of the organism with his environment, expression is the key to further interaction and development. Expression is never individual, but always social in character. It involves others besides himself. Whether accepted or rejected in the social milieu, the organism is reconstructed, undergoes change.

Furthermore, the organism is always creative in expression, for the action is from within. Impressions are not stamped in as connections, but energize the resources of the organism to action. Expression is the exercise of the organism's resources in relation to his environment. The whole-person-in-action is involved in expression. He does so in the style of life he has come to develop in his milieu.

There is a third angle. It is the security angle. Man is a security hunter from the beginning. The infant in mother's arms discloses this trait. Express himself he must, for so he is constituted. But his expression may prove a threat to his security, as do crying and squirming when they call forth a gruff voice from the parent. Tension increases, followed by more expression, and of the undesirable kind. Continued expression under such circumstances develops a personality in conflict. Wholeness and consistent action become impossible. Learning is expression. Teaching is guiding expression of the whole-person-in-action in security to desirable ends.

Current Theory and Practice

Momentarily educational theory represents dominantly a combination of the insight, experience, and creative expression theories. In practice, that is, in the classroom, we still see many influences of the connectionist and association theories. The substance theory of mind with the accompanying theories of assimilation and mental discipline have all but vanished. The reaction that has set in to contemporary educational theory and practice is focused largely on the fruits, not on the underlying theory involved.

Appraisal

By way of appraisal let us note first of all that there is truth in each and every one of these theories.

The I does assimilate ideas in the knowing-life of the whole person, and he organizes these ideas for a purpose. And the I orders the dimensions of his personality according to the disciplines he has come to accept in the psycho-somatic.

The I does associate ideas according to certain basic principles. There are divine ordinances for the whole-person-in-life, and therefore for every dimension of his personality.

The nervous system in its multitudinous connections does afford the I a mechanism in which he is organically involved for innumerable possibilities. Add to this the potential afforded the I through a glandular structure of the psysiological-life and we lose all comprehension of the intricacy of the psycho-somatic.

And, too, the whole-person-in-life comes to expression in his own life style. The depths of life are sounded again in recent psychology. Even total depravity becomes relevant. Regeneration is talked about in some psychological circles. Recent psychology has broken with the romanticism and optimism of the past.

All of this is true, but only when set forth on the basis of a scriptural anthropology.

The faculty psychology violates the basic unity of the person so clearly taught in the Scriptures. It does hold to spiritual substance as the principle of life in man, but it dichotomizes or trichotomizes the person, and compartmentalizes the knowing-life.

The association psychology destroys the spiritual identity of the person. Original sin becomes impossible and redemption is made unnecessary. The power of man rests in ideas.

The connectionist has become a rank materialist. Thorndike's laws of learning are too atomistic and mechanistic to interpret animal learning, not to speak of human learning.

Our "insight" psychologists, with the best of intention to give learning some wholeness, do not escape the mechanism of the connectionist.

And our social educational theory and practice, democratic and collectivist alike, deal with man as a social animal, of considerable refinement, to be sure, but an organism of basically animal propensities just the same.

Though the creative expression people tend to take heed what the depth psychology has to say about the unconscious, they fail to grasp the meaning of expression, for they fail to understand man in his true depth. They want self-expression. Do not understand them wrongly. They do not seek unrestrained expression. Not at all. As a matter of fact some psychotherapists advocate rigid control of expression. But it is self-expression that they want just the same. In the eyes of God self-expression of the broken-I is self-righteousness on which Jesus pronounced the severest judgment. Man is to be the self-expression of God, for in His image is man created.

VII. The Child's Learning Process

I trust it has become clear that we shall have to reconstruct our conception of the learning process if we want genuine Christian education. We cannot be satisfied with any modification or combination of the theories we discussed. The truths contained therein must be recast into another mold and given another direction.

Let me try to summarize with the view to considering the bases for a reconstructed theory of the learning process. I claim no originality for the attempted reconstruction, but I shall not burden you with documentation and quotation. Let me say that I owe the main slant to our Reformed brethren in the Netherlands, though I have tried to delve into other sources, too.

Bases for a Reconstructed Theory of the Learning Process

The first thing I should re-emphasize is that man is religious in the I. In the I he is spirit of God's Spirit. The I is breathed-in of God. In that he is a living soul. Being religious, therefore, is not an attribute of the self or personality. Man does not choose to be religious or non-religious. Being religious is descriptive of the I as spirit of God's Spirit. Created, of course, but in a very special sense, *viz.*, breathed-in.

In this fundamental truth the learning process has its inception, its direction, and its goal. The I as created spirit is motivated religiously. His greatest need is commitment, surrender in keeping with what he really is. It is for the I to accept life in the fellowship of God's love or to dissipate his very person, spirit, in the disintegrating tensions of the phycho-somatic. In the former he will find the fulfillment of his created nature. In the latter he commits himself at best to momentary equilibrium among the tensions of life, but to ultimate collapse in his person. The learning process begins with a view to commitment and finds its consummation in acceptance or commitment. Hence, on scriptural ground we may say, nothing is learned until it is accepted in the heart.

From the clear teaching of the Scripture that man is religious follows another. Because the I is religious, he is rational-moral-social. And these attributes of the I define his freedom and responsibility. In being spirit of Spirit he can know the truth, he can choose the good, and he can fellowship in love.

Here we have another basis for viewing the learning process aright. It is in the knowledge of the truth, in conforming to the good, and in the security of the fellowship in love that the I comes to acceptance thereof, and to commit himself freely and responsibly. In the learning process the child must be confronted with the truth, bow before it in obedience, and in love accept it.   The Christian educational structure, love, faith, and obedience, must be built in the life of the child.

A third basis for a reconstructed theory of the learning process we see in the I organically involved in the psycho-somatic.   The needs of the psycho-somatic become impulses and drives which call for direction and integration by the I as he gives expression to his religious need in acceptance and commitment.   Learning is motivated.   It is based on needs.   Needs give rise to drives.   The needs and impulses of the psycho-somatic become effectively motivated in the I as he consciously focuses them for commitment.   There is no learning without motivation.   The religious nature of the I organically involved in the impulses and drives of the psycho-somatic gives rise to this motivation.

In our recognition of the broken-I we have another basis for the understanding of the learning process.   In viewing the disharmony of the broken-I the previous considerations are not nullified, but their implication is greatly qualified.   What can be the nature of the commitments of a person hell-bound?   How free is he in his rationality, morality, and sociality?   How can the I under the law of sin order the psycho-somatic in its drives into a degree of harmony?   What we can say, according to the Scriptures, is that in God's keeping providence, in his "common grace," amidst the darkness of a hell-bound life spots of grey are visible; that not all is complete darkness.

But we are not left with the tragedy of the broken-I.   In Christ God restores a race of men to the fellowship of his love.   In the I refocused upon God and kept by his power the considerations we spoke of as bases for the learning process acquire new significance.   In the disharmony of the psycho-somatic, the I turned to God dwells in the light, though still subject to the tensions from within and to the degenerating forces of the world from without.   Total depravity does not mean that the divine ordinances for human development were nullified.   But it does mean that the learning process must take account of the ravages of sin in the dimensions of personality and in the world.

A fifth basis for interpreting the learning process aright we have in the unity of the person.   We cannot single out one dimension of the personality for development.   Our efforts will always be directed upon the whole-person-in-life.   The interaction of the dimensions of the personality in the I makes the learning process unitary in character. Though the school as a cultural institution directs its program necessarily upon the knowing-life primarily, failure to take account of the other dimensions will tend to defeat the learning process in its true intent.   Needs and drives arising in the social-emotional dimension of the personality little understood by the teacher, not at all understood by the learner, may divert our efforts in the knowing-life. In hidden recesses of the personality escapes and compensations may be built up in the learner which arise later to plague the child and those associated with him. The whole-person-in-life is involved in the learning process.

And finally, expression belongs to the very nature of the child as a religious being, to the I, the spirit. So he is created. He comes to express himself in a structure. Momentarily it will be the structure that affords him immediate security. His development-urge demands expression. The teacher can guide (inspire, instruct and discipline) the child in his expression by the structure he builds in his life. As he comes to express himself in this structure he forms himself.

What Is Learning?

We now come to what is in some ways the most difficult phase of our subject: How do we learn? We ask this question with reference to child life. Let this be clear. We are talking about childhood. It is the stage of life we regard as immature. And Scripture clearly refers to child life as the immature stage of human life. It implies divine ordinances for child life (Cf. Prov. 22:6; Mark 10:14; Luke 18:16; I Cor. 13:11; Col 3:21).

Learning is the process by which the I comes into conscious control of the self in his interacting with the environment. In and through the psycho-somatic the I or person is constantly interacting with the environment. In the dimensions of his personality, changes occur which the I integrates in the whole-person-in-life. These changes become a permanent ingredient of the total personality as the person commits himself to them.

As a child in the course of the learning process comes to accept life, he is said to mature. This means he is coming to order the dimensions of his personality responsibly. In the child of God the I is coming to order his total self in keeping with God's will. He comes to accept life responsibly as a member of the body of Christ, as a citizen of the kingdom of God.

Modificatory Factors

Before we study the learning process as such more closely, we should take note of certain factors which, if not always determinative, are at least of a qualifying character. I mean to say there are factors which affect the learning process though they are generally not considered parts or phases of the process. Several might be mentioned, but I shall mention three.

The word "readiness" has come to occupy a large place in educational theory. It generally has reference to a certain stage in the maturation of a child when he can learn certain things. We speak of "reading readiness" and a child's "readiness" for number work. In the thinking of some teachers it seems to indicate a "favored moment," now or never.

Let us make sure of what we mean when we speak of "readiness." A child of two is not ready to deal with the written or printed word. The first grader in school is not ready to understand city government. Does it mean that in the life of a child a specific time or moment arrives when he can learn to do these things? Hardly. Rather than think of a "favored moment," we should view "readiness" in relation to the development-urge of a child. His development-urge makes constant demands upon him. It is the urge for maturity of the whole-person-in-life. It is continuous and avails itself of every opportunity presented. Not always as desired by adults, of course.

Now note this. If we seek to energize the development-urge with reference to, and direct it upon, a medium in which the I cannot order the self in the dimensions of his personality, learning as we desire it cannot take place. We say a child is not ready for it. Learning is an active process of the person. We must know a child in his development-urge and the demands it makes upon him to know whether he is "ready" for a certain medium, or what we more commonly call a step in the learning process. It is surprising, however, what "short cuts" some children can take. The development-urge will not be bound by our carefully arranged steps. This becomes evident in a rural school where there are several grades in a room. How the children of lower grades will "pick-up" work of higher grades!

There is a second very important factor. It is that of social-emotional security. The younger a child, that is, the more immature, the greater the qualifying effect of this factor. In his development-urge he may reach out in a new medium. He may go exploring. But he must constantly feel a sustained strength he has not in himself. The presence of mother affords this in the very young child. The approval of the teacher is needed later, in early school years. And the standing in his peer group becomes important in later childhood.

Love as understood in the Christian educational structure affords a security to child life every child needs. "Perfect love casteth out fear." A teacher who causes children to feel the warmth of her love for them can undertake difficult ventures with them in the knowing-life without a serious threat to their security. As a child matures in a new medium he wants to feel the challenge of the novel without the threat of insecurity beyond what he can bear as a child.

I must mention one more modificatory factor. We often speak of it as motivation. But let us make certain of what we mean by this term, too. The development-urge as it comes to expression in child life is based on needs. In a general sense we all know what needs are. A child needs food. He needs warmth. He needs activity. He needs a feeling of success at times. And so we might continue. Every dimension of a child's personality, the physiological-life, the social-emotional-life, and the knowing-life, has needs peculiar to itself. Central to all these needs is the need of the I, surrender to God in a life of obedience and the consequent enjoyment of the fellowship of God's love.

How shall we define needs? Let me suggest this definition, at least for the present. *A need is the tensional state (unrest of the whole person) brought about by the absence of the necessary requirements for one's fulfilment as the self-expression of God.*

Our needs give rise to drives, in the psycho-somatic as well as in the I. In the broken-I the drives in the psycho-somatic threaten to engulf the whole-person. In the man of God, the I restored to the fellowship of God's love, they, the drives of the psycho-somatic, often resist disciplining in keeping with the commitment of the I. In the I drives become purposes, foreseen ends upon which we focus the whole-person. Motivation is the focusing of the whole-person-in-life upon foreseen ends.

Please note that motivation must not be understood in any such superficial sense as "making a lesson interesting" or "making it lots of fun." It is the enlisting of the whole-person-in-life in an activity.

There is no learning, as we have defined it, without motivation. The child cannot provide his own motivation in the learning process if learning as we desire it is to result. This the process of teaching must provide. Learn he will, because he has the development-urge. In the absence of right motivation he provides his own.

I call these modificatory factors: the development-urge, social-emotional security, and motivation. They operate without our seeking them. We must take them into account if we would teach at all.

The Learning Process

And now the learning process itself. Perhaps it is well that we begin with an actual learning situation as it might occur in a classroom.

A fourth grade teacher is planning to bring her pupils into understanding relationship with the urban community in which they live. We say they should become good citizens, yes, now, on their level, be good citizens of this community. Cognizant of the modificatory factors discussed above, the teacher begins to plan this unit of study. She realizes that on their level they are not "ready" to deal with life in the community as a unit in a political or governmental system. But they have matured in their social-emotional life as well as in their knowing-life to the point that they can view their community in relation to themselves and their responsibility in it. Their life has become sufficiently differentiated through home and family experiences, through their activity among other children in the community, and through the activities in their school community.

The development-urge of the children calls for a systematic, organized attack upon the problem. Reaching out into this medium will present a challenge, but not beyond the point of ability to experience the joy of achievement. Greater social-emotional security in the community will result from the right understanding of relationships: that the policeman is our friend, for example, but that he is also the man clothed with authority; he has a right to make demands upon me. The children too can be made conscious of real purpose in attaining well-conceived goals.

Inasmuch as there is a park in the immediate vicinity, the teacher decides to use the children's contact with it as the taking-off-point. The management of parks and our task in co-operating with recognized and established authority for parks will introduce government and our responsibility to it.

From the park the study continues into the wider areas of the community. For this study the pupils need sources of many kinds. They read in books and magazines; they make excursions, real and/or imaginary; they construct charts, maps, etc.; they organize a bulletin board display; they discuss and make reports. Letter writing may become necessary.

Finally what has been learned about community life is organized in a form that is conveniently retained as basic knowledge by fourth graders. Drill for mastery becomes necessary.

When the work is completed, the teacher proceeds to appraise the development of the whole child in this meaningful work. The appraisal may indicate that some remedial measures must be taken with certain pupils. This work must take precedence over new work for these youngsters.

So much for the illustration. What is the teacher trying to accomplish? She is trying to challenge every pupil in all the resources of his total personality to enter into the understanding of his place in the community as a citizen. What are the demands of God upon his life in this area? To what basic truths must he come to commit himself to be the self-expression of God in his whole-person? These and similar objectives are in the teacher's mind as she guides the pupils successfully through the stages of learning.

The teacher recognizes too that if the pupils are to come to express themselves as they should on their level, opportunities for successful mastery of basic knowledges and skills must be provided. Momentarily a certain skill, such as legible writing, must receive attention. A writing lesson is necessary. The teacher guides pupils to personal commitment to standards of legibility in keeping with their maturity. She holds them responsible for this maximum effort in this direction. And so a child in the Christian school commits himself progressively to relationships-in-life in the Christian educational structure and continues to express himself accordingly.

What I have been trying to say here is that the learning process does not consist of a ready-made series of steps or formula for mastery. But it does involve activities on the part of the learner in his wholeperson that can be psychologically circumscribed. The educational medium we employ in the school, generally known as subject matter, must be organized to call forth these activities in the learner if the desired result is to be attained, namely, the maturing of the wholeperson-in-life as a child of God.

Preceptual Field

Learning has its origin in a perceptual field. A child learns to handle numbers and number relations as he deals with things in quantity and in sequence. He develops sentence sense in language in communicating about things and their activities. The dog is a thing that barks before it is an animal. There are two dogs before they are dogs as a class. Things have their first relationship to a child, not in isolation, but in a perceptual field. The in-life means to him first of all what he experiences through his sense organs and relates together in their activity.

Note that I speak of perceptual field, not of percepts. From the very beginning the perceptual is a relationship. The warmth of the nursery, the bottle and what it does or brings, the mother and cuddling, etc., are inseparable to the infant. The park for the fourth graders and the nature and meaning of community life are integrally related.

The thing to observe here is that a child learns through relationships and that the first relationship is perceptual. They remain dominantly perceptual till the conceptual has been built up out of the perceptual, till thinking has been built up out of direct contact with things. It is always in-life that the immature takes his first steps in learning. The more mature the youth in a given area of learning the less important the perceptual in continued learning.

Every learning situation calls for a clear understanding of a child's perceptual fields and his ability to apprehend the relationships involved. Suppose the fourth grade we spoke of is located in a rural school, forty miles from a city. Would the community park be a good taking-off-point in the study of the community? No. The auction sale down the road might be a better one. No one would begin with a text-book assignment of words, words, words, etc., of course; still less with a lecture in outline form. These ignore the perceptual field entirely, except in so far as the pupils provide it from their own background. This is not teaching, but only talking.

Thinking and Reasoning

The I can conceptualize the perceptual. Being rational-moral-social, as we saw earlier, he reproduces, not only, but also reconstructs the perceptual. A small boy of four was standing at a window in his home. He was looking for pigeons in the field adjoining, for they often flew down in numbers to feed there. But this day they did not seem to come. In his keen disappointment the little fellow said, "If God said, 'Let there be pigeons,' there would be pigeons, wouldn't there, mommy!" The four-year old, yes, even the two-year old conceptualizes. But it originates immediately out of the perceptual field. Every word and phrase stands for something concrete to him as a child.

The elementary school child conceptualizes out of his perceptual field. The fourth grade teacher did not begin the study of the com-munity with a definition of community, or a discussion of the com-mission of parks in the city, or with a list of duties of the voter, etc. A child does not learn to conceptualize by assimilating ready-made, logically organized, adult subject matter, predigested for him.

As the immature youth begins to mature in all dimensions of his personality, his conceptualizing begins to form the perceptual. What he begins to experience in relationship perceptually will be determined by what he is looking for. This is called expectancy or anticipation. He begins to see and hear, not merely with the physiological eye and ear, but with the psychic eye, yes, even the eye of the spirit (Eph. 1:18, "eyes of the heart"). Thinking is conceptualizing the perceptual. Reasoning is organizing the conceptual to foreseen ends. The solving of a problem, for example.

Now what important principle of teaching do we learn here? Let me illustrate. The understanding of fractions begins for a child in *his* perceptual field, not in that of the teacher, no matter how it is simplified. What is a child's perceptual field for the understanding of parts of a whole? He has used fractions often. He has said to his brother, "Do you want half of mine?" Or he has remonstrated with mother, "You gave me the smaller (perhaps he said littler) half." Right out of the child's life comes the perceptual field of fractions. Fractions are not new to him in *his* perceptual field. But now to make the transition so that he can think ½ of 14. This is conceptualizing. It is a big step; and yet, not so big, depending upon how meaningfully it is developed out of his perceptual life. Oh, yes, I know, one catches it more quickly than another. But in every case the teacher must understand a child in-life to help him understand fractions.

Expression

Expression is native to the child. In his total personality God made him to be the self-expression of God. He is creative by virtue of being spirit. It is out of *his* conceptualizing that he comes to express himself. In his expression he continues his conceptualizing. If in our teaching we confront the child in his perceptual field with truths in-life and direct his conceptualizing accordingly in the Christian educational structure, he comes to express himself according to these truths in this structure. That is, he begins to express himself thus in the totality of his personality.

Express himself he must and will. And he will express himself in some structure. He may take a test and give the teacher back on paper what he thinks the teacher wants. But his conceptualizing and expression may take place in another structure. It may be one that is neatly arranged to cover up an inner revolt. This is the constant threat of an intellectualism in education.

A child must come to love truth in the understanding if he is going to accept it in his heart. But love, as we saw earlier, involves the whole person. When the whole-child-in-life is challenged in his perceptual field, when he is guided in his conceptualizing to face truth, when he is encouraged to express himself in his conceptualizing in the Christian educational structure, the stage is set for the child's loving in the understanding. As the truths of community living are conceptualized by the fourth graders in their perceptual field, these truths come to touch the children's lives. When expression takes place in the structure of love, faith, and obedience, the children can come to love these truths in their understanding. We have then done all that is humanly possible, as far as we can understand child nature according to divine ordinances, to prepare the way for the consummation of the learning process.

Commitment

What follows? The truths the child has come to love he must lay up in his heart. In the I a child must come to accept these truths and order his personality accordingly. Nothing is learned until it has been accepted in the heart. There will be no heart surrender to truths which a child has not come to love. Commitment is the consummating phase of the learning process because man as a religious being, that is, bent on God, finds his fulfilment in God. It is not for us as parents and teachers to give. We can only prepare the way in keeping with divine ordinances for the child life. For the present I shall not go further with this phase of our subject.

The Teacher as a Guide

The learning process in the Christian educational structure is distinctive, for it recognizes not only the sovereignty of God in adult life, but also that the development-urge of childhood has a divine sanction. But then the Christian teacher has a distinctive task, too.

In the thinking of some people the teacher comes to class with a ready-made system of knowledge that he has acquired over the years and that he now tries to pass on to pupils in small doses. Because these doses prove distasteful to many, and at times to all, he also brings with him a bag of tricks by which he makes the pupil's assimilation of the regular dosages as pleasant as possible. Periodically he asks the pupils to give back to him what he has given them to check on their progress in the accumulation of knowledge. If and when the children are able to repeat the required amount, they pass on to another grade. Or on another level they get so many units or hours of credit. When they have accumulated the required amount, they graduate, they go on.

We should realize that this thinking is predicated on the thought that the child has a mind that acts like a container. It has the capacity to store up ideas as entities for future use. It also acts like a muscle that is strengthened with use to do certain things. For one thing, it can pull out ideas when called for. I am not trying to present a common misconception facetiously. The sad fact is that the language some use to describe learning seems to imply this conception of the human mind.

Laying aside all systems of psychology, past and present, for a moment, we turn to the Scriptures. And we saw earlier that the Bible presents an entirely different picture. In sum and substance we learn that a child is a subject who in his person creatively orders the psycho-somatic in all dimensions of his personality, according to what he comes to love in the understanding. He lays up in his heart what he in love embraces in the knowing life.

What, then, is the task of the teacher? The learning process as I have tried to describe it needs control to terminate in desired ends. The child in his immaturity is not capable of determining the ends, nor exercising the controls. He must do the learning. The teacher is at the controls. And the teacher knows the end from the beginning. He understands too how a child can get there. He understands a child in his active development-urge. He understands too the medium the school affords to direct the developmental process.

The task of the teacher is three-fold. The teacher must *inspire* a child in the active pursuit of ends. They are ends that make contact with child life in a child's perceptual field. The teacher seeks to energize these ends as stimulating goals for a child. The purposeful activity in which a child engages in pursuit of dynamic ends, growing ends, generates a feeling of mastery and confidence. With self-assurance and security the learner goes about his task.

The teacher *instructs* a child. Instruction is the process by which the teacher furnishes materials for self-activity of the learner. These materials may be stimulating ideas as well as objects to be observed. He may do so directly by communication. He is then telling the child. He may also do this indirectly by surrounding the subject with source material for understanding and mastery. Direct communication may prepare the way for indirect presentation, or the other way around likewise. Direct instruction may also be a summation of what has been learned indirectly. In instruction the teacher informs the pupil, that is, brings him into contact with that according to which he should form himself.

The teacher *disciplines* the child. This means that the teacher exercises the necessary controls that the self-active subject may be held to his task with some firmness. No child feels secure in a task without the firm support of the teacher. The administration of the controls depends upon the self-control of the teacher and his grasp of the development-urge of a child in a given situation.

What name shall I give to this three-fold task? I prefer to call it guidance, for that is what the teacher really does. Not guidance in the sense of giving some friendly advice. No, it is the authoritative directive in the life of the child. The teacher's authority is that which follows from the second part of the covenant, to bring up a child in the "new obedience." The authority is administered in love for Christ's sake. Allowing for the teacher's authoritative position, I still speak of guidance. Only the Lord can do more. He can turn the I. Teachers can only take a child "in hand" and lead him to the goal.

The School

One of the objections, I know, that will be raised against some of the things I have been saying is that the school has a place of its own and must not enter the area of the home and of the church. My answer is as follows.

If what I have said so far with reference to the unitary character of the person in his religious motivation; if what I have said about a child in his educability; and if what I have said concerning a child's way of learning are correct, then the task of home, school, and church must be thought of as one. It cannot be "pieced out" to separate units. And what is this task? To bring up a covenant youth in the "new obedience."

However, the school as a necessary extension of the home in our modern civilization has a medium in which the task must be accomplished. This medium is the cultural product. This is not the medium of the home, nor of the church. But how can our complex cultural product in its many ramifications serve as a medium to bring up a child in the "new obedience"? I must limit myself to five considerations that must guide us.

1. Our cultural product must be simplified, for in its common form it presents too complex a form for fruitful learning.

2. The continuity of child development demands that the cultural produce be graduated. Every stage of development must be meaningfully integrated with what has gone before and what is to follow.

3. Areas of the cultural product must be organized for momentary abstraction from life for analysis and mastery. So-called subject matter areas are necessary.

4. Our mixed culture must be subjected to critical appraisal for levels of child development. Children must make choices, but they can choose only in-life as they have come to live it. As they mature they make commitments, for they are basically religious in their motivation.

5. The cultural product is integrated in-life as the child comes to face the truths in relationship to life. The cultural product will serve as a medium to mature the whole-child-in-life as he comes to accept life according to the "new obedience."

VIII. In the Totality of Life

A Child In-Life

When talking about the whole-child-in-life, we should note, first of all, that there are three factors involved in child development. Not merely two, as modern psychology constantly holds before us. They speak of nature and nurture, or heredity and environment.

There is our racial continuity. It includes our biological heredity, our ancestry. This phase of our racial continuity contributes to our limitations and our potentialities. Genetics, the science of heredity, can make valuable contributions to our understanding of child life when its findings are interpreted in right relationship to other important factors in child development. But the child of God also experiences a restored racial continuity in Christ. When the Lord pleases to lay hold upon the lives of children we do not know. The new life may be present long before we have evidence of it. But when he does implant the new life, biological heredity is not set aside. God can, and may overrule it in a child's life, of course. But we labor with the child in faith and obedience. We take account of what we can know of a child's heredity, his ancestry. But far be it from us to ascribe more power to it in a child's life than the Scripture permits.

A second factor in child development is the community in which he matures. It touches every dimension of a child's personality. Since I shall have more to say of a child's development-urge in relation to his community further on, I merely mention it here.

A third factor is the person of a child, or the I. The I is not to be counted in the racial continuity biologically. Spirit does not reproduce itself in cellular division and differentiation. We face a profound mystery at this point. Perhaps the best we can say on the ground of Scripture is that God provides the I in the germ cell that gives rise to the life of the psycho-somatic. God has in creation adapted the psycho-somatic to the life of the spirit when he breathed in man and he became a living soul.

The I is the life principle, the "moment," involved in the psycho-somatic structure from the very beginning in conception. As a child matures the I consciously takes over in ordering the dimensions of his personality according to foreseen ends. He begins to establish a line of action in his total personality.

In teaching a child we address the I as subject, not as a behaving organism that develops self-consciousness as one of its many qualities. We address a person who comes to express himself in the three dimensions of his personality.

Development-Urge

When we observe an infant in his early stages of development, the characteristics of a behaving organism are very much in evidence. It is not at all surprising that psychologists who believe that man is an animal have concluded that man is essentially a behaving organism who develops traits that may be called human. Similarities to animal life are evident in instinctive reactions, in the first stages of the learning process, in early random movements, etc. A child's animality furnishes the basis, it is thought, for the more complex behavior of the later development.

But it is only the pre-scientific commitment of the secular psychologist that could lead him to conclude that a child is a behaving organism. The early random movements of the infant are the first stages of a differentiation in the unity of the person that in later integration become purposeful action. These little legs will soon run after a ball, and in a co-ordinated way the little arms will reach for it and throw it to daddy. The babbling of infancy develops in the course of development in childhood into connected, purposeful discourse. Such development cannot meaningfully be interpreted as the integration of organic behavior in interaction with the environment. It is the budding *I* coming into conscious control of drives in the psycho-somatic. It is the development-urge of a person pregnant with the self-expression of God.

A child must be understood in his development-urge, which according to the divine ordinances for child life is the motivating power in his development to maturity. The development-urge is the expression of the religious motivation of the I becoming integrated with the motivations of the psycho-somatic. It comes to expression first of all in the physiological-life. Think of the hunger urge of the infant. The social-emotional soon becomes involved. Think of the contentment of the infant in mother's arms. The knowing-life begins to express an urge for development early. Think of the child beginning to explore his toys whereas earlier he merely threw them around or clutched them in his little fist. Watch him as he begins to act "on his own." See him launch out in all dimensions of his personality. He comes to express himself with greater self-assurance. Watch him in his progress as he learns to walk, talk, seek out his playmates, etc. You begin to see *the person* in action. Every new step, every new venture, every attempt to establish himself among his peers, etc., represents the whole-child-in-life in his development-urge seeking maturity. You do not come to understand a child in his momentary emotional reactions or mastery of skills. He must *be understood* in his development-urge as he comes to express himself in-life. And he must be so appraised.

The Community

Above I referred to a child's community as a second factor in his development. I now want to speak of it as the counter-part to a child's development-urge.

God places in every child the urge to realize the potential of his resources. These resources are those of the I as spirit and of the psycho-somatic adapted to the I. God has a purpose for every person and endows him in his total personality with the potential needed to realize this purpose. In his inscrutable providence God too places every person in a community that affords the opportunity for realizing the potential with which a person is endowed. In his development-urge the person, as endowed, comes to realize his potential in all dimensions of his personality in interaction with his community. The community is the counterpart to the person in his development-urge. So a child must be understood as the whole-person-in-life.

This process of development is, however, tragically distorted in the devastation wrought by sin in the harmonious relationship of the person and his community. On the one hand the development-urge is that of the broken-I. On the other hand the community is the product of a race enveloped in the darkness of sin. How is any degree of integration still possible?

We know, too, according to the Scriptures, that God is accomplishing his purposes in endowing men and placing them in certain communities that they may be productive of that which will contribute to bringing about the consummation of all things as God wills it.

It is in God's ruling and over-ruling providence that his divine ordinances continue to make their demands upon human life. So it is too that the disharmony of sin does not nullify the divine ordinances of child-life according to which a child is brought to maturity in his development-urge. We as Christians particularly are to take heed to these ordinances as we bring up a covenant child in the "new obedience." Of the obedience in the covenant of works he is no longer capable. But what the law could not do, grace does, so the Apostle Paul informs us. God enables his own to develop in the "new obedience." We seek to establish for our children a community relationship that will afford the development-urge of child-life the opportunity for the expression of the truth and commitment to it.

Three Responsible Agencies

Who will assume the task in keeping with the Lord's ordained ways among men? Our Covenant God has assigned this task to parents only. They, the parents, are the channels through whom the Lord in his providence calls into being the succeeding generation. What a blessing parenthood is when we view it in this light! Parents do not merely in animal fashion perpetuate their kind. In giving birth to children they are the self-expression of God in his generating power.

And then to be a Hannah, or a Zachariah and an Elizabeth, or the mother of Moses. To be the parents of a John Calvin, Dwight L. Moody, John Wesley, Abraham Kuyper, etc. What a blessing it is to bring sons and daughters of God's own choosing, even to the most humble, to the Kingdom of Christ! God pleases to center this great responsibility in parents. God wants us as parents to take *his* children and in their development-urge lead them through their community relations into the "new obedience."

To us as parents this great task is entrusted. God has never committed this charge to anyone else. How dare the state, or even the church, usurp this divine responsibility? Only in a much distorted community relationship in which parents completely neglect their duty may another take over. When children are deprived of their parents, another parental home should be found, if possible, so that the work can be carried on in keeping with divine ordinances.

The school derives its task from the divine mandate to the parents. In the second part of the covenant parents assume the responsibility to bring up their children "in the Lord." However, they may call in assistance to "cause them to be instructed" as well as do it themselves. Modern life has made the school a cultural necessity. Parents cannot perform adequately the bringing up of their children in the modern cultural life without the aid the school affords. The school is the extension of the home, and on this basis only does it find its justification.

Though we recognize the necessity of the school, we must not ignore the unity of child life as we came to see it earlier. The educational task in its objective cannot be divided between the home and the school. The task is one, to bring up the child in the "new obedience," because the child is one. He cannot divide his personality between the home and the school. His development-urge is the expression of his total person in all dimensions of his personality. In his whole-person-in-life he goes to school. But the in-life aspect of the child's unity also demands that the "new obedience" be relevant to the community in which his development-urge comes to expression. It is for the latter especially that the school is equipped. The school has the cultural product of man as its medium. In this the school has an area of operation of its own.

But let it be clear that no school is Christian which fails in its community to challenge a child in his development-urge as a religious being by the primary claim of the gospel upon his life. Why do I say this with reference to the school? Because only the gospel is the power of God unto salvation (Rom. 1:16, 17). The gospel in its saving power must be central in the cultural medium of the school if we expect the learning process to terminate in the divine call upon the lives of our children. What I am saying is this. No more than a life of service can be Christian in which worship is not central, can education be Christian which is not centered in the gospel as the power of God unto salvation.

A word about the church before I try to show how we can implement the principle of totality centered in the gospel. John Calvin repeated the statement of St. Augustine with affirmation, I believe, that "No one has God for a Father who does not have the church for a mother." Some have questioned this statement because they interpreted church to mean the body of believers in institutional form, or as organized institutionally. But we surely all agree that if we think of the church as the body of Christ in its universal scope, that is, the one Holy Catholic (Universal) Church, this statement is very true. What I am interested in at this point in our discussion is the reference to the motherhood of the Church of Christ. It is for the church to mother us in the most holy faith, in the life hid with God in Christ. It is the church that places the seal of baptism upon us, by which is signified the washing away of our sins. It is the church that brings us up into spiritual maturity.

It is in the function of motherhood that the church comes to the help of parents in their responsibility of bringing up their children in the "new obedience." Hence the responsibility of the church in relationship to the covenant youth is two-fold, one might say. First of all the covenant youth is a member of the church. Secondly, the church comes to the aid of the parents by instructing the covenant youth in the truth of the Word as committed to the church.

In summary we may say this. The parents have the God-given mandate of nurturing their children to maturity in the "new obedience." The school as extension of the home assumes part of this task for the parents insofar as it can supplement the home in a cultural medium. The church as the mother of the saints of God aids parents in their task of maturing their children in the life hid with God in Christ. Together they accomplish a major task in the kingdom of God on earth. And the task is one.

Implementation of the Principle of Totality

I have been trying to emphasize the interrelatedness of the whole child and life. There is a wholeness about this interrelatedness which must not escape us would we view a child rightly in his development to maturity. In our attempt to analyze the whole in its various aspects or phases we may forget that every part can be known only in its interrelatedness in the whole.

That we must analyze to come to understand anything is quite evident. We are creatures. We are finite. We cannot have the perspective of the Infinite, of the Creator. Furthermore, we are sinners subject to the divisiveness of the power of evil. What sense of wholeness man had in the beginning has been badly distorted. In the unbroken-I Adam had immediate apprehension of a wholeness we do not possess today. He named the animals. God brought them to him for this purpose. He had a communion with God in his universal revelation which we no longer possess in that degree even in the restored-I. In the broken-I the appreciation of wholeness is fully distorted. From within and from without man has been thrown into disharmony. So we analyze in our broken-I. And what a mess we make of it! We build up our little systems, and we proceed to view the whole from the confinement of our systems.

As I indicated before, systems of thought have their place. We need them. But let us realize their limitations. No human system has a monopoly on the truth. Even when we orient it in the Scriptures. For as a system it is still human. What I am trying to say is that in our systems we are apt to neglect, or even completely ignore, the totality of things. This mistake has been made over and over again. We are making it today.

The Bible comes to us first of all not as a system of doctrine, but as the living Word that speaks to the totality of man-in-life. We thank God for the guidance of the Holy Spirit as the Church of Christ through the ages has sought to confess its faith in creedal form. But our creeds are not infallible. I believe it was Herman Bavinck who cautioned the Reformed churches not to confuse the confession of our faith with faith in the confession. The former is necessary. The latter places the creeds on a par with the Scriptures. We believe in the whole gospel, for it is the power of God unto salvation. In it God speaks to us infallibly. Only out of it can we view life in its true unity or wholeness.

Understanding a Child

We must view teaching and learning according to the principle of totality, as a child lives and learns in-life and thus develops into maturity. I shall try to implement this principle first of all with reference to the child and then with reference to what is generally known as method. I am speaking of the school only.

A child comes to school as a person-with-a-history. Several years have preceded in which the development-urge in his appointed community has enabled the I as equipped by God to come to expression in a three-dimensional personality. This is Dickie as he comes to school. He comes as a whole-person-in-life. Now what the school is apt to do is to put Dickie in a class of thirty or thirty-five children as a member of a class. As soon as possible he must be "fitted" into a ready-made-pattern of control that required learning may be possible. For he must "toe the mark" of the first grade, second grade, etc. He must not "stay back," of all things, no!

I am not saying that all of this is wrong. No, not by any means. Some of it is unavoidable. This is not my point just now. But *this is* my point. Dickie is a whole-person-in-life. He is a person-with-a-history. And though all these thirty or thirty-five children have very much in common because life itself is common, what Dickie says and does must be understood in *his* history. And his history includes a God-appointed I in an ancestral psycho-somatic having come to expression in the dimensions of his personality.

Dickie as a person-with-a-history may give the teacher plenty of trouble. He may also prove a child who readily enters into the life of the classroom and the school. But in any case he must be understood. God will have his way in Dickie's life. He has endowed Dickie with a potential. He has also established, ordained, a way of child life, as we saw. He has placed Dickie in his development-urge in a community that can afford Dickie the opportunities he needs for self-development. We pray that the Lord may lay his hand on Dickie early in life. We shall guide him in the Christian educational structure, that he may come to love the truth in his understanding and commit himself to it.

I heard one of our psychiatrists of the Reformed faith say recently as he spoke to a group of Christian school principals, "What would you have done with Joseph, the dreamer, in your classroom today? And timid David? How do you appraise a child? In terms of an A or a B on the report card? Or as one teacher did when she wrote on a report card 'He wastes time.' Whose time? Was it wasted? How did the teacher know?"

Among the primary requirements for teaching in a Christian school is the understanding of a child in his life-style. Psychology and sociology are very helpful, but as a teacher I must see these in-life in Dickie, otherwise they are comparatively meaningless. Some mothers have more intuitive insight into child life, though they never studied psycology, than some teachers who have a college degree and among their courses have completed several in psychology. These mothers have come to understand themselves in relation to their children and live with them in love. The teacher must do likewise.

How does a teacher come to know Dickie? A few suggestions must suffice.

1. A study of child life as viewed according to the Scriptures.

2. A survey of significant facts pertaining to Dickie, as intelligence test scores, achievement test scores, profiles, playmates and their relations, home, church, special interests, etc., and an interpretation of these data in relation to one another as seen in Dickie's life style.

3. One or more visits to Dickie's home. The P.T.A. is no substitute for home visits in their value to the teacher, to the parent, and to Dickie.

4. Personal concern for Dickie in a teacher's prayer life.

5. Consultation with others, as the pastor, principal, a psychologist, etc., who may be able to give helpful suggestions.

Broader Concept of Method

The second example I wish to use to show how we can implement the principle of totality is that of method. As soon as we use the word method it conjures up in the minds of some people the tricks and devices teachers are said to use to get youngsters to study and master knowledges and skills. And in a sense they are right. This is what method means to many teachers. At teachers' institutes one can hear the question often, "What would you do when or if . . ." The implication seems to be that for a given situation there is a certain formula. And if learning and education are primarily the assimilation of knowledge and the training of the faculties of the human mind, I suppose method is just this and not much more. Some one has said that the old didactics asked, how can I get the distasteful stuff down their throats, and modern method asks, how can I get them to like the disliked. Fact is that both miss the point, and both violate the principle of totality.

School is a phase of the total life process of a child. The Christian school is the place where the development-urge of God's child as a whole-person-in-life, in his personal history, develops into maturity according to the "new obedience" in a community which employs the cultural product of the race. Can you envision all of this as your task, my fellow teacher? You are to guide — inspire, instruct, and discipline — Dickie in this setting as you come to understand and appraise Dickie. You understand Dickie. You understand life and accept it in the "new obedience." You understand child life as viewed in the divine ordinances for it. You are master of an area of the cultural product which is your medium, and you can view that area in its interrelations. Your understanding of these in their relationship to one another is your methodology. Method takes form in your person as you make all of this meaningful in Dickie's life. Why do we still need methods of this or that?

I know the "ceiling is low." By this I mean that almost everything in school is geared to a "lock-step" program of learning. And my writing about a broader concept of method seems so unrealistic. But you and I want to work toward greater distinctiveness in Christian education. The principle of totality as I have tried to develop it is, I believe, necessary to get from under the intellectualism of the past and avoid the pragmatism and activism of our current educational theory and practice. We have a tremendous task ahead of us as we try, in the Lord's strength and in the light of his Word, to develop a distinctively Christian school.

CORNELIUS JAARSMA
"The Child — His Nature and His Needs,"
Christian Home and School,
September, 1951-June, 1952.

Key Thoughts:

1. A child must be understood as a religious being, created by God for fellowship with Him in love; mandated to exercise his potential as a created person in loving obedience to his Creator; subject to disintegration in his person because of voluntary disobedience, inherent in the fallen race and manifest in life by choice; in the light of the antithesis which is a religious distinction, a race not in Christ and a race restored to the fellowship with God in Christ.

2. On the basis of the religious nature of the child in his being we may state the following principles as basic for Christian education:

   a. The child is a person in the spirit, an I, an ego.

   b. As person he is directly linked to God who is a Person.

   c. His mandate as person is religious in character.

   d. His deepest and most comprehensive need is religious in scope.

   e. The religious need is the focal point in the child's education.

   f. It is in meeting the child's needs as a religious being that we find unity or integration in learning and in teaching.

   g. The child's religious need as a person is satisfied in love.

   h. Love is the basis for the Christian educational structure.

3. The child must be understood in a two-fold unity: the unity of the race as a collective whole and the unity of his person. A child

is a person-with-a-history racially involved in the human race. Out of a dying human race God is ingrafting a new race in Christ. This forms the basis for the covenant of grace which is an expression of the restored unity as realized in the church of Christ. The covenant youth, therefore, must be understood in his personal and racial unity as restored in Christ.

4. We must view a child too in the dimensions of his personality: the physiological life, the social-emotional life, and the knowing life or understanding. In these dimensions the person or spirit expresses himself in relation to his world about him. It is in these dimensions that he is characterized as a whole-person-in-life. Learning and teaching are to take full account of this God-ordained unity if they are to be effective in their avowed purposes.

5. We can build the Christian educational structure in the life of the child according to faith and in the way of obedience. We inspire, instruct, and discipline a child in this obedience. In this structure the child comes to commit himself to the truth and express himself accordingly.

6. Degree of educability in school has reference to the child's ability to avail himself of the medium presented in this structure. The appraisal of this ability rests with the teacher as he comes to know a child in his life style. Recently divised tests and scales can help, but are only tools in the hands of a teacher who gains insight by more personal observation and communication.

7. A reconstructed theory of learning is essential according to a psychology scripturally oriented. Current and earlier theories will not do for the Christian school. The learning process is to be set up for acceptance of and commitment to the truth as made known by God in Christ.

8. In keeping with our discussion thus far, learning must be expressed as the activity of the person in all the dimensions of his personality as he comes in conscious control of the processes of integration. He comes to accept life responsibly as a member of the body of Christ.

9. The learning process involves three qualifying factors in a child's development to maturity: the development-urge of the whole person, social-emotional security, and motivation. These must be understood in terms of a child's life style.

10. The learning process has its beginning in the perceptual. On the basis of the perceptual experience the child conceptualizes. In

conceptualizing he comes to understand. As he comes to understand in the structure of love, faith, and obedience he comes to commit himself to the truth and order his life accordingly.

11. In teaching, one directs the learning process of the child. The teacher does this by inspiring the learner in the active pursuit of ends, by instructing him in the skills and understanding necessary to attain those ends, and by disciplining him in the process.

12. The principle of unity causes us to see the educational task as one. It cannot be "pieced out" among various agencies. However, the spheres of operation of the home, the school, and the church can be well-defined. The school as extension of the home brings up a child in the totality or unity of life in the medium that the school only can provide, the cultural medium.

13. The child learns in the unity of life. When we select a given area for momentary analysis, we must remember that only its relation to life is ultimately fruitful in bringing up a child to maturity. Life is always more true than any system we abstract from it. We may slay a child with our systems. Systems help him only when they help him in-life to experience its unity.

14. The implications of the principle of unity are several. They apply to curriculum and methodology, as well as to the understanding of a child. Rightly interpreted this principle will avoid the Scilla and Charibdis in education, the intellectualism of the past and the pragmatism and activism of the present.

8

Humanism in the Life of the School

One who does not know humanism in its modern form cannot understand why, for example, a given language lesson must be termed humanistic. That the Christian school is distinctive by virtue of its basic principle and that it is not in accord with the "spirit of our age" are commonly accepted. But if foreign penetrations are to be removed from school practice, it is imperative that we learn to understand this spirit, and we may detect them in the common, everyday smaller details. This is not merely a fad of philosophers and educationists, but the calling of every Christian teacher. For this spirit stands squarely in opposition to the spirit of Christ. This spirit of humanism has slain its thousands by means of the school.

I desire to point out some major features of this humanism with reference to education, schooling in particular. Historically, humanism operates between two poles, which we may conceive of as two centers of power within the same principle. On the one hand we have the *personality ideal,* in which everything revolves about human personality. On the other hand, we see a striving for *knowledge as the ideal,* in which every activity is bent toward erudition or learning. The two poles have in common that they make men sovereign, that they deny God's sovereignty or ignore it, that the creature is glorified above the Creator who is to be praised to all eternity. The last humanism has in common with the idolatry of the pagan.

A. We shall first of all point to some illustrations of the poisonous character of the knowledge ideal for our children.

1. First, we call attention to the awful exaggeration of mathematical thinking, as if only this kind of thinking gives real certainty. It has been said: "$2 + 2 = 4$, this I know, this is absolutely certain; but what the Bible says is not certain, that I can 'only believe,' but no one knows." In this case $2 + 2 = 4$ is presented as reliable knowledge, more certain than the Word of God. In brief, human knowledge is more reliable than God's communication. Thousands have fallen into this error and have become unbelievers. And the school has frequently contributed to this. The school has taught the grandeur of number

and mathematical certainty as if we ourselves are the creators of number and has not pointed to God as their author and that our mathematical certainty is a gift of God. Thus the entire sphere of number is viewed as a human product, and we no longer think of God as sovereign in mathematics. Hence, God is not given the glory due him. In this, too, we must choose between God and current thinking.

2. Another characteristic of humanism in its knowledge ideal is the *overrating of the natural sciences* as if they furnish the predominating knowledge.

3. When children begin to relate their mathematical thinking — regarded more certain than the Word of God — with the predominance of the natural sciences, it is obvious that acceptance of the biblical account of miracles becomes more difficult.

4. A fourth characteristic of humanism that follows directly from the foregoing is what Prof. Dooyeweerd has called *the abstraction-fallacy of humanism.* When the concept is made the real and takes the place of and placed above the actual creature of God, it is abused. God created actual birds in a manifold variety of form and color, in an amazing multitude of kinds. And now man tries to form some concepts to help him understand the great works of God. He begins to classify animals under a certain concept; thus the heron is a bird, the sparrow is a bird, the blackbird is a bird and the robin is a bird. If the concept 'bird' serves to call attention to the birdness of the actual sparrow, robin, etc., and to recognize the unity amidst the diversity, this is very well. All genuine scientific study does this. But when in pride the concept is made to dominate God's creature, and the concept supercedes what God created, our troubles commence. Then the riches of God's creation becomes mere 'bird,' and 'birdness' becomes the real. With the concept, 'bird' dominates the entire bird world. If you desire to see a bird-concept, ask someone to draw a bird. He will not draw a sparrow, or a duck, or a stork, but something like a pigeon, with wings, a beak, and two small paws. This is the actual bird concept. Poor student of bird life who must be satisfied with this kind of bird!

Well now, the outworn, schoolish concept world of humanism compares with the rich world of God's creation as the bird concept does with the sparrow, the robin, etc. The concept is of value when it helps us grasp the truth of God's marvelous creation. The concept is only a means. It tells us something about God's creation. Just as the conventional drawing of a bird is real art, for it lets us see something of the bird world. But when the concept dominates and even replaces God's creation, things become sterile. Then the abstraction fallacy of humanism prevails and destroys genuine scientific learning and real knowledge, and degenerates into a musty school affair. The humanist attempts to popularize knowledge, and thereby makes a caricature of true knowledge. History of education can relate striking incidents of the abstraction fallacy. Alas, it is full of it. It has been called intellectualism. That is the first stage. Then the concept replaces knowledge. Then one rushes from things to knowledge, which can be learned apart from things. One can study Africa without thinking about it, that Africa lies yonder, way over there. But of what account is Africa to me if I only have the knowledge?

The second stage is still easier. Verbalism is directed to the practical. Academic concepts help no one. One can learn without concepts — just master words, and names. But for an examination, there is this risk involved — the examiner may ask for knowledge instead of words. Hence, the school has happily not dared to implement the practical implications of verbalism. They that have are exceptions. Instead instruction should be an imparting of concepts. This has been preached as pedagogical wisdom for a long time. Protest has come from practical workers in the school, rather than from Herbartian educational theory and practice. In practice, many have considered the accumulation of concepts as a stifling activity, and have, in spite of Herbartian theory, presented things in the place of concepts. They discussed actual chickens instead of the chicken.

Alas, humanism, like weeds, is tough. There have been school personnel who thought it a pity that children showed so little interest in *the* chicken. For this reason, they introduced pictures of chickens to make the experience more attractive. They even got the idea of bringing an actual chicken into the classroom as object lesson. Note, a creation of God as illustration of a man-made concept. What a glory for the creator of this animal concept, for man!

Really, we are not talking of pedantry. Here we have the sin of humanism, the sovereign thinking about God's creatures. The result of this kind of instruction that imparts ideas or concepts is evident in the schoolish composition written by a child whose father has eighty chickens. The child gathers the eggs in the evening and knows the chickens very well. One is his close friend and eats out of his hand. This child writes the following composition in a humanistic school.

THE CHICKEN

The chicken is a bird. It has feathers. It has two wings, two paws and a beak. The chicken lays eggs. The chicken is a useful animal.

You see, here the school — no, the sin of humanism — has broken something into pieces.

Up to this point I have called attention only to the formal errors of humanism; namely, the exaggeration of mathematical certainty, natural science overstepping its boundaries, control of God's laws of nature, and the abstraction fallacy. Let us note to what systems the knowledge-getting ideal of humanism has given rise. We confine ourselves to the elementary school.

1. The state school system. I am, in addition to being father of my family, member of the church, and principal of a school, also citizen of the kingdom of the Netherlands. This is one function among many. But if that concept of citizenship is elevated to an all-inclusive, dominating idea, as in the days of the French revolution when people embraced each other in tears only as citizens, then there is complete equality among men. Then logic demands some dominating power over this citizenry. And this is the state. But this state is principally different from the idea of government. This state acknowledges no sphere sovereignty, neither in the church nor in the school nor in the family. Hence, this state is sovereign over the school too. Buildings, curriculum, program, teachers, parents, and children — they are all the charge of the state. The school becomes a state institution.

2. A second institution of humanism in the area of the school is the *neutral school,* the school which practices tolerance of different faiths and convictions.

3. A third institution of humanism is the *modern common school,* school for all the people.

4. A fourth is the so-called *general education idea,* a minimum amount of knowledge, that must become the possession of all.

5. The knowledge ideal found its way into all methodology.

B. The second center of power is the *personality ideal.* Then it is not knowledge that step by step in its methodology becomes dominant, but the living person of the instructor or the pupil. Then every teacher may proceed according to his own insight. And sooner or later, every child does as he pleases. Then the human person becomes sovereign, as knowledge becomes sovereign at the other pole. It is to be expected that this likeness ends in an ignominious failure. Instead of the idea or concept being dominant, the person becomes dominant. And this is equally dangerous. Individualism in expression leads to boredom as much as does formalism of idea and concept. Not knowledge, nor personality, but God is sovereign over all. Let us in these serious times, in which we face a crisis of the humanistic ideal of knowledge-getting, not take our recourse in the personality ideal, but let us pray to God to give us the courage and the wisdom to serve him in the face of the spirit of the age.

In this period of transition and crisis, let not the conservatives among us defend the knowledge-ideal of humanism, and let the progressives be on their guard against a striving for the personality ideal. Let us together on the present basis work out the distinctive character of the Christian school and clean house of all humanistic infiltration. May God help us to this end.

A. JANSE
The Distinctive Character
of the Christian School, pp. 7-29.

Key Thoughts:

1. Humanism turns up in the schools of today in one of two forms or in a degree of compromise between the two. On the one hand the knowledge-getting ideal is glorified. On the other hand the personality ideal is given primary emphasis. Both are known to turn up in Christian schools too.

2. The knowledge-getting ideal makes either concepts or things its basis for learning. The personality development ideal makes the teacher and his guidance of the pupil primary while subordinating the values of instruction and discipline.

3. The Christian school must be saved from the infiltration of both humanistic errors.

Comment:

The Christian schools arose when nineteenth century intellectualistic humanism had the upper hand in education. They developed while secular education became largely influenced by the social and personality ideals. Many teachers recognized that the reform movement had something to contribute to the Christian school largely dominated by a knowledge-getting ideal. A genuinely Christian education will integrate both the knowledge-getting ideal and the personality-development ideal in a meaningful whole which transcends both.

9

The New Obedience

When we speak of obedience — one of the thorniest and most important issues of our time — it is first of all necessary that we clearly state the given conditions and formulate our problem. I do this in connection with a story taken from a small book by Laura Richard entitled *Go and Come*.

"Sonny," says the maid, "it would be better if you did something. Your little garden needs weeding. Go out and weed it as a good boy."

But the little boy had no desire of weeding his garden that day. "I can't weed," he said.

"Oh yes you can," said the maid.

"But I would rather not," replied the boy.

"But you must," said the maid. "Don't be naughty, but get to work at once and do as I say."

She went back to her own work, for she was diligent. But the little fellow sat still, and thought that he had not been treated very nicely. After some time mother entered the room and saw him sit there. "What's the trouble, sonny?" she asked, for his expression reminded one of March weather.

"She said I should weed my garden," said sonny.

"Oh," said mother, "I think that's a good idea! I love to weed, and it is a beautiful day! May I go along to help you?"

"Of course, you may," replied sonny. And both weeded the garden and had a joyful hour.

This story presents us with the following:

A. A diligent maid, one of the old-fashioned kind, who sees what needs to be done and does it, and takes pride in being a hard worker. Gardens full of weeds annoy her, as do idle people. No wonder that she thinks that idleness is bad for the boy and wants to put him to work. To this end she uses the following arguments: (1) It would be better if you did something, (2) Your garden needs weeding, and (3) If you do this at once, you're a good boy. A good boy, you understand, as she is a good, hard-working maid. If the boy gives heed to her arguments and obeys, then she has imparted to this small boy her life's ideal, and that he is as courageous, diligent, useful and amiable as she. I would be the last to discredit the diligence of a maid — but I must at least say this; that in this case she fails to understand completely the child, child life, and the bringing up of children.

I would raise the following serious objections. The greatest objection is that she makes herself the norm for the child. She fails to understand that God created each thing with a nature all its own, and that divine ordinance for child life is not the same as that for a servant girl. A number of errors follow. A maid may not be idle; neither the child. A maid must keep the garden weeded; the child has the same responsibility. A maid does her work as quickly as possible; the child is to weed the garden quickly. A diligent maid is a good maid; therefore, a diligent, obedient child is a good child.

That the Lord has not given the child a life task, that he has kept the child free from cares, that the child is not expected to hurry to get to a job, that the Lord has not made the child to be a small adult, but that he must grow as a child — the diligent maid has no conception of these matters. No wonder that this diligent maid can serve to characterize the nineteenth century school with its appropriate and useful accomplishments and Christian social virtues of adults.

B. We should turn to the second point given us in the story quoted. The small boy finds weeding the garden very distasteful, at least for today. He believes too that it would be a good thing to be busy, as is the maid. He knows too that there are many weeds in the garden, and they should come out. And he recognizes that he will be called a good boy if he does the weeding soon — but the ideal of the maid arouses in him an aversion. The result is, "I don't feel like it today!" If he should say this openly, he would no longer be called a good boy, and to be so regarded is rather pleasant. He seeks a way out. Feeling unequal to the adult ideal held before him, he seeks to escape in the thought, "I cannot weed." And this is true. As the maid thinks of work, the child is unequal to it. But she says, "You can weed the garden." This is also true. He *can*. But at once, his distaste for the whole thing overmasters him, and he says positively, "I'd rather not." He would even forego being called a good boy. He won't. The nineteenth century school that held the adult ideal before children has known: 1. Obedient children who did as they were told and were known as good boys. 2. Children who felt the oppressiveness of the adult ideal and said, "I can't." 3. Children who revolted and boldly asserted, "I won't."

C. Now our third point given here. A coercieve nurse maid who becomes enraged because her arguments are not accepted and her ideals are not followed out. "But you must," takes the place now of reasoning about what is useful and good. Over against the idea of the good boy, she places the terrifying image of the bad boy. And the "Quickly, then you are a good boy," changes to "Get to work at once and do as *I* say!" Humanistic schools have known them, those teachers who became angry because the child did not seem to understand the value, necessity, and good of the instruction given, who shouted, "quickly" and "naughty" and "do as *I* say." And all this without reference to higher authority. I tell you — with the greatest emphasis on that *I*.

D. Our fourth given. A small boy who doesn't feel like it, does not want to, is disobedient, and doesn't do what he is told by the maid; a naughty boy, and yet — he feels that he is ill treated. And in this feeling he is right. The humanistic school has known them by the thousands, those children who didn't care for the instruction given and who sought some kind of escape, who didn't want to and were naughty and — who, notwithstanding their awareness of not being good children, felt that they were ill treated.

E. Now our fifth given. A mother who understands her child better than anyone else, and who has entered into the life of her child. She sees him "as the last rose of summer," and she wants to enter into his grief. There are in our time many teachers who see in this mother their ideal, and who would make the following adage their goal:

> He who the child would understand,
> Must learn his way in kiddie-land.

They despise the adult ideal of being virtuous, of being good and diligent as the ideal for the child. They see the child in his childhood and regard child-likeness more important than virtue. The little pranks of youngsters they find most interesting. Those kiddies are real types for funny sketches of child life in school. And they are such "cute" youngsters.

F. There is a sixth point given. A mother who knows the play-way. Weed the garden for the fun of it; it's such a beautiful day. But it is childhood play — it is the boy's garden and it is his game. And mother says, "May I go along and help you?" We have them in our time who play with the children — reading, figuring, writing, singing, speaking — but it is the children's game; it is their fun, and the teacher plays with them — and asks whether she may help. The child remains a child in keeping with his nature. Isn't this progress?

G. And there is a final point. A boy who feels like weeding his garden and goes to work joyfully. And quickly too. A child who doesn't bother about the value of what he is doing, nor does he especially feel that he is a good boy, but he is no longer naughty and feels that he is treated decently. There are thousands of children today who eagerly go to work at school without insight in the value of it, who go to school joyfully, and protest when father and mother think they should stay home. These children are treated as children and, as a result, are unusually willing and obedient. Teachers can get them to do anything and everything. And when father tells the teacher that his child is very disobedient at home, it stands to reason that the first thought that occurs to the teacher is: that is your fault; you do not treat him as a child. If that father could come to understand the secret that evokes the new obedience, as the new school does, things would be different at home. What is the modern problem? It is this: How can the naughty boy who doesn't feel like it, will not, and doesn't, and therefore extremely disobedient in the main, become suddenly a lovely, obedient, willing boy for mother?

Is this real? May I give you another example from literature to clarify the problem further?

Jan Ligthart tells in his *Memories of Youth* of a catechetical class held in school which the teacher could not control. The rascals took the cards containing memory verses and texts and made spitballs out of them, which they used to throw at one another. At one time the disorder became so great the teacher yelled in desperation, "You're possessed of the devil. He controls this class. But soon the Lord Jesus will come to punish you all." At this moment, the door opened and the principal entered, an avowed atheist, who had no regard for religion. Immediately the rascals rushed to their seats and were silent. His presence was enough to banish all devilishness.

And now I ask again: How is it possible that a class of rascals with no respect for anyone is suddenly transformed into a group of obedient children who go to their seats orderly?

Is this real? Mother knows. Treat the child as a child, for he is but a child. And then you can do with him what you will. She is right. And the principal says, "You've got to be firm with such rascals, then you can wind them around your finger." And he is right. But the maid says, "I have no time to play, and I came here as a maid, so this boy must do as I tell him; otherwise, I might as well leave." And I believe she is right too. And likewise, the teacher of the catechetical class who says, "Those rascals, they have no respect for God's Word, but they do for that strapping, bossy principal. They are still far from the true obedience." And surely this man is right too; he speaks a serious truth. And so, I am no further with my problem.

And if I had to choose between the maid who commands, "Do what *I* say," and the mother who asks, "May I help you?"; between the teacher of the catechetical class who has God's Word but no tact, and the principal without God, but who knows how to be firm — if I had to choose one to teach obedience — in all seriousness, I wouldn't know.

And if you ask me to choose between the boy disobedient to the maid and the boy who permits his mother to help him, between the orderly rascals of the principal and the rascals of the catechetical teacher — if I must point out where true obedience is found — really, I don't know. I couldn't tell you. For obedience surely is to listen to a command, to accept in one's heart an admonition, to give heed to guidance of those placed over us.

The little boy of mother is "nice," but there is no obedience, for there is no command. And the orderly rascals seem to listen to the demands of the principal, but in reality, they are the same rascals who return to the seats quietly, merely because they dare not to do otherwise. They fear the principal more than the devil. They are afraid. And I don't know what is worse: disobedience or sham-obedience. I really don't know.

It is the modern problem of obedience of the well-disciplined school where everything is conducted in military style, but often produces lawless people outside of school, and the free school where child life is honored, but children do not learn to bow before law imposed upon them because they are not asked to do anything contrary to their desires. It is the problem of the old nineteenth century humanistic school and the new school of today. The old school is stuck with the question: How can I teach children to obey from their hearts? The new school is just as stuck with the question: How do I teach the children to obey? The old lacks the tact rooted in love. The new lacks the command.

Today we find ourselves in the midst of the struggle between the two. Both sides are severely critical of each other. Read what Montessori, Ligthart, and others have to say about the old school. And then listen to the criticism of the old guard. But neither gives us a solution to the problem of obedience.

In the sketch of Laura Richard and in the memories of Ligthart, the modern problem of obedience is clearly presented. And we saw that the maid and the mother, the teacher of the catechetical class and the principal are equally right — or if you will, equally wrong.

You realize the problem cannot be solved in this way. As so many problems, it is stated wrongly. The question is not, How can I get the child to weed the garden gladly or against his desires? The question is not, How can I get this class to be quiet? But the question is, How can I teach the child to obey the fifth commandment, and every commandment and ordinance of God? Now the problem is stated not in the modern sense, but as the Christian views it. That we have a solution to this pressing problem, we owe to the Word of our Lord Jesus Christ.

Have you noticed that in stating our problem according to modernity only two parties are involved? The maid and the naughty boy. The mother and the sweet little boy. The catechetical teacher and the boys throwing spitballs. The principal and the quiet class. The teacher and the pupils. Montessori and her youngsters.

In stating the problem according to the Christian view, three parties are involved. The two mentioned here on earth, but also, in heaven, the Almighty, the King of Kings, our Lord, whose ordinances have priority.

Some seem to think that the difference between the modern school and the Christian school lies in a difference in teachers and in pupils, but the difference is to be found chiefly in the fact that in the Christian school God is acknowledged as sovereign over all men and over all human learning, over all things. And if teachers and pupils in the Christian school are different — and it is to be hoped they are — it is because of this fact.

God is not acknowledged in the modern school — at the most he is assigned to a subject as religion, but for the rest he is excluded. This is the root of all our objections to the modern school. And this applies, too, in the case of the problem of obedience. The modern world faces no such problem for it takes no account of God's commandments. The Christian school can state the problem of obedience meaningfully for it recognizes the fifth commandment. And it has an answer to the problem because Christ came.

Let us view the given facts of the situation we discussed in the light of the Word of God.

The maid has been engaged by mother as nursemaid and exercises limited authority over the child according to God's ordinance in behalf of the mother. Therefore, she may command. If she may not, she might as well leave. But God has assigned the child a sphere of life characteristic for him as a child; he plays; he is free from care; he is not full-grown. This ordinance of God for child life the maid must respect. She fails to recognize this fact and runs into conflict which proves embarrassing. Her appeal to self-confidence and to naughtiness if he fails to heed her, all are evidence of self-defense. She backs out.

The catechetical teacher makes the same mistake and then commits the grave error — no, the great sin — to attribute his failure to-get-along-with-children to the devil and tries to use the Lord Jesus as a discipline measure. As the maid, he should be in another job.

Mother understands the child. But she forgets that God has commanded: Honor thy father and thy mother. And she forgets that she must exercise her authority which she also delegated to the maid. She fails to teach her child obedience for God's sake. The principal knows how to tighten the reins of control, but in his own self-satisfaction he is blind to the fact that the rascals learned no obedience, neither to the unfortunate principal, nor to God whom he disregards.

The little boy does not recognize that he must obey the maid, and he fails to see that mother needs no permission from him. The fifth commandment is entirely lacking. The rascals do not acknowledge their conduct as sin against God, as disobedience to his Word; and being driven by fear in slavish obedience to the principal, they haven't accepted the fifth commandment.

This conclusion is very disheartening, as well for those more at home in the old school as those that have adopted the new in education. True, genuine obedience is more than adjusting oneself contrary to his nature under the threat of the severity of a master, but it also is something else than giving mother permission to help. True obedience is in one's heart to be submissive to authority placed over us by God; it is giving heed to a command, guidance, admonition of one placed over us; it is listening with all one's heart to government ordained of God. Whether it is in harmony with or contrary to our nature, to our liking or not is of less importance. Severe masters, too, one can obey with all one's heart as a Christian. God asks this of us. Taken from this Christian standpoint, we all fall short, children too, of obedience; there is much transgression of God's command.

If we had no more than the command, we might well despair. A mountain of disobedience would rise up before us when we reflect on our past life, and at school we should hesitate to speak of obedient children. That commandment would slay us as far as obedience is concerned and would make ridicule of our traditional obedience as well as of the modern version; and declare both insufficient in the sight of God. In all fairness we would have to admit that it is useless to teach others to obey, and we might as well cease demanding of others what we cannot attain ourselves.

We might try to state the problem with relation to God's law thus: Do with all your heart what God commands, honor all authority, obey its commands. But to put this into practice and to answer the question, how do I teach children to obey, that is beyond us. We should then perhaps arrive at the pedagogic of Jesus Sirach of the Pharisees, who by severe demands of the Law caused others to go down under the burden, but failed to take any cognizance of the Law himself. Jesus Sirach wrote in this spirit in his Book of Wisdom of Jesus Sirach's son, chapter 30: "He who loves his son will use the rod freely that in it he may reap joy. Who whips his son, heals his wounds. Caress a child and he will frighten you; play with him, and he will grieve you. Do not laugh with him that he pain you not and that in the end you gnash your teeth. Give him no privilege in his youth and do not disregard his ignorance. Bend his neck while he is young, and break his limbs while he is a child."

You see, this is teaching obedience under the Law by men who know only the Law, but who have not come to contrition by the Law, who have not died unto the Law by the Law, as Paul, but who remained erect in the face of the Law. Once again, had we only the Law, only the fifth commandment — with reference to obedience, the case would be hopeless, both for us and for our children.

But besides the solution of the Jewish Rabbi, thank God, there is another, a better solution — by the Rabbi of Nazareth, by our Lord Jesus, the Christ, and this is the Christian solution to the problem of obedience. Our obedience cannot stand in the sight of God. But He was obedient to death on the cross. He is the propitiation for our disobedience; He removes our guilt. He counts those who believe in him as never having disobeyed; He forgives; He loves with an eternal love; through his spirit He creates in us love in response to his love. And this blessing of the covenant He seals to us in baptism.

This is the Christian, the complete solution of the problem of obedience, or rather disobedience. The problem is completely solved; it is no half job, no humanistic embellishment, no "good boy" pedagogy, no corporal cruelty to assure greater fortitude as a Pharisee, no straight jacket but neither nullifying of the command, no satisfaction with sham submission (old school) but neither lawlessness (new school), no striving Excelsior, ever higher. It is very simple — go to Jesus with our disobedience and that of our children and ask for pardon, and confess guilt, and believe.

Whoever is not satisfied with this solution — it is much too simple for our sophisticated culture — will have to seal his broken cisterns that constantly lose their water content. But Christians of all time have rejoiced in the obedience of Christ who has conciliated our disobedience. And they have through the ages praised the sufficiency of his redemption. And they have — not with flogged bodies nor in timid suspicion — but with all their heart and soul bowed before him as Lord. With all their heart they submitted to his rule and renounced all that was in conflict with it. And when they felt unequal to the true obedience, they strengthened each other in love, and reminded one another in love of the obligation of the new obedience, well expressed in: "Whereas in all covenants *there are contained two parts, therefore, are we by God through baptism, admonished of and obliged unto a new obedience,* namely, that we cleave to this one God, Father, Son and Holy Spirit; that we trust in him, and love him with all our heart, with all our soul, with all our mind, and with all our strength; that we forsake the world, crucify our old nature, and walk in a Godly life."

We can learn from the new school to give heed to divine ordinances for child life; we can learn from Montessori, Ligthart, and others; with the old school, however, we shall recognize authority and command — but we shall view authority and command as of God and shall constantly confess guilt and seek forgiveness. And then we join in love to him, and listen to his Word in new obedience. No, we shall not be talking about it all the time; but it will constitute the basis for all we do and leave undone; we shall teach these truths and implement them in practice.

Then the firm voice of the teacher may at times resound with "do as I say," and yet it will not sound harsh. When in the afternoon, this teacher bows in contrition before God with the children, that *I* will occupy a very secondary place. Then a motherly teacher may ask at times, "May I help you?" and yet not resemble the modern attitude to child life, for in all reverence she led the children to the throne of grace in prayer and then does not hesitate to command in the name of God. Then someone will pull the reigns of control tightly at times, but the fear he seems to engender is soon allayed in that he fears God and, too, confesses guilt; this children never forget. Then a catechetical teacher can act very stupidly at times and irritate an energetic group of rascals — but many a rascal will come to regret action and the catechetical teacher will confess his sin; both will be forgiven, and both will in all earnestness seek to live according to all God's ordinances.

Think not that all this passes by the children unnoticed. They do not reflect on it as such. But observe it they do. A boy soon feels that the Word of Christ is being honored. They are aware of the fact that the teacher bows before God's Word, that he knows himself to be of Christ, that he practices the new obedience. To make the pupil aware of this he need not testify to his own conversion in so many words. He need not display his inner life externally in tears or give expression to his religion in long-faced piety. No, daily life is the best indicator of the true nature of the man. And to this children are very alert, you can be sure.

We must teach the truth concerning Christ revealed in his Word. If we are sincere, time and occasion will arise to prove us genuine. What is not genuine will disappear in fiery test of practice. And this will detract from our words about the Bible. It will not detract from God's Word, for without our example it can lay hold upon the soul, to stimulate it to resist (then woe unto us; then we become objects of scorn) or to acceptance (and then our learners gladly forgive our deficiencies).

In the grace of God the coming generation, the seed of the church, will grow in the new obedience and increase in favor both with Jehovah and also with men (I Sam. 2:26). And — in the future, join *him* who was subject to his parents, and was filled with wisdom and grew in favor with God and man. This means that a schoolboy increases in favor with God.

Yes, I know, there are others, but of this I am certain, God maintains his church, also among the children as the children increase in genuine obedience to the fifth commandment; they increase in their awareness of guilt, in their faith in Christ's forgiving love, they increase in the new obedience, and thus increase in favor with God and also with man.

May their teachers grow along with them. Our Lord is worthy of our most devoted, loving obedience. One day He, God himself, will wipe away all tears of our disobedience and say, "Don't mention it; all guilt is removed; enter thou faithful one. I will make you ruler over much," as though we had always obeyed. To know this gives rest to our soul.

Christ's work is complete, for us and for our children. He has solved the pressing problem of disobedience. That may not be so obvious in present practice — but, the practice of Christian obedience by us and by our children points to the time that we, like the angels, stand ready to serve God. We ask this daily as we pray, "Thy kingdom come."

A. JANSE

*The Distinctive Character
of the Christian Schools,* pp. 49-64.

Key Thoughts:

1. It is the new obedience that we seek to achieve in the lives of our children.

2. The first requisite is that this obedience is evident in the life of the parent and the teacher.

3. The parent and the teacher are mandated by God to exact obedience from the children.

4. In the exercise of this authority the parent and teachers are called upon to:

   a. Be penitent in their own disobedience.
   b. Be firm and consistent in their demands upon children.
   c. Honor the ordinances of God for child life in its development to maturity.

Comment:

Discipline administered in love and penitence is an integral part of Christian education in the home and in the school. Neither the arbitary command of an authoritarian teacher nor the sentimental appeal to the good will of the child constitute Christian discipline. Discipline in the Christian school is administered in the name of God, for He is the source of our authority over the child. It is carried out in love, for Christ has merited God's love for us and our children. It honors child life, for our children are the lambs of the flock of the Lord Jesus. God has ordained the ways of child life. These ordinances are authoritative for parents and teachers in directing child life to maturity.

10

Education for Self-Direction

If the child is to attain the true self-direction, he must recognize his place and adjust himself to God's ordinances for child life; therefore, he must be a child, not an adult. If we as Christians are to bring up our children for true self-direction, we shall have to take position four-square against the modern emancipated man, and fight this modern position in our own sphere of life and in our own hearts, and that with the Word of God as our armor.

The modern idea is this: man is autonomous, is a law unto himself, acknowledges no higher authority than his own better self, directs his world (micro-cosmos) according to his will as a little god within, thinks that as autonomous, free, independent subject he has free reign in all his decisions, purposes, and choices, often looks upon the actual world about him as antagonistic to his desires and would mold all things to his liking.

Over against this modern idle fancy we posit the following truth: independent, self-directing is the man who in the place assigned him by God subordinates himself in obedience to God's ordinances; who carries out his life's task; who voluntarily chooses to do so; who knows what he chooses and why; who in his choices recognizes God's ordinances for every sphere of life; who regulates his life as led by God; who does not ascribe his misdeeds to extenuating circumstances but to his own poor judgment and sin; and finally, who does not regard adversity in life as obstinacy of his environment but as God's providence in life to which he learns to be submissive.

How shall we bring up the child in this true self-direction, and how shall we guard him against the false independence? If we desire the child to develop into a self-directing person, have him practice self-direction now, a self-direction in keeping with his childhood. Let him practice childlike independence, and protect him against vain pride and foolish self-assertion by instructing him in God's Word.

The clear expression of God's Word, "Children, be obedient to your parents in everything; for this is well pleasing in the Lord" (Col. 3:20; Eph. 6:1) is not an undeserving limitation placed upon the actions of a free person and necessary only to realize the better-self in him, but is a divine command; and the Lord still knows best how a child is to be brought up. As Christians, we maintain this over against all plausible modern slogans of the liberation of childhood, which end in practice in the greatest slavery.

But — let us never forget this — as educators we too must be obedient. We may not act as autonomous beings any more than the children. No, we do not obey the child. Neither do we obey nature — especially not the nature of the child which is corrupted by sin. We must obey God. And he has told us, "Fathers, do not fret and harass your children, or you may make them sullen and morose" (Col. 3:21).

We can by arbitrary action frustrate children that they snap and lose heart, that in a defeatist spirit they go through their childhood feebly and burdened. We then break their independence with which God endowed them in creation. We may place burdens on our children too heavy to bear, beneath which they succumb. We can restrain all independent action, frustrate all self-control, deprive them of reaching conclusions by themselves. Then we do not resist his evil nature, but the nature of the child as created by God. We oppose the ordinances of God's creation — and break down many worthy potentialities in the child.

This the old school has done with its rigid grade division. You see, this "old" school, with its ideal of a carefully measured dose of knowledge that everyone must know whether it interests him or not or whether he can assimilate it or not, with its ideal of general education, has harassed the child and deprived him of his necessary opportunity for self-direction.

In reaction to this school that took no account of God's ordinances for child life which says that the child needs a certain amount of freedom of action, a measure of self-interest, of self-activity, of independent thinking, of self-direction, there has arisen the so-called new school that takes the very opposite position. The new school has seen what the child needs. It dares to allow a measure of childlike independence. It permits the child self-activity, independent thinking, decisions and action. And as a rule it achieves marvellous results, incredible to the minds of our teachers of the old school.

No, I would not praise the modern, new school in everything. When it undermines authority and sets aside the divine command, "Children, be obedient," it has violated even the true independence of the child, but especially God's law. Therefore, our demand for the Christian school in which God is honored stands in the face of the modern, new school. But we must give the new school credit for honoring divine ordinances for child life. And those Christian schools still one-sidedly oriented to the old school should haste themselves to learn from the new school how God desires that children be treated. We shall give them the independence appropriate to child life that they may practice self-direction and thus grow up to act as independent, self-directing people in the larger areas of life. For this is a very serious truth that if a child does not learn to carry out his childhood activities independently, there is great danger that he will be unprepared to take his place in life.

A. JANSE

*The Distinctive Character
of the Christian Schools,* pp. 65-78.

Key Thoughts:

1. The child must attain to self-direction in obedience to God.

2. He learns self-direction by being permitted and enabled to practice self-direction in keeping with his maturity.

3. Modern education has learned to understand the needs of child life as earlier schools never dreamed of knowing. These needs are God-ordained ways of child development that must be honored if we are to bring up children rightly.

4. But the modern school undermines God-ordained authority when it fails to relate the child's needs to obedience.

5. Christian education must understand a child in his needs and develop him into a self-directing person according to the "new obedience."

Comment:

Self-direction in the "new obedience" is a mark of maturity for the Christian. Precept makes its contribution when the precept takes account of the needs of the child life in a given stage of development. But active participation by the child in responsible activity does far more. It is by participation that he begins to feel secure in the activity.

And a child needs security in his person if he is going to learn at all.

11

The Problem of Giving a Child a Biblical Conception of his Fourfold Relationship in Life Through the Classroom

Briefly I shall picture the present need for a Biblical conception of life in its inclusive sense, the nature of this scriptural interpretation, and the general task of the classroom teacher in this matter. The discussion of the need of a Bible outlook centers around the question "why?"; the analysis of this outlook deals with the "what?"; and the possible solutions answer the question "how?"

Why the Modern Child Needs a Biblical Conception of Life

There is today probably as never before in the schoolroom an acute need for nurturing the child in an atmosphere of true piety and respect for authority. In our present western Christian civilization, Christianity in its original purpose expressed in its simple yet profound tenets is, as far as the average elementary schoolroom is concerned, quite completely ignored. It has gone out of the picture. "They have taken away my Lord," is a plaintive cry that may be uttered by most of the classrooms in our United States. At one time the Christian philosophy is openly mocked and laughed out of court; at another occasion it is entirely omitted, or simply forgotten, or boldly eliminated. Here, pupils know nothing of the life treasures of the Christian religion; there Christianity is simply but purposely crowded out. It has no standing room. At best it is motioned to take a seat upon the floor. It is dethroned in the classrooms, and the lofty aim of Mathurin Cordier — a teacher of the great John Calvin — to make every schoolroom a theocracy, has been substituted by the general purpose of dedicating the schools to human progress. Its glory is departed from the halls of learning. For millions of people, Christianity is about equivalent to doing a bit of good service to mankind at marriage feasts, at births, at funerals, at sudden disasters, and at graduation exercises. It is treated as a periodic luxury instead of a continuously fundamental human necessity of the first order. It is largely and merely ornamental, and that only intermittently at stated intervals. Indeed, there is a wide gap between John Calvin's applied religion on the basic belief that the sovereign and omnipresent God is the governor of our souls in all circumstances of life, and the present day rather prevailing practice of treating God and His Christ as available beings suddenly to be used and then as promptly to be shelved again till more opportune time.

Christian piety and reverence? Humility and child-like obedience to divine laws? Instead, there is a growing pagan arrogance. There is no fear in the hearts of men. The ruling philosophy is, "Help yourself." The cardinal law of Christ, "Seek ye first the kingdom of heaven and its righteousness, and all other things shall be added unto you," seems to be recast into this mold, "Seek ye first all other things, and the kingdom of heaven and its righteousness shall be added unto you."

And why is this Ichabod-condition in regard to Christianity commonly found in the classrooms — those salient sources of any civilization — so prevalent? Floods of secularization have for the last five centuries in ever rising volume swept the world of thought in this Christian civilization. The cultural calling of man, once imbedded in a Christian outlook upon life here and hereafter and producing our Christian churches, our Christian states, our Christian society, our Christian family, etc., has now quite largely been divorced from the Christian way of life. Christianity, once occupying the central place in the lives of individuals, of families, of communities, and of nations, has now been shoved so far to the utmost circumference of human concern that it is for most people well-nigh lost out of sight in the common-place of life, and for many totally lost. This secularization now so powerfully entrenched in the homes, the schools, the daily papers, the magazines, and even in many so-called Christian churches has practically inundated every domain of human activity. Where ideally true Christianity should be supreme in every department of life, a mighty shift of emphasis has taken place, and a worldly philosophy now seems the Alpha and Omega. Nearly everywhere the spiritual atmosphere, if not supplanted by a material philosophy on the part of the masses, is charged with a secular outlook on the part of leaders. This shift is so overwhelmingly thoroughgoing that even the strongest bulwarks, such as the Christian homes and Christian societies, that battled for centuries for Christianity and against its enemies, too often have succumbed to the onslaughts of secularization.

Now it must be remembered that this process of replacing Christian homes and other Christian institutions by secular institutions and of substituting a secular outlook for a Christian way of life has not happened recently. Christianity always has had this foe within the gate and without. Never before, however, has a secular mind so controlled this Christian civilization as it does at present. Never before has Christianity lost so much ground as it has now. Never before, it would seem, were the interests of the Christian religion threatened as they are in this age. Why this stranglehold? Why this throat grip?

History, it seems to me, has the answer, and instead of a few decades, five hundred years were needed to bring about this leavening of our Christian civilization by foreign elements which finally succeeded in so transforming man's regard for a supernatural religion, for the Bible, for the Church, and for Christian principles of sin and grace that today it appears as though the word "Christian" is a mere label and a conventional name for what once was.

For the convenience of tracing more readily this colossal change from the Christian mind to a secular mind, the four following stages in this change since the fifteenth century ought to be kept in mind; *viz.,* man appearing on the scene in the successive roles as humanist around 1400-1500, as rationalist around 1600-1700, as naturalist around 1800-1900, and as scientist today. In viewing history for our purpose in these four periods we should note three general characteristics of these four movements; *viz.,* that they have one common denominator named secularization which is bound to develop an unbiblical God-concept and man-concept contrary to what was taught by Christianity; that the order in which they appear is significant, one preparing for the other; and that their destructive work in undermining Christianity is cumulative, each successive force or movement reinforcing the attack made by the preceding one. Thus, man as a humanist laid the strong foundation of an antagonistic philosophy subversive to the teachings of Christianity — particularly in the matters of sin and grace; man as a rationalist continued this warfare in other quarters by systematizing and organizing humanistic ideas into a whole; man as a naturalist boldly attacked the main citadel of Christian philosophy — the supernatural; and man as the scientist, while producing most disastrous results for Christianity, adapted consciously or otherwise strategic measures most readily suggested by our technical use.

The first most serious onslaught Christianity suffered after it was firmly established in Europe was that called "Humanism," finding expression in what is termed the Italian Renaissance. Whatever good features it revealed in other respects, it was characterized by a philosophy opposed to authority, dogma, and institutions of the church. More than this, it was devoted not to Christian virtue but to a sheer experimenting with Christian morality and Christian theology till nothing of either was left. Freethinkers were adored, and ever since 1400 their offspring loudly proclaim the failure of the historical Christian view of life, of God, and of man.

One of the best authorities on the moral-religious nature of these Italian humanists and on their new philosophy or way of living says: The study of the classics and the effort to assimilate the spirit of the ancients, undermined their Christianity without substituting the religion or the ethics of the old world. They ceased to fear God; but they did not acquire either the self-restraint of the Greek or the patriotic virtues of the Roman . . . they wallowed in sensuality . . . and devoted their ingenuity to the explanation of foulness that might have been passed in silence. Licentiousness became a special branch of humanistic literature. Under the thin mask of humane refinement leered the untamed savage; and an age that boasted not unreasonably of its mental progress was at the same time notorious for the vices that disgrace mankind. (J. A. Symonds, *The Revival of Learning*, pp. 520-521).

Haughty, conceited, unreliable, setting aside every Christian virtue, custom, and convention, they in every act rebel against a mode of living colored by certain definite forms of restraint and inhibition, and thereby introduced a new order of things. Christian morality as well as doctrine is set aside. The Christian religion is in principle, if not openly, sacrificed by these individualistic humanists of the fourteenth and fifteenth century to the old pagan ideal that man is the measure of all things. The Christ of the Scriptures was again labeled foolishness, and the humanists of that time were the first organized group with a new outlook upon life to keep that label intact and pass it on downward through the ages. The foundation of humanism without God was laid. Conceit in man, so characteristic of practically all the Italian humanists of that time, was brazenly practiced as the root principle, and the grace of God, that all-pervasive teaching of Scripture used as the basic theme by the Apostle Paul in his thirteen epistles, all of which proclaim the plan of redemption, and all of which begin with the salutation, "Grace unto you" and end with the prayer, "Grace be with you all," is spurned. Paul knew man's need of divine grace, but the Humanists denied it. The antithesis became organized on this point in more definite form of two opposing and hostile camps. The longing of man to be like God but not in the God-appointed way was firmly rooted in the hearts of these humanists, and their descendents have worked away at this innate desire to this present day. These humanists made the beginning of the process that was to result in a de-Christianized western civilization with its seemingly uncontrollable harvest of confusion and despair. And, in spite of the Christian Renaissance of the North (Holland and Germany), headed by the Brethren of the Common Life, and the Reformation of Luther and Calvin, both Christian movements of that time trying to restore a Biblical conception of life, the humanistic tendencies of 1400-1500 grew into the more formidable convictions of the rationalists of 1600-1700, who with their "Enlightenment" or "Verlichting" more definitely replaced Bible standards for life here and hereafter by man's reason as the final criterion and highest tribunal in determining the True, the Good, and the Beautiful. The humanist placed himself above the Church and its Christian institutions and Christian morality; the rationalist exalted himself above the Bible, and instead of the Light of the world offered his light of reason that would fain serve as a lamp for our feet and a light upon our pathway. It is again the same antithesis: God or man; divine grace or human reason. The Bible conception is again rejected, but the approach is more refined.

And this sad story of disintegration of the Christian philosophy is repeated when this humanistic rationalist has the self-complacent audacity of advising man to turn back to nature. The supernatural is now ruled out. The first reckless step was to declare man the measure of all things; the second step inevitably to follow is that man's reason is to be the criterion for ultimate reality; and the third step that must be made is to change from defensive tactics to an offensive campaign. The sovereign God is denied. The natural is the only object in our horizon. The lights of heaven are extinguished. The supernatural is erased from man's thinking, often so completely that not only the supernatural in Bible revelation but even the supernatural in man's natural religion is denied the means for subsistence. The result is that the humanistic, rationalistic, and naturalistic man now concerns himself only with the observable, measurable, and tangible. He is a scientist — satisfied with the material — and is now ready to worship the God of his own making; *viz.,* the marvelous technique of this age and the physical luxuries it brings. Truly, a study of history of Western civilization for the last five hundred years, it would seem, reveals rather clearly that one is justified, when beholding the arrogant position of the humanist over against the simple teachings of early Christianity such as sin and grace, denial and holiness, etc., to cry out, "Ichabod"; and, again, when meditating on the pride of the rationalist, to lament, "Ichabod"; or, once more, when witnessing the complete abandon of the naturalist, to sob, "Ichabod"; and, lastly, when viewing the final result of how man has robbed himself of his own glory by worshipping the creatures of his own hand to cover his face with shame and weep, "Ichabod."

The Biblical conception of life as an absolute norm for individual well being and group welfare has been practically crowded out. The need of the hour for our so-called Christian civilization is a return to the fundamentals. Everywhere there is an underlying need for reform, for betterment, for reverence for God, for respect for authority, and for love for others. The right remedy is that true Christianity and true piety are first requisites for right living. We must go back to the fountains of Scripture, to our antecedents, and among those more particularly turn with our children in our classrooms to our origins in the Reformation. The loss is a Bible view of life. Our duty then is for the sake of our children, our homes, our schools, and our civilization to supply that need in the form of a Bible conception of life.

What that Biblical Conception Is

What do we mean by giving the child in the classroom a Biblical conception of life? It should be at once clear that any proper answer to this question must contain at least one of the cardinal principles of Christianity. Many appropriate answers are possible, but an outstanding characteristic of every good answer is that we as human beings, and our children with us, cannot possibly have the right conception of life without the grace of God operating within us. This position we must hold at any cost. Paul, as mentioned before, does not fail in any of his letters to make this grace of God the essential human need for all true living. Therefore, we do well to listen to Paul and for a while study his remedy for developing in man a proper biblical outlook upon life. In his epistle to Titus, the second chapter, verses eleven to thirteen, we find the following program for Christian living: "For the grace of God that bringeth salvation hath appeared to all men, teaching us that, denying ungodliness and wordly lusts, we should live soberly, righteously, and godly, in this present world; looking for that blessed hope, and the glorious appearing of the great God and our Savior Jesus Christ."

This Biblical summary of Christian living satisfies universal human needs, for "salvation hath appeared to all men"; it provides for life here and hereafter, for this salvation is "looking for that blessed hope"; and it takes care of any relationship any individual may possibly develop, for this grace of God has a teaching program both negative in "denying ungodliness and worldly lusts" and positive in sober, righteous, and godly living; both inhibitory and assertive; both repressive and expressive. It instructs the individual how by sober living he may provide for his own well being, how by righteous living he may love his neighbor as himself, and how by godly living he may love God above all. By carrying out this program as an ideal he will approach a balanced life, a perfect life, yea, even eternal life. And the glory of this program is that its fullness, its sufficiency, and its absolute character are incontrovertibly assured by the grace of God. Here is the Biblical conception. Here is the teaching program for those teachers who wish the children to lay a relatively firm hold, consistent with their immature minds and souls, on an outlook upon life divinely appointed and historically developed. Here we find the children's four possible types of life's relationships as so many large divisions of life's calling.

An analysis of this teaching program reveals how salvation in Christ and it alone contains the true spiritual directory for man's relationships to himself, to his neighbor, and to his God. The only way to attain to the ultimate reality of right living for self is by sobriety; the only scheme to bring us to the eternal verity of civic well being is by living righteously; and the only plan to realize the abiding values in life is by living godly. Paul's program once for all excludes man's vain imaginations. These three types of relationships are closely related to a fourth kind — the relation of the individual to his material universe whose laws he needs to know for sober, righteous, and godly living. The whole sweep of life is included. Nothing truly human is slighted. The program is unique, absolute, final. No substitute will do. No revision will be made. No modification will be allowed. The Lord spake, and it was done! He commanded, and it stood fast! The grace of God as the power house and its teaching program are sufficient. Every substitute of humanist, rationalist, naturalist, and scientist as well as every random imagination of man's heart must forever hopelessly fail and should be emphatically shunned.

In this Biblical conception of life man is not the measure of all things. According to this message man of himself does not know what healthy humanism, ideal rationalism, true naturalism, and exact science are, unless through the grace of God that appeared unto all men. The Bible alone can function as the lamp for the feet and as the light upon the pathway for any real humanist, rationalist, naturalist, and scientist. The genuine Bible humanist will humbly exclaim when contemplating on this grace of God, "Lord, what is man that Thou art mindful of him, and the son of man that Thou visitest him!" The serious Bible rationalist will promptly but meekly respond to the divine invitation, "Come now and let us reason together!" The naturalist, once seeing the glory in the grace of God that appeared unto all men and accepting this Pauline program of teaching, will shout, "Come, let us see the works of God." And the true Bible scientist, likewise prompted by the grace of God, will lay all discoveries and inventions at the feet of the Lord saying, "Thou art worthy, O Lord, to receive glory and honor and power; for Thou hast created all things, and for Thy pleasure they are and were created."

It is a program that includes the study of self, of fellow beings, of God's revelation of Himself in Scripture, and of the material universe about us. There is nothing in any curriculum for any school that cannot be classified under one of these four types of relationships. And a course of study for any classroom cannot possibly require anything outside the scope of this Bible program of teaching and living. The task then of the classroom teacher in introducing the child to the world of self, of others, of God, and the universe itself is to do this by the grace of God in accordance with the Biblical norms, directions, and mandates bound up with the words of this program, "teaching us" and "looking for." No other program could possibly satisfy human needs and divine laws governing those needs. We would violate laws for true human well-being if we would — while trying to teach the children the first approaches to a relatively rounded out body of knowledge — ignore the source of all true living; *viz.,* the grace of God. We would not be able to inform the children about the proper duty of denying ungodliness and worldly lusts, if we would not expect our all and all from Him who is the Redeemer of man. We could not possibly teach sober living, righteous living, and godly living if we had not the grace of Christ who by His mediatorial work is the only great Restorer of all these relationships, as True, Good and Beautiful. And we would forever be silent about "that blessed hope," if He who was, is, and is to come could not be presented as Savior of men and as such of man's relationship to self, to his neighbor, to his God, and to the Universe. Then our program of teaching would be unbiblical, and the schoolroom would fail to give what the child as image bearer of God and as to his very nature and very need demands; *viz.,* a Biblical conception of life.

In opposition to all man-made schemes of equipping the child in the classroom with a world and life view, with an interpretation of life in its manifold aspects, and with a sound and sane program of living in strict harmony with the laws of his very being, we want to hold high the Bible plan of redemption, whereby we may be taught of the Lord the only way to live soberly, righteously and godly. Then we are in God's way. Then we may expect His approval and His blessing. Then we can justly, rightly, and fervently pray, "Lord, establish Thou the work of our hands upon us; yea, the work of our hands establish Thou it."

How this Bible View can be Developed in the Classroom

In the attempt of giving the child this divinely appointed conception of life, the classroom of today looms larger than ever before. The scope of its opportunities for doing this has greatly been enlarged. There are at least three good reasons for maintaining that the present day classroom has far more possibilities for molding and shaping the child's outlook than ever before.

In the first place, the education of the child of today is much more formal, and of late much of what the home used to supply in an incidental way is now transferred to the school and there given in a formal way, so that the classroom occupies a more conspicuous place in rearing the child than formerly. As a result the course of study is much enlarged and possibly enriched by this new and more institutionalized and formalized education.

In the second place, education is democratized. Every child may go to school. This also increases the importance of the classroom, for its opportunities to guide the child into a life view are thereby extended to all children.

In the third place, school attendance is made compulsory, both in the matter of daily attendance and in reference to the number of years the child is by law compelled to attend, so that the child spends more time in the school annually and attends there for a larger number of years than ever before.

The remarkable feature about these three factors, it would seem, is that they prove not only a greater need on the part of the child while in the classroom for a Biblical conception of life, because his range of relationships due to a more prompt and more prolonged attendance is greatly broadened, but also an ever growing number of opportunities on the part of the teacher for applying this Biblical, Christian, and only truly human way of living to an ever increasing number of teaching situations. With this fact before us — the fusion of both greater need and larger opportunity for teaching this Christian outlook — it may in justice be said that today more than ever Christian day-school education is a crying need. It also reveals stronger and clearer than ever the immense responsibilities of the Christian day school teacher in sensing this need and in applying this Pauline program. His calling viewed in that light may well prompt us to attach a bit more significance to Dr. Martin Luther's unique confession, that at times the work of the Christian teacher seemed yet more vital to him than that of the Christian pastor.

How then is the teacher to accomplish this task as far as teaching subject matter is concerned? How is he going to satisfy this great need for true piety and true knowledge in the classroom? How is he going to make the best of this all important fusion of classroom need and classroom opportunity for true piety and true learning? How is he going to develop this Biblical conception of life if he thinks of the results of all teaching and studying? Are these outcomes or results not knowledge, skills, abilities, and attitudes? And are not "attitudes" the main product, also even as far as knowledge, skills and abilities is concerned? Should not all knowledge, skills, and abilities have the primary object of wholesome Christian attitudes? The goal then for the classroom teacher to strive for, it would seem, is to develop attitudes and nothing but attitudes in the souls of the pupil — all in accordance with the program set forth by the Apostle Paul. Then, what are the means to be used to make the child in the classroom grow into Christian attitudes while getting knowledge, skills, and abilities?

Imagine that we enter a classroom. We are looking for tools, or factors, or means to rear children in a Biblical way. We at once notice that there are really two distinctive groups of factors; *viz.*, material and spiritual. If a teacher and a class discuss the beautiful poems, "Teach me to Live" or "A Song of Trust" — both taken from a Lutheran School Reader — we at once label these gems as "material" means to give the child a Bible interpretation of life. In this group of means or factors also belong sacred history, Christian literature, Christian songs, rules for Christian conduct, the course of study, the daily schedule, pictures on the wall, story telling, class discussion, pupil activity, etc. But there is another type of means — the spiritual. It is invisible, yet real, and possibly more real than the material. Take, for instance, the Christian personality of the teacher and the Christian atmosphere of the room — of which the former is undoubtedly the first and therefore more important. Indeed, the teacher's Christian personality with its Christian outlook and its innumerable Christian attitudes is the decisive factor. It is quite possible, therefore, that a true Christian teacher gives the child a biblical conception of life, even though she does not teach Bible history as such, and even though she does not select *per se* Christian literature.

For our convenience, let us, in view of the supreme importance of a Christian personality, think of four teachers. The one has a Christian personality, is familiar with the real issue of a Biblical conception *vs.* a de-Christianized outlook, knows the historical development of this issue, is through God's grace proud of her historical-religious antecedents, and has ability to teach. She is trying to teach Christian attitudes in everything, though her subject matter is wholly secular. Yet, she knows her position, and in season and out of season asserts her Christian way of life. The second teacher has the same traits, and teaches the same way, but uses the best of Christian literature and of secular literature. The third teacher is indifferent as to the issue, has a secular mind, and uses secular material throughout. A fourth teacher likewise thoroughly secularized uses the best Christian and secular materials. Try to imagine that you successively visit these four teachers. Is there any doubt as to whom you would desire as the educator of your children? The second is, of course, your ideal.

Our conclusion then, it seems, must be that in order to develop in our boys and girls a Biblical conception of life, we want first of all a capable teacher with a Christian personality, and wherever possible the best Christian and secular material at his disposal so that he may equip children with a Biblical view of life.

Surely, the motive for parents, school boards, and teachers themselves in desiring this aim is the loftiest imaginable. It is to stem the tide of de-Christianization in the present age; it is to do the will of God; it is to be once again Biblical in the most important business in the world; it is to be truly historical, truly human.

Bible history or sacred history occupies the place of honor in bringing all subject matter properly to the child. From its towering heights, the teacher tries by God's grace to show the child through the eyes of God all the beauty, all the glory, and all the riches of the plan of God in history, in science; in the humanites as well as in the social and the physical and the biological sciences. "For all is of Christ; and Christ's is God's."

HENRY VAN ZYL

Address before the National Union of Christian Schools Convention, Hull, Iowa, August 19, 1931.

Key Thoughts:

1. The dechristianization of our western civilization since the fifteenth century makes the return to a Biblical conception of life in the classroom more imperative than ever.

2. The Biblical conception of life that should underly all classroom instruction is well expressed as sobriety, righteousness, and godliness. A careful analysis of these will show that they are inclusive in human relationships, self, fellowman, God, and the world.

3. To accomplish the development of the Biblical conception of life knowledge, skill, and abilities must have as primary objective wholesome Christian attitude.

4. Two groups of factors provide the means for this development: the material and the spiritual. To the former belong the more tangible elements of instructional materials, as course of study, classroom appearance, songs, etc. To the latter belong the Christian personality of the teacher and the Christian atmosphere of the classroom.

Comment:

The principle of unity (unity of the person, unity of the collective whole, and the unity of life), so clearly taught in the Bible, demands the primacy of love. Love only gives expression to the person in his wholeness. The Biblical conception of life demands that love be made primary in education, in learning and in teaching.

The ability to love is not some incidental by-product of knowledge-getting or a trait in the total personality. It involves the whole person in the fullness of life.

12

Learning Through Understanding

What a contrast between the child psychologist, Decroly, observer of and experimenter with child life, who lived and moved among children all his life, and Herbart, the man of self-observation, who wrote: "For twenty years I have studied metaphysics and mathematics and have schooled myself through self-observation, experience, and all kinds of testing to find a basis for valid psychological insight. And the motive in all this work was the conviction that many of the weaknesses in our pedagogical knowledge can be accounted for by our lack of knowledge of psychology."

One must respect in Herbart the untiring effort of a seeker after knowledge. But this does not remove the fact that he erred. For by his self-observation in psychological study he came to know only the adult. His psychology must of necessity fail when applied to the education of the child. Herbart has given us many practical educational suggestions, but he was no child psychologist. What he taught, namely, that the part is easier to grasp than the whole, that in teaching we must proceed from the compounded parts to come to understand the complex, that one must always proceed from the particular to the general seems true. And it is indeed — for the adult. It is logical. But for the developing child it is not psychological.

Many investigations carried on by psychologists of different countries, frequently not knowing of each other's work, led to the same conclusion; that, contrary to Herbart's conclusion concerning the adult, the child finds the global, the whole, easier than the detail, because he observed not first of all the parts but the entire object. The child assimilates the world about him, not in detail or in parts that constitute a whole, but in its total appearance, vague and indefinite. Only later does he come to analyze the parts. The child's observation, and therefore his development, does not proceed from the constituent parts to the whole, but from the total image to the elements.

By proceeding in the method of instruction in a logical rather than in a psychological manner, one works contrary to the natural growth of the child's thinking and gives rise to difficulties which at a given stage constitute insurmountable hurdles. Because the memory of the child functions with rote efficiency, he retains the material, but — not in understandable form. Instruction thereby degenerates into verbalism.

P. LANKAMP AND L. VANDER ZWEEP
General Introduction to a Course of Study for the Christian Schools, pp. 69-70.

Comment:

A child can retain logically what he has come to understand. Only what he understands transfers effectively to other areas of his life. Our knowledge of child nature and his needs has given us to understand that it is in the unity of life that a child learns meaningfully.

13

Intellectualism in Education

To note the derivation of the word "intellectualism" is not sufficient for understanding of its present meaning. Derivation helps us secure a clearer insight in the meaning of a word, but in addition to this one must note the more common use of it. In our daily life, but particularly in scientific communication, words may have contrasting meaning. Only he who recognizes the contrast will understand the word correctly. So it is with the words *intellectualist* and *intellectualism*. If everyone who has high regard for intellect and tries to develop it should be called an intellectualist, nearly everyone could be labeled such. And even if the word is to be understood in a fuller, deeper, more pregnant sense, as one refers to a man as a thinker not merely because he thinks but because he thinks sharply and deeply; if one would mean by an intellectualist, a person who values highly the intellectual, the word would still be inadequately circumscribed, for to value highly the intellectual it is not necessary to discredit the significance of feeling and willing. Only when a conflict arises, in the sense that the intellect is given priority at the expense of feeling and willing, can one really speak of intellectualism. This does take place in philosophy, in scientific knowledge, and in education.

In the meantime, we must not overlook the fact that Christian education can go ashore on the rock of intellectualism. The danger is all the greater, because we must travel so close to the rock. Developing of the ability to think, the exercise in understanding is a first requirement in all instruction.

To ask a child to read, listen to, and memorize what he does not understand is not only useless, but does positive harm, in that it cultivates indolence, superficiality, blind imitation, and mechanical expression, all of which is contrary to the Christian principles we confess. The question of Phillip, "Understandest thou what thou readest?" the more than once recorded, "hear and understand," and the words of the apostle, "I will pray with my understanding, too," and "I will sing praise with my understanding too," indicate this clearly. But to understand and to understand are two different things. One cannot get children to understand to the same extent and in the same depth as their elders. This rock threatens not only, however, when we ask too much of understanding, more than it can lay hold upon, but also where the intellect alone is called into action, be it for a reasonable extent, apart from feeling and willing.

P. LANKAMP AND L. VANDER ZWEEP
General Introduction to a Course of Study
for the Christian Schools, pp. 117-119.

Key Thoughts:

1. The epithet "intellectualist" does not apply to the cogent thinker who balances thinking with feeling and willing.

2. Intellectualism constitutes a constant threat to Christian education for the latter must emphasize ability to think and understanding.

3. The thinking of a child is to be understood in terms of child life, not in terms of adulthood.

4. Especially in child life thinking must be integrated with feeling and willing in the whole person.

Comment:

The principle of unity in the development-urge of child life demands integration of thinking, feeling, and willing to achieve a commitment to the truth. Instruction directs itself to the understanding. But understanding takes hold of the whole person only when in love he can commit himself to the knowledge he has aquired. We learn only what we come to accept in our hearts. Development of the intellect or knowing function apart from the feeling and willing functions closes hearts to the truth instead of leading to acceptance of it.

14

Knowledge and Wisdom

We want to draw one parallel. Dr. J. Waterink ended his brochure, *The Educability of the Child's Intelligence*, with an appendix in which he points to wisdom as the most precious gift of God in our life. "Intelligence without wisdom does not make for happiness. Thinking without wisdom leads more often to rupture than a binding together. Not methods of thought and not intellectual power are the most important in life, but *wisdom.*" This appendix fits into our discussion and contains at the same time a directive for the thousands of children and young people who go through life as nervous, sensitive, and asthenic humans.

In 1887, Dr. Woltjer likewise wrote about wisdom. He wrote about wisdom in relationship to knowledge, thinking, and doing. "Discipline in association with instruction must lead to wisdom, Christian wisdom, the highest good. Without knowledge there is no wisdom, but knowledge is not wisdom. Knowledge that breeds wisdom may result from experience, but generally it is a product of instruction, closely associated with experience. Knowledge, however, must be applied in wisdom; it gives knowledge the right insight for action, for it is purposeful. Christian wisdom is from above and a gift of the Spirit of God. It has learned to view things according to the wisdom of God, revealed in his Word, in which it finds unity, calm trust, power, and true modesty. It finds its source in Christ Jesus, who has become unto us the wisdom of God (I Cor. 1:30); it teaches us to view all things, temporal and eternal, through his eyes, and to follow in his steps (I Peter 2:21). It does not, therefore, despise the knowledge of the world, but learns to value it aright and put it to right use. It keeps in view the final purpose of all things, the glory of God.

"The practice of this wisdom is demanded of all Christians (Eph. 1:8, 17). Hence the cultivation of it in school is asked of the teacher above all things. This wisdom is the ideal that the child, too, must keep in view; all knowledge and discipline must be made serviceable to the achievement of the first principles of this wisdom, according to his level of understanding. It does not conflict with the childlike nature.

"Of Jesus it is said that he as a child not yet twelve years of age was filled with wisdom, and later that he increased in wisdom (Luke 2:40, 52). And the highest wisdom says, 'Now, therefore, hearken unto me, O ye children, for blessed are they that keep my ways' (Prov. 8:32)."

P. LANKAMP AND L. VANDER ZWEEP

General Introduction to a Course of Study for the Christian Schools, pp. 122-123.

Comment:

A knowledge-getting school often achieves mastery at the great expense of disrupting the dimensions of a child's personality and deepening hostilities. Such a school cannot achieve wisdom in its education program.

An education seeking personality development without the norm of truth achieves momentary adjustment, not wisdom. The wise man knows the truth and accepts it as the discipline for his life.

Only Christian education is capable of this wisdom.

15

The Discipline of the Christian School

Discipline unquestionably is a distinctive, perhaps even the most distinctive feature of Christian education. For what is discipline? According to the *New Standard Dictionary* discipline is "systematic training or subjection to authority; especially, the training of the mental, moral, and physical powers by instruction and exercise, and by authoritative control and direction; as, educational discipline." Discipline, then, is not only — not even in the first place, what we popularly mean by punishing children. This popular notion is altogether too limited; it refers only to the extreme of correction by the rod. Discipline is first and foremost *education*: training of the mental, moral, and physical powers by instruction and exercise.

The necessity of discipline for such as hold that "education is implication into God's interpretation," as Van Til tersely put it, is self-evident. For this means that in obedient submission, we accept with the heart God's definition or explanation of all things in heaven and on earth; that we accept God's explanation of ourselves, of the standards of right and wrong, good and evil; that we acknowledge ourselves bound by His law as the expression of His sovereign will which we honor and adore as only and always holy, wise and good. Implication into God's interpretation means on our part the admission that we know nothing of ourselves as we ought to know, and that we therefore look up to God that He may interpret to us all things as we ought to know them. This implication into God's interpretation demands obedient acceptance with the heart all that our great and only Teacher explains unto us, that in such attitude of heart and mind we may be built up after the image of Christ in Him. Obedience to Christ is simply the receptively reconstructed attitude of the human being once more. We become disciples of Christ, and He it is that gives to our lives authoritative control and direction. Remove discipline from Christian education, and then, if you can, tell me what there is left of it. Discipleship without discipline is a contradiction in terms.

If discipline must be considered as the heart of Christian education, it is equally true that it fits in no other philosophy of education. What ever of discipline you may observe in anti-theistic systems of education has found a place there as a concession to the inexorable demands of practical life; must be imputed to the imperfections of the educators: a perfect educator would have no need of discipline, said Schleiermacher. It follows, then, that teachers in Christian schools must solve their own questions and problems of discipline since they concern no one else. In matters of administration, in the methodology of the branches we may often profit from the labors of worldly men and women; but how shall we profit from those who by their own confessions may not even admit the problem of discipline? True, the "moderns" have their "control technique"; but the very term flouts the idea of discipline. Seen in its true light, it is nothing but a miserable fig-leaf which must serve to cover the shame of the nakedness of modern educational philosophy. Can there possibly be found any among us who desires to borrow this device which out-Gandhies the Indian apostle of the simple life in the scantiness of his girdle?

Practical people of the world are by no means satisfied with the results which this whooped-up freedom of the New Schools produces. Indeed, the results of the system of "control" by pupil government and student council, which is to demonstrate man's inherent ability for self-determination, offer in the notorious crime record of modern youth plenty incriminating evidence to send the advocates of this system hunting for alibies. Let me introduce a couple of witnesses for the prosecution. Garry Cleveland Myers in his article "Spank it Out" (*Forum, Feb., 1931*), remarks "While Mr. Wickersham is looking for the basic causes of increasing crime, he would do well to observe the general breaking-down of parental authority in the American home."

Miss Edna Yost, a former teacher, turns the searchlight of her own personal observation upon the control technique of the New Schools. I am sorry that time will not allow extensive quotation from her article on "Freedom in the New Schools" (*Forum*, Feb., 1930). I will briefly give you her *puzzle* and her *disappointment*. First then the puzzle: "What interests me more than anything else in the whole situation is the psychological urge in some of the leaders of the New School movement which has led them into their emotional point of view and held them there. What is it that makes immovable desks a symbol of slavery to them, and movable little chairs and tables a symbol of freedom? Why is it that they write so vehemently about how children have always hated the old schools and how they love the new?" That is her puzzle. Is she looking for foundations on a sand ground?

And here is the way she registers disappointment in her conclusions: "The more I think of it (i.e., of this New Freedom) abstractly, the more beautiful it seems. But the more I see of it actually, the funnier — or ghastlier — it all becomes." Incidentally this ex-teacher confides: "To this day, I am not able to go by a school building without a wave of thankfulness passing over me that I stepped out." We may perhaps be pardoned for relating the tidal wave of the New Freedom and this "wave of thankfulness" as cause and effect.

Our last witness is Katharine Fullerton Gerould. Born in Massachusetts and educated as a child in France, Mrs. Gerould taught for nearly ten years at Bryn Mawr. In 1910 she married Mr. Gerould, an author and a professor of English at Princeton. In her article on "Educating Girls for Marriage" (*Forum,* Jan., 1931) she touches upon the question of discipline in home and school as follows: "We like to think of our children as uncoerced. This spoiling of children, this 'leaving them free' — the course of our generation of parents — is already having disastrous effects in the field of manners and education. Part of our bad American schooling is due, no doubt, to our general passion for experimentation; but surely a lot of it can be charged up against the unwillingness of parents to have their children burdened with work."

Now, however much we can appreciate these complaints of weary parents and disgusted teachers, so long as they with Miss Yost confess that the *theory* appears more beautiful the more one thinks of it, just so long are they justly suffering from the natural consequences of their own iniquitous thinking, they are "receiving in themselves (and in their children) that recompense of their error which was due." To us it is evident that Christian educators cannot hope to find profitable instruction for the progress of their cause from those who know no progress in the real sense of the word; but who only turn round and round in the vicious circle of man's destructively futile anti-theistic reasoning. We have "the Word of prophecy made more sure; whereunto we (ye) do well to (that ye) take heed, as unto a lamp shining in a dark place, until the day dawn, and the day-star arise in our (your) hearts: knowing this first, that no prophecy of scripture is of private interpretation. For no prophecy ever came by the will of man: but men spake from God, being moved by the Holy Spirit" (II Pet. 1:19-21).

Does not this word of Peter call to your mind Van Til's definition of education as implication into God's interpretation? Truly in God's Light only do we see the light. This is our "declaration of independence." Our complete and exclusive dependence upon God delivers us from the thraldom, the servitude of man.

*   *   *

Having thus satisfied ourselves that discipline is an essential, even the *chief principle* in Christian education; that it is at the same time an *exclusively theistic* principle, the very idea of which must be consistently repudiated by any and all anti-theistic educationists who themselves refuse to bow before the absolute authority of God, it follows that we must find the solution for the problems of discipline, that is, the proper way to work out the training of the mental, moral, and physical powers by instruction and exercise, and by authoritative control and direction — that we must find our guidance as educators from Christ, the Son of God in whom at the end of these days God has spoken unto us.

To him the receptively reconstructive mind turns as the thirsting hart to water brooks. He is the Restorer of all things. He, the second Adam, restores us, in the words of Peter, unto "an elect race, a royal priesthood, a holy nation, a people for God's own possession, that we (ye) may show forth the excellencies of Him who called us (you) out of darkness into His marvelous light" (I Pet. 2:9). In Christ we are restored as prophets, priests, and kings unto God. So understood we appreciate criticism with reference to those who would make use of the Christian school as "a soteriological life boat and institute of conversion." How can we be a "royal priesthood," how can we "show forth the excellencies of Him who called us" if it were not true "Christ came to bring man *and his cosmos* — i.e., the entire world, or universe — back to the God of creation." Christian discipline has indeed to perform a function which is decidedly *diesseitig;* it fits men and women for their earthly careers. It is intensely practical. Receptively we accept Truth from God as the Holy Spirit reveals it to our understanding hearts that reconstructively we may again learn to think His thoughts after Him in order that we may prophesy, i.e., teach the excellencies of Him who called us in all His works. Thus only do we become once more in principle kings of creation that as a royal priesthood we may dedicate all things to the God of creation who in Christ is also the covenant God of our salvation.

*   *   *

What does all this mean for the discipline of the Christian school? Though far from exhaustively treated, I believe that the foregoing thoughts contain briefly everything that determines the discipline of our schools. It fixes the status of our pupils, the means and nature of our discipline, and the function and authority of our teachers.

Since grace restores what sin had spoiled in nature so that by grace nature becomes truly *natural* once more, we hold that organic redemption, in distinction from individual salvation, is, with due recognition of God's absolute sovereignty in election, the correct view. Grace has restored the human race, and is, through the operation of the Holy Spirit in the hearts of men, perpetuated in the natural line of successive generations. The Christian school therefore deals with children who are Christ's and God's by the gift of the Holy Spirit.

But some have objected, how can you maintain that every child of the covenant is truly a child of God since experience seems to prove the contrary, and Scripture itself demonstrates the error of the supposition? The answer is that we do not maintain anything like that. We must steer clear from individualistic interpretation and prognostication with reference to the covenant. In Adam the entire race of man was given; and in Christ also, as in the second Adam, the entire body of believers as the new-born humanity are contained. Our Lord employs the figure of a tree when He says: "I am the true vine, and my Father is the husbandman. Every branch in me that beareth not fruit, He taketh it away: and every branch that beareth fruit, He cleanseth it, that it may bear more fruit" (John 15:1, 2). Furthermore our Lord continues in loving admonition: "If a man abide not in me, he is cast forth as a branch, and is withered: and they gather them and cast them into the fire, and they are burned" (John 15:6). Now since our Lord explicitly declares that the Father removes the unfruitful branches, it seems evident that no man dare presumptuously arrogate unto himself the work — no more than to know the times and seasons which the Father hath set within his own authority (cf. Acts 1:7). On the other hand, the knowledge that "they are not all Israel that are of Israel," should beget in the hearts of educators increased zeal to seek for the fruits of righteousness among the children of the covenant. For as such and none other must he receive them by faith in the covenant God.

* * *

What then are the means, and what is the nature of discipline in the Christian school? Let us call to mind once more that discipline is "especially the training of the *mental, moral,* and *physical* powers by *instruction* and *exercise,* and by *authoritative control* and *direction.*"

The book of Proverbs which does mention the rod, indeed, devotes more attention to the training of the mind by instruction. And rightly so, of course, since instruction is indeed the *chief* as well as the *first* agency employed in discipline. Our Fall into sin in Paradise was prompted by the anti-theistic self-assertion of our human, carnal wisdom in opposition to God's absolute wisdom and authority. Our sinful pride challenged God's absolute wisdom to a duel with finite human reason: man crossed swords with the Almighty on the super-abundant confidence in his own understanding.

And now, says Dr. A. Kuyper: "And as his fall, so also must be his *restoration*. Redemption must come from *without,* act upon our *consciousness,* and bear the form of *knowledge*. To affect and win us in our personality we must be touched in the very spot where sin first wounded us, *viz.,* in our proud and haughty self-consciousness. And since our consciousness mirrors itself in a world of thought — thoughts expressed in words so intimately connected as to form, as it were, but *one word* — therefore it was of the highest necessity that a new, divine world of thought should speak to our consciousness in a *word,* i.e., in a Scripture. And this is the work of Holy Scripture."(*The Work of the Holy Spirit,* p. 61).

The Christian school instructs and through its instruction *disciplines* in the *first* place the mind of the children of the covenant so that, in the words of Paul, they may learn to "cast(*ing*) down imaginations, and every high thing that is exalted against the knowledge of God, and to bring(*ing*) every thought into captivity to the obedience of Christ" (II Cor. 10:5) thus acquiring the correct mental focus which will enable them "to live in all righteousness, under our only Teacher, King and High Priest, Jesus Christ." The discipline of the mind is of the first importance.

The study of the Bible as the revelation of God's wisdom for the correction of man's perverted near-sightedness is the core of all instruction, and controls the presentation of all other subject matter, giving significance, tone, and color to the child's spiritual, mental, and physical environment. It is the light upon the pathway of his life, a lamp before his feet. For the child of the covenant it is vastly more important that his spiritual vision be rectified in as thorough a manner as the school may possibly accomplish than that his head should be crammed with all manner of facts which have not been related properly by the light of divine revelation. To see in history the battle between the Seed of the woman, and the seed of the serpent, between the Church of Christ and the kingdoms of the earth, disciplines the mind "by authoritative control and direction" in a more fruitful way for its genuine spiritual growth than the accumulation of numerous facts and dates. On the other hand the truths of revelation should as much as possible be directly related to the contents of the course of study.

In the child's immediate environment: home, school, playground, and street, he finds a natural sphere for the practice of the demands which his spiritual enlightenment imposes. Implicit obedience to the will of God and self-denial in his dealings with others are undeniable claims which confront the child at every turn of the road. And right here we meet the struggle which no child of God escapes, and which ends only with death. The moral powers of the child, residing in the will must be trained to respond accurately, and ever more promptly to the known will of God. This is the battlefield of spirit and flesh. Discipline, in the popular and narrower sense, in the form of admonition, rebuke, coercion, and correction — if needs be with the rod — must stand by the spirit when the flesh is weak. The discipline of the Christian school must insist that the pupils bring forth fruits of repentance and faith.

The Christian school, functioning in behalf of the parents has the sacred task to "stand by" the daily conversion of the child. Instruction, admonition, rebuke, and correction: all work together such that the child learn to see his rebellion as a loathsome, horrible leprosy so that he will more and more detest himself, as, gradually, the true picture of his sin-defiled nature looms before his awakened and horror-struck consciousness in all its repulsiveness. Progress in the development of the new life runs a very individualistic course in accord with the personality of each child, for the Lord, our Redeemer, respects and restores his own work as Creator. The school, for that reason, must shun all schemes of discipline which in the name of justice, so called, advocate a uniformity in corrective measures which fails to recognize the great variety of soul structure in different personalities.

There are, *e.g.,* children who show in their daily life a studied effort to walk in the ways of the Lord. They eagerly welcome suggestions for improvement in conduct and study; and from all appearances they seem to conform from inner constraint to whatever comes to them as the expression of the will of the Lord. For such instruction is all the discipline they need, with, perhaps, an occasional reminder.

But there are also other types of character. Who does not know those children that outwardly conform to the Christian life and even excel in the punctillious discharge of routine duties, who even are always ready to perform some special task, *always* as long as these good works get them the praise or procure them a little reward from the teacher. They seem to possess an almost uncanny faculty to insure observation of their unflagging devotion, and they know how to collect their rewards. When, however, these little formalists think that their "goods works" pass by unnoticed they stumble; and they find it well-nigh impossible to forgive and forget real or fancied insults. For them it is hard to find grounds for loathing and humbling themselves. They are of the primly smug, self-satisfied type. Here the educator is called to the delicate task of unmasking the child to itself, of making it understand that the Lord desires mercy more than sacrifice. This type needs what the missionaries call *personal work* on the part of the teacher; and this personal work must serve to bring home to the child the discipline of the Word of God as presented in Bible lessons and other teachings in the classroom.

If you want to compare this type to the elder son in the parable of the Prodigal Son, his contra-type, the younger, reveals itself in the happy-go-lucky extrovert nature which looks upon life as a rather interesting round of pleasant games and outings, agreeably seasoned to his particular taste with here and there a few pranks and some larks. He is not at all necessarily hard to go around with, a good sport often, and he enjoys generally a large popularity among his fellows. School he looks upon as an opportunity to have a good time. As long as he lands a passing mark, honestly, or sometimes, otherwise, he is not concerned much about school. He is a regular hedonist in the bud. For him, too, private talks emphasizing lesson material which brings the message that we are not our own but the Lord's, that we are bought at a price, and must with our lives serve the Master and our fellow-men, are in order.

Now, it would be so convenient if every child presented a clear-cut character of standard type! We might then consult a sort of *vademecum* containing an alphabetical list of "symptoms" with a corresponding list of remedies, prescribing the proper doses for the various classified constitutions. But the Lord has not made any two exactly alike, and the ingredients of character have often been so heterogeniously mixed that many personalities defy classification. And yet, most individuals possess some leading characteristic, and it is the teacher's business to discover this predominant trait. For he must, in the interest of a well-rounded, full-orbed life guard against a one-sided development on the one hand, and on the other he must seek to bring out in the fullest possible measure the strength that lies in that dominant characteristic.

* * *

We have already referred to corporal punishment as the extreme discipline for the stubborn child. We must touch upon this measure a trifle more fully, in the first place to consider the fact that a predominant, anti-theistic, and therefore anti-biblical philosophy of education has succeeded in "protecting" the child by legislative enactment against the rod in the hands of the teacher. In the second place there is the undeniable fact that against the temperamental weakness of some hot-tempered teachers, children *do* need protection; not only — perhaps not even in the first place — because of the unmeasured severity which inflicts excessive physical suffering, but chiefly on account of the tragic possibility that such temperamental outbursts of uncontrolled passion defeat the very aim of the administered correction. To forestall such a possibility, Dr. J. Waterink recommends the application of two safety devices which appear altogether reasonable and also reasonably effective. In the first place, he lays down the rule that no teacher should be allowed to administer corporal punishment without permission from the principal, and, secondly, he holds that corporal punishment should be administered only after class hours.

As to the "protection" of the child by our humanistic legislation we accept the Word of the Master that it is even "profitable for us (thee) that one of our (thy) members should perish, and not our (thy) whole body be cast into hell" (Matt. 5:39). We perceive in that so-called "protection" the inverted emphasis of the sinful mind that rates secondary things higher than things of first importance. The anti-theist who refuses to acknowledge the authority of an absolute God may indeed not have recourse to the rod. If man is good — only imperfect as yet, you know — why, then no kind of punishment whatever is justified, and surely such a degrading, insulting castigation with the rod must be branded as a brutal outrage upon the dignity of the child-man. With people of scriptural principles things appear different, as observed from the text just quoted and from several other statements of Scripture. Dr. J. Waterink urges that schools which, as parental institutions, are free should make efforts to have corporal punishment re-instated. Some parents insist that the school has no right to inflict corporal punishment and since the law sustains them in their opinion, teachers who feel in duty bound to apply the rod to children of such parents expose themselves to the liability of unpleasant litigation. This ought not so to be. When the school, as suggested above, takes proper measures to safeguard the children against temperamental abuses, then there should not be any question as to the need of heeding Solomon's dictum: "He that spareth his rod hateth his son; but he that loveth him chasteneth him betimes" (Prov. 13:24). May I here call attention to this word "betimes"? Experience proves that the school has very little if any occasion to make use of the rod for children whose parents loved them so truly that obedience had been "betimes" instilled into them. Similarly, I must in this connection observe that parents who allow their children "to get wind of it" that father and mother will not allow teacher "to lay hands on them" are by that much making sure that an occasion for such action on the part of the teacher will soon, and frequently, arise. It seems that both Scripture and experience prove the occasional need of the rod.

When for a moment we consider the nature of discipline in the Christian school, parents surely will readily be convinced that to banish the rod from the schoolroom is to oppose human arrogance against divine wisdom, and therefore shows to the child not love, but hatred. For the nature of discipline in the Christian school is the same as that of the Christian home, not to "get even" with him, or to "take him down a peg or two," but to bring him back to the way of Christ where he departed from it. The relationship of teacher and children is regulated by the Word of God, which has been concisely expressed: "That I show all honor, love and fidelity, to my father and mother, and all in authority over me, and submit myself to their good instruction and correction, with due obedience; and also patiently bear with their weaknesses and infirmities, since it pleases God to govern me by their hand." So does the apostle Paul ordain submission of our children to their teachers, when in that familiar passage, Romans 13:1, he says with reference to the source of all authority: "there is no power but of God: and the powers that be are ordained of God."

This being the case our teachers function as servants of Christ, and must know themselves responsible to Him. Functioning then as servants of the Lord Jesus Christ, the teacher in the Christian school will never forget that Christ bore the punishment for the guilt of our sins and for the sins of these His little ones, that for this reason pedagogical discipline in distinction from judicial retribution must always proceed from love and aim to correct, that it is therefore in the nature of chastisement. Moreover it follows that the teacher as he exercises this authority must never forget that this authority is not inherently his; it is the Lord's. Let him beware lest he substitute personal notions and ideas for the will of God. Moses and Aaron did this when they struck the rock instead of speaking to it as they were commanded to do.

Especially should educators at all times be aware of the fact that discipline is a *positive*, a *liberating* power the purpose of which is *not* to keep the child *down* or *to break* him, but to *lift* him *up* or to *heal* him; for that reason discipline may be called upon *to repress only* in order *to set free*, to train children in the exercise of the *freedom* of the children of God. Hence, when our children grow older there should be a progressive relaxation of exterior discipline on the part of the teacher that the child may have opportunity to practice self control from that inner restraint and constraint which is the fruit of the Spirit registering increase in the knowledge and in the sanctification of the Lord.

How far one may go in the matter of these exercises in moral training cannot be ascertained without a thorough understanding of each particular class, of each individual child.   The ubiquitous school problem of excusing children to leave the room readily lends itself for a practical exercise for the whole class.   In the primary grades pupils naturally must ask for permission to do so.   When children have reached the fifth or sixth grade, it may be expected that they have caught some inspiration in the fight against indwelling sin from the appeal carried to their hearts by daily instruction and admonition.   This appeal the consecrated teacher will tactfully present to the mind of the children. Need it be pointed out, especially in this respect that the example of the teacher himself is needed to clinch the appeal brought by the written and the spoken word?   The desire for service which the children often manifest may at the proper psychological moment be capitalized in the interest of their own training by giving them permission to leave the room, when necessary, without asking permission. Much of course depends upon the way in which this exercise in self-control is introduced to the class.   Here you have the one occasion which not only permits but *demands* an appeal to the fighting instinct. The soldiers of the Lord are put in training for service, and while they are trained, they already actually serve.   Prepared in such fashion, the exercise will teach the class that Christian service begins at home with the conquest of self.   Sin is the enemy, and this enemy attacks us from within.   To yield to sin is weakness, it is suffering defeat.   What if defeat comes to some of them?   Shall the privilege be taken from the class?   Never — unless the whole class needs this severe measure of discipline.   If you must deprive some of the privilege, let it be for a time only.   Never rob them of the support their weakness gains from the constancy of the others.   Make sure that the whole class and each member individually is convinced in his heart that to sin is to suffer defeat, is weakness.   That true principle rooted in the hearts of the children is the most valuable ingredient in the composition of that indefinable, but most potent influence of the classroom which we call *atmosphere* or *class spirit*.   When you have succeeded to create such a class spirit you have done much to promote that loathing and humbling of self on the part of the children which is the first step toward conversion.

* * *

So "laboring that Christ may be formed in these little ones" (Gal. 4:19), the teacher must possess boundless patience.   This he may obtain, if he does not naturally possess that inestimable and essential qualification of an educator.   In the school of Christ no diplomas are awarded upon earth; one is never "through."   And the better we have learned and continue to learn our own weaknesses, the more able we will be to assist Christ's little ones in their slips and stumbles. The deeper the drafts which the teacher quaffs at the fountain of God's forgiving grace, the better he will be able to lead these little ones toward the same source of comfort and strength. Besides patience a teacher must possess firmness. Patience must not deteriorate into indulgence. The goal must always be kept in view, and that goal is *absolute* and *implicit obedience*. Complete submission in joyfully rendered obedience is not alone the only correct attitude for sinful and finite man; but upon the intensity of this attitude depends also the degree of intimacy, of fellowship with God, to which he may attain. For it is our sins that hide His face from us. Paraphrasing by the substitution of just one word, we may with reference to Christian discipline, appropriate the famous utterance of Daniel Webster: "Obedience and liberty, now and forever, one and inseparable!"

The more clearly we teachers see our high calling as co-workers with God, the more earnestly will we seek our pupils with *chastisement;* and we will seek them with a love which, in wrath, remembers mercy. Modern pedagogy vociferously proclaims in cant phrases the idea that teachers and parents must serve the child; but the glib authors have not even begun to understand the value and the nature of that service to the child which prompts the educator to seek it early with chastisement. Christ, the only Teacher of children and teachers both, washed the feet of the apostles that they and we might learn the true meaning of authority in the Kingdom of God. The Son of man, who came not to be ministered unto but to minister and to give his life a ransom for many, instructs also the teachers of his little ones that the proud and harsh authority of gentile masters does not obtain within his kingdom; but that "whosoever would become great among you shall be your minister; and whosoever would be first among you shall be servant of all" (Mark 10:42-45). When there is warfare between the spirit and the flesh in the heart of the child, it is the teacher's duty to succor the new creature born of the Spirit, and he can only do this as he remembers that to serve the child, he must serve none but Christ. To be a co-worker with the Lord he must be acutely conscious that human sympathies and humanistic theories of education are contraband in the Christian school; for the philosophy of education that underlies the discipline of this institution which is a recruiting camp of soldiers of the Cross is not a man-made product, but is a heavenly gift communicated to us — and exemplified for us — by Him whose meat and drink it was to do the will of his Father that sent him, and to accomplish his work. This philosophy of education may then once again be summed up in the words of Van Til: "Education is implication into God's interpretation."

* * *

Who is able to do these things? The best of us will most often be depressed with an almost crushing sense of his utter inability to do aught of himself as it should be done. But he will also experience that the Lord's strength is fulfilled in our weakness and that Christ also died in atonement for his sins as an educator. This will enable him to continue in the glorious conviction that in this respect, too, "we are more than conquerors through him that loved us" (Rom. 8:37). And thus he will be all the more able to comfort the little sinners in their moments of depression with the comfort wherewith he himself has been comforted. Together, teacher and pupils will, in Christian love and fellowship, make progress on the way of sanctification in Christ.

Where thus the Christian school seeks in love to train its pupils unto the obedience of Christ, should Christian parents then thwart this work by raising humanistic objections to corporal punishment? Would they not be found to sustain the rebellious carnal mind in the struggle between sin and grace in the hearts of these little ones?

There remains yet one question. Christian discipline, we have pointed out, proceeds from the conviction that since Christ bore the punishment for guilt of the children, no punishment may be meted out to them. Yet among those that heartily subscribe to this conviction, different opinions are held with regard to the question whether or not children may ever be punished. To me it appears that Dr. Waterink in agreement with Dr. H. Bavinck has given the proper solution. He reasons briefly as follows: Since Christian citizens must be punished by the government when they transgress the law, say by stealing, so also must the child be punished when it breaks one of the commandments. The government, however, recognizes the exclusive authority of parents over their children, and for that reason does the right of punishing the children devolve upon parents and all others who in the name of these parents are called to assist in the education of the children. The nature and the measure of such punishment visited upon immature and hence not fully responsible subjects is of a type all its own. And even this punishment is subservient to the improvement, the correction of the child, and not exclusively retributive. Nevertheless the idea of punishment must be maintained. In Hebrews 12, the chapter on Christian discipline, the Holy Spirit admonishes the saints "not to grow weary and faint in their souls because of the chastisement of the Lord." This may also sustain children.

A. S. DE JONG
Address before the National Union of
Christian Schools Convention, Hull,
Iowa, August 19, 1931.

Key Thoughts:

1. Discipline rightly understood is perhaps the most distinctive feature of Christian education.

2. Accepting Van Til's definition of education (education is implication into God's interpretation), we see the relationship of discipline to education. Implication into God's interpretation demands obedient acceptance with the heart all that our great and only Teacher explains unto us, that in such attitude of heart and mind we may be built up after the image of Christ in Him, our God and Father.

3. Discipline so interpreted fits in no other philosophy of education. Other philosophies place discipline over against freedom. They say discipline if you must. The Christian philosophy of education says that we find freedom in disciplined life.

4. In the Christian school, discipline is "the training of the mental, moral and physical powers by instruction and exercise and by authoritative control and direction." It looks upon the children as God's children in the organic process of the new race in Christ.

5. The Christian school instructs and through instruction disciplines. Discipline of the mind is of first importance.

6. Study of the Bible as the revelation of God's wisdom for the correction of man is primary and the core of all instruction.

7. The child's immediate environment affords a sphere of practice of the demands of God and implicit obedience to his will.

8. The Christian school, functioning in behalf of the parents, has the sacred task to "stand by" the daily conversion of the child. The Christian school is no "soteriological lifeboat," but it seeks by instruction, admonition, rebuke, and correction to help the child abhor his sinful nature and seek the development of the new life in Christ.

Comment:

Discipline is an integral part of Christian education. It is not merely a momentary means to establish control in order that instruction may proceed without interruption. It is much more than that. Instruction directs itself to the understanding of a child. Discipline is directed to his will-function. When instruction integrates understanding with the feeling and the willing of a child in keeping with the needs of child life, it disciplines him in his total person.

To accomplish this integration a teacher must understand the needs of child life on a given level of development, know how to activate these needs for self-activity in the learning process toward true ends felt by the child as worth-while. This discipline activates a child in his love capacity with a minimum amount of developing hostility or estrangement.

Discipline may require stern and firm measures. But it will not be interpreted in child life as hostility and threat when the child is understood in his needs. Among these needs will be that of chastising unto righteousness of a sinful heart. But he must experience this as a child, not in adult fashion. Adult experience thrust upon him he will reject as a threat to his whole person.

Positive, constructive discipline supports a child in the battle of life as he learns to accept life in the "new obedience."

16

Discipline in the Christian School

Mr. Jones, a junior high school teacher at School X enters his nine-thirty class in mathematics. He picks up a group of papers which he had looked over previously. He is about to return them to the pupils. With mixed feelings, the pupils rivet their eyes upon him with considerable anticipation.

"Well, I marked your papers. I want to tell you that this is positively the worst class I ever had. I have seen many stupid mistakes made, but you beat them all." In disgust, Mr. Jones throws the papers back on the desk, and continues, "The trouble with you is you don't listen to me in class and you don't study the problems. You don't take time to read a problem. Most of you just seem to take a guess at the answer."

Mr. Jones walks to the front board to work a problem for them on the board. As he turns, someone blows his nose violently. Others giggle. And more blowing of noses follows. A regular epidemic breaks loose. Jones turns suddenly, and asks, "Who started that?" No reply, but suppressed laughter is in evidence. "All right," continues Jones, "if you think this so funny, we'll finish this after school. I'll return your papers then. Everybody return to this room at three-thirty, and we'll see how funny this is. Now take out your books, turn to page sixty and work the first five problems. No loitering. At work at once."

Have you ever witnessed a situation like this or nearly so when you went to school? Do such things still occur? In Christian schools too? This description may be somewhat exaggerated, but such practices are still found in schools today.

We are going to visit another type of classroom. Miss Townsend's fifth grade has been working on a transportation project. They have been tracing the history and recent development of transportation. Their study is about to be concluded. As we walk in, the children are very busy. One is completing a railroad bridge on a large mural posted on the wall. Another is putting the finishing touches on a cornfield in the distance on the mural. Three children are putting covers on a booklet they prepared together. And so we might continue. Miss Townsend is checking on last-minute completing activities.

When everyone is about ready, Miss Townsend walks to the front and taps on the desk lightly. Everyone responds by turning to her for an expected announcement. "We seem to have completed our project," she begins. "Will you all take your own seats now so that we can talk about what we have done."

Promptly and orderly, all pupils find their seats. Miss Townsend continues, "Now that we have all worked so hard to complete our project, what remains to be done?" Several raise their hands. "Yes, Jack, will you tell us."

"We should see whether we all did a good job," answers Jack.

"You have a good idea. How shall we find out?" asks Miss Townsend.

Many suggestions follow, from which she finally culls this thought. "We know what we set out to do. Have we accomplished our purpose? If so, we did well. If not, we were not very successful."

A few moments of appraisal follow. On the whole, everyone agrees that what they set out to do has been achieved, namely, understand how people travelled long ago, how they improved travel and shipping, and how it is done today.

"It seems to me," Miss Townsend concludes, "we all did a good job. Let's give everybody a good hand." Applause follows.

Did you ever see a classroom like this? Do you prefer it to the other? Is this the kind of discipline you advocate? "The fundamental reason why children do not act right is because they do not have the conditions for right action." So said Francis W. Parker, educational reformer of the nineteenth century. Create right conditions and you will have good children. Was this what Miss Townsend believed too?

What Is Discipline?

You will notice that in the two scenes I briefly pictured to you, teachers are engaged in teaching. Mr. Jones is trying to teach arithmetic. Miss Townsend is likewise engaged in teaching social studies. Well, is this discipline, you ask?

One of the mistakes teachers are apt to make is to think of discipline as something that becomes necessary when class conditions are not favorable to teaching. It is thought to include such things as calling a class to order, reprimanding a pupil, keeping a child after school, and the like. In other words, discipline is thought of as a function in a teacher's task detached from teaching as such. Mr. Jones apparently thought of discipline in these terms. Not Miss Townsend. She realized that teaching includes discipline, that learning and discipline are closely related in the educative process. Does this, in part at least, account for the difference of classroom atmosphere in the two scenes?

Perhaps you are ready to ask now, "Well, then you approve of Miss Townsend's procedure?" And you ask this question with some suspicion, I believe. I know what you are thinking. You are wondering whether I am going to end up in the camp of those known as Progressives. Do not draw conclusions too hastily. Let us see.

The principle I would like to establish at the outset is that discipline is an integral part of the teaching and learning process. For the first supporting evidence of this, I would ask you to turn to the Scripture. First, in Proverbs 22:6, we are told to bring up a child *in the way of his going*. The phrase "in the way of his going" includes both the child-like way and the end or purpose or goal. It is the child-like way that I want you to note. The Scripture recognizes childhood not merely as a prelude to adulthood, but as a necessary stage in developing to maturity. We may speak of God-ordained ways of child development. Child life is one continuous process of development. In the teaching process, the unitary character of this development must be respected. To violate it is to retard and disturb normal progress to maturity.

I want to point you to a second evidence from Scripture. In such passages as Acts 7:22; 22:3; and Titus 2:12, the Greek word *"paideio"* is used. This word includes two main ideas integrally related, instruction and discipline. The implication seems to be that instruction must be disciplinary, and discipline seems to mean directing to the right end. In instruction, we direct ourselves to the thinking of the child; in discipline to the willing. What do we get in these thoughts, then? This, as I see it. We are so to instruct and discipline the child in the child-like way, according to God-ordained ways of child life, that the right end be reached in his total personality.

Recent studies in human development, particularly in the area of motivation, have emphasized the truth of the idea that instruction must be disciplinary, that is, direct the child to the right end, to be effective in the development of the total personality. Unfulfilled needs give rise to tension. Tension creates unrest and imbalance, which in turn cultivates a feeling of insecurity. The unrest gives rise to action aimed at relieving the tension. This is motivation. The person experiencing a state of unrest goes into action to equalize the tensions and balance them. Instruction is directed to the understanding of a child to help him meet his needs rightly and to create awareness of new needs that subsequent motivations may lead to action. The action which ensues is directed to right ends that abiding goals may be realized in the pupil as a person.

Instruction and discipline are essentially two facets of the same process. Precede these two by inspiration, and we have the three-fold function of the teacher in the classroom. They are inspire, instruct, and discipline. This three-fold function of the teacher is better expressed in the Dutch word, *opvoeden,* which means to bring up, or the German word, *Erziehen,* or in the Latin word, *educare.* Our English word, education, has come to mean so many varied things that it no longer conveys the idea.

What is the right end, according to the Scriptures? Obedience that springs from faith (Rom. 1:5). It is the new obedience which is the expression of love of God in Christ and love of our neighbor. To quote a Christian educator from across the Atlantic, "The secret of Christian education is the leading of children to Christ, that they may learn to love in the school of Christ, whereby they find peace notwithstanding the adversities of life."

Discipline is the control of child life motivated by love for Christ's sake. In school, it is an integral part of instructional activity, which meets the needs of child life in the child-like ways of development. Thus Christian discipline becomes what the Christian educator quoted above calls, "the guidance and support that parents (and others designated) practice in seeking the daily conversion of their children, called to perfection and holiness."

The teacher engaged in effective, well-planned teaching is disciplining the child, directing him to the right end for his life. A well-controlled classroom in which the conditions for effective learning are present is primarily the product of well-planned teaching. Discipline is not first of all some antecedent function or supplementary task necessary to make effective teaching possible, but is essentially involved in the total teaching process. Hence, we do not speak of a disciplinarian as a good teacher. He has divorced instruction and discipline. We speak of a good teacher, and to qualify for this designation the teacher constructively controls child life by well-planned instruction.

Mr. Jones is not a good teacher. This is obvious. Is Miss Townsend? This question is not so easily answered. We should explore our study a little further before we try an answer.

Basic Specifications for Christian Discipline in School

I shall mention five though one might carry the analysis further.

First, discipline to be positive and constructive must follow from a well-planned instructional program. A well-planned instructional program in Christian education has purpose in keeping with the Christian commitment. There is also concerted effort at a growing realization of this purpose, in the consciousness of the child. The learning process is laid out in keeping with this purpose. Knowledges and skills to be mastered are selected with reference to this purpose. Responsibility for mastery and good workmanship are engendered. The plan includes a conclusion involving appraisal, summary and needed repetition. Every such plan is an integral part of a long-range plan aimed at the maturity of pupil personality.

A second specification. Child nature and needs in a given stage of development must be understood, and a child must be accepted by the teacher in a given stage of development. A child can be motivated to effective learning only when he is accepted in his given stage of development, understood, and inspired. The God-ordained ways of child development are to be honored and skillfully employed to stimulate pupil self-activity in keeping with the learning activity in hand.

In the third place, a high degree of cooperation and participation by the pupil, in planning the learning activity, is essential. As an immature learner, the child becomes aware of a need or needs by actively participating in planning a learning activity, not by the teacher's prefixing the value that can accrue to the learner. Only as he has a growing awareness of needs does motivation function.

Note, too, in the fourth place, that acceptance in the peer group becomes increasingly stronger as the child matures. A child will feel more secure in the learning process when group opinion supports the activity. Hence, the teacher must seek group consciousness for the learning process in which he wants the children to engage.

Finally, the pupil must be encouraged to work independently of constant teacher approval and disapproval. He must come to appraise his weaknesses, attack them independently and seek to emulate his own record. A spirit of self-confidence supported by group acceptance tends to maturity.

Such are the specifications for the administering of Christian discipline.

Now, can Miss Townsend qualify? On many counts she can. She has apparently an over-all plan. She enlists pupil participation according to her understanding of child life. She aims at independence in a group consciousness. But . . . there are essentially two basic errors.

The first grows out of her perspective. There is occasion in this unit to view transportation in relation to the work of Christ's gospel among men and a development of standards of our use of transportation in keeping with the Christian life. The only reference is social and economic. Discipline is viewed as social and economic acceptance, not as obedience to God's will for our life.

And the second error is a common one today. A well-planned instructional program includes thorough mastery of knowledges and skills. We cannot obediently serve God with partial efficiency. God requires our full effort according to the level of our development. Modern education frowns on optimum efficiency and encourages social proficiency. Respect for child nature and needs in modern education follows from an optimistic view of man. Improve the environment and we shall improve man, it is thought. No account is taken of the inner resistance of a distorted soul-life because of a sinful heart.

Yes, Miss Townsend's teaching operates in the wrong perspective and with an optimistic view of man based on human autonomy. Her assumption is fallacious, and no matter on how many other counts her teaching is admirable, her work cannot accomplish true education.

Other Specifications

The discussion of discipline may not stop here as every teacher soon recognizes. The teaching process is not completely determined by the teacher's professional competence in directing a learning activity. There are conditions which do not fall in the area of the basic specifications as such that can upset the best laid plan. Let me mention only two to make clear my point.

Unconsciously, as well as consciously, a teacher's emotional life may reflect inner tension. Children, especially younger ones, are very sensitive to a teacher's emotional expression, in voice for example. What ordinarily does not phase the teacher may prove very irritating. It will take special effort to accept a child under these conditions. When a teacher finds himself ready to snap at a child, he should pause for self-examination.

Another example may be taken from the vicissitudes of child life itself. The energies of childhood, its tensions and conflicts too, seek expression, and frequently in channels very unacceptable to their adult superiors. They feel restrained and hemmed-in, often with resentment, and do not understand. There will be wandering minds in the classroom, talkative mouths, noisy feet, etc. There will even arise critical moments of distraction.

These conditions call for another kind of discipline, one that is more direct, and apparently less related to the teaching process. We may call it *preventive discipline*. The teacher "rides" her eyes over the class and through the pupils, as it were, to alert herself to every possibility. "Teacher just seems to see everything," is Jackie's way of putting it to his mother. During the discussion a group becomes very disturbing. The teacher pauses, looks at them with some firmness, anticipating immediate cessation of the interruption so that "we may go on" as she expresses it. Stopping the little things may prevent major breaches of good order. A teacher who knows how to apply the "tricks of the trade" wisely has time to look into the causes of the disturbance later to avoid more serious outbreaks.

But this preventive discipline must be Christian too. To accomplish the desired results in the daily conversion of children, this discipline must be motivated by love as well as all other work of the teacher. A firmness of the teacher which springs from a heart filled with love for the child for Christ's sake will be tempered with the kindness that wins children rather than repel them. It will give them the security they so unconsciously desire as they seek to maintain themselves among their peers.

There is still another form of discipline which must be administered at times. We call it punishment. Perhaps we should think of it as *remedial discipline*. For by means of it, we seek to correct a child's conduct after the wrong has been committed. In more serious types of misbehavior, too, the child should come to accept responsibility for his conduct. In school, too, his conduct involves the order of right and wrong. Here is where Christian education makes a vital difference. In more serious offenses the child must come to recognize that he has violated the divine order. Wrong conduct is an affront to the sovereignty of God and may not remain unpunished. God has ordained authority for this purpose.

But discipline dealing with major offenses must seek to correct that which went wrong. Hence, the person involved must be understood in his needs (Read Eph. 6:4). There is no simple formula for the teacher's procedure. Every case must be dealt with on its own merit and demerit, for it is the person we seek to reach, not merely the behaving organism.

Shall we use prayer and the admonition of the Scripture? Never should they be used to make the child feel that they are a means in the teacher's hand to threaten him. They are to be used remedially to undergird the child in his confession and penitence. A Christian teacher prays for his pupils. But he also prays with them, and often with a single pupil when he has been brought to a receptive mood for prayer. The Word of God can be used in the life of the immature child to help him realize his dependence upon God. Threats only raise barriers of self-defense in the soul-life of the immature.

We conclude that discipline in the Christian school is an integral phase of education. The teacher is to inspire, instruct and discipline the child according to the stage of his development. The God-ordained ways of child life in a world where both the child and the world are corrupted by sin, and the goal God holds before us, namely, holiness and perfection, constitute our criteria. The Christian teacher seeks to understand the child in this Christian perspective. He thus proceeds clinically, but knows the "tricks of the trade" and is capable of administering them that minor offenses may be avoided or checked in their inception to forestall major offenses or give him time to study them.

In the Christian school, discipline is first of all distinctive in its motivation. Control is administered in child life from a heart filled with the love of Christ. And they are the lambs of the flock entrusted to the Christian teacher's care, lambs whom he disciplines. But Christian discipline is distinctive too in its ministry to the person of the child. It seeks to reach the heart of the child as the dynamic of his personal life. Though the Christian parent and the Christian teacher know they must begin with external obedience in bringing up a child, they realize too that only obedience fully internalized, that is accepted by the person, is genuine obedience. We as Christian teachers work toward personal acceptance of and commitment to the truth. Only Christian discipline is aimed at personal commitment.

Cornelius Jaarsma

Address before Eastern Christian
Teachers Institute, Boston,
Massachusetts, October, 1952.

Key Thoughts:

1. Constructive discipline in the classroom is the result of well-planned teaching motivated by love.

2. Effective planning requires the understanding of the medium of instruction (subject matter and related activities), the nature and needs of child life, and how to activate these needs in the consciousness of a child in the medium of instruction.

3. The specifications for administering Christian discipline, positive and constructive, declare both knowledge-getting and personality development wanting as objectives in Christian education.

4. Every teacher must resort to less desirable forms of discipline at times, the forms we may call preventive and remedial. They are very necessary inasmuch as neither teacher nor pupils have attained or will attain unto perfection and holiness in this life. The Lord

chastises his children. Teachers too must chastise children in their classrooms. But even these forms of discipline must be administered in love from the heart for Christ's sake. That love may not be immediately in evidence, but will break through before long to give the child the feeling of security rather than feeling rejected in his person.

17

The Great Office of the Teacher in Preparing the Child for the Complete Life

What is the complete life or the "full-orbed life" for which the child must be prepared? To put it briefly: A complete and well-balanced life is a life that enters into and responds normally to all the relationships for which human life is designed by its Creator. It is a life that makes efficient contact on all sides with its many-sided environment. And when we say efficient contact, we mean two things that are involved in efficiency, which are perfectly correlated.

Efficient contact with my environment means a contact by which all the elements of my environment (each one according to its nature) are properly appreciated and absorbed by me, so that I make them contribute to the full extent of their possibilities to the satisfaction, the growth and expansion of my life.

In the second place efficient contact implies that, on the other hand, I am fully aware of my own value, of the worth of my own personality and equipment, and that to the fullest extent the significance of my life finds expression in that environment.

A complete life, therefore, is made possible only by efficient contact, a realization of the relation in which the world stands to me and I to the world. It is both absorbative and contributive. It is a relation in which I make the world in which I live count to the full in my life, and conversely, in which I make my life and energies contribute to the fullest extent.

As has already been said, these two elements are reciprocal. It is not possible to attain the highest satisfaction of which I am capable except as through the pathway of achievement I enter into the awareness of the value of my own life and personality in the lives of those about me. On the other hand, I can serve effectively only as I learn to enrich my own life through the channels of life's manifold contacts. I can contribute only as I absorb and as my appreciations become more expansive, more deep and more vivid.

Bringing this two-fold truth to a focus we find that a genuine interest in the treasure-trove of our environment is reached only as we are sincerely interested in exploiting this wealth as a means of service. The fundamental relationship in which human life moves is a fourfold one. Naming them in ascending order we find that a complete life includes everything that is demanded by the relationship in which man stands to the world round about him, to his fellow man at his side, to the world of life that stirs within him, and to the God who stands above him. None of these factors can be ignored. Life is complete only as it responds to each one of these relationships in the full and constant diastole and systole of receiving all that these relationships offer, and sending all forth again into the manifold channels of constructive endeavor. This is the fulness into which God would lead every man and it is the complete life for which each generation as it arises is to be prepared.

With all these facts in mind, we ask the question: What is the peculiar task of the school and of the teacher with respect to the child? How should the teacher function as an agent to lead the children committed to his care into a life that is fully developed and equipped, and that is truly restored to a right relation to God and God's world?

Before attempting to present a few thoughts in answer to this question, it is well to remind ourselves at this point that the teacher does occupy a unique place, but that he is by no means the only agent in the development of the mind and life of the child. And when all the forces that mold and shape the mind and character of the child are taken together, it cannot even be said that the teacher wields the most decisive influence. The most unique, most intimate and most significant contact, as we all understand, is that between the child and his parents. Growing up day by day from the complete helplessness and dependence of babyhood, it emerges from unconsciousness to consciousness, to its first lisping prattling and faltering steps, to all the interests and activities of early childhood under the influence of parental love and care and guidance that are focused upon it every hour of its existence. And even after the child enters the school this home-life remains a continual and paramount factor in the development of the child. It is in the atmosphere of the home that the child's mind begins its first unfolding, that a definite trend is given to his outlook upon the world around him, and that the foundation of character is laid deeply in his soul. It has been well said, "The child looks out upon the world from the threshold of its home." This is so true that any attempt to reform education or to advance its cause which does not include the home must of necessity prove to be a dismal failure.

It is quite necessary to keep this fact in mind. It will prevent the mistaken assumption on the part of many of the teaching profession that everything depends upon the child's work and activities in connection with the school. Certainly, the teacher should have a profound sense of the essential importance of the school work and the school life. But, if we are not mistaken there is today a marked tendency so completely to monopolize the interests and time of the child that little opporunity is left for the home or even the church to contribute their legitimate share to his education and training.

We know that there is today a theory of education and of the educational control that entirely dismisses the home. Russia offers an extreme example. But the same spirit has been rife for many years, and has been noticeable even in many Christian schools. I fancy that I know the reply that will be given to this statement. "There is so much work to be done! Such a tremendous field must be covered to meet the demand created by modern conditions. Time is so short. The curriculum is so crowded that all the time in school and much of the time outside of school-hours must be utilized in order to get through with it all." We do not pretend to be able to solve this problem, we merely point to the fact that it is there and that it does call for a solution that shall do justice to the proper claim of the home and church as well as of the school.

We may also remark in passing that there is another sphere of influence which profoundly effects the development of the child-mind and child character. This is found in the field of voluntary association which he soon learns to make for himself. It is in this play-world which he occupies with his companions that his primary interests find full expression, that his social instincts are rapidly developed and undergo profound readjustment, and that his personality emerges with increasing capacity for self-evolution. In fact, in early adolescence when the "gang spirit" has him in its grip; the contagion of the group spirit sways him more surely than any other power; and how his boon-companions rate him moves him more deeply than all the smiles or frowns of parents or teachers or preachers. A teacher that takes stock of his own position and of his own share in the molding of child life will also take the influence of this life of voluntary association into due consideration.

All this, however, does not mean that we seek to minimize the place of the school and the importance of the teacher. The very opposite is true. We can come to a real sense of the value of the teaching and training given in the school only when we recognize all the influences under which the child is growing up, and then take note of the special place which the school occupies in the midst of them. The function of the school and of the teacher in the development of the child can be understood and appreciated only as we recognize the unique place which it occupies among all the other agencies.

What is this unique place? In the home the relationship is one that is largely personal. It is intense, but it moves within narrow confines. The home is a little world within the world. But the school represents the interest which society at large has in the child. It is the peculiar agency to open up for the child-mind the wide field of interest and opportunities offered by the life of the social group as a whole. Its function is particularly to initiate the child into the heritage of knowledge, of ideals, and of incentives operative in the wide field of world-life that is beckoning him, and on the other hand by training, by discipline, and by the awakening of new enthusiasms to prepare him to take his full share of that world and to contribute his full share to it. The point which we seek to make is that the school stands at the gateway where the footpath of the home widens out into the broad avenue of the life and activity of the wide, wide world.

Preparation for life in its broadest aspects the home can rarely give. Not merely because parents are seldom able to teach their children those branches of knowledge which have become essential because of modern conditions; but, as we have said, the home represents a sphere of intensely personal and markedly restricted interest. To the parents the child is their child upon which under God they lay their claim. To the school the child is a world-child upon which under God it places its stamp of ownership. We are presupposing here the Christian home and the Christian school.

In this school with its great and hallowed task, it will be readily admitted, the teacher is the paramount factor. The teacher is not all of the school, but he is the center of it, the moving genius in it. What the school is, what it stands for, what it means to the child and will continue to mean to the young life that has been nurtured in it, depends almost entirely upon the man or woman under whose guidance the child makes his way from day to day. It is the teacher who stands as mediator between the child and the world that awaits him. And his mediatorial position lies in this, that he represents both. It is sanctified in this, that his heart goes out to both. And that is the reason that he is pre-eminently qualified to bring them together in fruitful union.

What are the requirements of a teacher that he may thus perform his holy office to do his share in the unfolding of the child and in preparing it for a complete and significant life? This is our most pertinent question. In answering this question we point to three elements that are of necessity implied in the position and work of a real teacher. The first is *authority*. The second is a vital *interest* in the child. The third is a genuine *enthusiasm* for the ideals of life for which the child is being prepared. Let us say a word about each.

The teacher stands in a position of authority, not because he has received this authority from the parents, but because he has received it from God. He stands under authority, he is answerable before authority, and therefore he has authority. That is true of the parents in their position. It is true of the teacher in his position. This does not mean that parents and teachers have nothing to do with each other or are not to consult with each other. Both are dealing with the child who is in the first place a child of the home. And therefore the parents have the right and the duty to elect or erect such schools and to appoint such teachers as will give assurance that their children will be educated and trained for their life in the world in accordance with the faith and convictions that obtain in the home. But it does mean that the teacher is not a servant of the home; and that, when he teaches and trains and disciplines the child, he does so not primarily because the parents want it done, but because he sees in it a sacred task to which God has called him.

This conception of authority is essential if it is to be a real and fruitful element in the development of the child. Never can the child be prepared for any real leadership in any phase of life unless first of all he has learned to obey and to have reverence for the laws of God that govern the world in every sphere in which man is called to live and to labor.

We venture to say that the idea, fostered by man, that the authority of the teacher is delegated authority derived from the parents has not infrequently done much to work havoc with the discipline of our Christian schools and in many cases has wrought great harm to the pupils. In the home parental authority will be ineffective unless the child is taught to feel that parents have received this power from God and learns to obey in the name of God. The same is true of the school. Teacher and pupil both must feel that they stand before God, the one as divinely appointed to rule, the other to obey.

This does not mean, however, that the teacher is to parade his authority as right to command, to exact obedience and to correct. The less this authority has to be dragged out into the open, the more successful he will be as a teacher. Standing alone and naked this authority is a ghost that walks and haunts the schoolroom as a hateful presence. It will effectually frustrate the purpose of all real authority. Some of the pupils will be cowed, others will fawn and again others devise devious means to heal the wounds of injured personality by revolt. But none will be moved by a sense of genuine respect and glad obedience.

This authority is certainly not to be relinquished or neglected. Neither is it to be masked as something that is a necessary evil. But it must be made vital by being incorporated in the teacher's ability for real leadership.

The first requisite for this coveted leadership is undoubtedly that the teacher is thoroughly equipped for his task. That he is thoroughly a teacher, that he has a deep professional interest in his work. When we say "professional" we do not mean the cold, unemotional and impersonal attitude which is a connotation often associated with the term. We mean exactly the opposite. Genuine professional interest means the warm and whole hearted enthusiasm with which the teacher engages in his work, engendered by the fact that he is thoroughly at home in the things that he teaches, that he carries with him the sense of the supreme worthwhileness of his task, so that he would rather do that than anything else in the world.

This professional attitude presupposes that the teacher is master of his subject and is master of the art of teaching it. But it also requires that the teacher is diligently and perpetually studying to gather new ideas. The teacher himself must grow, if he would see his pupils grow in wisdom and grace under his hands. He must bring to his class the contagion of fresh enthusiasm that is born of newly discovered truths and ideals, if he would inculcate into his pupils a reverence and love for the subject which he teaches.

You have probably heard the story of the Scotchman who prayed for his preacher. The preacher was long and rambling in his prayers, as he was in his sermons. In his prayer that was getting nowhere in particular, the preacher constantly reiterated the petition, "Lord, give me power; Lord, give me power today." The old Scotch deacon in the front pew had another petition however. He said, "No, Lord, give him ideas!" A preacher without ideas which make for a fresh and convincing presentation will survive longer on old, shop-worn and threadbare material than a teacher in a similar plight. The preacher is exposed to his audience only two hours or less in a week. The teacher faces his class five hours every day. And more than that, the teacher's audience is much more merciless and much less burdened with conventions than the preacher's. School children discover very quickly, much more quickly than we are prone to think, when a teacher is not master of his subject, when he is not prepared to teach it, when he is proceeding with uncertainty in his own mind, or when he is making a stab at it and using his position in the class to bluff his way through. And when they do discover it, all his opportunity for real leadership is gone.

A thorough education, a wide grasp of the subject which he is teaching, and a knowledge of the art of teaching it effectively are the first requisites for real leadership. Authority must be vitalized by ability and sincere interest, if the minds and the hearts of the children are to be reached and to be inspired with respect for the teacher and a love for the subject which he teaches.

May I be permitted to remark here that I believe that it is the bane of many schools, that a large number of teachers have no genuine professional interest in their work. Many, especially of the lady teachers, look upon the school as a means of being employed in a genteel fashion during the years between graduation and marriage. They have no intention of making teaching their career if they can help it. Hence they come to their task as skimpily prepared as the law will permit, they do not delve for themselves any further than the class work immediately requires, and they do not carry with them any great enthusiasm for their work. They may get by, but they certainly will never set the minds of their class on fire. The same may be said of many young men who use the school as a stepping stone for something which they consider better. The interests of the school are rarely served by teachers of this class. Whatever of financial considerations may lead school boards to engage teachers who are after all but transients, the fact remains that the great importance of the work, the vast equipment required, the fund of experience that must be gained through the years, and the real leadership that must be given — without which the children are defrauded of the most essential part of their education — all call for men and women who are truly professional teachers and who bring the best that is in them to this great task.

In the second place, if the teacher is to guide the pupil upon the way to a complete and efficient life, he must understand the pupil and have a genuine interest in him. This means more than a study of child psychology and pedagogy. One may learn to read notes and to use proper fingering on the piano, but he will never be more than a mechanical player unless in his soul there is a true appreciation and love for music. In the same way the laws that govern the mind, its development, and various activities may be studied, but if there is no real interest in the child as such, there will never be a real insight into the operations of his mind and heart.

To the teacher it should be the grandest thing in the world to be permitted to teach children and to help them on the way to a fuller equipment for life. "My fingers fairly itch for a knife, when I see a surgical case," a prominent surgeon once said to me. So it is also true that the urge is present in the soul of every real teacher to use his tools, his equipment, and all the powers that he possesses upon the child in the classroom before him. It is his greatest delight to impart knowledge, and he experiences the keen joy of a master workman when he is utilizing the laws that are operative in the child's soul and when he sets in operation all the means at his command to see the child life expand, its knowledge grow, and its character develop under his skillful hands.

When a teacher is truly a professional teacher and his heart is sincerely absorbed in his work, he will also have profound interest in the child itself. He will not look upon the child merely as a piece of raw material in the laboratory, but as a human being and as a child of God with marvelous capacities and wonderful possibilities in life. When this genuine personal interest in his pupils is felt and exhibited by a teacher, the gateway to the heart of the child us unbarred, and the way for true and fruitful leadership is open. Let us not deceive ourselves on this point. Let us not think that the child will ever commit his heart to us unless we first give ourselves to him. "Honor thy father and mother," is the injunction with which God comes to children in the fifth commandment. But obedience to this commandment is made possible only when parents themselves honor their children as a precious heritage from God and see in their children the real possibilities of life and joy and usefulness which God has bestowed upon them.

This is also true with respect to the relation between teachers and pupils. Going back into my own childhood days, I see one of my teachers who truly came to me as a godsend in the midst of my many perplexities as an immigrant boy in a strange land. Other teachers had consistently treated me as a rather difficult and unpleasant case with which they were obliged to deal, and consequently they left little more than a spirit of indifference if not of rebellion in my heart. It was not until a couple of years after entering into this country, when being placed in the seventh grade, that I found a teacher who seemed truly to understand me and who clearly showed a personal interest in me. In the very first week she had won my heart, and that teacher from that moment on could do anything with me that she wanted. I would have jumped out of the window for her or gone through a fire, and I would have followed her to the ends of the earth. I cannot at this moment recollect one single individual that has done more to impress me with the worthwhileness and the beauty of the real ideals of life. Honor the child; honor God's laws operative in him; honor God's purpose, and behold even in the most ragged youngster the eternal possibilities that lie enwrapped in his soul, and only in this way will God honor us and deem us fit and worthy to lead that child in the green pastures and to open for him the way to the fuller life.

Let the teacher ever keep this truth before him, that if he is to be God's instrument to lead the child into the fullness of life, he himself must possess that life and must have entered in through the gate. His own heart must beat with love and enthusiasm for life's great ideals.

It is especially at this point that the Christian teacher will remember that the process of preparation for the full life is a twofold process. It is a process of growth, from the immature to the mature. A host of problems ranges itself around this fact, problems of which every teacher is keenly aware. The fundamental problem that arises out of this situation is this, that the teacher is dealing with the immature and growing soul, that he must observe at every step the laws that are at the present moment operative in the child mind, and yet, that at the same time all the work of the teacher has in view the equipment of that child for its task in the world as a mature man. The problem of co-ordinating harmoniously in education the immature state of the child and the mature life for which preparation must be made is indeed one of the major problems of education.

But in the second place, and this should never be forgotten, the process of preparation for the full life is one not only of development, of growth from the immature to the mature, but also one of restoration from the abnormal to the normal. In other words, the Christian teacher is cognizant of this great fact, that the power that must lead the child to a life that is truly life, that is a full and significant life, is accomplished, not in the first place by the operation of natural laws, nor by the efforts of the teacher, but by the saving grace and power of God. Without that saving power all education is but the loading of a doomed and sinking ship.

What position does the teacher occupy with respect to the child in the light of this great fact, that it is not only an immature being who must grow and develop, but that it is also a sinful human being who needs a change of heart, who must be restored and be drawn back to God if he is even to catch a glimpse of the life that is truly complete and fruitful? Should the teacher feel that his task is only a partial one? Should he take the attitude that he can serve the child only with respect to its natural development and equipment but that he must leave this restoring process that must take place in the child's life to God? Assuredly not. Also here the teacher in his peculiar place is appointed as an agent of God to labor for this greatest need of the child.

It is his task under God's authority, strengthened by God's power and dealing with God's laws, to work for the development of the child's native powers. But it is equally true that in his peculiar position he has received a task from God to lead the child into contact with the forces of God's restoring grace as these stand revealed in his Word and as they are operative in the world. Right here lies the very peak of his high office, and it is this that gives the Christian teacher his character as Christian teacher. It will of course be readily felt that in order to be God's instrument here the new life must surge through his own soul; he himself must have been brought under its spell and control, and the Kingdom life must be the life that fills his horizon and that supplies his soul with a warm and abiding enthusiasm for God's great ideals in the lives of men.

Standing upon this soil of the new birth and the new life, the Christian teacher realizes deeply that it is not enough to lead the child to the feet of the world's great men. The consummate courage of a Washington, the high idealism of a Lincoln, all the wonderful visions of poets and the marvelous achievements of the men of science will not suffice to touch the deep wells of the child's soul or to draw him toward the way of life unless he is first of all led to the foot of the cross of the Redeemer of men.

And so it is the task of the Christian teacher to lead the child to a vision of the healing that is found under the wings of God. It is his privilege to show from God's Word how God's grace is manifest in all his works with which he stoops down to the children of men, to point to a world steeped in sin and at the same time to the footsteps of redeeming grace that fill the earth and sea and sky. Upon every blessing with which God comes to us is placed the stamp of the Cross that hallows it and makes it a treasure beyond price. Through every event runs the plan of God so that we meet Him every step of the way. In every task lies expressed the purpose of God, so that all of life and all of man's energies are to be brought in glad and proud bondage to God's great redeeming work, which He is constantly carrying on through the ages in every sphere of human endeavor and through every channel of the renewed and surrendered lives of his children.

There lies the peak of the full-orbed life. To bring the children committed to his care in contact with that fullness is the task, the most glorious task, of the teacher. He is appointed to be the captain of the young life, to lead it to that mountain-top. Captain, because humbly and gladly he himself follows the great Captain of his faith. Teacher, because he himself is a hungering pupil at the feet of the Master. And standing upon this holy ground, he takes the sandals from his feet, and stands amazed that God deems him worthy for so glorious a task. And there he prays, "Lord, if I may be permitted to make my life count in the lives of these little ones, to lead them to a vision of that Kingdom of Thine, to influence them to choose for a life for Christ in the midst of the world, and to equip them so that they may carry on thy great work when we are departed hence, Lord, then my life will have been worth living, its fruits will be worth a hundred fold all that it has cost in labor and in sacrifice, and then Lord, let thy servant depart in peace, for my work will be done."

G. W. HYLKEMA

Address before the National Union of
Christian Schools Convention, Hull,
Iowa, August, 1931.

Key Thoughts:

1. The complete life is the well-balanced life that enters into and responds normally to all relationships for which human life is designed by the Creator.

2. The teacher is to function as an agent to lead the child into the complete life.

3. In distinction from the home and the church, the school represents the interest of society to orient the child into the world-life that is beckoning him.

4. The teacher is clothed with authority not delegated by the parents to the teacher, but received from God.

5. The teacher must have a deep professional interest in his work.

6. To guide a child in the complete life the teacher must understand child life and have a genuine interest in children. Only as the teacher gives himself to the child can the child commit his heart to the teacher.

7. To lead a child to the fullness of life, the teacher as agent of God must possess that life himself.

Comment:

When the principle of unity, set forth in various places in this book, is implemented in the instructional program of the Christian school, the complete life or life-abundant enters into the understanding of the child. It is the function of the teacher to guide the child into the complete life. This is achieved when in the communication of the spirit of the teacher and the spirit of the child both experience inner security. When teacher and child are a threat to one another, intellectual mastery may still be attained in the life of the child, but wisdom or heart commitment or the complete life is not attained.

18

The Teacher and Vitalized Teaching

All vitalized teaching stands or falls with the ability and aptitude, the diligence and devotion of the teacher. This statement has become famous because attention has been called to it time and again. Therefore we wish to re-emphasize it and then especially bring to the fore that this diligence and devotion must spring forth from a love for youth and a delighting in their very nature resembling the joy of parents in beholding their dear children. The teacher must take real delight in his class if he would create an atmosphere of buoyancy and cheerfulness, a mutual attitude of trust and sympathy that makes schoolwork a delight (this is possible!) for pupil and teacher and makes the orderly classroom a perfectly natural phenomenon. Way back in the early centuries of the Christian era, Augustine said that the chief concern of the teacher is not the organization of subject matter, not the method of teaching, but to take delight in teaching. All other desirable qualities of the teacher follow naturally from a keen sense of duty, tact, and patience.

To avoid misunderstanding, something must be added: a teacher must love his pupils, exercise sympathy in his relation with them — but he must do so intelligently! *He* must remain the leader; he must give them his confidence without fraternizing and losing a certain distance between himself and his pupils. Hence, if necessary, the rod should be used! But all such punishment is a last resort and is used for the welfare of all concerned, never a reprisal or a means of establishing prestige. To refer again to Augustine, "Only he is competent to execute punishment who has mastered in love the anger aroused in the one offended." Practice demonstrates, however, that where a natural, constructive control prevails, the more severe modes of punishment are rarely necessary. Pupils do make mistakes, but they soon recognize their own error.

H. Vander Zweep, G. Wielenga and J. W. Hulst
Guide for a Course of Study
for the Christian Schools, pp. 5-6.

Comment:

Vitalized teaching is possible only when the teacher feels thoroughly at home in the classroom. A teacher may be ever so competent a student and even well-integrated and balanced in his total personality, but lacking the joy that comes from the love of youth, he cannot inspire. But love must be intelligent to generate confidence in the hearts of youth. The competence referred to cannot be missing.

19

Choice of Technique in Teaching

Though keen observation and accurate experiment in psychology have disclosed many significant facts concerning the functions of the soul-life of the child in memory, observation, thinking, etc., we are not ready to apply these to education without further qualification. They constitute valuable elements that we can use in teaching, but essentially they are no more than valuable technical tools. Technical equipment, adequate instruments, good tools, and the like, are indispensable, but they are no more than means to be used for ends previously determined. All depends on the proper choice and effective use of the tools. With the best of means one can do much damage, and if plan, design, and draft are not sound, the best apparatus will not help us. It is especially this that we observe in modern education.

One can note a sharp contradiction in the new education when he takes note of what it does with the proposition that the child is not a small adult. On the one hand it seeks to apply this truth, psychologically established, and holds in its methodology rigidly to it, that the child in every period of his development must be viewed as a unity with his own world of experience. In contrast with this practice, on the other hand, we see that as a result of a false world-view all child psychology is set aside and the child is assigned a task properly belonging to the adult. This is demonstrated visibly in experimental schools in many lands guided by this false world-view. The imitation of the parliamentary system in the school community together with a "liberal discipline" is contrary to the very nature of the child, not to speak of the delusion cherished that a school organization of this kind prepares children more adequately for their task in society. The best results of research in psychology will not reform education if their application is accompanied by so much nonsense.

The child needs a leader and — the child desires to be led. Because of the denial of this truth, the child is allowed too much independence in the accomplishment of his task, as if he possesses the insight and ability for systematic organization of the adult. Let the teacher remain in the background, it is said. Only when the child can no longer proceed must he inject himself. In the meantime much valuable time has been wasted.

The "old school" demonstrated the very opposite picture. Its methodology was based on a false psychology and set the young heads to work on mental gymnastics far beyond their years. But for the rest the child remained a child in the discipline and in the assigned task of the teacher. The "old school" would have nothing to do with a playing around with self-discipline.

Which is better? This question has been widely discussed. We must not choose for the old system, afflicted with obvious error, nor for the new, which reminds one often more of destruction than instruction.

One is reminded of the drunkard mentioned by Goethe who slid off his donkey on one side. Because he could not remain hanging in this dangerous position, he was lifted to an upright position, only to slide down on the other side. The "new" school is more disappointing to date than the "old." It cannot boast of glowing results. It cannot serve as model for the common school.

A common earmark is the one-sidedness of educational practice. Contrasts are created that do not exist in fact. So much is made of activity that receptivity is forgotten; so much agitation is made against the mechanization of instruction that all drill is discarded; so much is made of the self-activity of the child, that a systematic explanation by the teacher is too often set aside. In this way the totality idea (the whole child) is poorly applied. One-sidedness leads to excess, and both unite to send the school in the wrong direction.

Christian educational practice must avoid these errors. It must not be a one-sided product. One-sidedness and excess can be avoided when we approach the child not only experimentally and observe the child according to our natural insight, but when we earnestly search out and in faith accept what God says about the child in his Word.

P. LANKAMP AND L. VANDER ZWEEP
*General Introduction to a Course of Study
for the Christian Schools*, pp. 89-91.

Key Thoughts:

1. The many significant facts about the soul-life of the child which psychology has brought out must be interpreted in the light of the more basic truth of child life.

2. Failure to do this has led much of modern education into a classroom practice contrary to child nature. For example, failing to

give the child the firm discipline he needs for inner security as a child.

3. The "old school" ignored the facts of child nature as a child. The "new school" gives these very facts the wrong setting.

4. Let Christian education avoid one-sidedness and find a solid basis in what God says about the child in His Word.

Comment:

Our dissatisfaction with the "modern school" and its superficial character should not create a reactionary spirit in us to return to the "old school." There are Christian schools which have taken very little account of what psychology has disclosed to us about child life. But there are also classrooms in Christian schools where the "new" has been uncritically absorbed.

We need a thorough study of Christian education based on what God's Word says about child life, one that takes account of what, also by God's grace, is disclosed in recent studies of children and learning.

20

The Social Trend in Education

The forming of the individual to the full development of all human values and thereby to qualify him for service in the community is desired. To accomplish this, instruction in school is to be individualized more than before and, at the same time, socialized to a greater degree in a system whereby spontaneous interest and spontaneous activity receive their just due. We regard this of no little value and acknowledge gladly that the contemporary graded school manifests a weakness on this account. Through the community life among children in the school, we must cultivate a consciousness of social responsibility, as is done in the home. As in the home, so in the school every assertion and restraint, every act must produce a sense of community life in the child. We can profit greatly from the social-psychological views of the social educators of our time.

We must note this caution: we have a duty in the reform of our graded school system to test every move by the standards of a Christian sociology. And then we must place in the foreground what Dr. D. H. Th. Vollenhoven has expressed: "A human being is not an individual, but an individual member of the one human race. And even this relationship is subordinated to the relationship of the human race to God." Only according to the distinction and in the relationship as here expressed by a biblical philosophy can we find the synthesis of the life of the person and of the community. In their unity according to the ordinance of God's creation, distinguished but never separated, they must serve to the eternal glory of God. Christian educators are impressed here with their sacred task.

Also in the social life our chief concern is to have the glory of our Lord manifested in His image. He, in His sovereign wisdom, entrusts one with five, and one with three, and still another with one talent. Divine election is also manifest in this case. If there is one thing that appeals to us in the current trend, then it is this, that on the basis of these differences among men instruction is individualized to a greater degree and our graded system must be revised accordingly. Greater justice must be done to the individual, it is thought. We gladly agree to this trend, if the difference of endowment among individuals is viewed in the light of God-given talents. Because they are God-given, man must put them to use. It is the task of education in the school to cooperate in guiding the child that in the self-realization of his God-given talents he may develop his personality qualities to the glory of God. To lead our society into right channels, we, as Calvinists, must hold without fail to this basic truth.

Social education does not merely consist of introducing a new system whereby children are permitted to help one another and carry out a task jointly, in contrast with the old graded school where mutual help was forbidden and considered a misdemeanor. Purposely, we permit the extremes to be heard here. In the social education of this kind we could assent to the reform presented by Dewey and other social educators.

The basic law for individual and social life God has laid down for us in the decalog, of which Christ gave us the following summary: "Thou shalt love the Lord thy God with thy whole heart, thy whole soul, and thy whole mind. This is the greatest and foremost commandment. And the second similar to it: Thou shalt love thy neighbor as much as thy self. The whole of the law and the prophets is summed up in these commandments" (Matt. 27:37-40).

The Lord, your God, you are to love. This is the greatest and foremost commandment: fellowship with God in Christ. Your neighbor you are to love: the fellowship of the human society.

How shall we give the child this religious, and at the same time, social instruction? We shall teach him these principles according to his ways. But to do this, we teachers must know "his ways": child psychology.

We believe we are in line with Holy Scriptures when we say that religious education includes the social and also that in this connection the demand is made that we correspond to what is of the child, to the opportunity his way affords, that is, his age, his comprehension, his feeling capacity. And when we lead the child according to this way in the active cultivation of his God-given talents and potentialities for the service of God and of the community, we are emphasizing that this must be done in keeping with God's demands with his whole heart, with his whole soul, with his whole mind, and with all his strength. Here we have the application of the idea of totality, of the whole person in education.

P. LANKAMP AND L. VANDER ZWEEP
*General Introduction to a Course of Study
for the Christian Schools*, pp. 91-94.

Key Thoughts:

1. The Christian school calls for more individualized instruction
   while at the same time developing greater community consciousness.

2. On the one hand we recognize that every child is endowed by God
   with a measure of personal capacity. This must be discovered and
   developed for greater glory to God.

3. On the other hand the person is always a unity in the larger whole,
   the race. His community obligation is not exhausted in living together. He must love his neighbor, that is, give himself wholly
   and freely.

4. The principle of unity or totality calls for the individual and the
   social to be developed in the person for effective service.

Comment:

In Christian education we have still to learn what it means to
make the summary of the law effective for the learning process.
Neither the knowledge-getting school nor the personality development school is capable of it. We shall have to give the nature of
child life greater consideration in setting up curricula and in
guiding the learning of children.

21

Philosophy and Educational Trends

Varying religious convictions and philosophical opinions with reference to the meaning of the world and life, and in relation to these more particularly the origin, nature, and destiny of man, have given rise to an educational spectrum with the color rays here and there running into one another, but in which the main colors can be clearly distinguished. Modern, Roman Catholic, and Reformed outlooks upon life cast varying light upon educational theory and practice. In spite of these differences, schools of thought in education manifest similarity of trends, chiefly because education is influenced not only by philosophical thinking but also by forces originating in social life.

There is first of all an agreement in negation. Slowly, but with certainty, a concensus has taken root in all educational thinking with reference to the intellectualism that dominated educational theory and practice for years. It ended in bitter disappointment. It provided stones for bread and must be reformed in keeping with current psychology and sociology.

Paralleling this disillusionment is the growing conviction that we need an educational theory and practice, on the one hand more socially oriented, and on the other hand doing greater justice to the individual. The educational reform demanded today is saying that education must do greater justice to both the personal and the social and that these two are not to be placed in opposition to one another but must constitute one organic, harmonious unity. Many social educators are striving for a synthetic community ideal by which the welfare of the whole community is sought in the cultural development and enrichment of the individual accompanied by the development of a strong social consciousness.

Individualism arose as a reaction to the depersonalizing of men by modern industry. The compulsion of the machine, which enslaved the masses, gave rise to a counter-urge to seek social fulfilment. Individualism sounds forth the call to freedom. It demands that every man cultivate the potentialities of his personal life through the cultural product.

431

The complexity of modern life has led to greater dependence of the individual as a member in the social whole. He has meaning only as an "instrument of labor" that has been stricken with impotence by being severed from social ties and made meaningless. The educational consequence of this fact is the demand that we educate for a consciousness of solidarity and a sense of calling, in which the Christian view of life gives priority to the calling that comes to us from God relative to our place in society, state, and industry.

The faith that God is our Father in Christ and that He leads us by His providence is the true ground for our sense of calling. In it originates the true inspiration, on the one hand to improve working conditions, and on the other hand to test daily by prayerful trust in God the adequacy of our task. It hardly needs saying that this Christian-social creed is held by comparatively few. Social education and personality development have originated in contemporary cultural and social milieu, but they are variously interpreted according to the world view to which one is committed.

P. Lankamp and L. Vander Zweep
General Introduction to a Course of Study for the Christian Schools, pp. 35-37.

Key Thoughts:

1. The intellectualism of the nineteenth century school has given us stones for bread. Its knowledge-getting ideal left the heart cold and uncommitted. It divided rather than bound together what belongs together.

2. Individualism arises from a depersonalization in modern industry. Social educators seek a synthetic answer to extreme individualism and depersonalization.

3. Christian education turns to the call of God upon one's life to give priority to service.

Comment:

The Christian school of our time needs a fresh approach to the educational problem. We are not going to make the school Christian by more of this and more of that, by greater mastery of this or that. While optimum achievement by a child is basic for Christian education, it is one of several considerations. Even more fundamental is the nature of child life in its development to maturity. When this is ignored, education cannot be Christian. God has ordained ways of child development. These we must understand and be guided by them.

Modern education has observed the ways of child life on the basis of the natural man, immanentistically, without the light of God's Word. Christian education seeks to understand the goal, the child, and the medium in the light of what God says about all three.

SECTION FOUR

CONCLUSION

1

Antitheses in Education

The principles by which believers live are squarely opposed to the principles by which unbelievers live. This is true in the field of education as well as in the church. Accordingly we speak of antitheses in education. These antitheses cover the whole educational field. They cover first the field of educational philosophy. This is of basic significance, but is often overlooked. In the second place these antitheses appear in the field of what is to be taught, i.e., the curriculum. Finally these antitheses appear when we consider the child or the young person to be instructed. Under these three aspects we shall try to bring out the antitheses in educational philosophy.

Non-Christians believe that the Universe has created God. They have a finite god. Christians believe that God has created the universe. They have a finite universe. Non-Christians therefore are not concerned with bringing the child face to face with God. They want to bring the child face to face with the Universe. Non-Christian education is *Godless* education. What is of most importance to us in education, which is absolutely indispensible to us, is left out entirely.

Godless education ignores or denies that man was created responsible to God. This implies that sin is not a transgression of God's law. Hence Christ did not need to die in our stead. Godless or non-theistic education is therefore also non- or anti-Christian education. Godless, non-Christian education naturally becomes humanistic, i.e., man-centered. If man does not need to live for God he may live for himself. If then we want a God-centered and truly Christian education we will have to break away completely from the educational philosophy that surrounds us.

Non-Christians believe that man is surrounded by an absolutely unknowable Universe. Man is grasping in the dark, except for the little light that his own mind is radiating as a headlight in the midst of the mist. Christians believe that originally man lived in the light of the revelation of God and that in Christ as the fact-revelation and in Scripture as the word-revelation, man is in principle restored to that true light of God.

Accordingly non-Christian education dashes then this way and then that under the delusion that it has pierced the darkness, or it stops altogether in utter despair. Often non-Christian educators do away with the idea of a definite aim or purpose in education altogether. They talk of "functional adjustment" to environment. But if man does not know the road and drives in the mist why should he "step on the gas"? As Christians we *know* the purpose of education. We also *know what* should be the content of education. Finally we *know* that a definitely Christian method is to be used in the instruction of a definitely Christian content.

Non-Christians believe that in so far as man knows anything, he knows apart from God. Man's mind is not an electric bulb that needs a current if it is to show any light but it is rather an oil lamp that carries its own supplies. Christians believe that everything is dark unless the current of God's revelation be turned on. We cannot even see any "facts" without this light. Non-Christian teachers will accordingly sometimes think they really have and know the "facts" and can teach the child all about them, and then again when they see that the "facts" are really in the dark they will give up in utter despair. Christian teachers know that not a single "fact" can really be known and therefore really be taught unless placed under the light of the revelation of God. Even the laws of arithmetic cannot be known otherwise.

We need to become more conscious of these basic distinctions. Unless we are conscious of them we shall never have genuinely Christian schools. To be conscious of these distinctions does *not* mean that we must spend much more time on the direct teaching of religion than on teaching other matters. If we teach religion *indirectly,* everywhere and always we may need less time to teach religion *directly.* To be conscious of these distinctions *does* mean that the plan of curriculum is to be God-centered. Man exists for God. But in the created universe other things exist for man. Hence in this sense the curriculum must be man-centered. Only thus can it become God-centered.

Non-Christians believe that the personality of the child can develop best if it is not placed face to face with God. Christians believe that the child's personality cannot develop at all unless it is placed face to face with God. Non-Christian education puts the child in a vacuum. In this vacuum the child is expected to grow. The result is that the child dies. Christian education alone really nurtures personality because it alone gives the child air and food.

Non-Christians believe that authority hurts the growth of the child. Christians believe that without authority a child cannot live at all. Non-Christians do speak of the authority of the "expert" but that is not really authority. Christians want authority that is based upon the idea of God as man's creator and of Christ as man's redeemer.

Thus we see that the antithesis touches every phase of education. To try to enforce the idea of the antithesis at one point and to ignore it at others is to waste your energy and your money. We cannot afford this.

I. The Antithesis in Educational Philosophy

The whole Christian church is based upon the antithesis idea. But, if anything, it is still more pointedly true of Christian instruction in particular than of Christianity in general that it is based upon the idea of the antithesis. Oh, yes, I know there are voices heard on every side that we must not always emphasize the negative and the destructive but that we must emphasize rather the positive and the constructive. We are told that such is far wiser in the end. Now we all wish to be positive and constructive. But in this world of sin no Christian individual and no Christian organization can be positive and constructive till *after* they have been negative and destructive. To deny or to ignore this fact is to deny or to ignore the fact of sin. For anyone who recognizes the fact of sin in its unadulterated Biblical connotation of insult to God on the part of man under the leadership of the devil, antithesis is in the nature of the case basic to synthesis. He that seeks to bring good tidings and to publish peace, he that calls upon Judah to perform her feasts and pay her vows, is a false prophet unless he offers as a reason for his optimism the assurance that the "wicked one will no more pass through because he is utterly cut off."

Non-Christian Idea of God

In seeking to bring out something of the antitheses in education we wish first of all to stress the fact that there is really only one antithesis. It is fully in order to speak of antitheses if only we remain conscious of the fact that all the differences in educational theory are reducible to that of the question of a personal God.

Every education program seeks to bring the growing personality that is to be educated into the best possible relation to its environment. But such a term as environment is in itself perfectly colorless. And so if we should say that education is "adjustment of the growing personality to its environment" such a definition would be quite without significance unless one would specify what one means by the environment to which the growing personality is to be adjusted. And when it comes to the question of the meaning of the term environment it will be seen at once that the Christian-theistic and the non-theistic theories of reality stand diametrically opposed to one another. The former affirms while the latter denies that the environment to which human personality is to be adjusted is ultimately personal.

It is true that there are plenty of non-theistic theories of reality which speak of superhuman personality or personalities. But this does not make their views *ultimately personalistic*. No theory of reality can properly be called "personalistic" unless it thinks of God as an absolute personality. It is quite possible and quite common to speak of a personal God and yet not to think of him as absolute. Such a monotheism is not theism in the proper sense of the term any more than an outspoken polytheism is. It is clear that if the god or gods to whom the child is to be adjusted must themselves be adjusted to a Fate or a Universe or a Reality that is beyond or independent of them, that in that case we may just as well look beyond such intermediaries and say that the child must be adjusted to this Fate or Universe or Reality or whatever else we may choose to call that which we think of as most ultimate.

Now it seems to me to be incontrovertible that the educational philosophy of today presupposes an ultimately impersonal and therewith antitheistic environment to which the child is to be adjusted. If one searches the pages of modern speculative thought one may find here and there statements about belief in absolute truth and in absolute verities, and these may then be identified with the term "God" so that men may even speak of God as absolute, but when men speak thus they speak metaphorically. The "God" of modern philosophy is at most an impersonation of certain ideals that men have set for themselves and of which they are ultimately themselves the judges. Accordingly a metaphorical God is for all practical purposes a finite God.

It is to this Universe, this Reality then that according to current educational philosophy the child must be adjusted, and it is this adjustment that constitutes his education. It follows that we have not grasped the depth of the educational antitheses until we have traced them back to this absolutely determinative antithesis of an ultimately personal and an ultimately impersonal surrounding. And no more basic difference is thinkable. The whole of the educational program built upon an impersonal background must be diametrically opposed to an educational program built upon a personal foundation. We shall seek to bring out something of this below. Suffice it for the moment to call attention to the fact that for better or worse every Christian educator should come to grips with this point. And anyone who comes to grips with it at all will sense the impossibility of thinking of Christian education as being ninety or sixty or thirty or ten percent like other education, the only difference being that Christian education adds certain elements or emphasizes certain elements that secular education neglects. When viewed from this absolute standpoint Christian education is not even a fraction of one percent like public education. The different conceptions of God that underlie the two educational theories cover every point on the whole front and cover them before and behind, without and within.

At this point I may interject that when I thus emphasize the absolute antithesis I am not denying or even for a moment forgetting the doctrine of common grace. That doctrine does not militate against but here as elsewhere confirms the doctrine of the absolute antithesis. Common grace does not overlook ultimate differences. Nor does it when correctly understood, in any way tone down those ultimate differences. On the contrary, common grace helps to point out that things which look alike are not ultimately alike. Common grace points specifically to the fact that similarities between the people of God and the people of this world are but proximate similarities and that these proximate similarities play before the background of ultimate differences. If people do not believe in common grace or do not know what it means, they are likely to raise proximate similarities to ultimate similarities or to raise proximate differences to ultimate differences with the result that the absolute differences are toned down. It is this which has often taken place in non-Reformed churches. There it has been thought that religion is a condiment that may be added to the otherwise neutral territories of life. Because they knew not the doctrine of common grace they took it for granted that no ultimate difference could be hidden behind the statement of a Christian that two times two are four and a statement of a non-Christian that two times two are four.

Now the fact that two times two are four does not mean the same thing to you as a believer and to someone else as an unbeliever. When you think of two times two as four you connect this fact with numerical law. And when you connect this fact with numerical law you must connect numerical law with all law. The question you face then is whether law exists in its own right or is an expression of the will and nature of God. Thus the fact that two times two are four enables you to implicate yourself more deeply into the nature and will of God. On the other hand when an unbeliever says that two times two are four he will also be led to connect this fact with the whole idea of law but will regard this law as independent of God. Thus the fact that two times two are four enables him to get farther away from God. That fact will place the unbeliever before a whole sea of open possibilities in which he may seek to realize his life away from God. And it is this basic difference between what two times two are four means to the believer and what it means to the unbeliever that the doctrine of common grace has helped us to see. It has enabled us to focus our attention upon the antithesis without fearing that we are doing injustice to any of the facts that surround us.

Let us look then more fully at this antithesis and what it means for education. The first thing we would observe is that if the Universe to which the child is to be adjusted is thought of as impersonal the one supreme result is that there are then no antitheses between the child and the universe. We may say, if we wish, that as Christian-theists we have a life and world view in which the antitheses of life are not overlooked while non-theists have a life and world view in which the antitheses of life are overlooked. For that reason every Christian knows that he cannot begin to build till he has first broken down, while every non-Christian thinks he can begin to build without any necessity of first breaking down.

Godless Education. Perhaps one of the most important points in this connection is to note that on the impersonalistic basis of our opponents there is no forensic relationship between man and his environment. How can anyone stand in a forensic relationship to an impersonal law? You cannot get any notion of what it might possibly mean that you should be legally responsible to law as such. Now the whole structure of Christian ethics or morality presupposes this forensic relationship. Scripture defines sin as a transgression of the law of God. Without the possibility and the actuality of a forensic relationship between God and man, the whole doctrine of sin falls by the board. And if sin falls by the board the only thing that can be done with the evil in this world is to knit it into the constitution of the Universe. Accordingly we find that both ancient and modern philosophy have maintained that negation is as fundamental as affirmation and that the devil is as old as God. Thus all ethical distinctions are reduced to metaphysical distinctions. What ought to be is, and what is ought to be, is not philosophy of certain philosophical schools merely but is the philosophy of all non-regenerate thought. And a consequence of this is that no Christianity is possible. There would be no sin and therefore no sin to remove. And if there were sin to remove there would never be anyone able to remove it since it would be impossible that any one person appearing at any one point in the course of history should occupy the absolutely unique position that Christianity has attributed to Christ.

From these considerations it follows that if any ethics or morality is to be taught in schools that are based upon this impersonalistic philosophy it must be pagan ethics or morality. So too if any religion is to be taught it must be pagan religion. Everything that is truly Christian is in the nature of the case excluded.

In the second place the complete removal of all antitheses between the child and its surroundings appears still more fully in the fact that the impersonal conception of the universe has of necessity led to a complete relativism of all things. The "eternal ideas" of Plato did not for long remain eternal. Plato himself injected temporalism into them when he insisted on the ultimacy of evil. He therewith made the ideal world dependent upon the temporal world. Time became a moving image of eternity. In modern days this motif has been worked out fully till Pragmatism openly avowed an exclusive temporalism while Idealism made time and eternity correlatives with the "Concrete Universal." It could not have done otherwise. The impersonal means nothing if not related to the personal. If the impersonal cannot be related to and derive its meaning from the absolute personality of God it will in the nature of the case be subjected to the personality of man. The evolution theory is only a particular manifestation of this general tendency. It is quite hopeless to fight evolution in the public schools and think that therewith you have gone to the bottom of the trouble. Back of evolution lie relativism and impersonalism.

It will be seen at once that upon such a relativistic basis there can be no antithesis between man and his environment. On such a basis God and man are mutually dependent upon one another. And if you say that this very relativism provides for an infinity of antitheses, it is true in a sense, but in such a case there is no one to settle the antitheses and they are therewith rendered meaningless. Man does not stand higher than God and God does not stand higher than man. Who is to judge the other?

Humanistic Education. Now a Christian will recognize in this process of the history of philosophy the realization of the plans and purposes of Satan. The first thing he did for the human race was to tell Eve that nothing would happen to her if she ignored what she thought were the laws of God. He instilled into her mind the notion that the Universe is neutral, that is, that there are no antitheses in it. The devil told Eve that he was just as old as God. The devil told Eve that there was an impersonal law above both God and himself. He did not openly deny the personality of God. He implicitly denied the absolute personality of God. Satan is not opposed to personalistic philosophies. He can sometimes use them more effectively than outspoken impersonalistic philosophies when he wants to make non-Christians believe that they really are Christians.

Now when the educational curriculum of a school is based upon such a relativistic educational philosophy the child is sure to learn that it really matters not at all what it does. Oh, yes, it does matter as far as getting through this life is concerned. It is still the best policy to be honest. Yet if you are dishonest that too does not matter as long as you can "get away with it." The whole universe is then a place to "get away with" things. "The Lord doeth no good neither doeth He evil." The "Lord" is but a symbolical expression for the impersonal laws of nature.

When Zephaniah the prophet noticed this sort of attitude getting into the lives of those who were Jehovah's covenant people, he preached the antithesis in its highest possible expression. He preached the judgment day as a day of wrath and of tribulation. God's people could not possibly insult their maker and redeemer in any more gruesome fashion than by having anything to do in their educational policies with those who said that God was dead. When God was no longer recognized either in his promises or his threats the climax had been reached of all the devil could possibly desire. To ignore God is to go to perdition without so much as a bump.

God-centered Education. It goes without saying then that our first duty as Christian educators is to face this education without antitheses and take a thoroughly antithetical attitude toward it. Modern educational philosophy gruesomely insults our God and our Christ. How, then, do you expect to build anything positively Christian or theistic upon a foundation which is the negation of Christianity and theism? Here it appears that we must be negative before we can be positive. We must negate the negation of the educational philosophy about us in order that thereafter we may be truly constructive. All your construction and all your synthesis that has failed to negate this negation of modern philosophy is itself negative and destructive. Here lies *the* antithesis in education.

Non-Christian Idea of Mystery

And now to look at the same antithesis from the point of view of knowledge rather than from the point of view of reality we must note that according to modern educational philosophy man is thrown entirely upon his own resources. This is but a natural concomitant of an impersonalist theory of reality. In an impersonal universe God can at the most be given the place of a collaborator with man in the field of knowledge. The void surrounds both God and man. Accordingly man makes himself the standard of truth. Nothing will happen to him if he thinks wrong about the nature of reality. Nothing will happen to him if he does not choose to think about the nature of reality at all. Says D. C. Macintosh, "There is no law human or divine to force man to waste his time on matters on which he feels no real concern; and since the human capacity for interest is limited at best it perhaps is just as well that he should keep to the things to which his special bent inclines him" (*Religious Realism*, p. 5). In Tolstoy's *Anna Karenina*, one of the main characters expresses it as his opinion that the gods will certainly not take it amiss of us if we have made some mistakes about them inasmuch as we have done the best that we could. Now such a way of presentation presupposes that man has never had any contact with God and has never had any information about the truth of reality so that it would be an insult to God to think mistakenly about him and his universe.

And how does man feel now that he has for centuries tried for himself the task of interpreting reality without any reference to God? He has done his best. He has courageously entered the field with the crow-bar of his intellect in order to conquer all mystery or if you will, conquer *the* mystery. When his intellect failed him he tried to descend into the lower levels of his existence in order there to receive some feeling of what it is all about. And when that failed he was driven to the conclusion that reality is *essentially irrational*. That is the prevailing view today. We are told that a surd remains no matter how carefully and exhaustively we may study any particular fact. And as for the notion that men can have knowledge about reality as a whole, it is said to be based upon conceit. The philosopher of today has given up every attempt to understand the meaning of the whole of reality. "Die Ganzheitsbetrachtung, die Meinung, wissen zu können, was das Ganze, geschichlich und gegenwärtig, sei, ist ein Grundirrtum; das Sein dieses Ganzen ist selbst fraglich." (Dr. Karl Jaspers, *Die geistige Situation der Zeit*. p. 22.) And yet the philosopher is also conscious of the fact that all things are related. He knows that unless we know the whole we cannot really know any part of the whole. The question of the one and the many is to him as insoluble as it was to Plato and Aristotle. The whole of reality is in darkness and consequently a surd surrounds every particular fact.

The net result of all this is that modern man feels himself adrift as a derelict on a shoreless sea. He is overwhelmed with a sense of the utter futility of it all. More than that, he feels terrified. He speaks much of *"Lebensangst."* "Angst steigert sich zu dem Bewusstsien, wie ein vorlorener Punkt im leeren Raum zu ver-sinken, da alle menschlichen Beziehungen nur auf Zeit-gelten scheinen." (Jasper, *op.*

cit., p. 56). Man feels that he is somehow significantly related to that ultimate irrational existence about which he has no knowledge and over which he has no control.

Looking at this modern Irrationalism what else can we do but reject it *in toto*? If we give to God his rightful place as absolute selfconscious personality we have the very opposite of Irrationalism. In that case we know that our knowledge is analogical of God's knowledge and therefore true. We live and move and have our being in the revelation of God. And as for Scripture it is then but the means of the reinstatement of man into the original revelational atmosphere in which man was created. We make no apologies for regarding Scripture as the textbook of the philosophy of science. Granted the existence of God and granted the existence of sin the imperative necessity of redemptive revelation follows unless God should fail of his purpose with man. "If ye believe in God believe also in me," said Christ. As theism is the presupposition of Christianity, so Christianity is the implication of theism. We are in no doubt about either. Fear of the void is the controlling motive of the unbeliever's life. Confidence in God is the controlling motive of the believer's life. And you cannot be positive on a basis of fear. You cannot construct into the void, especially when you stand upon the void. Here again we must negate the negation of modern education before we can really be constructive in anything that we do.

Uncertainty and Fear. And if now we turn to the educational picture that surrounds us we find that it corresponds exactly to the educational philosophy that we have been discussing.

In the first place we would note the excited interest in matters educational. The number of books on education is legion. Man throws all his hopes on the education of the next generation. He is conscious of the fact that the present generation is in a hopeless condition. "Ein Zeitalter, das sich selbst nicht vertraut, kümmert sich um Erziehung, als ob hier aus dem Nichts wieder etwas werden könnte." (Jasper, *op. cit.,* p. 94.)

In the second place there is no centrality in the educational policies of the day. How could there be if no one knows what the center of human life is? Instead of following a policy that is based upon a definite assurance that human life must be lived for the sake of God, we find a hasty and nervous series of experimentation into the unknown. One demagogue after another arises to proclaim: Lo here is the Christ and lo there is the Christ. Since man thinks he has no knowledge of reality but at most a glimpse now and then as to what he may accomplish in this world; his educational policies are split up as to purpose, as to content and as to method. Educational theorists are out of breath. They dash after one thing and then after another as dogs do after a ball that is carelessly thrown out. What else then can we do but negate this negation of a center and a goal in education?

As to the purpose of education we are told that it is to teach the growing personality a method of adjustment to the environment in which it may be placed. This purpose is set in opposition to what is said to be the older conception of the purpose of education, namely to give the child a certain informational content. Functional education is substituted for ideational education. But if we look for a minute at this so-called functional theory of education we notice that it cannot possibly function. The reason for this is that nothing will function in the void. It is perfectly selfcontradictory to say that the purpose of education is to teach men adjustment to environment if we nor anybody else can have any notion whatever as to what that environment may really be. There can be no preparation for the void. In trying to prepare for the void modern educational theory has missed all sense of direction.

In contrast with this we can readily see that only the Christian conception of education can really be said to be the functional conception of education. Upon a Christian basis there is assured a conviction as to what the growing personality will meet in the environment with which it will come into contact and functional adjustment can be made accordingly. It becomes evident how absolutely imperative it is for any teacher who becomes enamored of the modern idea of functional education to ask himself whether such an idea of education is consistent with the Christianity that he professes. All too often have Trojan horses come into the Christian camp.

Knowledge and Confidence. The case is similar with respect to the content of Christian education. Here, too, we shall have to be increasingly fearless in letting the controlling concepts of the Christian-theistic life and world view determine what shall be the center of the curriculum. If we constantly keep looking over the fence to see how many hours are spent on this subject and how many hours are spent on that subject, we shall not get very far. If we are always worried about the criticism of our opponents, it is a sign that we have not yet learned the lesson to build alone. Again, this does not at all mean that we cannot learn from our opponents. During the World War the Germans no doubt learned from the Allies and the Allies learned from the Germans. Yet it is equally true that the Germans never failed to use what they learned from the Allies against the Allies and the Allies never failed to use what they learned from the Germans against the Germans. Thus, too, we can afford to take over from our enemies only that which will fit into our own program of constructing a covenant personality. No educational content that cannot be set into a definitely Christian-theistic pattern and be conducive to the development of covenant personality has any right to appear in our schools.

And finally this is also true of educational method. Here, too, the temptation besets us that we should be very keen to watch the methods that are used about us. Now this too is in itself altogether commendable and necessary. It is commendable because every good soldier should know the tactics of the enemy. It is commendable too because perhaps some of the methods used by the enemy may be transformed and used by us. But *transformed* they must always be. We cannot afford to say that if only we place a different content before our pupils we need not worry about the form because the form is a neutral something. If a glass has contained carbolic acid you do not merely pour it out in order then to give your child a drink of water. How much more impossible will it be to take a spiritual content and pour it out of its form in order to use the latter for the pouring out of a definite Christian-theistic content? The connection between form and matter is too much like that of skin and flesh to allow for the easy removal of the one without taking something of the other for us not to be on our guard with respect to the educational methods of our opponents. We can never, strictly speaking, use their methods. We can use methods that appear similar to theirs, but never can we use methods that are the same as theirs.

So, then, our conclusion with respect to the educational philosophies and the educational policies that surround us is that we must be intensively and extensively negative or we can never be intensively and extensively positive in the Christian-theistic sense of the term. The fundamental principle of the antithesis upon which Christianity is built demands nothing less than that. We must more and more dare to be consistently peculiar in our educational policies. If we dare to be peculiar we will be "peculiar" in the eyes of the world, to be sure, but we will not be "peculiar" in the eyes of God. If we are not peculiar, we will be "peculiar" in the eyes of God and be twice "peculiar" in the eyes of the world.

II.   The Antithesis in the Curriculum

And now if you will speculate with me a little I would like to look at some of the features that, it would seem, should always characterize the curriculum of a Christian school. I purposely say that I wish only to look at some of the features that should never be missing. I do not presume to lay down a program.

In order to consider the curriculum in its broad outlines and not to lose ourselves in details, we may say that it deals with nature and history. It deals with "facts" of space and with "facts" of time. It matters not what subject you teach; whether it be mathematics, sewing, cooking or music you are dealing with space-time "facts." I speak of *space-time* "facts" even in preference to "facts" of space and time in order still further to simplify and centralize the question. All "facts" are inextricably interwoven with space and with time. We cannot intelligibly think of "facts" without thinking them in space and time. We may speak of space and time, if we will, as the form of the "facts" if only we recall that form and content too are inseparable. Empty space and empty time are meaningless concepts. We may say then that the curriculum deals with "space-time—facts."

The Non-Christian's Selfsufficiency

One more preliminary point we would make in this connection. A sharp distinction is usually made between "facts" and "laws." It is taken for granted that you have explained the "facts" if you have referred them to the "laws" according to which they work. But this is misleading. Laws are nothing but ways in which "space-time facts" behave. It is therefore more to the point to say that laws are aspects of the "facts" or are themselves a part of the larger "fact" that we are seeking to learn about the "facts." An historical "fact" is perfectly meaningless unless seen in the relation it sustains to all other historical "facts," or in other words unless seen according to the law of its operation. So, then, for our purposes it is better to include the term "law" under the term "fact." The phrase "space-time facts" would then include all the "facts" and all the "laws" in their concrete relationship.

And now with the consideration of these preliminary matters we have also prepared the way for a direct attack upon the problem as to what should be the main feature of any Christian school curriculum. This main feature, it would now appear, is that the whole of "space-time facts" should be set into the pattern of the conception of the absolute personality of God.

We have seen that a "fact" without its relation to space is to us without significance. It is unintelligible. It is a mere abstraction. It is wholly unthinkable. And for these reasons it is *altogether unteachable*. Similarly a "fact" in space without time is a mere abstraction and unteachable. You cannot tell anyone anything about such a thing because it does not mean anything to yourself. And it seems still to be a requirement that he who tries to teach should at least have some remote notion as to what it is all about.

Teaching without reference to God. Now, just in this way the whole of "space-time facts" is to a Christian a mere abstraction, wholly unintelligible and therefore altogether unteachable unless it be seen in its relationship to God as its presupposition. We may express the same idea by saying that no "fact" is seen as it really is unless it is seen in its correct relationship to God. Since God has made the space-time facts their relation to God is naturally the most important thing to know about them. But more than that, it is not really enough to say that the most important thing to know about a "fact" is its relationship to God because that very relationship to God exhausts the meaning of the fact. When you have seen the "space-time facts" in their relationship to God you have for the first time seen the *fact* about the "facts" that is, you have for the first time seen the *facts* in distinction from bare facts. Accordingly, anyone who does not see the space-time facts before the background or in the pattern of the absolute personality of God does not see any facts but only thinks he does. It is not true to say that everybody has the facts to begin with. On the contrary, only a Christian-theist has the facts because there are none but theistic facts. Non-theists deal with "bare facts," that is, with abstractions that have no meaning.

We are purposely bringing the matter to this irreducible level in order to get away from the dangerously misleading confusion that appears perhaps more glaringly in the educational field than anywhere else, namely, that a fact is fact for everybody alike, unbeliever as well as believer. Now this is either a truism or a satanic falsehood. It is a simple truism if we mean that Christianity is either true or it is not true. If it is true, then this truth does as a matter of fact exist for the unbeliever as well as for the believer, and the unbeliever will learn to know the facts when it is too late, as the parable of the rich man and Lazarus teaches us. But it is a satanic falsehood to say that a fact is a fact for everybody alike, if it is taken to mean as it is usually taken to mean that there is a realm of space-time fact that is known to all men alike. The whole point in dispute between a theistic and a non-theistic interpretation of reality is this question, whether "facts" can be facts without being theistic. It follows then that to say that the facts are facts without saying anything further is to give yourself over soul and body to the mercy of your enemy, which likes nothing better than that you should give up the battle before the first blow has been given. As theists our contention is that there are no facts but theistic facts, while the contention of our opponents, expressed or unexpressed, is that facts are facts whether God exists or does not exist. For us to admit this at the outset is a complete admission of defeat and spells utter bankruptcy as well as the uselessness of Christian education.

Teaching with reference to God. What sense is there in spending money for teaching arithmetic in a Christian school rather than in a so-called neutral school unless you are basically convinced that no space-time fact can be talked about and taught unless seen in its relationship to God? When speaking thus of the absolute antithesis that underlies the educational policies of our schools, it is not too much to say that if any subject could be taught elsewhere than in a Christian school there would be no reason for having Christian schools. The only reason why we are justified in having Christian schools is that we are convinced that outside of a Christian-theistic atmosphere there can be no more than an empty process of one abstraction teaching abstractness to other abstractions. No teaching of any sort is possible except in Christian schools.

No, please do not say that this is an extreme statement or an overwrought accusation. Plato knew it and said so. He knew that he could do nothing with the profound notion that two and two are four if he looked at two horses and two cows. He found that he would somehow have to make a reference to the ideal world and speak of twoness abstracted from horses and cows and everything concrete. But twoness — what was it? Plato knew that he did not know. He knew that the ideal world was not within his grasp. But he also knew that he was helpless without it. And this was true with respect to everything that he saw in this world. It was true of mathematics but it was also true of ethics. Can virtue be taught? he asked. Well, to teach a thing we must know that thing. But do we know virtue by looking at it in this world? No, for there is no virtue here that is not mixed with vice. Any virtue driven to extremes becomes a vice. To get a true idea of virtue, then, we must look at the ideal world again. But even there we cannot find virtue totally by itself because among the ideas of good things there are those terrible ideas of mud and hair and filth. In the ideal world, too, Plato thought the positive does not exist without the negative, the devil is just as old as God. So then the idea of virtue as Plato saw it remained an ultimate mystery. Plato admitted that he was before an ultimate dilemma of thought. He knew that he knew nothing and that he could therefore teach nothing.

As for modern philosophy it knows still better than Plato did that it knows nothing, but the pity is that it is not willing to admit as Plato was willing to admit that it cannot teach anything. Bernard Bosanquet has labored to understand what it means that five plus seven are twelve. He calls it an eternal *novelty*. He also calls it an *eternal* novelty. By that he means that no law of arithmetic means anything to anybody unless such a law is related to a body of absolute truth. His argument was the same as Plato's when he said that to know what it means that two times two are four we must know what twoness means. Now here we have a full admission of the indispensibleness of Christian schools. The ground for the necessity of Christian schools lies in this very thing, that no fact can be known unless it be known in its relationship to God. And once this point is clearly seen, the doubt as to the value of teaching arithmetic in Christian schools falls out of the picture. Of course arithmetic must be taught in a Christian school. It cannot be taught anywhere else.

Consciousness of Antitheses

We have purposely taken up this matter of two times two are four because that seems to be the black beast in Christian instruction. Many are willing to admit that it is quite reasonable that the Christian religion and Christian ethics should be taught in Christian schools but are not willing to admit that subjects which lie on the educational periphery should be taught in Christian schools. The most they will admit is that of course it is nice to have the children in a Christian atmosphere at all times and that such a Christian atmosphere can be supplied by Christian teachers only. Sometimes some say sneeringly or at least doubtfully, "How can you teach arithmetic to the glory of God?" or, "How can you be specifically Christian when you teach the children that two times two are four?" Well our answer is that if you cannot teach arithmetic to the glory of God you cannot do it any other way because it cannot be done any other way by anybody. And by this I do not mean that you have breathed a sort of Christian atmosphere about the problems of arithmetic in the sense that you have opened the school session with prayer a couple of hours before. By a Christian atmosphere I mean first of all that deep conviction on the part of the teacher that no fact is teachable except when brought into relationship with God. For it is not till the teacher has this conviction that he will radiate any ethical atmosphere that is worth the having. Emotional Christianity does not flower well on a hard clay bottom of intellectual paganism.

Now I well know that it is easy to figure this thing out in theory and most difficult to bring it into practice. We do not speak of it as an easy matter, but we speak of the impossible as possible because the possible has become wholly impossible. Ah, how large a portion of the grace of God it requires to be a teacher of the children of the covenant! But do we not sometimes too lightly dismiss the matter as beyond our power altogether? When we say that arithmetic must be taught to the glory of God we do not mean that the child shall at once understand the full implication of all that it means that two times two are four because God has made the space-time world according to certain laws and that these laws express something of the very being of God. We need not at all despair when the first grades do not understand this matter. But you may as well despair if your eighth or tenth graders do not begin to get an inkling of it. They ought to begin to see these things and if they do they will later learn to see more of them.

Then, too, there is a sense in which the subject of arithmetic lies at the periphery of the Christian school curriculum. Not as though arithmetic should take less time than other subjects. It is quite possible that a subject should take a large share of the available time and yet lie at the periphery of the curriculum. Arithmetic and all other subjects that emphasize the space aspect of the space-time world lie in the nature of the case at the periphery of the whole area of the creation of God. This is due to the arrangement God has made in his creation, namely, that man should stand at the center of it. And since man is a selfconscious and active being his most characteristic human traits will manifest themselves more fully in the movement of time, that is in history, than in the immovable atmosphere of space. Accordingly it is easier to bring out the more specifically human and the more specifically Christian interpretation of reality when teaching history than when teaching nature. Consequently, we cannot expect the same intensity of emotional response to a really Christian instruction of arithmetic that we can expect to a Christian instruction of history. And for that reason, too, we should again realize the close connection between the facts of space and the facts of time. Since the more definitely temporal facts lie closer to the center of the glory of God we should connect the spatial facts with the temporal facts and use the latter as media of transmission of the glory of the spatial facts to God. In a symphony every individual instrument need not be individually conspicuous. In a good picture there is much background that is little noted but none the less indispensible. The curriculum of a Christian school should be an organism in which some members seem less important but cannot be amputated.

May I interject again that when I have maintained that no teaching is possible except in Christian schools I have not forgotten the doctrine of common grace. Of course arithmetic and for that matter everything else, including religion and Christianity, is teachable if by being teachable you mean nothing more than making susceptible to a temporary pragmatic manipulation by unbelievers. But we are not speaking of that now. We are speaking only of specifically Christian instruction and of absolutely ultimate matters.

The Natural Precedes the Spiritual. While speaking of the curriculum we have emphasized the all important point that every space-time fact must be set before the absolute personality of God because we feel that if this point is once clearly seen all other problems can be solved in the light of it. We cannot speak of many of these problems. Let us however look for a moment at this question of centrality in the curriculum on which we have already touched. It goes without saying that if there is centrality in our Christian life and world view there is of necessity also centrality in our educational curriculum. We have spoken of the lack of centrality in the educational policies that surround us and found that such a lack of centrality was due to the lack of centrality in the educational philosophy that surrounds us. So also there is a lack of centrality in the curricula of the schools that surround us. It could not be otherwise. No one can make a curriculum that has a center if he has no center for his own life and world views.

We are all familiar with the mad rush for the study of nature at the expense of the classics and the humanities a number of years ago. Now we are not interested in the details of this question. We only wish to point out that this tendency was indicative of an emphasis upon man's environment at the expense of man himself. And if now we recall that according to modern educational philosophy man does after all know nothing about his environment, it becomes apparent that the modern educational curriculum is built upon the silent admission that we do not know who man is and that we do not know what his surroundings are. Accordingly man is wholly adrift, and all that he can do is turn as fast as he can to anything that he may fancy himself to see in the distance.

The curriculum of a Christian school will naturally maintain the exact opposite of all this. We know who man is and what his surroundings are. Moreover we know that man is the center of the created universe. And this knowledge lies at the foundation of our curriculum building program. As builders of a curriculum for Christian schools we do not dash wildly back and forth, then, in this and then in that direction. We will always place man at the center of the curriculum. God has made man's environment subject to man instead of man subject to his environment. It follows that history can never be relegated to the background. It is in history that the acts of man appear most conspicuously. Note well, we are not speaking first of all of the quantity of time required to teach these subjects. Nature study is good and useful if only it is not separated from the study of history.

All Things Are Ours. But we have not said enough if we say that man must always be at the center of the curriculum. We must add that man as the Christian must stand at the center of the curriculum. Hence sacred history in which the program of redemption is held to view is at the center of all the teaching of history. Again I speak not primarily of a quantity of time. To say that sacred history should stand at the center of the curriculum is not inconsistent with spending many hours on subjects other than sacred history. It only means that when nature is brought in connection with history and secular history is brought in connection with sacred history does man as redeemed stand at the center of the curriculum and only thus can any and every fact of the space-time world be brought into relation with the absolute personality of God. Only thus is there no abstract separation of the *that* of education from the *what* of education. Only thus can teaching become really concrete. Only thus can the emphasis be laid where it ought to be laid. It will enable us to set forth the really important figures in the history of the human race and in the history of the redemption of the human race without being all the while afraid that we are spending too much time on Moses rather than on Mussolini. Only thus can nature be set forth as the picture book of God, that is, as the moving picture book of God. Only thus can we provide the atmosphere that is so indispensible if Christian education is to be worth its name.

III. The Antithesis in regard to the Child

And now that we come to a consideration of the child that is to be educated, we can be very brief. We have already discussed what the modern educational philosophy thinks of man. It will naturally think the same thing of the child. Out of the maze of the void and out of the infinite depths of irrationality there has somehow come forth upon this world these specs of rationality that we call human beings. And each human being recapitulates this process of the race as a whole. The adjustments that the tiny spec of developing rationality is to learn to make seem all to deal with temporal things, but there is a misty haze of possibilities surrounding him. Accordingly the child must be placed before an infinite series of open possibilities. The most common term used for this supposed process of adjustment is the term or phrase of "integration of personality" into its surroundings. The concept of personality is used over and over again. The whole of education is said to be the development of personality. And it is said that only now that education is liberated from the trammels of mediaevelism which made the child subject to the curriculum instead of the curriculum subject to the child has personality any real chance for development.

Non-Christian Idea of Personality

This question, then, of personality and the possibility of its development is the point in dispute between our opponents and ourselves. What shall we say in answer to the charge that in our type of curriculum personality cannot develop at all? It is clear that we are once more face to face with an ultimate alternative.

Vacuum Fed Babies. When discussing the philosophies of education we saw that our opponents in the nature of the case think our position wholly untenable and that we think our opponents' position to involve nothing short of chaos. When discussing the curriculum we saw that the real issue was whether upon a non-theistic basis anything at all was teachable. And we have maintained that upon the educational foundation of our opponents nothing at all is teachable. That was our answer to the charge made by our opponents that we cannot teach because we are hide-bound in the formation of the curriculum. What else do you suppose can be our answer now to the charge that personality cannot well develop in our system of education, than to say that on their system of education personality cannot develop at all. Here, as along the whole front, we must begin with an absolute negation before we can be positive and constructive at all.

Genuine Nurture. Our reason for holding that personality cannot develop in the educational system of our opponents is that on their view finite personality is, as we have seen, placed in the midst of an absolutely impersonal atmosphere. Our claim is that finite personality cannot develop unless it be placed face to face with absolute personality. We have contended that no space-time fact in general can have any significance except when placed in its proper relation to God. And personality is a space-time fact. But more specifically than that the fact that nothing in this universe can be known except when placed into its relationship to God appears most clearly in the case of human personality. You cannot think of personality without thinking of rationality, and finite rationality is by itself unthinkable and without meaning. To think of finite personality by itself is to think meaning into the void. The impersonal cannot be a foil to the personal. Taken in an absolute sense personality must be completely selfsufficient. And taken in a finite sense, personality may have the impersonal as its foil only if back of this impersonal foil is the absolute personality of God.

It was the impersonalism of the educational philosophies that reduced all antitheses to nothing and reduced the universe to a neutral universe in which nothing would happen. So now again it is this same ultimate impersonalism that reduces finite personality to nothing. Consequently, nothing will happen in the way of the development of personality. If then the finite personality is not placed face to face with God and the "facts" about which the finite personality is to learn or the environment to which it is to be adjusted is not placed face to face with God, there cannot possibly be any fruitful contact between the subject and the object of knowledge. To have knowledge at all, both the knower and the known must be in contact with God. Only through God can the two be brought together.

Non-Christian Denial of Authority

And this brings us finally to remark on the question of authority in education. The relation of one person teaching another brings out at once the question whether the one has any authority to present his interpretation as absolute truth. Is there any authority at all? Will not authority when exercised by one upon the other hamper the freedom of the other? Our opponents hold that strictly speaking authority and freedom are mutually exclusive. True, they will allow for the authority of the expert in the sense that one person knows a little more about the actual performance of the universe than another, but authority in the ultimate sense, that is authority in the juridical as well as the expert sense, they will not allow.

Expert Authority. Now we are not pleading for the substitution of juridical for expert authority. But what we do claim is that on the basis of our opponents there is no authority at all and that without authority no teaching is possible. That there is no authority on the basis of our opponents is clear from the fact that on their basis there is no knowledge at all. And if there is no knowledge possible, no expert knowledge is possible.

Real Authority. Authority is nothing but the placing of the absolute personality of God before the finite personality of man. It follows then that if nothing can be taught unless it be taught in relation to God nothing can be taught unless it be taught with authority.

It is this that makes the position of the teacher so infinitely difficult and at the same time so infinitely valuable. On the basis of our opponents the position of the teacher is utterly hopeless. He knows that he knows nothing and that in spite of this fact he must teach. He knows that without authority he cannot teach and that there are no authorities to which he can appeal. He has to place the child before an infinite series of possibilities and pretend to be able to say something about the most advisable attitude to take with respect to those possibilities, and at the same time he has to admit that he knows nothing at all about those possibilities. And the result for the child is that it is not furnished with an atmosphere in which it can live and grow. In contrast with this the Christian teacher knows himself, knows the subject, and knows the child. He has the full assurance of the absolute fruitfulness of his work. He labors in the dawn of everlasting results.

CORNELIUS VAN TIL

Address before the National Union of Christian Schools Convention, Holland, Michigan, August, 1932.

Key Thoughts:

1. Non-Christian education seeks to develop personality in an environment ultimately impersonal.

2. Christian education develops personality in an environment which is personal because God as absolute personality is the ultimate.

3. In non-Christian education the curriculum consists of "bare facts."

4. The curriculum in Christian education consists of "space-time facts" placed under the light of revelation, the fact-revelation in Christ, and the word-revelation in the Bible.

5. In non-Christian education the plan of the curriculum is man-centered.

6. Christian education makes God the center of curriculum planning, for man exists for God. Inasmuch as the created universe exists for man, the curriculum in relation to man's finite environment is man-centered.

7. Non-Christian education makes nature the "core subject" of the curriculum.

8. Christian education places all subjects in the periphery except history which is central for it deals with man. And at the center of history is "sacred history," Christ and his redemption.

9. Non-Christian education views authority and freedom as mutually exclusive.

10. Christian education regards authority based upon the idea of God as man's creator and Christ as man's redeemer the basis of genuine freedom.

Comment:

As Christians thoroughly committed to the necessity of Christian education in the school, we seek *good* schools that are *soundly*

Christian. We want schools that understand their task as schools. We want schools that carry out their task as Christian schools.

We are not always clear on what constitutes a *good* school, and what makes a good school *Christian.* This is one of our major difficulites in Christian education today. The antithesis of Christian education and non-Christian education may seem clear to us on paper. When we get to work on the educative process itself, this paper work is not always so obvious.

When a Christian school places major emphasis on marks or tests, on report cards, and on passing from grade to grade in lockstep fashion; when a non-Christian school takes account of the needs of child life in a unitary way and sets up a cooperating community of children actively engaged in worth-while learning — then where is the Christian education? Or what can Christian education mean? These are not hypothetical situations, but based on facts. Not that every Christian school is a lock-step institution and every non-Christian school a cooperating community of learners. Let's not draw such generalizations. My point is what constitutes Christian education when we seek personality development in a personal environment?

We have much work to do on this subject. Seeing the antithesis clearly will help. But let us not forget it took non-Christian education to teach us the value and dignity of child life, while we could have known it from the Bible centuries ago. Why did we fail to apply to education what the Scripture so clearly taught; that the divine ordinances for child life are basic in child development?

2

All Men Knit Together As One Man

The work of our Christian schools is a glorious pursuit well worthy of our united efforts. Advancing Christian education is the duty of everybody — the minister in the pulpit, the laymen in the pews, the members of the school society, the parents of the pupils attending, the principal, the teachers and children in school, the school board, etc. I should like to give some suggestive hints as to how "everybody" can carry out their task. In attempting to do so I desire to begin with the teachers, for the teacher indeed is the life and the soul of the school. Edward Everett is quoted as saying, "What considerate person can enter a school and not reflect, with awe, that it is a seminary where immortal minds are training for eternity?" But Chauncey P. Colegrove who gives the citation adds, "The average young teacher does not have this inspiring view of his work." Presumably not, but at least the teacher in a Christian school *should* have it.

Let us now suppose that you have but recently graduated from normal school. Are you acquainted, from a theoretical viewpoint, with at least some of the difficulties that will confront you? Work, I would advise you, work diligently in school; and continue just as diligently after school hours. Find out what teaching is, and what its aim is. Is it merely imparting knowledge? Preparing for exams? Or, does the element of training enter? And training for what? Training of minds that have not learned before to study; of wills that have not yet learned to obey law cheerfully. Were such men as Locke, Pestalozzi, Froebel right when they virtually asserted that character is above learning; hence character the supreme aim of all instruction?

Study, then, books on pedagogy, on method in education, on principles of teaching in order to obtain even a distinctly adequate hold on the three requisites of teaching: knowledge of matter, knowledge of method, knowledge of mind. And in your classroom try to practice upon your scholars the useful hints you may find as so much canned wisdom in books.

Again, as a teacher in a Christian school, have you any duty toward training *Christian* character? If so, how will you undertake it? If

460

Colegrove in his laudable book, *The Teacher and the School,* says to the public school teacher, "Teach him to covet earnestly the best gifts, to aspire to the things that are true, honest, just, pure, lovely and of good report: these are the ultimate aims of the school" (p. 114), how about Christian-school teachers who do not even reach out for these? And here let me raise a question: Do you think it possible to strive after such an ideal without Him who said, "Apart from me ye can do nothing"? Do you think that Paul, when writing those words, meant to say that the Corinthians, the Philippians could reach after these things apart from Christ? Is, then, a Christian school necessary, and is a thoroughly Christian teacher needed in order to make the school Christian?

You should also know something about *the distinctive features of the Christian school.* For even a good teacher (and that already means much) is not *ipso facto* a good teacher for a Christian school.

In your intercourse with *the children* you will meet with discouraging facts. In your classroom will be children that are physically unfit through the ignorance (sometimes criminal ignorance as I heard a physician brand it) of parents. Some children do not get sufficient sleep because selfish parents refuse to sacrifice unnecessary pleasure to the child's health, dragging their tired little ones along upon evening visits instead of staying home with the children. Others do not receive the right kind of food; their digestion and elimination in the morning is not looked after by busy mothers. You will have to find the cause of wilfulness and backwardness of such children. A little personal talk, a visit to the home after school hours, may work wonders.

And you will meet with as many different characters as there are pupils. This is difficult as they all have to be taught the same subjects. Yet it is also charming. For all are characters in the making. They are headed for various occupations and spheres of life. And you, through the attitude of sympathetic understanding, will be able to put your soul's imprint upon these various future characters. What an ideal!

This attitude of sympathetic understanding, however, carries with it that you at all times bear in mind that you are dealing with children. And children are easily fatigued. It is not so much the effort required for study as the manner, method, and spirit of the teacher that is responsible for the amount of fatigue produced by school work. Will your method and personality produce, or arrest fatigue? Will you conserve the vitality and nervous energy of the children, or waste it by your own fretfulness, anger, nervousness? Do you see that in order to be a good teacher you have need of a sanctified personality having your own passions well in hand?

Even public school men agree that the school room is a silent teacher of morals. "There is scarcely a sounder principle in pedagogy," says the *Massachusetts State Report* of 1895, "than that care begets care; order, order; cleanliness, cleanliness; and beauty, beauty. Things conspicuously good command the respect of children, invite their imitation, and in ways real, though obscure, sink into their souls and mould their beings." If Pestalozzi at Stanz completely changed the nature of a school of seventy or eighty pupils, most of whom "on their arrival were very degenerated specimens of humanity," "skeletons, with haggard, careworn faces and shrinking looks; some used to begging, hypocrisy, and all sorts of deceit; others broken by misfortune, patient, timid, suspicious, and entirely void of affection"; if Pestalozzi transformed these children so that in a few months he said of them, "Amongst these wild beggar children there soon existed such peace, friendship, and cordial relations as are rare even among actual brothers and sisters"; and if he accomplished this miracle (as he said himself), "trusting in the natural powers that God bestows on even the poorest and most neglected children" — then how could you despair either of yourself or of your pupils, you who believe in the regenerating influence of the Holy Spirit?

What is needed, then, in a Christian school teacher is first of all a native and ingrained love for children. Should this be absent, retrace, I beseech you, your steps. Turn to stenography. Sell Chevrolets, silk hosiery, electric stoves, anything. But do not teach. Search your heart, I pray you. Why did you take up teaching? Did perhaps an ambitious mother advise you that there would be "better chances" because forsooth Dorothy Dix says, "School teachers have always been preferred risks in the matrimonial market"? Did you now, maybe, think, "I have gone through high school, through college anyhow; so I might as well use it for something before settling down"? Please, change your mind. Teaching is a calling; and teaching in a Christian school is as much a calling as the ministry of the Word and sacraments. I wish to emphasize that. It may not be a calling for a life time; it should be viewed as a divine calling while it lasts.

Secondly, what is needed is a deeply rooted sense of one's accountability to God. You may either mar or beautify these God-given and God-directed lives which have but just begun. Do not spoil the opening bud by the touch of rough hands. Realize your dependence upon God, and, trusting in Him, put high your ideals. Man always falls far enough below them at the best. But the higher one aims the greater the satisfaction as time goes on. It may be more difficult to climb the mountain than it is to ascend the hill; the landscape from the mountain top is more gratifying than is the scenery on the hill side.

Your attitude toward community and church will be determined by your attitude toward school and pupils, not vice versa. Let me quote from the rules of the school board of Cleveland: "It shall be a duty of the first importance on the part of teachers to be models in personal appearance and conduct for pupils under their care. They are especially enjoined to avail themselves of every opportunity to inculcate neatness, promptness, politeness, cheerfulness, truthfulness, patriotism, and all the virtues which contribute to the effectiveness of the school, the good order of society, and the safety of our American citizenship." Dr. Colegrove, to whom I own the reference, adds himself, "The unconscious tuition of the teacher is one of the most important factors in school training. It is the alchemi of the teacher's influence that counts most in giving pupils the desire to do better and to be better" (pp. 66-67).

This radiant personality of the teacher is a force not only during school hours. How could it be, since it is one with him? Wherever it is extant, small children will not come home with disconcerting reports of how wild teacher acted after school.

I might add that in the beginning at any rate, you will not have much time for social activities. I would not go as far as certain school boards in North Carolina go, who were recently reported offering applicants for teaching positions contracts containing these sentences: "I promise not to fall in love or become engaged or to secretly marry. I promise not to go with any young man except insofar as it is to stimulate Sunday school work." Such strict rules, I am convinced, will work out more to the benefit of the Sunday schools than for the day schools which they are supposed to help. At the same time however, she makes poor material who, upon discovering that the teacher is the belle of the community, avails herself of every opportunity to spend hours early and hours late with companions of the opposite sex. Better wait a while. I heard it said the other day in quarters where I should not have expected it, that it really is a pity to have young girls bury their teen years by teaching school since in that way they so soon reach the hopeless age of twenty-five. Do not believe it. Rather believe me: an educated girl's best opportunities for marriage occur after her twenty-fifth year. A serious-minded and educated man simply has not the time to enter into such a hazardous situation until he himself is at least that old. Nor is he ready to propose to a young lady before he has had some certainty at any rate of a position in the world. Let the young woman meanwhile increase her value by continuing her own preparation for life. It may be true that the early bird catches the worm; it is a mere worm too, and aften a small one at that. Better specialize along the lines of child psychology for a few years. Make training children the object of your devotion rather than an experimental study of adolescence. You will thereby not only increase your intrinsic value, but also your self-respect, something that is to stay with you throughout your life. Paul's advice to Timothy to be at it "in season, out of season" you would do well to write over your desk.

Closely related to this is a word or two in regard to your behavior in church. The *don't's* I am respectfully submitting are taken from the sad school of experience: Don't take a back seat in church. Don't whisper during services. Don't be a leader in following extreme styles, or in wearing suggestive clothing. Don't exhaust your artistic talent in the field of face decorating, a sort of painting after all which reveals little genius, taste, or originality. A whited sepulchre remains a sepulchre for all that. Now I should not be saying this but for the fact that these and similar things do happen. And where they occur, some staunch supporters of the Christian school are disappointed; some other members of the church think, if teacher does this, we can safely go a step farther. Wherever a Christian school and a public school exist side by side, and the Christian-school teacher through appearance or loud manners creates the impression of being more worldly than her public-school colleague, there will be at least some people who will leap at the conclusion that the public-school system is superior to the Christian. And while this conclusion is unwarranted there is this much truth in it that it is the personality of the teacher which makes or unmakes the school. Be not guilty therefore of breaking down Christian schools while serving them and while living through them.

Let then your conduct at all times be above reproach, your behavior courteous. Make too socially inclined people understand that you have not joined the ranks of the professionals for a good time, but for serious work during the school term. On the other hand, should you be sometimes obliged to decline invitations, let it be done pleasantly. Let your bearing be at once modest and dignified; your face sunny. Avoid all coarseness of speech.

* * *

I hesitate when coming to principals. You are responsible not only for work done in the upper grades, but for results, and for good school organization in the rooms of your subordinates also. These you are to supervise, to assist with your counsel, to encourage; and you know that the younger teachers have by no means an easy task. You are to map out the courses of study for their rooms; to trace the progress their classes make. You are to know how much time your teachers spend with recitation; you are to find out whether their children recite mechanically or intelligently; whether staff members make an effort to teach the pupils *how* to study; and if they know how to assign lessons properly. Whether lessons are assigned merely by pages, or if helpful suggestions are added as to the preparation of the lesson. Are ideas conveyed to the pupils by the facts and names they memorize? Is any part of the school hours of their scholars squandered? As pedagogues do you know if your teachers help pupils overcome harmful individual peculiarities and sins? Do they continue their studies, or are they in danger of reaching the dead-line? Do they prepare the lesson before or after assigning it to the class? Are they interested in school problems, in educational literature; and is theirs the proper *esprit de corps?* To be a principal worthy of the name you will have to instruct the teachers in these matters.

As to modern educational methods, it is decidedly the part of you principals to know what is going on in the school world at large. And, since the Christian school should never be behind the public school as a school (for how could that be distinctively Christian which is inferior to the creation of the men of common grace?), you are either to introduce whatever is said to improve the school in any sphere, or to differ as to the suggested aims and results, and you are to know *why* you disagree.

If the teachers are the heart of the school, the principal certainly forms its inmost core. Hence he is to watch the walk of his fellow teachers. He is to keep his own heart with all diligence, for out of it are the issues of the life of the Christian school. And as to the school board, he will but seldom meet a body of men who are his equals in understanding school problems. Therefore, while in a sense their subordinate, he should never fail to remember that he is to help the board along in aiding him. Suggest to them needed improvement. And, if sometimes disappointed by a somewhat niggardly treatment, keep high your ideals, and do not lose your faith in men. Be an educator of men as well as of children. Above all, lay your numerous difficulties before your heavenly Father. And, never allowing yourself to become sour of disposition, be sure that, in school matters too, "Faithful is he that calleth you, who will also do it" (I Thess. 5:24).

* * *

I now turn to school boards, parents, and church members in general. I must needs be short. There is no harm in that though. You are aware that I think highly of the importance of our teaching staff, and that I consider their task by no means a sinecure; do not think of them less highly. If we want our Christian schools to be Christian schools indeed, let us receive our teachers in the Lord with all joy; and hold such in honor (Phil. 2:29). Let us not expect perfection. Let us not discuss the imperfections of our teachers in the hearing of our children. Rather begin the day with a family prayer in which the children's teachers are remembered by name.

School boards should assume a kind attitude toward teachers. They should not look upon teachers as upon enemies of the common weal when they suggest improvements that may look like luxuries to school board members, but which students in normal schools were taught to consider necessities. They should rather invite teachers (and not the principal only) to their meetings occasionally, and, through discussion, aim at reaching a common ground of mutual understanding and appreciation. They should encourage struggling young teachers; and as to poor ones, warn them of their faults rather than simply ditch them. In case, however, a teacher proves to be a misfit, it would be sinful to recommend him to the board of another school merely to avoid an unpleasant situation. It would indeed be sinful for Christian-school boards either to re-appoint, or to inflict upon others teachers whose religious character is not above that of the average young church member.

Parents should begin to co-operate with the Christian school long years before their little ones are first sent thither. Proper sleep and nutrition, those major offsets to fatigue, should be given, as well as respect for authority instilled from earliest infancy. When children have not learned to respect authority at home, it must be expected that there will be a conflict before they learn to respect the authority of the school. To permit children to grow up without respect for some authority is a crime.

Children should not be sent to a Christian school that parents may pass on the duty of Christian training, but that they may receive help in performing this task. It would seem that parents, whether themselves educated or not, whether extremely busy or less so, could at least do as much as this: let the children at the supper table tell the Bible story teacher has told during the day; and let it thereupon be read from the Bible. In this way the children will receive some inkling that the home and the school are working together. At the same time opportunities will hereby arise quite naturally to imbibe the children with appreciation of their teachers.

* * *

I shall make but a few remarks applicable to all parties outside the school proper.

Giving the children of the church a religious training is as much work demanding concerted efforts as is preaching in slums or teaching

Nahavo children. It should be emphasized that it is a sacred privilege as well as a duty to contribute toward a better and larger Christian school; and that this privilege and duty does not commence when one enters upon the state of matrimony, far less when baby has reached his first birthday, but as soon as independent wages are earned. Here is work for ministers and elders. All church members, including ministers should do their Christian duty by tithing their incomes; every tithe should be divided into three equal parts, marked *church, school, outside purposes*. But besides money we need attractive and up-to-date schools, the kind that can compete with the public schools. We have the Holy Spirit, and *He* has the money, the talents and everything that is needed. "For the eyes of Jehovah run to and fro throughout the whole earth, to show himself strong in the behalf of them whose heart is perfect toward him" (II Chron. 16:9).

Some people need to learn how to treat teachers. A good room, a quiet resting-place and opportunity for study are necessities in order to have teachers fit to give the best that is in them. It now happens that a young girl, after accepting an appointment in a strange town, finds it next to impossible to locate a boarding-place. No one seems to want "those teachers." And this is very unfriendly, and very discouraging at the start. There is also the mistaken notion among some women that they cannot board teachers "because then you always have to have something extra on the table." Many a girl who feels hurt because no one seems to care for her soul would be surprised to know that this seeming carelessness proceeds from an overzealous care for her stomach.

Dr. Colegrove in his book *The Teacher and the School* to which I have frequently referred, makes this startling statement. "The illustration that Paul uses in I Cor. 12 is just as appropriate when applied to a school as to a church: 'For the school is one body and hath many members. And the teacher cannot say to the parents, 'I have no need of you'; nor again to the school officers, 'I have no need of you.' Nor can the school officers say to the tax payers, 'I have no need of you.' And whether one member suffer, all the members suffer with it; or one member is honored, all the members rejoice with it." This is well said. Yet, with him this is an ideal of *social cooperation*. A public school, by common consent, is a school without the Christ of the Scriptures, even though Bible reading without comment may be tolerated, or even required.

* * *

The Christian Statesman was mistaken when calling Christian schools an un-American and foreign institution, which cannot work in the land of the Pilgrim fathers. Professor D. S. Sharp of Boston University was wrong when before the Teachers' Institute at Atlantic City he denounced private schools as an Old World educational idea at variance with the idea of a democracy and tending to breed antagonism and suspicion. We can well afford to smile at such sweeping statements. Professor B. S. Winchester, Assistant Professor of Religious Education in Yale School of Religion, and Chairman Commission on Christian Education of the Federal Council of the Churches of Christ in America, reminds us in his book on *Religious Education and Democracy* how much of our democracy and of our school ideas is a legacy of Calvinism. Says he, "When the townships came to unite under a common government, the model after which the state was patterned was the religious republic of Geneva. It was this Puritan religious commonwealth which set the fashion for democracy in the United States and first gave impulse to the movement for compulsory popular education." While another American educational authority, Professor Philip Vollmer, states, "The *Parochial* school has been in the past one of the greatest blessings to America, for until recently it was the only opportunity for educating the plain people. While the system is fast dying out there still remain thousands of these 'schools with the Bible.' "

But after all we had perhaps better not pay too much attention to opinions pro and con the Christian school. While religious America admittedly is at sea as to the proper method of religious training, let us study anew our Calvinistic inheritance. No doubt we shall find that it can be neither undemocratic nor foreign nor anti-Christian-school when properly understood. We only need better schools, better equipped teachers, more freedom from the fetters of imperfection and sin.

J. K. VAN BAALEN

Address before the National Union of Christian Schools Convention, Grand Haven, Michigan, August 31, 1927.

Key Thoughts:

1. A Christian school is first of all a gift. Appreciating every gift of common grace, we use these gifts in the education of our boys and girls.

2. The challenge of making the school Christian comes first of all to the Christian teacher. Working with children in love as unto the Lord is his chief task.

3. The principal of the Christian school too occupies a place of importance in the internal unity of the school. As administrator he should enable every teacher to give of his best.

4. The Christian community as represented in the school board, parents, and church members in general are to assume their responsibility in cooperation with the teacher to make Christian education effective in the home and in the broader areas of life.

5. The Christian school is not foreign to American life as some would hold. It belongs to the early Calvinistic contribution to colonial life. Statism in education is a later import.

Comment:

Making the school Christian is the responsibility of the entire Christian community. The professional personnel must give the leadership, but must also enlist the entire Christian community to realize the potential of the Christian school for the Kingdom of God.

The integrity of the Christian home and the fellowship of love centered in service of God in Christ are indispensable as bases for the Christian school. Where these are missing or weak, the Christian school runs into serious problems.

Then too, Christian parents are to be alerted to developments in the understanding of the bringing up of children. The school should give leadership in this area to establish cooperative relationship. Much good material is constantly made available. This must be appraised for use in Christian education. Our professional personnel of the school might discuss this material and make it available to parents. Thus home and school will grow cooperatively in doing a better job of Christian education.

And the Church? The boys and girls attending the Christian school are lambs in the flock of Christ. The church is their mother too, as well as mother of the parents. How interested is the mother in what care is given to the babes in Christ at school? We of Reformed persuasion oppose church schools on principle. Rightly so. But, has the church exhausted its responsibility when the membership is urged to send the children to the Christian school? The Christian school needs a more positive link to the Church. This too, must be explored as we study Christian education.

3

The Road Ahead

A pioneering task lies ahead. Will anyone take issue with this statement after he has adequately informed himself about Christian education? We have an urgent mission. The work that needs to be done cannot wait till we have satisfied ourselves on every issue. Complacency now will cost us the Christian school. What is the task?

We find ourselves in the midst of attempted educational reform going on all around us. I say attempted educational reform. Good, bad, or indifferent — and it has evidences of all three — the attempted reform is reaching into our homes, our schools, and our churches. Where are we going, and who will show us the way?

The nineteenth century school in which the Christian school movement arose made knowledge and skills primary. It was thought that it is by intellectual mastery and practice that we are disciplined in the truth. A disciplined mind is the end of education it was said. The mind of the child was thought to be a small, undeveloped mind that needed the discipline of the adult mind to form it according to adult norms.

But the nineteenth century school ignored, violated or assigned a secondary place to the ways of child life in child development. No education that fails to take account of God-ordained ways of child development can be Christian. No amount of Bible study, prayer and devotional reading, or Bible-centered interpretation of subject matter makes a knowledge-getting school Christian. It took the twentieth century school to awaken even Christian teachers to the needs of child life and its place in the learning process.

Is the twentieth century school with its emphasis upon human relations the answer to our educational problem? How can it be when it views the needs of childhood apart from the spirit, the I, or the person who finds his fulfilment in the fellowship of love first of all of God and then of his fellowman? And this is precisely what the twentieth century school tries to do. Human relations are based on enlightened self-interest. Each individual is a self among selves that must learn to maintain and develop himself for the good of all.

The twentieth century school is worse off than the nineteenth century school in spite of the former's greater recognition of the child and his needs. It lacks norms of truth for effective self-discipline. It knows neither where it is going nor what it is doing. It is just doing, and trying to do it graciously and gracefully. Make friends and influence people — this is the extent of it. The blind leading the blind, and the ditch is not far hence. God save us from the twentieth century school. I fear we have imbibed more of it in our Christian schools than we realize.

In charting the course for our Christian school we must build on another foundation than either the nineteenth century school or the twentieth century school have to offer. It is the laying of the foundation for positive Christian education that constitutes our pioneering task. A Christian view of child life in its needs and development; a Christian view of the curriculum that affords a medium for a child's development in the school; a Christian view of guided learning in the classroom; a Christian view of educational objectives for the school. These are some of the issues that need clear exposition for teachers in Christian schools. We may wait no longer with this task. It needs doing now. May the Lord provide the leadership as we all work at it with consecrated hearts.

CORNELIUS JAARSMA

BIBLIOGRAPHY

Bibliography

The following list of sources is not intended as a comprehensive bibliography covering the subjects discussed in this book. Rather does it seek to give the teacher a selected list of helpful readings. Teachers who are eager to improve their classroom teaching along the lines indicated in the foregoing pages will find many helps among the pages of these books. The Christian teacher is urged to read critically in the framework of thinking underlying and contained in the fundamentals of this book. Every one of the following books merits careful study.

Burton W. H. *The Guidance of Learning Activities.* Revised Edition. New York: Appleton-Century-Crofts, Inc. 1952.

Develops principles of learning and organization of teaching on the basis of an organismic psychology. Emphasizes the unity of the child in the unity of life. Worth diligent study.

Campbell, L. and Roberts, P. J. *The Life of Christ — A Resource Unit for Grades Three and Four.* Chicago: Moody Press. 1952.

One of the unit series for Christian elementary schools. Others are to follow. A help to Christian school teachers in the organization of units for their grades. The organization of this unit is applicable to all areas of activity and study. The central idea of topic can come from geography or natural science as well. Teachers who gradually wish to break with the traditional assignment-study-recite procedure will find this unit very suggestive and helpful.

Eavey, C. B. *The Art of Effective Teaching.* Grand Rapids: Zondervan Publishing House. 1953.

This book represents an attempt by a Christian teacher of evangelical Christian faith to guide Christian teachers in the appraisal of the contribution of the "new education" to effective teaching. Unfortunately the author is not sufficiently critical because his Christian philosophy of education lacks unity and consistency. In spite of this weakness the book is replete with helpful suggestions for the Christian teacher in gradually applying a clearer grasp of learning and teaching.

The same author wrote a book for Christian parents too. The title is *Principles of Personality Building for Christian Parents.* Teachers can profit from the reading of it themselves and recommend it to parents. Again, though orthodox in religious views, this book too must be read critically.

Grambs, Jean D., and Iverson, W. J. *Modern Methods in Secondary Education.* New York: The Dryden Press. 1952.

The Christian high school teacher who seeks to implement the principles discussed in the selections preceding will find much help in this volume. Not that this volume is written from a Christian point of view, but it does suggest theory and practice which properly appraised and adopted can be rich in helps.

Havighurst, R. J. *Human Development and Education.* New York: Longmans, Green and Co. 1953.

A source of this kind will help teachers greatly in the firsthand study of their pupils. Be guided in your appraisal by the Christian approach as set forth in selections preceding.

Helping Teachers Understand Children. (By the staff of the Division on Child Development and Teacher Personnel of the Commission on Teacher Education.) Washington, D. C.: American Council on Education. 1945.

Do you know how to observe a child, to record your observations, to observe patterns of development, and to interpret them? A teacher should be able to do this, especially in a Christian school. Here is a good source when appraised rightly.

Jersild, A. T.: *In Search of Self.* New York: Teachers College, Columbia University. 1952.

This little volume can help a teacher to understand himself better. Self-understanding is essential to any degree of understanding others. Read this book with great care, and critically, and you will profit greatly from it.

Mehl, M. A., Mills, H. H. and Douglas, H. R., *Teaching in the Elementary School.* New York: The Ronald Press. 1950.

Better ways of teaching in keeping with principle of unity are introduced gradually as a teacher gains security in the use of them. A book of this kind can help greatly in the transition.

Mursell, James L. *Developmental Teaching.* New York: McGraw-Hill Book Co. Inc. 1949.

How can one carry out some of the better ways in the subject matter fields? Teachers should and want to make the transition intelligently and gradually. This book is very useful in helping one in the transition.

Vander Zweep, L., Wielinga, G., and Van Hulst, J. W. *Guide for a Course of Study for Christian Schools* (1949); *Manual for a Course of Study for Christian Schools* (1952). Groningen, The Netherlands: J. B. Woltjers.

These are prepared to guide educational reform in the Christian elementary schools of the Netherlands. The Dutch titles are here given in English. The books appear in the Dutch language only. Read for yourself what leaders in Christian education in the Netherlands are saying about needed educational reform. If you do not read the Dutch, you will appreciate an oral translation by some one. Teachers will find this material inspiring.

Waterink, J. *Principles of Education.* Kampen, The Netherlands: J. H. Kok, 1951.

This book too appears in Dutch only. It is a must for Christian school teachers. The author has given the greater part of his life to develop a Christian approach to learning and teaching. This volume was preceded by three earlier volumes on problems and history of education, also written from a Biblical point of view. A book of this kind gives the Christian teacher solid ground for his pedagogical feet.

INDEX

Index